ARTHUR POLLARD (Born 22.12.22,
Lancashire) is Professor of English at the
University of Hull. A graduate of Leeds
University, he subsequently studied at
Oxford and taught at Manchester,
where he became Director of General
Studies in the Faculty of Arts.

His publications include *Mrs. Gaskell,
Novelist and Biographer* (1965),
Charlotte Brontë (1968) and an edition
of the *Letters of Mrs. Gaskell* (1966)
(with J. A. V. Chapple). He has also
edited *New Poems of George Crabbe*
and introduced the Everyman edition
of Mrs. Gaskell's *Sylvia's Lovers*.

HISTORY OF LITERATURE IN THE ENGLISH LANGUAGE

HISTORY OF LITERATURE
IN THE ENGLISH LANGUAGE

Vol. 6 The Victorians

The Victorians

EDITED BY ARTHUR POLLARD

BARRIE & JENKINS
London

In association with
Sphere Books Ltd

First published in Great Britain in 1970 by Barrie & Jenkins Ltd
2 Clement's Inn, London W.C.2

© Sphere Books 1970

A paperback edition of this volume is available from
Sphere Books

PR
463
P6
1970

Set in Linotype Pilgrim

SBN 214 65082 0

Printed and Bound in Great Britain by
Hazell Watson & Viney Ltd,
Aylesbury, Bucks

CONTENTS

BIBLIOGRAPHICAL NOTE

The place of publication of books mentioned in the text or bibliographies is London, unless otherwise stated.

INTRODUCTION

It is difficult to characterize in brief compass a span of time as long as that in which Queen Victoria reigned over England and her realms beyond the seas. Not only did it cover so many years, but those years also witnessed political, economic, intellectual and scientific change previously unparallelled in British history. In his brilliant survey of the period, *The Victorian Frame of Mind*, Mr. W. E. Houghton cites many who felt themselves to be living in an age of transition (op. cit., p.l); 'an awful moment of transition' was Tennyson's phrase (quoted by Houghton, p. 317). Writing of the 1840s, J. A. Froude declared:—

> It was an era of new ideas, of swift if silent spiritual revolution. Reform in Parliament was the symbol of a general hope for the introduction of a new and better order of things. The Church had broken away from her old anchorage ... Among the middle class there was the Evangelical revival. The Catholic revival at Oxford had convulsed the university and had set half the educated men and women speculating on the authority of the priesthood as the essential meaning of Christianity ... Physical science, now that it was creating railroads, bridging the Atlantic and giving proof of capacity which could no longer be sneered at, was forming a philosophy of the earth and its inhabitants, agitating and inconvenient to orthodoxy but difficult to deal with. Benthamism had taken possession of dominions which religion had hitherto claimed as her own, was interpreting morality in a way of its own, and directing political action.
>
> (*Carlyle's Life in London*, 1891 ed., Vol. I., pp. 310–11)

In the 1840s the half had not been told. By the end of the century Britain exercised 'dominion over palm and pine' with assurance and with a sense of responsibility that in retrospect looks both more beneficent and less self-interested than it was once fashionable to regard it. The Navy imposed a *pax Britan-*

nica on many parts of the world. Trade and Christianity followed the flag. At home successive Reform Acts made democracy more and more a reality, and when after the 1867 Act it became necessary, in Robert Lowe's words, to 'educate our masters', universal elementary education was instituted in 1870. Science and technology together testified to man's adventure and achievement. Darwin and his associates gave man an entirely new view of himself and his place on earth, whilst technical advances extended and completed the revolution in industry that had begun in the previous century. These technical advances were themselves accompanied and in some ways made possible by the changes which brought into being the necessary commercial and financial structure of modern capitalism. Men confidently saw change as progress.

If progress is one Victorian watchword, freedom is the other. The twofold (and opposed) inspirations of the period, Utilitarianism, secular and rationalistic, and Evangelicalism, other-worldly and fideistic, agreed at least in their stress on individualism. Men must be free. As a result free trade replaced protection, government interference in industry and social organisation was resisted, competition was extolled (though there were important contrary voices—see Houghton, op. cit., pp. 191 ff), the Dissenters opposed the claims of the Established Church, the Evangelicals emphasised the necessity of personal salvation, and some people found courage to espouse agnosticism. It all amounted in Arnold's phrase to 'doing as one likes'.

His was the most prominent of a series of dissentient voices. The contrasted ideal and threat that are represented in his title *Culture and Anarchy* remind us that, though it may have been an age of progress and achievement, the Victorian period was also an age of doubt and anxiety. The middle-classes were supreme. They were immensely, self-confident, commercially successful, scornful of the old establishments of aristocracy and Church, but though they often showed a fine sense of social responsibility (they formed the backbone of the humanitarian movement—Mrs. Gaskell is a fine literary example of their conscience in this respect), most of them failed to see the relevance of culture, of an organic view of society. They did not realise, sometimes indeed actively scorned, the importance of authority and traditional values. These modern 'Philistines' were blind to the 'sweetness and light' of the Hellenistic ideal, blinded in fact by their own subscription to a Hebraistic caricature, an arid Puritanism of narrow conduct and narrower dogma. Most Victorians would have accepted with Carlyle that *ernst ist das leben* (epigraph to *Past and Present*—from Schiller) (cf. their attitude to work), but there were some who thought that life need not be ugly as well. Amongst these, with Arnold, were to be found Newman with his appeal to the historic, authoritative Church, Carlyle in his cult of the hero and Ruskin with his vision of art and society. These several medievalisms were all lifelines in vain.

Hope was not fulfilled, confidence ebbed, and the last years of the century were marked by reaction, resignation and disillusion. Though men failed to realise it, the imperial heyday was passing and economic prosperity had gone beyond its peak. The old rigid social hierarchy had disappeared and in its place was social flux, the product of an individualism that issued in discontent and strife. The old certainties of faith had evaporated; those who continued to believe were, perforce, less sure and those who disbelieved were often unhappy. It all amounted to what Mark Pattison described as the 'present mood of depression and despondency' (*Fortnightly Review* XXI, p. 351). Tennyson was discouraged, Hardy gloomy, Shaw devastatingly critical, Wilde scintillatingly cynical. Arnold had lamented the age's 'sick hurry, its divided aims'; at its end it came to worse than this. It appeared to have lost all sense of purpose. There were sad ways by which the Victorian era seemed to have gained the whole world and lost its own soul. A period in which so many contrary forces interacted so intricately and energetically cannot fail to be interesting. Its writers, expressing the spirit of the age with all the resources of imagination, feeling and thought, abundantly reveal their response to their time and the effect it had upon them. In the following chapters an attempt has been made not to mention everybody but to cover both the major figures and others who, though less than major, yet have an interest and importance which demand that they should be considered.

BIBLIOGRAPHY

The following is a list of some books of general interest on the Victorian period.

The New Cambridge Bibliography of English Literature, Vol. III (1800–1900), 1969.

E. Batho and B. Dobrée (edd.), *The Victorians and After*, revd., 1950.

F. E. Faverty (ed.) *The Victorian Poets, A Guide to Research*, 2nd edn., 1968.

L. Stevenson (ed.), *Victorian Fiction, A Guide to Research*, 1964.

A. Briggs, *Victorian People*, 1954.

—— *Victorian Cities*, 1963.

—— *The Age of Improvement*, 1959.

J. H. Buckley, *The Victorian Temper*, Cambridge, Mass., 1951.

W. L. Burn, *The Age of Equipoise*, 1964.

O. Chadwick, *The Victorian Church*, Part I, 1967.

A. Cruse, *The Victorians and Their Books*, 1935.

R. C. K. Ensor, *England, 1870–1914*, Oxford, 1936.

H. N. Fairchild, *Religious Trends in English Poetry*, Vol. IV, 1957.

J. Holloway, *The Victorian Sage*, 1953.

W. E. Houghton, *The Victorian Frame of Mind*, New Haven, 1957.

Ideas and Beliefs of the Victorians (B.B.C. Talks), 1949.

G. Kitson Clark, *The Making of Victorian England*, 1962.

D. C. Somervell, *English Thought in the Nineteenth Century*, 1929.

R. Wellek, *A History of Modern Criticism*, Vol. IV, 1966.

B. Willey, *Nineteenth Century Studies*, 1949.

—— *More Nineteenth Century Studies*, 1956.

R. Williams, *Culture and Society, 1780–1950*, 1958.

E. L. Woodward, *The Age of Reform, 1815–1870*, 1938; with corrections, 1946.

G. M. Young, *Victorian England: Portrait of An Age*, 1937.

and the following periodicals :-

Nineteenth Century Fiction [originally *The Trollopian*], Berkeley, California 1945– .

Victorian Poetry, Morgantown, West Virginia, 1963– .

Victorian Studies, Bloomington, Indiana, 1957– .

VICTORIAN THOUGHT

A. O. J. COCKSHUT, Hertford College, Oxford

To understand how men thought we need to know their feelings, their hopes and especially their fears. Of the early Victorians it is pre-eminently true that they pondered on the
things that worried them, in some cases on the things that
terrified them. For few, if any, of the great names is it useful to
consider their thought as a closed intellectual system. The
apparent exceptions—John Stuart Mill is one—have a way of
proving only apparent while Newman, the man of most finely-
tempered speculative intelligence of them all, characteristically
chose as his motto 'Cor ad cor loquitur.'

The 1830s and early 1840s were a time of reaction against
abstract theoretical solutions, or what Newman called 'paper
systems'. The most striking single fact about the literature of
the 1840s is the entrance of industrial England, with its smoke,
grime, misery and oppression into serious literature. Carlyle,
quickly followed by Disraeli, Dickens and Mrs Gaskell, and
later by Ruskin, brooded on the life actually led by the men
who worked in the factories of Lancashire and by their children. Where the radicals at the time of the Napoleonic wars
had talked of abstract rights, Disraeli talked of tommy-shops
(in *Sybil*), and in *Hard Times* Dickens was soon to talk of a
piston 'Like the head of an elephant in a state of melancholy
madness'.

The absence of any sign of serious interest in industrial
society in literature before 1830, and its abundant presence
after 1840 is deeply significant. For the Industrial Revolution
was not, after all, a new thing. Arkwright, the pioneer of the
spinning-mill, died in 1792, the year Shelley was born. But

Shelley was too abstract, Wordsworth and Keats too introspective and personal, Byron too scornful and cosmopolitan, to
give much attention to the consequences of what he did. The
men of the new age were different, and Dickens, who was
twenty-five when the Queen came to the throne, may stand as
typical of the new interest in *facts* and the new distrust of reforms which were merely constitutional and legal and not
adminstrative. What difference had the Reform Bill of 1832
really made after all the ardour and excitement that had gone
to its making? We can find the answer in Trollope's political
novels which show the social composition and the political
instincts of the House of Commons still mainly aristocratic
even in the 1860s.

But if the men of the new generation were very different
from the Romantic poets in this respect, there were also
ways in which they were like them. A very significant point
which Wordsworth, Shelley, Carlyle and Dickens all have in
common is a grudging, or at times a downright contemptuous
attitude, towards eighteenth-century literature and society. It
is startling to find how cavalierly Coleridge could dismiss a
great man like Samuel Johnson; and the portrait of Sir John
Chester in Dickens' *Barnaby Rudge* (1841) shows a characteristic early Victorian view of eighteenth-century man. He is
polished, gentlemanly, heartless and false. For the early Victorians, as for the Romantics, lack of heart, lack of natural feeling, is the ultimate transgression. Any form, any custom, any
constitutional principle must be informed with living faith
and love; otherwise it was merely, in Carlyle's words, that he
loved to apply both to the French and English eighteenth century, 'buckram' or 'sham'. The early Victorians and the Romantics were alike, then, in their reverence for feelings, and what
an unfriendly critic might call their hunger for sensation. But
there is also a shift of emphasis. The early Victorians were
seldom dreamy, and not markedly introspective. The feelings
they cultivated were social, beginning with the primary family
affections and stretching out to the unknown man at the
bottom of the social pyramid. They did not always understand this man very well; the remedies they suggested for his
lot were not always well-advised. But they always wanted to
understand him and thought it their duty to try. In this connection the development of Ruskin's thought, with which we
shall deal later, is significant. Here was a man naturally inclined to be egocentric, possessed of the strongest aesthetic
sensibilities, and of the money and leisure to gratify them. Yet,

under the influence of *Zeitgeist* of the forties and fifties, he gradually turns his attention more and more to social questions and makes the most urgent, though largely ineffective, attempts to communicate with the poor and to benefit their lot.

To question *idées reçues*, to ask laws and customs to justify themselves, may be salutary, but for the enquiring mind it involves very awkward problems. Carlyle, Newman and Mill were all caught up in an agonizing search for origins and principles. Men of their age in that they jumped intuitively to affirmations derived from their deepest feelings, they were also men who felt the need, even the duty, to justify what they felt by study and argument. Sometimes this led them to modify their first instinctive affirmation, and when it did, the process was painful. This quest for origins, this need to justify established forms by showing their relevance to men's deepest emotional needs, is highly characteristic of early Victorian thinking. It is first clearly seen in two publications of 1833, four years before the Queen's accession, Carlyle's *Sartor Resartus* and Newman's first *Tracts for the Times*.

Carlyle is perhaps the easiest of all great Victorian figures to underrate to-day. His faults have often been pointed out, and can hardly be denied. He is turgid, repetitive, wilful and intemperate. He arrogates a divine prerogative of dividing the world into sheep and goats. It is frightening to see a man so absolutely sure that Cromwell was utterly right and Charles I was utterly wrong. But his importance, which it would be hard to overestimate, lies mainly in two things. Over and over again he was the first to ask the questions which soon became the general questions of the age. At the same time he was the strongest formative influence on the most talented of his younger contemporaries.

Sartor Resartus is a strange mixture, and has become in the course of time a mixture forbidding to most readers. Autobiographical fragments are interwoven with German philosophy, and a secular message is conveyed in the language of Calvinist preachers. German was a language not often studied in England in the 1830s, and part of Carlyle's authority (which is analogous to that of Coleridge in an earlier generation) sprang from an awed, ignorant respect for the translator of Goethe and the interpreter of unintelligible German metaphysics.

But Carlyle was not fundamentally Germanic. Above all, he was Scots. He was steeped from childhood in the stern, terrifying and thrilling world of Scots Calvinism. If in some ways

15

his intellect wandered far from this, his feelings were formed for life in its crucible. His account of the conversion of the hero of *Sartor Resartus* to the 'Everlasting No' has the true accent of the old Calvinist preachers who did so much to form the Scottish national consciousness.

I asked myself: 'What *art* thou afraid of? Wherefore, like a coward, dost thou forever pip and whimper, and go cowering and trembling? Despicable biped! what is the sum-total of the worst that lies before thee? Death? Well, Death; and say the pangs of Tophet too, and all that the Devil and Man may, will or can do against thee! Hast thou not a heart; canst thou not suffer whatsoever it be; and as a Child of Freedom, though outcast, trample Tophet itself under thy feet, while it consumes thee? Let it come, then; I will meet it and defy it!' And as I so thought there rushed like a stream of fire over my whole soul; and I shook base Fear away from me forever. I was strong, of unknown strength; a spirit, almost a god. Ever from that time, the temper of my misery was changed: not Fear or whining Sorrow was it, but Indignation and grim fire-eyed Defiance.

Thus had the Everlasting No (das ewige Nein) pealed authoritatively through all the recesses of my Being, of my ME; and then was it that my whole ME stood up, in native God-created majesty and with emphasis recorded its Protest. Such a protest, the most important transaction in Life, may that same Indignation and Defiance, in a psychological point of view, be fitly called. The Everlasting No had said: 'Behold, thou art fatherless, outcast and the Universe is mine (the Devil's); to which my whole ME now made answer: '*I* am not thine, but Free, and forever hate thee!'

(Book II, Chapter 7)

If we wish to enter imaginatively into the world of an intellectual young man, born between (say) 1805 and 1820, we must try to understand the intense excitement he will have felt on first reading a passage like this. It appeared to cut through tedious philosophical disputes, to make anxieties, both intellectual and social, irrelevant. It appeared to reach out at one and the same time to the ultimate forces of the universe and to the deepest impulses in the human mind. Here was an answer.

Several points which were generally overlooked at the time became obvious later. The message was stirring, but it was vague. A later chapter of the book, it is true, was entitled 'The

Everlasting Yea'. But this was just as vague and altogether less memorable. Carlyle was really setting a fashion which many later Victorians were to follow, of trying to use the language and emotional power of Christianity without accepting its doctrines. It would eventually become apparent that this was like trying to gather the fruit of a tree whose roots one had deliberately cut away. Meanwhile, the young responded to the deep earnestness of Carlyle, and they responded, too, to the fundamental idea embodied in the title *Sartor Resartus*. According to this, the fundamental verities of the universe were unchangeable, settled by Divine fiat for all eternity. These are respresented in the figure by the unclothed body. The dress required by this body is the concepts, the language in which we try to speak of the eternal verities. This can and does change. The clothes wear out; and when this happens, there is a time of crisis and despair. For most people will try to pretend that the worn-out clothes are not really worn out. They will cling to what no longer has power to express the truth, and therefore no longer has power to save them. Hence the need for a new statement, a new set of clothes, a new batch of ideas, and, consequently, a new social order and a new way of living.

When this attractive idea is understood, it will be easy to see why Carlyle went on to write the history of the French Revolution. Published in 1837, *The French Revolution* is Carlyle's most important book, and it exercised a general philosophical influence which very few other historical works have attained. It was a detailed concrete illustration, backed with considerable learning, and an imaginative insight into character, and conducted with a moving eloquence, of the central idea of *Sartor Resartus*. It showed the old eighteenth-century order, in all its aspects, ecclesiastical, political, intellectual and social, irrevocably rejected by destiny, and the birth-pangs of a new civilization, full both of pain and hope. Carlyle's mind worked, like a poet's, primarily in images; and the master-images of *The French Revolution* are the volcano and the phoenix. A volcano is irresistible, and it comes at its appointed time, irrespective of all human efforts to prevent or delay it. So, for Carlyle, is the revolution. And what is it that is erupting? It is the people, the common people who, in the past, have been anonymous in history, have been sufferers rather than actors. Now, first in France, but later inevitably, everywhere, they will acquire power to make and overthrow monarchs and even, perhaps, to form the whole of society in their own image. This is Calvinism secularized. The vision is

Calvinist in its sense of inevitability, which is at the same time a form of Divine Justice. The French Revolution is a judgment on a corrupt society, so that in one sense it is a punishment for collective sin. But it is an idea entirely foreign to Carlyle's thought that the Revolution could have been averted if aristocracies had been more generous or kings had been wiser. Sin and punishment are alike seen as inevitable. In true Calvinist fashion, Carlyle blames people for what they were inevitably destined to do.

But it is a secularized vision, because the Book of Revelation is no longer Scripture but History. In an earlier essay, Carlyle had stated this idea explicitly, calling history 'Universal Divine Scripture, whose "plenary inspiration" no man, out of Bedlam or in it, shall bring in question' ('On History Again,' *Fraser's Magazine*, No. 41 (1833)). Like many of Carlyle's ideas, this was a statement of great appeal in its stark simplicity, but essentially confusing in its wider implications. One knows who has won a game because there is a time limit. But in history there is no time limit. Did Cromwell 'win' and Charles I lose? Or did Charles I eventually triumph in the person of his son after Cromwell's death? or did Cromwell win after all, because part of the change he effected in the constitution was permanent? Carlyle was later to compose three whole volumes of admiring comment on Cromwell's life and writings without seriously trying to answer these obvious questions.

More disturbing still, the plenary inspiration of history can carry the implication that success proves right. It is fair to say that in the sense Carlyle meant it the phrase 'Might is Right' was free from the taint of the worship of brutal power and vulgar success. He meant rather that the universe was so constituted that the right thing would be found to possess the most might, not that mere strength is the highest moral principle. But the idea, nevertheless, is a slippery one, capable of infinite degradation in the hands of millionaires and military dictators. Nor can Carlyle himself, especially in his later years, escape entirely free from the blame of unconsciously degrading it himself. The link of the idea with his assertion of the necessity of hero-worship is obvious. At first his conception of the hero included the hero of the realms of spirit and intellect. But he was always tempted to set up the simple strong man as admirable. He later wrote many volumes (1858–65) in praise of the tyrannical Frederick the Great; and as early as 1849 in the essay ominously entitled *The Nigger Question* he was asserting a fundamental distinction between master-races and slave-races.

This essay was written as a prelude to *Latter-Day Pamphlets* (1850), which mark a watershed of Carlyle's reputation. He had more than thirty years still to live, but his pre-eminence as sage and prophet never recovered from the damage inflicted by this sour and violent volume. After 1850 people came more and more to realize that Carlyle, for all his great literary gifts, was a negative prophet. His No was memorable, when his Yea was platitudinous or unintelligible, or even, in the treatment of some of his heroes, downright sycophantic. Carlyle in old age is the sad figure portrayed by Froude, who records:

> 'They call me a great man now', Carlyle said to me a few days before he died, 'but not one believes what I have told them.'
> (*Thomas Carlyle*, New ed., 1896, Vol. II, p. 495)

Younger than Carlyle by six years Newman (like Mill) was one of the few thinkers of his generation powerful enough in mind to ignore the tidal pull of Carlyle's rhetoric. He was like him in that his fundamental assumptions were intuitive so that he, too, may be seen as one who developed the interior affirmations of the earlier Romantic writers. But he was like Carlyle in little else. Above all, he had the power that Carlyle lacked of bringing his subtle intelligence to bear upon his intuitions. Newman makes assumptions, but he is always able to state clearly exactly how much he is assuming. A deeply emotional temperament is checked and guided not only by deep learning but by a philosophical rigour of argument, in which Mill was his only peer among the thinkers of that age.

When in 1833 Newman began with his friends to compose the *Tracts* mentioned earlier, his primary assumptions were three; and of these two were to remain unchanged throughout his life, and one, under a long bombardment of reasoning and experience, was to change, with momentous consequences both for himself and for the future of the Christian churches in this country. The first assumption which never wavered from the time of his Calvinist conversion at the age of fifteen he described in his *Apologia* (1864) thus:

> Isolating me from the objects which surrounded me, .. confirming me in my mistrust of material phenomena, and making me rest in the thought of two and two only absolute

and luminously self-evident beings, myself and my Creator . . .

(Chapter 1)

In the fifth chapter he develops the idea thus:

Starting then with the being of a God, (which, as I have said, is as certain to me as the certainty of my own exist-ence, though when I try to put the grounds of that certainty into logical shape I find a difficulty in doing so in mood and figure to my satisfaction,) I look out of myself into the world of men, and there I see a sight which fills me with unspeakable distress. The world seems simply to give the lie to that great truth, of which my whole being is so full; and the effect upon me is, in consequence, as a matter of necessity, as if it denied that I am in existence myself. If I looked into a mirror and did not see my face, I should have the sort of feeling which actually comes upon me, when I look into this living busy world, and see no reflexion of its Creator.

This kind of instinctive, primary devotion to religious causes is rare, and its association with the finest intellectual gifts is rarer still. Its association with the best fruits of literary cul-ture is almost unique. (It is worth recalling that Matthew Arnold, whose religious position had nothing in common with Newman's, thought of him all his life as the epitome of the civilized intellect of Oxford.) All this makes it very difficult to do justice to Newman.

Newman's second assumption in 1833 was that the nature of this God in Whom he could not help believing was revealed in Christianity, and this was a religion both institutional and dogmatic. The mere sentiment of religion he calls 'a dream and a mockery'. This assumption also never changed. The third assumption, which did change, was that the proper home of this Catholic tradition and the proper seat of authority was to be found in the Church of England.

There is no space here to recount the gradual and painful stages of this change (see Newman, *Apologia pro Vita Sua*, 1864). But it is important to notice that it was more a change in the judgment of facts than in principles. Newman always held that the Catholic Church had authority because it was founded by Christ. The question was where to find the living voice of that authority in the nineteenth century. In this sense his original commitment to the Church of England, deep and fervent though it was, was conditional. Friends and allies like Keble, whose commitment was unconditional, found it hard to understand this and could be forgiven if, when he left the Church of England in 1845, they were unable to perceive the inner consistency of Newman's thought.

It is not easy for us to recapture the excitement or to feel the inherent importance of Newman's secession. Disraeli a quarter of a century later called his loss a blow from which the Church was still reeling. To understand this one needs to enter into the general unquestioning assumption of all parties in England that Protestantism in some form or other was the best of all religions and that England was clearly the best of all countries. The loss of Newman struck a triple blow. It was a blow at the intellectual superiority of Protestantism, for no one could doubt that Newman's was one of the finest and most theologically instructed of contemporary minds. It was a blow at the moral superiority of Protestantism. (Here, admittedly, Kingsley tried to draw a red-herring about Newman's sincerity across the path of evidence, but John Bull, however staunchly Protestant himself, was able, at least after the publication of the *Apologia*, to see that Kingsley was talking nonsense.) For Newman's selfless devotion to the cause of truth as he understood it did not admit of doubt. It was a blow at English insularity. It prepared the way for a new generation of intellectuals, whether Roman Catholic or High Anglican or agnostic, who were consciously European in their outlook, and, in some cases, like F. W. Faber, provocatively ultramontane and Italianate. A blow at insularity was thus a blow at what Arnold was later to call the philistinism of a great commercial country. The rapid growth of serious and discriminating interest in the arts bearing fruit eventually in such works as Pater's *The Renaissance* (1873) and J. A. Symonds's *History of the Italian Renaissance* (1875–86) can be traced in part to Newman's adhesion to a foreign ecclesiastical power.

Newman's literary power is best seen in the *Apologia*. The subtle complexity of his intelligence is best seen in *The Development of Christian Doctrine* (1845), which he wrote just before and published just after his reception into the Roman Church. It is a difficult book both in its material and its argument; great learning in early Christian history would be needed to follow every point. But it contains at its core an idea that can be expressed very simply. It is that an institution either grows or dies, and so, in the case of a dogmatic institution like a Church, the doctrines, too, must either grow or wither. Newman introduced a new term into the old debate between unchanging revealed doctrine and progressive ideological change according to the needs of the moment. As we have seen, Newman never doubted that religion involved dogma. By 'development' he did not mean change in the sense of abandoning the old in favour of the new; to hold that the original revelation could become outmoded was really to say that it had not been a revelation at all. 'Development' for Newman meant the gradual understanding of all the implications and corollaries of a fundamental principle. But he stressed that this process could involve very great changes in the appearance of things just as a root or seed does not *look* in the least like the full-grown tree or flower.

The importance of this idea for the future of Catholic theology was considerable. Its importance in general Victorian intellectual history was great, too. But it will be easier for us to see what it was when we have considered some of the alternative modes of thought. Meanwhile, we may briefly mention two other works of Newman. *The Idea of a University* (1852) shows Newman at his nearest point to Arnold, Indeed, *Culture and Anarchy* might be described as a satirical study of the social obstacles to the ideal of harmonious perfection of the intellect through study that Newman had proposed. *The Grammar of Assent* (1870), his most purely philosophical work, reveals his scepticism about abstract logic. He maintained that any study of the working of intellect must lean as much towards psychology as towards mathematics. The book is an enquiry into the way men actually reason and arrive at conclusions, and discovers profound differences between this and the arguments presented in text-books of logic. It is an extended comment on his saying on another occasion that reason is only the map of the mind's progress.

It is in this concreteness of approach that Newman differs most strongly from the one man in his generation who was his all-round intellectual, though not literary, equal. John Stuart Mill was the heir of an older tradition, anterior to the heritage of the Romantic poets of which we have been speaking. His father, James Mill, was the disciple and interpreter of Bentham, holding approximately the same relation to him in the eyes of the public as T. H. Huxley was later to have to Darwin. J. S. Mill, with his precocious intellectual powers, trained or overtrained by the extraordinary educational process later described in his autobiography, was the natural heir of the Benthamite tradition, and had already, before he came of age in 1827, a large share in the management of the new Benthamite organ, *The Westminster Review*. Mill has his niche in the history of philosophy as a technical discipline, especially through his *Logic* (1843), but his wider importance for us lies in his prolonged inner debate about the utilitarian tradition in which he was bred, and in the fascinating, though fragmentary, record of the inner struggle that appeared in his published work. The utilitarians were no exceptions to the general rule that men of the early nineteenth century were seeking for fundamental principles and origins to justify their practice. But they went markedly against the current in believing that a simple formula could cover every moral case. The celebrated principle of 'the greatest good of the greatest number' or felicific calculus was the sole guiding principle of all their thought on morals, on politics, law and on administration.

Now, of course, adhering to a simple principle does not imply the possession of a simple mind or the use of simple methods of argument. Characteristically, the early utilitarians were men of learning and heavy intellectuals, as a glance at the pages of *The Westminster Review* (to say nothing of Mill's account of his early study of Greek) will easily show. But the gulf between them and learned men of other schools, like Coleridge and Carlyle, was unbridgeable. Or was it? For one might say that the younger Mill spent his whole life trying to prove that it could be bridged.

It is obvious that the utilitarian principle if applied with rigour abolishes totally all right of appeal to instinct and tradition. The powerful conservative forces tapped by Burke and Coleridge had their origin in two ideas, which might be imprecise in their formulation, but which possessed a deep appeal to the feelings—the idea that society is like an organism or living body, not like a machine, and the idea that the human heart is a shrine of incomprehensible mysteries. Bentham and James Mill could see nothing in ideas of this kind but intellectual muddle and the self-interested special pleading of an aristocratic class and their intellectual satellites. One may say that the great debate between Bentham and James Mill on one side and Burke, Coleridge and Wordsworth on the other continued long after they were all dead, and indeed, it continues in some form to this day. It was (and is) a debate on which people take sides, as a rule, with a primary emotional commitment. J. S. Mill is almost alone in being deeply influenced by both sides.

He could not help being influenced by such a father; and though his personality was really very different from his father's, there are certain aspects of the father's thought that persist to the end in the writings of the son. There is a revealing similarity of prose-style. In each there is a kind of abstract precision. Their words are never formally unclear in their meaning, but they are often curiously remote from experience. Thus James Mill's *History of India* (1818) never gives any impression of what India looks like, feels like, smells like. It gives a very clear impression of the organization of the British administration. Similarly the son's most celebrated work, *On Liberty* (1859), masses the theoretical arguments for and against the liberty of the subject with consummate lucidity, but never gives any sign that the author felt deeply the experience of choosing, or had much curiosity about what Hopkins was later to call 'the selfless self or self' where fundamental choices are made.

For a full understanding of Mill the posthumous *Autobiography* (1873) is the key book, and any reader who came to it after reading all Mill's other works, as some of its first readers must have done, will experience a great surprise, a surprise which may help in the end to a salutary re-interpretation of what had gone before. He reveals that in 1826 he underwent a period of acute depression after asking himself whether, if all the utilitarian aims were realized, this achievement would be enough to make him happy. He continues:

> An irrepressible self-consciousness distinctly answered, 'No!' At this my heart sank within me: the whole foundation on which my life was constructed fell down. All my happiness was to have been found in the continual pursuit of this end. The end had ceased to charm, and how could there ever again be any interest in the means? I seemed to have nothing left to live for.

(Autobiography, Chapter 5)

A page or two later he adds the telling comment.—'To know that a feeling would make me happy if I had it, did not give me the feeling.'

He had no one to confide in, and eventually it was the reading of Wordsworth that initiated his recovery. Though Mill was much too modest to assume that his own case was of general importance, he came to see that he had accidentally stumbled at a very early age upon the central dilemma of utilitarianism and on one of the key problems of the age. What is the use of a system that would work very well for certain imaginary creatures in human form, but will not work for men as they are? Mill spent his life worrying at this question. His deep reverence for his father, coupled with his own intellectual character, loving clearness and suspicious of mystery, forbade him ever to renounce utilitarianism. In stead he pondered upon it, attempted to do what in strict logic was perhaps impossible, to make a synthesis of his father's system and others, even the most unlikely ally of all for a utilitarian:

In the golden rule of Jesus of Nazareth, we read the complete spirit of the ethics of utility. To do as you would be done by, and to love your neighbour as yourself, constitute the ideal perfection of utilitarian morality.

(*Utilitarianism*, 1853, Chapter 2, Sec. 18)

We can can only endorse the conclusion of one of Mill's most acute critics, Professor Plamenatz, who says, 'there is not much left of Benthamite utilitarianism when Mill has completed his defence of it' (*The English Utilitarians*, 2nd edn., 1958, p. 144).

To a large extent, as this last judgment will suggest, Mill was an unconscious rebel against his father's authority. His father regarded the passionate and sentimental relations between the sexes with contempt; the son believed his wife to possess superhuman gifts and virtues. The father had the usual utilitarian distaste for art; the son's essay on poetry shows a romantic taste and treats poetry as a private voice of pure feeling, overheard by the reader rather than publicly presented by the poet (*Thoughts on Poetry*, 1833; revised 1859).

But in calling his rebellion unconscious I am far from implying a charge of timidity against Mill. There was one occasion when his lucid mind (for confusions in Mill's thought always have an emotional, never an intellectual cause) actively confronted the utilitarian dilemma. In his articles on Bentham and Coleridge Mill with great acuteness discerned the main lines of the future conflict of ideas. Bentham for him represents the practical effectiveness and the limitations of the purely rational mind. He is the 'great questioner of things established'. Coleridge represents the unconscious reserves of life hidden in traditions, institutions and feelings, of which the rational defence is either difficult or impossible. Mill is aware of his almost uniquely cross-bench position when he writes:

The limited philosophical public of this country is as yet too exclusively divided between those to whom Coleridge

and the views which he promulgated or defended are everything, and those to whom they are nothing.
(*Mill on Bentham and Coleridge,* ed. F. R. Leavis, 1950, p. 103)

Mill's voice in this essay is the most temperate in a debate
that was not marked on the whole by temperance. Reading the
great early Victorian writers, especially Carlyle, Dickens and
Ruskin, one could derive the impression that utilitarianism
was a dead horse that everybody inexplicably insisted on
flogging. Linked with utilitarianism in their condemnations
was a doctrine of great practical importance, 'political
economy' or the economics of the great trading class. To some
extent the connection was fortuitous. It is true that Mill wrote
a book called *The Principles of Political Economy.* It is also
true that, as with utilitarianism, but more obviously, Mill eventually became a questioner, even a critic of the pure milk of
Adam Smith's doctrine. But the loose general association between utilitarianism and political economy aroused a new
kind of public interest, and stirred into an angry controversial posture men like Dickens who would have allowed an
abstract philosophical discussion to pass them by. *Hard Times*
is not a fair book; but its critique of utilitarian ethics and
Manchester business theories is brilliant and memorable. Its
fundamental assumption is the same as that which Mill, speaking in a much quieter tone, had found in Coleridge, that there
is a non-element in human nature which makers of systems
ignore at their peril. It is for this that the dying Mrs. Grad-
grind feebly gropes, as she takes upon her 'the dread solemnity
of the sages and patriarchs' (*Hard Times,* Bk. II, Chapter 9).
But the horse that Dickens and others were flogging was
dead only in a rather specialized intellectual sense. The debate was indeed one-sided, for Mill, whose loyalties, as we have
seen, were ambiguous was the only man of high intellectual
stature who carried forward into the mid-Victorian period
the tradition of Bentham and the early *Westminster Review.*
But the practical man of the world does not worry about intellectual consistency so long as he is making a profit. The great
political triumph of the Manchester School came in 1846 with
the repeal of the Corn Laws, and the next twenty-five years
were years of triumphant supremacy for the English businessman in the markets of the world. What did a commercial
nation that had coal and iron in plenty, that led the world in
the development of railways, need to worry about the
grumbles of intellectuals or the satire of a great popular

novelist? The first utilitarians, as we have said, had been scholars and thinkers, but their system also had great advantage for people who were nothing of the kind. By shifting the basic utilitarian principle a little, and using profit, not happiness, as the criterion (and does not profit make business-men happy?), these people were able to pursue their ruthless commercial aims in the conviction that they had an unshakeable basis of moral and economic theory on which to build. Most of them were too unintellectual, and all of them were too busy to answer Dickens or Ruskin. Perhaps Arnold's *Culture and Anarchy* is the best place to look for an impression of this oddly uneven debate as it appeared at the time. For Arnold gives us a sketch of these shadowy opponents who were so powerful in their day, even if it is hardly a fair one. But to see how far the tendency to treat human nature as a laboratory-compound could go, one should glance through the works of Herbert Spencer with their ominous titles like *Social Statics*. Spencer is unreadable to-day, but his immense prestige in his time, which extended as far as Russia, is a clear proof that complete ignorance of human nature will not necessarily prevent a man from becoming an acknowledged expert upon it. It is a reminder, too, that Carlyle, Dickens and Ruskin were not tilting at windmills.

In a time of rapid change thinking men look to the past for help in understanding the present. Some of the fundamental controversies of the age were conducted in the form of arguments about the past. The French Revolution, the Glorious Revolution, the Civil War, the Reformation all played their part; Carlyle, Macaulay, Froude and others found very different lessons in these great events. But one thing they had in common. All the time they wrote about history, they were really arguing about the nineteenth century, and so their more perceptive readers understood them.

The French Revolution was the nearest and the most insistent of these great historical events. Everyone read Carlyle's great book, and many were stirred by it, but its central message was ambiguous. Did it really say that revolution was inevitable, because the world, led by France, was moving into a new democratic phase, in which monarchies and aristocracies must either agree to abdicate or else endure to be deposed by force? Or did it say that the French Revolution was due to the inflexible selfishness of the French ruling classes so that the ruling powers in England could learn by the example and survive? Though terrible forebodings filled the minds of many in the 1840s, most people cautiously inclined to the second view. In this they were assisted, no doubt, by that hereditary feeling of superiority to the French in political and military affairs, which Tennyson so perfectly represented when he spoke of 'the red fool-fury of the Seine' and of freedom in England 'slowly broadening down'. There was a feeling expressed in Disraeli's *Coningsby* and *Sybil* that the new forces of organized labour were waiting for leadership from the educated and preferably from the aristocratic class. The comparative social peacefulness and increasing prosperity of the years from 1850 to 1890, coupled with the thoroughly ducal composition of the Cabinets of Disraeli and Gladstone as late as the seventies and eighties showed that this was not an illusion. Dickens, who had read Carlyle with attention, helped to implant in all classes a horror of mob-law by the terrible power of the crowd scenes in *Barnaby Rudge* and *A Tale of Two Cities* and a suspicion of demagogic trade union leaders by his portrayal of the insincere Slackbridge in *Hard Times*. But it is easy to forget that at least until 1850 the thought of revolution was in the air, and that Chartism seemed a much more formidable phenomenon to the first readers of Carlyle's essay upon it than it was eventually to prove.

This apparent digression is necessary because the more celebrated doctrine of progress, and the accompanying evolutionary ideas, are misunderstood if they are imagined as having nothing to struggle against. Those who accepted them were just as often worried men snatching at comfort as they were the smug, comfortable men of later caricature. For Macaulay, the most coherent and persuasive of all preachers of progress, the French Revolution was something that had to be explained away as not relevant to England. Macaulay called in 1688 to redress the balance which Carlyle had disturbed with his terrible account of 1789, and worse of 1793.

The germ of the argument Macaulay was to present with such learned and lucid ease in his *History* of the reigns of James II and William III (1849–61) is to be found in his long review of Hallam's *History of England* published in September 1828. He had already thoroughly absorbed the Whig habit, which was so useful in calming an inflamed public opinion in 1832 and after, of presenting moderate, even conservative, views in language that sounds revolutionary. Thus he calls Strafford 'the lost archangel, the Satan of the apostasy', but the accusation against him is that he had formed a design against 'the fundamental laws of England'. A society that has fundamental laws, which it is impious to question, and which remain un-changed in the nineteenth century as in the seventeenth, must be in many respects a conservative society; and Macaulay's idea of progress is conservative in the sense that nothing is ever lost and no real change of direction in the line or aims of advance is ever envisaged. He is fond of the image of the child and the grown man for the early and later phases of a society's development. The vigour of his denunciation of demo-cracy can still surprise those who have not grasped the in-herently conservative character of Whiggism and have not measured the power and insistence of the fears that Carlyle had started by speaking of a new democratic age inaugurated by a blood-bath in France.

When Macaulay wrote his review of Hallam, and to some lesser extent still when he wrote his *History*, the accepted view of seventeenth-century history was that given by the history of David Hume. Hume had made a sharp distinction between the issues at stake in 1641 and the issues of 1688. In 1641, Hume, with judicious deliberation but in the end with-out any doubt, had sided with the Royalists, and his portrait of Charles I is notably sympathetic. But he treated the revolu-tion of 1688 as an inevitable reaction to the reckless and un-constitutional actions of James II. Macaulay's aim was to break the traditional authority of Hume's antithesis and to represent that there had been a continuing inheritance of progressive and reactionary parties in the state from the Civil War down to the constitutional conflicts of 1832. Cromwell, the Whigs of the Exclusion Crisis in the time of Charles II, Charles James Fox and Lord John Russell are a strange team to carry the badge of uniformity, but Macaulay insists that they do so, for the strongest feature of his intellectual nature was a dislike of exceptions and anomalies. The great achieve-ment of his *History*, which made it so popular in its time and makes it so readable to-day, is that, with its mass of detail and its genuine depth of learning, it still contrives to give an im-pression of simplicity. All the detail, in the end, is shown to be related to two great unchanging tendencies, the reac-tionary and the progressive, and these great tendencies, in turn, are for ever linked to the two great parties in the state, Tory and Whig. And before the terms were invented, the realities they describe were already at work in the Civil War struggle.

Bagehot, his most acute contemporary critic, complained of Macaulay's 'inexperiencing nature' and pointed out that his original ideas on Indian education had not been altered in the slightest degree as a result of visiting India (*Collected Works*, ed. N. St. John Stevas, 1965, Vol. I, p. 399). He imagined him saying that 'Hampden was preparing for the occasion in which I had a part' and wryly noted that he treated existing men as 'painful prerequisites of great-grandchildren.' All these charges, with a little allowance for the rights of witty exaggeration, are true, but Bagehot was the first to say that they did not dispose of Macaulay. The fallacies in Macaulay (I think we must agree that the Whig view of history contains fallacies) were fallacies that a large part of his audience would have accepted without him. It is very human to treat the past as a mere introduction to the present, for how can any time in which *I* was not alive be as interesting to me as the time in which I am? It is natural for the citizens of a country whose trade and warships circle the globe to suppose that they must be on the right lines and that future development must only be an increase in the scale of the benefits already attained. Macaulay endowed these natural, though quite fallacious, assumptions with a civilized pedigree. Read with care, the celebrated third chapter of the *History*, with its prolonged one-sided comparison of the England of 1685 to the England of his own day, does not appear, as it is often said to be, a materialistic performance. Macaulay is just as zealous for progress in the 'useless' pursuits of intellectual culture as he is for the improvement of machines. But he is, admittedly, much less successful in demonstrating that the first must always be linked to the second. For the student of the period the final thought on Macaulay may be that in an age of cloudy prophetic writings and works of obscure and troubled genius it is refreshing to encounter a mighty simplifier, whose meaning is never for a moment in doubt.

Turning to Macaulay's great successor in the art of historical narrative, J. A. Froude, one is reminded to praise also Macaulay's unfailing geniality of tone. Macaulay is often sweeping, and sometimes unfair, but he is never ungenerous. Froude's history of the sixty years from the fall of Wolsey to the Spanish Armada (1856–70) is a brilliant work, marred by an ungenerous worship of the strong and triumphing over the weak. He tried to do for Henry VIII what Carlyle had done for Cromwell and he becomes ludicrous in an excess of barrister's zeal. To picture Henry, in his fifth marriage, as the innocent, pathetic victim of that designing harridan Catherine Howard and to represent the death penalty upon her almost as an act of lenity is to overstrain all ordinary credulity. Nevertheless, many of Macaulay's merits are re-captured. There is an extraordinary lucidity, an extraordinary power of arrangement in narrative form; and once again, the lesson Froude wished his readers to learn was a contemporary lesson. It was the same lesson that he tried to enforce in his Irish eighteenth-century history (1872–4). Froude offers a heady mixture of Carlylean hero-worship, English nationalism veering into racialism, and a kind of uncompromising secular Protestantism. I say secular Protestantism because it is not religious truth that is Froude's real concern. He believes that the Protestant system of belief leads on the whole to the growth of the civic virtues of veracity, courage and initiative, and that the Catholic system militates against these. Alternatively, he believes that Celts and Latins are naturally cowards, deceivers and sycophants, and that their traditional adherence to the Catholic system is an apt illustration of these congenital inferiorities. To a nation about to acquire, or already acquiring, great new tracts of land in many parts of the world, and determined to harden its conscience about its treatment of the Irish people, this reading of history had attractions.

Macaulay was a Whig and Froude was a Tory, but to a public taking its history in broad narrative doses and applying its lessons with the uncritical enthusiasm of the layman, both appeared to be saying similar things about the present and the future—that the new, the stronger, the more assertive nation or idea was also for that reason the better. The strength of this current of thought needs to be remembered in assessing the public reaction to the great scientific developments of the day.

Darwin was a very great man, whose achievements seem at least as important to-day as they did in his own time; as a general intellectual influence he has aften been taken out of context, misunderstood or overestimated. The great scientific changes for which he may always stand as a representative had begun before the close of the eighteenth century, and it was geology that opened the way to the new view of the physical development of animals and men. Sir Charles Lyell in his *Principles of Geology* (1830–3) had drawn together a great mass of evidence for the very gradual development of the existing formation of the geological strata in the earth's crust and had drawn attention to the changing pattern of animal fossils in the different strata and the presence of the fossils of extinct animals in the lower strata. It gradually became apparent that the earth was vastly older than had been assumed in previous centuries, and that the fossil evidence suggested that man was a comparatively recent arrival upon the earth (See S. Toulmin and J. Goodchild, *The Discovery of Time*, 1965). Through the 1830s and 1840s these matters did not excite the general public interest that they were to claim later, but a few people, among whom Tennyson is notable for us, brooded long and deeply upon them. The sensitive mind was likely to receive two main impressions from the process. The first was that things became less solid, because they were set against a time-scale indefinitely increased. In past centuries people thought of a river as flowing and a tree as still; they thought of spring as transient but of the orderly progression of the seasons as unchangeable. Now they were forced to ask whether all material things were not transient, a point perfectly expressed in Tennyson's line 'The hills are shadows and they flow' (*In Memoriam*, CXXIII). The second impression, equally important, had to wait longer for its full impact. A shadowy sense of direction was given to non-human processes, astronomical or geological. Part of the importance of Darwin was that he gave stronger ground for extending this second impression to the animal world also. He first, after a quarter of a century of patient research, in *The Origin of Species* disposed of many of the stubborn scientific difficulties in supposing that one species could be descended physically from another. It has become fashionable for later writers, especially the authors of text-books, with their precious gift of hindsight, to ascribe all these difficulties to prejudice, and especially to a narrow reading of the book of *Genesis*. This is grossly unhistorical, as can easily be seen by a glance at two points (out of many that might be given.) The first is that Newman welcomed the *Origin* because of its interesting analogy with his own idea of development in intellectual and spiritual matters. The second is that Darwin himself was to the end of his life worried by certain apparent discrepancies and obvious scientific difficulties. The most obstinate of these was that raised by Lord Kelvin about the time required for Darwin's processes of mutation of types. This appeared to be much greater than Kelvin's perfectly lucid calculation of the age of the earth derived from the time of cooling could possibly allow. Neither Darwin nor Kelvin could guess that later scientists would be able to suggest a much greater age for the earth, because they would discover that the interior of the earth could generate its own heat and thus retard the cooling process. Just as old Test cricketers, sitting in the press-box, never miss a slip-catch, later commentators are apt to think they would easily have solved difficulties insoluble at the time But, though unable to meet all reasonable objections, Darwin was convinced that the weight of evidence was on his side. His *Descent of Man* (1871) set out in full the arguments in favour of believing that men were physically descended from more primitive animal ancestors, though part of its argument, once again, had been anticipated by Lyell in *The Antiquity of Man* (1863).

The effects of all this on the general current of thought were oblique and variable. No deductions of a strictly philosophical kind could be made, but habits of thought and modes of feeling were deeply influenced. For some the increase in the time-span of the imagined past intensified that sense of loneliness in the universe, which is one of the most disturbing sensations of civilized man. The most sensitive literary expression of this idea is to be found in the works of Thomas Hardy. Others used evolutionary ideas to provide a kind of cosmic backing to Macaulay's Whiggish argument, so on this side the result was a strengthening of the Broad Church school of liberal theologians of whom A. P. Stanley was the most acute and Benjamin Jowett, because of his immense educational influence, the most celebrated. The volume *Essays and Reviews* (1860), to which Jowett contributed an article on the interpretation of scripture, and Frederick Temple, later Archbishop of Canterbury, an article entitled 'The Education of the World', may be taken as representative of the strong but ill-defined impact of science on this school of religious thought. The title of Temple's article is especially revealing, comprehending in one large gesture progress à la Macaulay, the traditional religious idea of the Hebrew *preparatio evangelica* and a vague bow to immense aeons of pre-historic time in which the Divine purpose may have been at work in ways newly suggested by the scientists. There were others, though the most notable of them, Nietzsche, is outside the scope of this essay, who saw Darwinian evolution as a kind of delayed death-certificate for humanity as we know it, which would become, upon the arrival of the pre-destined new race, an anachronism, like the extinct creature in the lower fossil strata.

One thinker is worth a more special mention here, because,

unlike the others, he found that the whole course of his intellectual life was changed and then directed anew by Darwin's discoveries. T. H. Huxley had all the gifts required for
the more serious kind of popularization. He was pugnacious,
lucid and well-informed. He scored some notable controversial
successes against men of more powerful mind than his own,
including Gladstone, when the latter ventured as amateurs
into territory where Huxley was a professional. But more
interesting than all this to-day is the impact of Darwinism on
his own meditations about the world. This is best seen in the
remarkable Romanes lecture delivered at Oxford in 1893 under
the title *Evolution and Ethics*. In this lecture he announced
the conclusion he had reached after more than thirty years of
meditation on Darwin's theory and its consequences. It was
simple, forceful and gloomy. He said that the evolutionary
process, which must now be considered an unquestionable
fact of nature, was unalterably opposed to the improvement
of human civilization and even to the very existence of our
moral institutions; but instead of saying, as others were saying,
that we must accommodate our petty human ideas to the
great cosmic forces revealed by the scientists, he said that we
must fight the evolutionary process with all our strength in
order to remain human at all. The more that mighty cosmic
forces decreed that the weakest must go to the wall, the more
we must tend with loving care our feeble grandmother or our
crippled, sickly child.

Huxley's is not the last word on evolution and ethics, though
his is the last notable voice raised within our period, but his
lecture brings home forcibly a point of the highest importance
that is very often overlooked. It is that Darwin's work does
not for general human, philosophical purposes point in any
direction at all. Once removed from the strictly zoological
sphere and allowed to have free influence over thought and
behaviour, Darwin's leading ideas become infinitely plastic.
The highest common factor of what intelligent late Victorians
found in Darwin is precisely nothing. Indeed, the testimony
of the rocks and fossils formed thousands or millions of years
ago was in this respect very like the testimony of the Civil
War or the Middle Ages. Many a serious and learned seeker
only found after careful study that his deepest instincts and
convictions about life were clearly confirmed.

Yet the Victorian interest in the Middle Ages was of deeper
significance than the interest in the Civil War and the Glorious

Revolution. The latter were studied to derive certain contemporary lessons and to prove particular points. There was scarcely a serious wish to revive seventeenth-century civilization. With the Middle Ages it was different. The point is most easily seen in the imaginative writers. The seventeenth century, by common consent a rich and various contributor to our literary heritage, had practically no influence on the best writers (It was left to the poets of this century to use and adapt the poetic treasures left by Donne and Dryden), but medieval influence in various forms, devout, socio-political, decorative and erotic, is obvious in authors as different as Tennyson, Ruskin and Rossetti, while the influence on architecture and painting is stronger still.

An important source-book for various kinds of medieval influence is Pugin's *Contrasts* (1836) in which an architectural argument is cleverly woven with religious and social ones to show the superiority of medieval to modern culture, and especially to all classical or 'pagan' revivals in the modern world. But Pugin was no more able than Darwin to control the fortunes in the world of the ideas he had presented. Pugin saw the Middle Ages as tense, heroic and radically Christian and Catholic. Rossetti, partly following Keats, saw them as dreamy, langourous and deliciously unreal. Pugin, certainly, conceived himself to be making a real historical statement. So, on the whole, did Ruskin, while Tennyson was more concerned with finding a medieval image of nineteenth-century dilemmas, and Rossetti cared little either for historical accuracy or for contemporary society. Nevertheless, all these and indeed all the different varieties of medievalizer had one very important thing in common. They all felt that the nature of the Victorian intellectual and social scene was such that the imagination could only grasp it obliquely. This is a point of prime importance about the society they lived in; and it is hasty to say that they must have been mistaken, and unfair to dismiss them all as escapists. The medieval cult, in all its forms, witnesses to the strain of living and thinking in a society where facts, theories and principles must have seemed to many sensitive people like an unintelligible whirl of atoms.

The most striking case of medieval interests leading to a prophetic re-appraisal of, and attack on, Victorian society is that of Ruskin. It is impossible here to do justice to the complexities of his long career, which is apt to seem even longer than it was because of the variety of his interests, the intensity of his feelings, and the long despair of his final years. His early works are specialist studies in art criticism, and need not concern us here. His later works are tangled and obscure and darkened by mental instability, though he was incapable at any time of writing anything that was not obviously the work of an exceptional man. It was his middle period, especially the works of the 1860s, that made the most valuable contribution to the Victorian intellectual scene. *Unto This Last* (1860) was the first distinguished work containing an attack conceived in analytical and theoretical terms upon the economics of the Manchester school. The title, drawn from the parable of the labourers in the vineyard, corresponds exactly to the intention, to show the gulf between Christianity and *laissez-faire* economics. Ruskin solemnly accused the commercial classes of having set up a doctrine systematically opposed to the first principles of their professed religion. The history of the publication neatly illustrated the point. The *Cornhill Magazine* had just begun under Thackeray's editorship, and it combined great popularity with a serious interest in ideas and in the arts. After three of Ruskin's essays had appeared the outcry against them became in Ruskin's own words 'too strong for any editor to endure', and the series had to be cut short. Had Ruskin, or anyone else, written attacks on the established religion of England, couched in the same decent and serious language as *Unto This Last*, the outcry would not have been strong enough to compel a friendly editor to such an extreme step. Ruskin's point was made. The Manchester doctrines were, in some sense, *more sacred* in the mind of the public than their professed religious beliefs.

Munera Pulveris (1863) is a fuller and perhaps more satisfactory statement of Ruskin's profound sense of the living inter-relation of religion, art, morality and economics. Ruskin was free from one of the chief difficulties felt by others in attacking *laissez-faire* capitalism. Its claim always was that it was on the side of freedom. The words 'Free Trade' had acquired, especially since the 1840s and the heroic days of the Corn Law debates, a special majesty of their own. Many people must have felt that the phrase was now consecrated as part of the tradition of *Magna Carta* and the precious personal rights of the citizen. But Ruskin had no difficulty about resisting this (rather specious) association, because he always believed it was more important to be right than to be free. He rejected altogether the idea that what the majority wants must be best, and he even went so far, in the fifth section of *Munera Pulveris*, as to compare an ill-informed democracy to a mass of beetles in Switzerland who tried to fly over a lake and all perished because they miscalculated the distance. His aim is always that the wisest and best should lead the weak and foolish. His radicalism had no trace of liberalism. He wanted the poor to have prosperity rather than the vote. Seen from this point of view, free trade becomes only the right of the rich and cunning to deceive the poor into spending what little money they have on shoddy goods. If one thinks of the poor man as a worker rather than as a consumer, the free-trade ethos comes in for an equally severe attack. To maintain his dignity a man needs to be a craftsman. (This is the original point of contact between Ruskin's original artistic interests and his social and economic ones.) The factory hand is not a craftsman, and his employer does not wish him to be one.

Ruskin replaces the current doctrine of freedom with a doctrine of society. Responsibility is mutual. The upper classes of England and France are responsible for the shocking crimes perpetrated in the streets of the new urban societies, though nearly all of them would, as individuals, be incapable of taking part in them. In this way Ruskin opens the door to a general corporate choice exercised by the state in many activities (like town planning) where most of his contemporaries believed that no general policy was desirable.

A great part of the difficulty many people have in understanding Ruskin springs from this union of radical social doctrine with a rigid paternalism. (Perhaps the most extreme case of the latter is to be found in *Time and Tide* (1867), where he actually recommends that the right to marry should not be acquired simply by coming of age, but by the completion of a term of satisfactory service to the community.) We are conditioned by the state of affairs we know to-day to assume that a man who thinks in this way will be on the political right. Ruskin's thought shows that there is no necessary reason for such an assumption. When we see this we shall begin to understand how it was the man, who always claimed to be a high Tory of the old school, was execrated as a socialist at a time when this was generally felt to be an ugly word.

Ruskin typifies, sometimes in exaggerated form, many of the characteristics of the leading men of the age. Like Carlyle, Mill, Gladstone and so many more, he is, above all, a crusader and a deeply emotional man whose distinguished intellectual powers could never operate in a cool, rational spirit. Like them, too, he possessed a versatility and a breadth of learning which is simply astonishing to our own age. In the end the most stimulating thing about the Victorian intellectual scene is this: a great debate, intelligent and passionate, was conduced by brave men who neither despised the public, nor pandered to its lowest instincts.

BIBLIOGRAPHY

A *Primary Sources*

W. Bagehot, *Estimations in Criticism*, ed. C. Lennox. 2 vols., Edinburgh, 1908–9.

T. Carlyle, *Sartor Resartus 1833*, [published anonymously].

—— *The French Revolution*, 2 vols., 1837.

—— *Critical and Miscellaneous Essays*, 2nd ed., 5 vols., 1840.

—— *Past and Present*, 1843.

—— *Cromwell's Letters and Speeches*, 3 vols., 1845.

—— *Latter-Day Pamphlets*, 1850.

C. Darwin, *On the Origin of Species by Means of Natural Selection*, 1859.

—— *The Descent of Man and Selection in Relation to Sex*, 2 vols., 1871.

C. Dickens, *Hard Times*, 1854.

B. Disraeli, *Coningsby*, 3 vols., 1844.

—— *Sybil*, 3 vols., 1845.

Essays and Reviews, 1860.

J. A. Froude, *History of England from the Fall of Wolsey to the Defeat of the Spanish Armada*, 12 vols., 1870.

—— *Thomas Carlyle*, New edn., 1896.

T. H. Huxley, *Collected Essays*, 9 vols., 1893–5.

C. Lyell, *Principles of Geology*, 3 vols., 1830–3

—— *Geological Evidences of the Antiquity of Man*, 1863.

Lord Macaulay, *Complete Works*, 12 vols., (Albany Edition), 1898.

J. S. Mill, *A System of Logic*, 2 vols., 1843.

—— *On Liberty*, 1859.

—— *Utilitarianism*, 1865.

——*Autobiography*, 1873.

—— *Bentham and Coleridge*, With an Introduction by F. R. Leavis, 1950.

J. H. Newman, *An Essay on the Development of Christian Doctrine*, 1845.

—— *Discourses on the Scope of University Education*, Dublin, 1852.

—— *Apologia pro Vita Sua* (the Two Versions of 1864 and 1865 preceded by Newman's and Kingsley's Pamphlets) With an Introduction by Wilfrid Ward, Oxford, 1913.

A. W. Pugin, *Contrasts or a Parallel between the Noble Edifices of the Middle Ages and Corresponding Buildings of the Present Day*, 1841.

—— *An Apology for the Revival of Christian Architecture*, 1843.

J. Ruskin, *Works*, ed. E. T. Cook and A. Wedderburn, 39 vols., 1903.

A. P. Stanley, *Essays Chiefly on Questions of Church and State from 1850–1870*, 1870.

B *Critical Works*

R. H. Hutton, *Essays on Some of the Modern Guides of English Thought*, 1887. A judicious summing-up, after the battle, by an intelligent Anglican.

R. W. Church, *The Oxford Movement*, 1891.

G. P. Gooch. *History and Historians in the Nineteenth Century*, 1913. Thorough, indispensable and dull.

J. M. Robertson, *A History of Freethought in the Nineteenth Century*, 1929. Thorough, though at times intemperate.

G. M. Young, *Victorian England: Portrait of an Age*, Oxford, 1936. A masterly account in brief compass.

B. Willey, *Nineteenth Century Studies*, 1949. A learned and lucid, though unexciting, account of the development of thought from Coleridge to Matthew Arnold.

B. Willey, *More Nineteenth Century Studies*, 1956. A sympathetic account of Victorian agnosticism from a modern equivalent of a Broad Church point of view.

J. Holloway, *The Victorian Sage*, 1953. A very intelligent and original account, from a point of view combining the philosophical and the literary approach, of the 'Prophets' from Carlyle onwards. Ruskin is unfortunately omitted.

W. E. Houghton, *The Victorian Frame of Mind*, New Haven, 1957. A sensitive and useful study of everyday feelings and attitudes, 1830–1870.

R. Williams, *Culture and Society 1780–1950*, 1958. An interesting and original, though very one-sided and at times scornful, account of the relation of the thinkers to the society in which they lived.

J. Plamenatz, *The English Utilitarians*, Oxford, 1958. A first-class philosophical study.

P. Geyl, *Debates with Historians*, 1962. A masterly enquiry into the moral and political assumptions of Carlyle, Macauiay and others.

J. D. Rosenberg, *The Darkening Glass*, 1963. The best general study of the development of Ruskin's thought.

W. L. Burn, *The Age of Equipoise*, 1964. Perhaps the best general study of mid-Victorian life in every aspect.

A. O. J. Cockshut, *The Unbelievers*, 1964. A study of agnostic thought, 1840–1890.

W. Bagehot, *Literary Essays*, ed. N. St. John Stevas, 1965. Bagehot is unfailingly acute, witty and realistic.

O. Chadwick, *The Victorian Church*, Part I, 1966. An admirable account for the years 1830–1860.

2

MATTHEW ARNOLD
(and A. H. CLOUGH)

KENNETH ALLOTT, University of Liverpool

The recognition of Matthew Arnold's distinction as a representative Victorian man-of-letters—and even T. S. Eliot, who found many of his ideas deeply antipathetic, has admitted that he was 'in some respects the most satisfactory man-of-letters of his age' (*The Use of Poetry and the Use of Criticism*, 1933, p. 104)—depends on an adequate response to both his poetry and his prose. For some students it is the critical prose that counts and the poetry is of less interest. Quite possibly Arnold might have agreed with them. Of Sainte-Beuve, his master in criticism, he wrote in 1869 with an unmistakable autobiographical reference:

> Like so many who have tried their hands at *oeuvres de poésie et d'art*, his preference, his dream, his ideal was there; the rest was comparatively journeyman-work, to be done well and estimably rather than ill and discreditably, and with precious rewards of its own, besides, in exercising the faculties and in keeping off ennui; but still work of an inferior order.
>
> ('Sainte Beuve' (1869), *Complete Prose Works*, ed. R. H. Super, Ann Arbor, 1960– , Vol. V, p. 305.)

Yet while sympathising with the French critic's predilection, he decided judicially that the criticism was first-rate, the poetry second-rate. He might have accepted amiably a similar assessment of the value of his own mixed productions, although he must have known that his poetry was much superior to Sainte-Beuve's. Arnold's example forbids us to make exaggerated claims on his behalf. The poetry has 'some want of flame, of breath, of opinion' ('Sainte Beuve', *Five Uncollected Essays of Matthew Arnold*, ed. K. Allott, Liverpool 1953, p. 72); the prose moves without constraint. In both verse and prose he was predominantly an intellectual, whose detachment seemed to cruder spirits supercilious. He was never in his own day a popular writer like Tennyson or Dickens appealing to a broad cross-section of the reading public. If towards the end of his life his poems were known to 'all lovers of poetry' and his prose was read by 'all who care for letters', the number of people in these categories was not large; and only one of his books, *Literature and Dogma* (1873), achieved the circulation of a best-seller. He spoke from the beginning to thoughtful and serious-minded people of some education, a group that remained faithful to him and grew in a modest way more numerous with the years. His success in catching the ear of the general public with phrases that epitomised his ideas—Barbarians, Philistines and Populace, 'to see the object as in itself it really is', 'the grand name without the grand thing', 'the remnant', 'that great rope, with a Philistine at each end of it talking inutilities' (of the Atlantic telegraph)—meant that some notion of what he stood for became familiar far beyond the circle of his actual readers.

Matthew Arnold (1822–88) began by being a poet and his literary career has two distinct phases, most of his poetry being written before 1857, the year in which he was elected Professor of Poetry at Oxford, and most of his critical prose after that date. As a Victorian poet he is usually ranked after Tennyson and Browning, but it is clear that Arnold did not think that his poetic achievement was of a radically inferior order to theirs, although he wrote fewer poems and was aware that he was master in them of a far narrower range of invention. Two years after his last original collection of poems, *New Poems* (1867), when Tennyson was still building up his Arthurian cycle of poems and Browning was enjoying his first great popular success with *The Ring and the Book*, Arnold wrote to his mother:

My poems represent, on the whole, the main movement of mind of the last quarter of a century . . . It might be fairly urged that I have less poetical sentiment than Tennyson; and less intellectual vigour and abundance than Browning; yet because I have perhaps more of a fusion of the two than either of them, and have more regularly applied that fusion to the main line of modern development, I am likely enough to have my turn, as they have had theirs.

(*Letters of Matthew Arnold, 1848–1888*, ed. G. W. E. Russell, vol. II, p. 9. Cited below as Letters)

His expectation that his turn would come has had a kind of fulfilment in the twentieth century. In his poems he speaks to us more directly and intimately than Tennyson or Browning, and his outlook is nearer to our own and therefore more congenial. His best poems are truthful, sometimes bleak, reports on experience, suggesting that he understood himself and the world he lived in and was not tempted to soften and blur the intimidating outlines of his vision. Although the poetry is suffused with melancholy and the prose is either high-spirited or more soberly cheerful, an impartial observer will recognize that the same wish 'to get breast to breast with reality' (*Letters of Matthew Arnold to Arthur Hugh Clough*, ed. H. F. Lowry, 1932, p. 86) is active in both and that both are aspects of a single 'criticism of life'.

As a writer of expository and critical prose Arnold's eminence depends most visibly on the variety of his interests and the intelligence and literary tact he brought to bear with such single-mindedness on the discussion of literary, social, educational and religious issues. He touched his age at more points than almost any other Victorian writer and is saved from the reproach of a mere miscellaneousness in his prose works, many of them made up of occasional lectures and contributions to periodicals, by the concern that runs through them all for the quality of the civilization around him—that is, both for the quality of the thought and feeling exhibited in the literature and public life of Victorian England, and for the quality of the lives Englishmen were able to lead when the material conditions of their existence were being rapidly altered and most of the values by which an earlier generation had lived were being disconcertingly questioned. He was a major literary critic—the only major critic between Coleridge and T. S. Eliot —partly because, like his predecessor and his successor, he could not be simply a literary critic: the seriousness with which he attended to literature compelled him to stray beyond literature for the real answers to literary questions and drove him to make up his mind about matters that divided theologians or the politicians framing social policies. But it was not only the tendency of literary questions to widen uncomfortably in a period of social transformation that led Arnold in the 1860s and 1870s to write on social and religious issues. He had been brought up by his father Thomas Arnold (1795–1842), the famous 'reforming' headmaster of Rugby School whose radicalism several times lost him the chance of a bishopric, to believe that a man was uneducated if he was uninformed about politics and religion. This bent was confirmed when, in order to be able to marry, Matthew accepted appointment in 1851 as a Government inspector of schools, a post he owed to the favour of the old Whig statesman, Lord Lansdowne, whose private secretary he had been since leaving Oxford, and came to have first-hand experience of the narrowness, unloveliness and self-satisfaction of Dissent in the manufacturing Midlands and North. As a layman he was at first restricted to inspecting Nonconformist schools—Church of England and Roman Catholic schools were inspected by clergymen. What these schools taught him about the life of a large section of the population ensured that a critical habit of mind would not be exercised solely upon literature. Yet when this has been said and *Culture and Anarchy* (1869) has been recognized as a classic, it is Arnold's literary criticism that we read and re-read for instruction and refreshment. 'From time to time, every hundred years or so', writes T. S. Eliot, 'it is desirable that some critic shall appear to review the past of our literature and set the poets and the poems in a new order . . . Dryden, Johnson and Arnold have each performed the task as well as human frailty will allow (op. cit., pp. 108–9). To which we may add, since this handsome judgement stresses the historical importance of the critic, that Arnold's presence and authority make themselves felt in contemporary critical discussion as frequently and almost as strongly as if he were still our contemporary.

This summary sketch of the nature of Matthew Arnold's critical activity would be incomplete without some notice of the manner in which he presents his views. Dr. Arnold had been a vehement controversialist on the liberal side in religion and politics—he was addicted, for example, to the use of such words as 'detestation' and 'abhorrence' in speaking of the opinions of his Tory or Tractarian opponents—and his son Matthew seems to have decided at an early age that vehemence was a less effective weapon in controversy than moderation if you wished to win over the opposition or to attract the uncommitted to adhere to your opinions. In 1863 he wrote:

Partly nature, partly time and study, have also by this time taught me thoroughly the precious truth that everything turns upon one's exercising the power of *persuasion*, of *charm*: that without this all fury, energy, reasoning power,

44

acquirement, are thrown away . . . Even in one's ridicule one must preserve a sweetness and good-humour.

(Letters, I. 201)

The adoption of an urbane manner prevented controversy on subjects about which men felt violently from degenerating into the printed equivalent of rowdyism and brawling.

The dominant impression likely to be left on most readers by a study of Arnold's prose writings is of a native good sense and balance, a combination of shrewdness, wholesomeness and fastidiousness. He urges his opinions positively but not as if they are his personal possessions, so that we are convinced that he will not consciously push an argument in favour of his case or play down one that tells against him (unconsciously he does both of these things occasionally in the social and theological essays); he does not parade his learning, but his reading is obviously wide; his prose style is sinuous rather than powerful, unheated (though there are traces of an uncharacteristic warmth in the first edition of *Culture and Anarchy*), and laced with wit and irony; and he is capable of the return on himself and his ideas that he so much admired in Edmund Burke. In his literary criticism he is customarily flexible and subtle in his response to the object of scrutiny, and in such early essays as *On Translating Homer* (1861) and 'Maurice de Guérin' (*Essays in Criticism* (1865)) there is something more: the exhilaration of a man who has come into his rightful inheritance. If in his social and theological writings 'the moral and social passion for doing good' is sometimes at war with disinterestedness and there is less sparkle in the prose, we do not usually feel that we are being browbeaten or unfairly got at, as we often feel in reading Carlyle or Ruskin. Arnold's techniques of persuasion are less flamboyant, they coax rather than overwhelm. His rhetoric is of the cooler, more equable sort that we find with individual variations in John Stuart Mill, George Eliot and John Henry Newman. What such different writers have in common with each other and with Arnold is the intellectual scrupulousness that is a distinctive moral resource.

The bulk of the poetry for which Matthew Arnold is now remembered belongs to the single decade 1847–57 and, within that span, is most thickly concentrated in the five years centred on 1850. From childhood his was clearly a divided nature, with on one side his father's seriousness and active itch to improve things and on the other the 'mobile, inconstant, eager' but passive temperament of the Romantic poet with its tendency to surrender to 'depression and *ennui*' (Arnold's own phrases). It was because the moral, energetic half of his divided nature so strongly disapproved of the 'dark disordered city' of his poetic self (the expression is from W. H. Auden's sonnet on Arnold) that his genuine poetic life was so short. Something in his make-up responded only too distinctly to his father's earnestness. For a while he was able to inhibit this response and evade care and responsibility. His remedy as a schoolboy and Oxford undergraduate, and during his bachelor years in London before his marriage, was to disappear behind a pose of insouciance and apparent frivolity. He hid himself so successfully that Dr. Arnold, who died in June 1842 when Matthew was completing his first year at Balliol, too gravely regarded him as an unregenerate spirit, and his family and friends were surprised by the seriousness and melancholy of his first collection of poems in 1849. He was then twenty-six.

At the risk of over-simplification it may be said that temperament speaks in much of the poetry and in the imaginative insights of the literary criticism, character and morality in some of the poems (usually the inferior ones), in the missionary impulses of the literary criticism, and more and more plainly in the social and theological essays. Arnold always insisted that his father, despite his many virtues, was not a poet. When he boasted in the 1860s and 1870s of being 'papa's continuator' in his criticism, he was really confessing that the once recessive moral fraction of his nature was now dominant. It began to take charge when he married in 1851 and, as the phrase goes, settled down. He often grieved over the loss of poetry, complaining pathetically in letters to his friend Arthur Hugh Clough, another divided nature, and to his favourite sister 'K' of the difficulty of composing poetry while earning his living at the perpetual drudgery of school-inspection. The difficulty was not exaggerated, but in his heart of hearts he must have known that broken leisure was not the real problem and that he had betrayed his muse. It has become a commonplace in critical studies of Arnold's poetry to observe that the death of the son Sohrab at the hands of the mighty warrior Rustum in 'Sohrab and Rustum' is a symbolic representation of the poet's sacrificial willingness to reject his poetic self in order to identify himself with Dr. Arnold's missionary vigour. To employ another phrase from Auden's sonnet, he 'thrust his gift in prison till it died' (*Another Time*, 1940, p. 58).

46

Inevitably Arnold's sense of what he could accomplish in prose with much less wear and tear to the personality than was demanded by poetic composition grew after 1857 when he was elected Professor of Poetry at Oxford and began to lecture. (He was the first holder of the chair to lecture in English.) Between 1857 and 1867, the period of his professorship, few poems were written, although one or two of them, such as 'Thyrsis', his elegy on Clough, and 'Obermann Once More', have an important place in the canon. Arnold's first two volumes, *The Strayed Reveller, and Other Poems* (1849) and *Empedocles on Etna, and Other Poems* (1852), were published pseudonymously—probably so that he might not benefit from his father's fame—and sold comparatively few copies. Already with *Poems* (1853), his third collection and the first to which he appended his name, the conflict in his nature was compelling him to censor and edit his work : the book contains pieces chosen from his two pseudonymous volumes, together with such new poems as 'Sohrab and Rustum' and 'The Scholar-Gipsy', and a remarkable preface, his first published essay in literary criticism, in which he defended his refusal to reprint 'Empedocles on Etna', attacked the subjectivity and the lack of concern for structural unity in the verse of the day (the real enemy being his own melancholy), and came out strongly against modern subjects in poetry. In *Poems*, Second Series (1855) Arnold rescued more pieces from his two early volumes, but there were only two new poems. One was 'Balder Dead', based on Scandinavian mythology, a companion epic fragment to the Persian 'Sohrab and Rustum' and, like it, an attempt to escape from a subjectivity Arnold felt to be dangerous because it gave expression to a sense of futility that he was determined to master. In the 1853 volume Clough had preferred 'The Scholar-Gipsy' to 'Sohrab and Rustum', but Arnold at once rebuked him for this preference.

Homer *animates*—Shakespeare *animates*—in its poor way I think Sohrab and Rustum *animates*—The Gipsy Scholar at best awakens a pleasing melancholy. But this is not what we want.

(*Letters to Clough*, p. 146)

The relegation to an inferior status of 'The Scholar-Gipsy', now recognized to be a masterpiece, and the suppression of 'Empedocles on Etna', which is certainly Arnold's most ambitious poem, are indications of the struggle to force his inspiration in a prescribed direction. Between 1855 and 1867 there was only *Merope* (1858), a tragedy on the classical Greek model. It illustrated very clearly the feebleness of the poetry Arnold was capable of writing with 'character' rather than 'temperament' in the saddle, and his voluble defence of it against the criticisms of his friends reveals that he was less satisfied with it than he claimed to be. *New Poems* (1867) was Arnold's last new collection of verse. It was blown up to a respectable size by the revival of 'Empedocles on Etna', but much else in the volume was not new at all—for example, half-a-dozen pieces were further salvaged from 1849 and 1852, and of two apparently new poems, 'Calais Sands' and 'Dover Beach', the first belongs to 1850 and Arnold's courtship of Frances Lucy Wightman, the second probably to 1851 in the months following their marriage. A group of religiose sonnets, which are with *Merope* the most depressing of all Arnold's poetic performances, begs us to accept good intentions as a substitute for creative imagination. The sonnets show up all the more badly in their awkward contrivance because they appear beside Arnold's bitterly truthful exploration of his feelings in 'Growing Old', a powerful short lyric probably provoked by impatience with the smugness of Browning's 'Rabbi ben Ezra'.

Even in *The Strayed Reveller* (1849) explicit moral intention intrudes and disfigures some of the poems. The most interesting poems in the book, apart from the lyrics 'To a Gipsy Child by the Sea-Shore' and 'In Utrumque Paratus', and the much longer 'Resignation', which by its final position gains authority as a personal statement, are the narratives 'Mycerinus', 'The Sick King in Bokhara' and 'The Forsaken Merman' and the tableau pieces 'The Strayed Reveller' and 'The New Sirens'. 'The Strayed Reveller' describes in free verse that recalls Goethe's poems loosely modelled on Greek lyric measures the burden of vicarious suffering the poet has to bear as

> ... the wild, thronging train,
> The bright procession
> Of eddying forms ...

sweeps before his mind: he is condemned to feel as a man and to see as a god. By contrast, 'Resignation', in which Arnold seems to have remembered some of Wordsworth's ideas in 'Tintern Abbey' for the purpose of disagreeing with them, sees the poet's role as simply that of a spectator. Nature seems to 'bear' rather than 'rejoice' and is quite indifferent to man. The poet

Whose natural insight can discern
What through experience others learn;
Who needs not love and power, to know
Love transient, power an unreal show;
Who treads at ease life's uncheer'd ways ...

should not be blamed for his detachment. Fate's ear is 'impenetrable', and it is only through our failure to see things as they are that we forget

In action's dizzying eddy whirl'd,
The something that infects the world.

In this first volume Arnold's selection of subjects and themes is less a matter of simple aesthetic choice than of a balance between this and the wish 'to get breast to breast with reality'. The second collection of poems in 1852 was inspired by a similar purpose. It contains the love-lyrics later to be distinguished as the two sequences 'Switzerland' and 'Faded Leaves', the narrative poem 'Tristram and Iseult', 'Memorial Verses' (an elegy on Wordsworth), and 'Stanzas in Memory of the Author of "Obermann" ', as well as a number of unrhymed lyrics, namely 'The Youth of Nature', 'The Youth of Man' and 'The Future', which Arnold seems to have thought of as 'pindarics'. Although all these poems are in varying degrees meritorious and worth detailed study, attention will have to be given here at their expense to the 'dramatic poem' which supplied Arnold with his volume's title.

'Empedocles on Etna' resembles Byron's *Manfred* superficially in form, but it is a better organized and more coherent work. The poem is seen in a proper perspective as Arnold's most serious attempt in poetry to gain the 'intellectual deliverance' which is 'the peculiar demand of those ages which are called modern' ('On the Modern Element in Literature', *Complete Prose Works*, I. 19). The attempt was a failure, but by a paradox it is the expression of this failure that is responsible for the poem's artistic success. Intellectual deliverance begins, Arnold says, when we grasp the general ideas which give the law to the multitudinousness of past and present fact, but it is not perfect until

... we have acquired that harmonious acquiescence of mind which we feel in contemplating a grand spectacle that is intelligible to us.

(ibid., p. 20)

There is an assumption here that intelligibility will issue in acquiescence, but what 'Empedocles on Etna' actually teaches is that acquiescence may be willed, but that it cannot be felt wholeheartedly.

The dramatic poem has only three characters, two of whom, Callicles and Pausanias, are there as foils to Empedocles, the mature poet and philosopher who commits suicide at the poem's climax by throwing himself into the crater of Etna. Callicles is a young poet whose happiness and ability to sing are as yet unshadowed by 'l'excès de douleur produit par l'abus de la pensée'. He represents what Empedocles was in his own youth and is seen only in the moist, fertile 'forest region' at the foot of Etna, as Empedocles, the man in whom the habit of analysis has destroyed the power to feel and the wish to live, is associated with and seen alone only at the 'charr'd, blacken'd, melancholy waste' of the volcano's summit. The Stoic preachment which Empedocles bestows on his friend Pausanias, telling him that the destruction of illusion and the contemplation of naked reality need not lead to despair if he moderates his expectations of life ('Because thou must not dream, thou need'st not then despair'), takes place exactly half-way up Etna at the point where the climbers come out of the shade of the forest into the burning sunlight of the upper slopes. This scene is set at noon; the earlier scene at the foot of the volcano (in which only Callicles and Pausanias appear) occurs shortly after sun-rise; the last scene at the summit, which contains Empedocles' long soliloquy punctuated by the songs of Callicles from below, is timed at midnight. This association of particular characters and attitudes to experience with particular times and places is one means by which we are led to see that the ascent of the volcano depicts the passage from innocence to experience. Empedocles cannot live by the resignation he has preached to Pausanias. Despondency is more real to him than the sentiment that 'Life still Leaves human effort scope'. With his move from comforting illusion into what Yeats called 'the desolation of reality' the spring of his life has snapped.

Arnold, like Empedocles, needed truth and joy, but as a poet found them to be incompatible.

> And yet men have such need of joy!
> But joy whose grounds are true . . .
> ('Obermann Once More')

Because the service of reason chilled 'feeling and the religious mood', because following 'the pale cold star of Truth' ('Stanzas from the Grande Chartreuse') destroyed the joy necessary for the fullest artistic creation, because he could bear no longer to juggle with the equal claims of two necessities, Arnold suppressed 'Empedocles on Etna'. Everyone has admired the songs and lyric interludes of Callicles, which break up and relieve the speeches of Empedocles, but a valid critical judgement of the poem must acknowledge the high poetic level on which the whole of the second act is sustained. Except in the magnificent *coda* of 'Sohrab and Rustum' and in a few lyrics, which have to include 'Dover Beach' and 'Yes! in the sea of life enisled', Arnold never wrote with such intensity or poignancy again.

Poems (1853), often described as the poet's most important single volume of poems, included 'Sohrab and Rustum' and 'The Scholar-Gipsy'. While 'The Scholar-Gipsy' celebrated what Arnold later admitted to be 'the *freest* and most delightful part, perhaps, of my life' in its recollections of undergraduate wanderings in 'that unforgotten Oxfordshire and Berkshire country' (Letter quoted in Mrs. H. Ward, *A Writer's Recollections*, 1918, p. 54), 'Sohrab and Rustum' had nevertheless to be preferred because it had been written to illustrate, in the words of the critical creed of the 1853 Preface, 'the all-importance of the choice of a subject; the necessity of accurate construction; and the subordinate character of expression' (*Complete Prose Works*, I. 12). After 'Empedocles on Etna' it represents a diminished ambition. In his defence of *Merope* (1858) Arnold spoke of a kind of poetry in which 'perfection' might be approached without 'an actual tearing of oneself to pieces', a perfection of form without 'perfection in the region of thought and feeling' (*Letters* I. 63); and 'Sohrab and Rustum', although charged with feeling by the personal significance the story developed for Arnold, is the first stage on the downward journey that leads through 'Balder Dead' to the nearly lifeless *Merope*. From the critical viewpoint which Arnold had reached in 1853 his satisfaction with 'Sohrab and Rustum' is understandable, but it is still surprising that he did not see that in its emotional tone and final effect on the reader it is close to 'The Scholar-Gipsy'. It is the influence of Keats that gives this pastoral lament for youth with its hopefulness and *brio*, which are sapped by living in the world, a sensuous richness unusual in Arnold's poetry. F. R. Leavis has urged the intellectual weakness of the elegy while admitting its charm, but this judgement seems to me too severe. The scholar gipsy, a Callicles magically preserved from becoming an Empedocles, is a figure borrowed from Glanvill to allow Arnold to criticize

Victorian civilization by opposing an ideal world to the actual. 'Yes', he writes to Clough in 1853, '—*congestion of the brain* is what we suffer from—I always feel it and say it—and cry for air like my own Empedocles.' (*Letters to Clough,* p. 130). It is not to the point to ask when

> ... wits were fresh and clear
> And life ran gaily as the sparkling Thames ...

if by juxtaposing two kinds of existence, 'the infection of our mental strife', which destroys the possibility of spontaneity and happiness, can be brought home. In 'Memorial Verses' Arnold had named Goethe 'Physician of the iron age', and here the imagery is all of sickness:

> ... this strange disease of modern life
> With its sick hurry, its divided aims
> Its heads o'ertax'd, its palsied hearts ...
> But fly our paths, our feverish contact fly!

I do not think it is true to say that 'What it was that the Scholar Gipsy had that we have not, Arnold doesn't, except in the most general terms, know' (F. R. Leavis, *Revaluation,* 1936, p. 191). He tells us in a succession of stanzas—with as much concreteness as we have a right to expect—what constitutes the scholar gipsy's health.

Nothing new in *New Poems* (1867) quite reaches the level of the best writing in Arnold's 1852 and 1853 collections. 'Thyrsis', the elegy on Clough, leans heavily on its predecessor 'The Scholar-Gipsy', with which it shares the stanza Arnold adapted from Keats, and its classical embroidery has a slightly self-conscious air. The sixth stanza is a good instance of the colour and fluency of the best descriptive writing :-

> So, some tempestuous morn in early June,
> > When the year's primal burst of bloom is o'er,
> > Before the roses and the longest day—
> > When garden-walks and all the grassy floor
> > With blossoms red and white of fallen May
> > And chestnut-flowers are strewn—
> > So have I heard the cuckoo's parting cry,
> > > From the wet field, through the vext garden-trees,
> > > Come with the volleying rain and tossing breeze:
> > > *The bloom is gone, and with the bloom go I!*

It is significant that the stanza is about something lost. 'Bloom' is a favourite word with Arnold; it signifies what is too easily destroyed. Arnold's recognition of the world's beauty and delight is heartfelt, but it cannot be for him a simple, unmixed feeling. The beauty traps us into falsity unless we also recognize, as he says in 'Dover Beach', that

> . . . the world, which seems
> To lie before us like a land of dreams,
> So various, so beautiful, so new,
> Hath really neither joy, nor love, nor light,
> Nor certitude, nor peace, nor help for pain . . .

'Obermann Once More' is another poem that must be adjudged inferior to its predecessor. 'Stanzas in Memory of the Author of "Obermann" ' belongs in its inception to 1849 and was 'conceived, and partly composed, in the valley going down from the foot of the Gemmi Pass towards the Rhone' (Arnold's 1869 note). This was towards the end of Arnold's relationship with the Marguerite of the 'Switzerland' poems, and the farewell addressed to the spirit of Senancour is also a farewell to her and to youth, irresponsibility and, ultimately, the writing of poetry. In 'Obermann Once More', which was written between 1865 and 1867, Senancour is constrained, in accordance with Arnold's sanguine hopes for the success of liberal ideas in the 1860s, to preach that the poet has a duty to fulfil to men in helping them to secure

> One common wave of thought and joy
> Lifting mankind again!

Here we note that thought and joy, once sadly judged to be incompatible, are forcibly coupled in an energy of inspiration. Sainte-Beuve's comment, 'C'est un Obermann transfiguré', seems just (quoted in C. B. Tinker and H. F. Lowry, *The Poetry of Matthew Arnold: A Commentary*, 1940, p. 271). He has come to have something of Dr Arnold's bearing. The symbolic dawn at the end of the poem, which is intended to herald a new age of hope by recalling the earlier dawn that broke on the exhausted Roman world with the advent of Christianity, is poetically quite unconvincing.

How are we to sum up? Although he objected aristocratically to any Byronic parade of his restlessness, and there is therefore always a discretion and an economy about the expression of the distinctive Arnoldian pathos, Matthew Arnold is, as T. S. Eliot says, 'more intimate with us than Browning, more intimate than Tennyson ever is except at moments, as in the passionate flights of *In Memoriam*' (*The Use of Poetry and the Use of Criticism*, p. 105). It is with fatigue, disenchantment and regret that essentially the poems have to do, and it is the resistance that Arnold offers to these feelings that prevents the poetry from being enervating. In this resistance the 'moral' Arnold is present, and yet the sense of futility is barely kept at bay by the struggle to practise Stoic composure. 'He had no real serenity', writes T. S. Eliot with an insight furnished, I think, by self-knowledge, 'only an impeccable demeanour' (ibid., p. 119). This is exact. The poems such as 'Rugby Chapel' or 'The Second Best' in which Arnold praises courage and perseverance or tries to promulgate hope are comparatively few in number. They are also usually inferior poems, being too obviously written with gritted teeth, metaphorically speaking, to suspend our disbelief. Arnold's deepest feeling in his poetry is that he has been born into an

> . . . iron time
> Of doubts, disputes, distractions, fears . . .,
> > ('Memorial Verses'),

that he is a wanderer between two worlds, 'one dead/The other powerless to be born' ('Stanzas from the Grande Chartreuse'), that his age in its 'true *blankness* and *barrenness* and *unpoetrylessness*' (*Letters to Clough*, p. 126) has made it virtually impossible for him not to be divided against himself. Therefore men must

> . . . waive all claim to bliss, and try to bear;
> With close-lipp'd patience for [their] only friend . . .
> > ('The Scholar-Gypsy')

He wrestles with discouragement because he is the son of Dr. Arnold and will not yield to despair. He believes that it should be possible to embrace the truth not only with an appearance of composure, but with real joy; he cannot feel this joy, however hard he tries; and he is unsure whether the fault belongs to his time or is partly due to some inadequacy in his own nature.

When Arnold fully understood the sombreness of his poetic nature, he stopped writing poetry, but by then he had produced a body of poetic work which, in spite of its restriction to a few themes and its lack of ease in execution, has permanent value. Sometimes lack of ease becomes clumsiness. He is undramatic—it is the elegiac rather than the dramatic note that is uppermost in the narrative poems 'Tristram and Iseult',

'Sohrab and Rustum' and 'Balder Dead', and it must be conceded that this makes for monotony. Poems of the type represented by 'A Summer Night' and 'The Buried Life' develop too haphazardly and are perilously close to the 'thinking aloud' condemned in Wordsworth. Yet Arnold is Wordsworthian rather than Keatsian (except in 'The Scholar-Gipsy', 'Thyrsis' and the third part of 'The Church of Brou'), and it is the Wordsworthian example supporting a personal voice that we find in the Cadmus and Harmonia interlude in 'Empedocles on Etna', for example, or in such a subdued 'average' passage of Arnold's verse as the following from 'Bacchanalia' :

> The evening comes, the fields are still.
> The tinkle of the thirsty rill,
> Unheard all day, ascends again;
> Deserted is the half-mown plain,
> Silent the swaths! the ringing wain,
> The mower's cry, the dog's alarms,
> All housed within the sleeping farms!
> The business of the day is done,
> The last-left haymaker is gone.
> And from the thyme upon the height,
> And from the elder-blossom white
> And pale dog-roses in the hedge,
> And from the mint-plant in the sedge,
> In puffs of balm the night-air blows
> The perfume which the day forgoes.

There is nothing extraordinary here—the language, the rhythms, the structure of the syntax are all simple—but it is writing that should win respect.

It is only in their poetry, since Clough's prose apart from the Epilogue to 'Dipsychus' is of little account, that the achievements of Arnold and Clough are in any way commensurable, and even this statement would probably have been regarded as dubious if not manifestly absurd a generation ago. But literary reputations are not stationary and at the present time Clough is deservedly enjoying a revival. Swinburne once wrote a limerick beginning 'There was a bad poet named Clough,/Whom his friends found it useless to puff', but the sneer has boomeranged. It is the Swinburnian logorrhoea that is now found tedious. It is no longer enough to think of Clough as the author of a single anthology-piece, 'Say not the struggle nought availeth'. Many modern readers of *Amours de Voyage*, 'Dipsychus', 'Easter Day', 'The Latest Decalogue' and 'Natura Naturans' would be willing to agree with the character in Graham Greene's *The Quiet American* (1955) that 'He was an adult poet in the nineteenth century. There weren't so many of them'. Clough is too unequal a poet and left behind him too much unfinished and unrevised work for him to stand appropriately at the side of Arnold, but in some respects he is a more original poet. His poetry deserves less cursory treatment than I am here able to give it.

Arthur Hugh Clough (1819–61) and Matthew Arnold were friends from their Oxford days, and there is a reasonable justification for classifying them both as Victorian 'poets of doubt' and dealing with them together in the same chapter. Arnold wrote to Clough in America in 1853, 'I really have clung to you in spirit more than to any other man . . . I am for ever linked with you by intellectual bonds—the strongest of all' (*Letters to Clough*, pp. 129, 130), and later in the same year on his return to England Clough acknowledged the nature of the tie between them in a letter to his fiancée complaining of some of his other friends :

> They have all got so *churchy*; there is no possibility of getting on thoroughly—Matt Arnold is not churchy . . . I am very glad I have not conformed *more* than I have—I shall pick up some misbelieving friends in London I dare say.
>
> (*The Correspondence of A. H. Clough*, ed. F. L. Mulhauser, Oxford, 1957, vol. II, pp. 460–1)

The sense of desolate loss experienced by the generation of those who were young in the 1840s when their religious certainties crumbled has never been more plangently expressed than by Clough in 'Easter Day' which is subscribed 'Naples, 1849'. Arnold's treatment of the same theme in 'Stanzas from the Grande Chartreuse' is more reflective. For full appreciation Clough's poem needs to be read at length since so much of its effect depends on the use of brooding, grief-stricken repetition, but the urgency of the feeling and the directness of its rendering can be sampled in the following extract :-

> Eat, drink, and play, and think that this is bliss !
> There is no Heaven but this !
> There is no Hell;—
> Save Earth, which serves the purpose doubly well,
> Seeing it visits still

With equallest apportionments of ill
Both good and bad alike, and brings to one same dust
      The unjust and the just
      With Christ, who is not risen.

Eat, drink, and die, for we are souls bereaved :
Of all the creatures under this broad sky
We are most helpless, that had hoped most high,
And most beliefless, that had most believed.
      Ashes to ashes, dust to dust;
      As of the unjust, also of the just—
         Yea, of that Just One too.
      It is the one sad Gospel that is true,
         Christ is not risen.

It is, in my opinion, one of the great 'religious' lyrics of the Victorian period.

Clough's terror of intellectual dishonesty, which grew at times so neurotic that he found it almost impossible to choose between two or several courses of action open to him, was the end-result of his total commitment to Dr. Arnold's beliefs and attitudes at Rugby and his inability to sustain those beliefs when he met the Tractarian doctrines at Oxford and faced the probing questions of W. G. Ward, his Balliol tutor, who was then on the path that was to take him before Newman into the Roman Catholic Church. Liberal theological opinion, to which Newman was bitterly hostile, was nevertheless admitted by him to have been 'invested with an elevation of character which claimed the respect even of its opponents' (Note A. Liberalism, *Apologia pro Vita Sua*, 1874 edn., p. 292) when Dr. Arnold's Rugby pupils went up to Oxford. Clough was one of these pupils. Although he was four years older than Matthew Arnold, he was in many ways less mature and less nimble of mind. His Rugby and Oxford experiences left him not only uncertain what he believed, but paralysed by the suspicion that if he made up his mind to believe or do anything it might be for 'factitious' reasons :

I do not like being moved : for the will is excited : and
   action
Is a most dangerous thing; I tremble for something
   factitious,
Some malpractice of heart and illegitimate process;
We are so prone to these things with our terrible notions
   of duty.

This is Claude, the hero or anti-hero of Clough's epistolary verse-novel in free accentual hexameters, *Amours de Voyage* (written 1849, but not published till 1858), but the fact that Clough could analyse Claude's disposition so dispassionately does not mean that he does not share this disposition (as one or two recent American critics have tried to argue). *Amours de Voyage* is the story of a man whose scruples about his sincerity cause him to hesitate, palter and delay until he has lost the girl whom he met in Rome during the siege of the city by the French. At first he is doubtful whether he is really in love. When she leaves Rome with her family and disappears, he becomes certain that he is in love and is stirred to action. He pursues her through Italy to the frontiers of Switzerland, but all his inquiries fail. Finally, he surrenders the chase and again wonders:

> After all, do I know that I really cared so about her?
> Do whatever I will, I cannot call up her image ...

Earlier in a state of deep depression at his lack of success in his search he hears a barrel-organ playing 'an English psalm-tune' in the streets of Florence, is sentimentally comforted by it, and thinks for a moment that he has gained 'a religious assurance'. But immediately in revulsion he brands this comfort as a temptation:

> I refuse, reject, and put it utterly from me;
> I will look straight out, see things, not try to evade them;
> Fact shall be fact for me, and Truth the Truth as ever,
> Flexible, changeable, vague, and multiform, and
>   doubtful.–
> Off and depart to the void, thou subtle, fanatical tempter!

The 'subtle, fanatical tempter' is externalized as the Spirit in 'Dipsychus', a dramatic poem which was published fragmentarily by Mrs. Clough after her husband's death at Florence in 1861 and has been known in as complete a form as its unfinished state allows only since the modern collected edition of Clough's poems in 1951. 'Dipsychus', set in Venice on a summer holiday, is a dialogue between moony, anxious idealism and cynically shrewd, worldly common-sense. From the names of Dipsychus (Faustulus) and the Spirit (Mephisto) in early drafts of the poem it is evident that Clough took a hint from Goethe, but his treatment of the subject is entirely independent. Many of Clough's poems deal with love and marriage, and in 'Dipsychus' he writes with a degree of sexual frankness that would have offended many Victorians. The Spirit's lively songs—' "There is no God", the wicked saith', 'How pleasant it is to have money'—have often been printed out of context, but, like the songs of Callicles in 'Empedocles on Etna', they lose by being separated from the speeches on which they are intended to comment. The Spirit stands for conformity to the ways of the world: Dipsychus should go into society, accept its conventions while seeing through them, build a career and make a good match. His scruples about such matters are as absurd as his Puritan ditherings when eyed by Venetian girls, sexual experience being to the Spirit

> But heavens! as innocent a thing
> As picking strawberries in spring.

The centre of the debate in a poem that develops slackly and lacks a firm shape is to be found in Scenes ix and x. In Scene ix Dipsychus, grumbling that God's 'newer will' is that

> We should not think of Him at all, but trudge it,
> And of the world He has assigned us make
> What best we can . . . ,

twists between the alternatives of 'waiting for the spark from heaven to fall' like the Scholar-Gipsy and what seems to him abject surrender. The Spirit warns:

> Devotion, and ideas, and love,
> And beauty claim their place above;
> But saint and sage and poet's dreams
> Divide the light in coloured streams,
> Which this alone gives all combined,
> The *siccum lumen* of the mind
> Called common sense: and no high wit
> Gives better counsel than does it.
> Submit, submit!

In Scene x the Spirit is given the dignity of blank verse for the first time for his savage portrait of the poetic idealist's inadequacies. His attitude to Dipsychus is very much that of the worldly uncle in the prose Epilogue. The young men of his nephew's generation, the latter says:

. . . seem to me a sort of hobbadi-hoy cherub, too big to be innocent, and too simple for anything else. They're full of the notion of the world being so wicked, and of their taking a higher line, as they call it. I only fear they'll never take any at all.

Dr. Arnold is responsible for making young men so high-minded and helpless—'It's all Arnold's doing; he spoilt the public schools'—but the nephew, although ready to admit that the young men may have been spoilt, objects to the attack on Dr. Arnold and attributes the trouble to the 'over-excitation of the religious sense' caused by 'the religious movement of the last century, beginning with Wesleyanism, and culminating at last in Puseyism'.

Clough's abandonment of 'Dipsychus' after his marriage has been paralleled with Arnold's suppression of 'Empedocles on Etna', but in fact after 1853 Clough wrote virtually no verse until his final break-down in health. On sick-leave from the Education Office in 1861 he produced 'Mari Magno or Tales on Board', which, owing its framework to Chaucer, its manner more to Patmore than to Crabbe (the latter being one of Clough's admirations), picks dispiritedly at old themes and is a sad declension from Amours de Voyage and 'Dipsychus'. It is in Clough's poetic career what Merope is in Arnold's. But these comparisons between Clough and Arnold may be misleading. Their poetic ideals were in many respects opposed. Clough favoured the subjects from modern life that Arnold impatiently dismissed in his 1853 Preface. Arnold discovered a want of concern for the beautiful in Clough's lyrics and never did justice to the intelligence or raciness of the verse-novels and satirical poems, although he did prefer Amours de Voyage to Tennyson's Maud. He would have found 'Dipsychus' unsettling and objectionable. Some of Clough's shorter poems are properly described as drab, dully surfaced and ramshackle, but there are others—for example, the charming and original 'Natura Naturans' and the unexpectedly elegant 'Epithalamium' —which are free from these faults. In part of his censure at least, one suspects, Arnold was denying himself an individual response to his friend's poetry out of deference to Victorian notions of the poetical in subject and treatment. 'Thyrsis', though a poem of affection, has contributed to a false view of Clough's achievement. There is a tragi-comedy of imperfect sympathies. Neither Arnold nor Clough really understood or sympathized with what the other was doing in poetry, and each censured in the other weaknesses he feared in himself. It is curious that Arnold's wit and sociability were expressed exclusively in his life and in his prose, the poetry being the vehicle of seriousness and melancholy, whereas Clough, who after his Oxford days was often glum and taciturn in company, in his poems gives us the fun and high spirits of the reading-party in the Scottish Highlands in *The Bothie of Toper-na-Vuolich* and the wit of 'The Latest Decalogue'. Arnold has had his critical due as a poet. Clough's own neglect of his poetry explains in some measure the critical neglect of it in the twentieth century. With the new editions of the poems and letters now available and the recent biographical and critical studies of Clough we are now in a position to see him steadily and see him whole. His reputation is bound to grow as his position as one of the most interesting and attractive minor poets of the Victorian period is more widely recognized.

To Arnold his prose writings formed a single web. 'Whoever seriously occupies himself with literature will soon perceive its vital connection with other agencies,' he wrote in the preface to *Mixed Essays* (1879), adding pertinently '. . . literature is a part of civilization; it is not the whole.' (*Works*, 1903–4, Vol. X, pp. v–vi). It is with civilization or 'the humanization of man in society' that the serious critic has to do, Arnold asserts, and in 'Heinrich Heine' he sets out his special task in Victorian times.

Modern times find themselves with an immense system of institutions, established facts, accredited dogmas, customs, rules which have come to them from times not modern. In this system their life has to be carried forward; yet they have a sense that this system is not of their own creation, that it by no means corresponds exactly with the wants of their actual life, that, for them, it is customary, not rational. The awakening of this sense is the awakening of the modern spirit. The modern spirit is now awake almost everywhere; the sense of want of correspondence between the forms of modern Europe and its spirit, between the new wine of the eighteenth and nineteenth centuries, and the old bottles of the eleventh and twelfth centuries, or even of the sixteenth and seventeenth, almost every one now perceives; it is no longer dangerous to affirm that this want of correspondence exists . . . To remove this want of correspondence is beginning to be the settled endeavour of most persons of good sense. Dissolvents of the old European system of dominant ideas and facts we must all be . . . what we have to study is that we may not be acrid dissolvents of it.

(*Essays in Criticism* (1865), *Works*, Vol. III, pp. 109–10)

This preaches the gospel of an inevitable transformation, but we should note that in his dislike of acridity Arnold implies that the genuine reformer is also the true conservative, and that without an imaginative appreciation of how well 'the old European system of dominant ideas and facts' once served civilization we are likely to fall into doctrinaire Jacobinism, namely 'Violent indignation with the past, abstract systems of renovation applied wholesale' (*Culture and Anarchy* (1869), *Works*, Vol. V, p. 109). The same belief that a willingness to accept necessary change is in practice conservative—since it is a force making for social cohesion—inspired Dr. Arnold's liberalism.

If the prose writings were a single web to Arnold, to us some parts of the web are more valuable than others. The theological essays, in which the instinct to conserve fights for its existence and survives only by a slippery piece of mental legerdemain that deceived its author, were important to Arnold but are less important to us. 'At the present moment,' we find him saying in 1875, 'two things about the Christian religion must surely be clear to anybody with eyes in his head. One is, that men cannot do without it; the other, that they cannot do with it as it is' (*God and the Bible* (1875), *Works*, Vol. VIII, p. xii). On the one hand, the *Zeitgeist* had shown theology to be a pseudo-science. It is convenient to retain the word God as a shorthand sign for '*that stream of tendency by which all things seek to fulfil the law of their being*' (*St. Paul and Protestantism* (1870), *Complete Prose Works*, Vol. VI, p. 10), but Christianity must be demythologized. On the other hand, conduct is three-fourths of life and, since religion is essentially 'morality touched by emotion' (*Literature and Dogma*, ibid., Vol. VI, p. 176), it is only religious feeling that is capable of converting unappetizing ethical precept into an inspiration acting on men's lives. Arnold's analysis of the way in which theologians have distorted the language of the Bible is acute, but his belief that men will still be fired to action and heroic self-sacrifice by his watered-down version of Christianity is optimistic. He wishes honestly and valiantly to assert nothing that is not verifiable, but when from the unenlightening but unobjectionable 'stream of tendency by which all things seek to fulfil the law of their being' God becomes 'the enduring power, not ourselves, which makes for righteousness' (*Literature and Dogma*, ibid., Vol. VI, p. 200), Arnold is already reading history with a squint and creating a new unpicturesque myth in place of the old picturesque one. As Lionel Trilling points out, the author of

Literature and Dogma is not at ease in his position—'That Christianity is true: that is, after all, the one thing that Arnold cannot really say' (*Matthew Arnold*, 1939, p. 364).

What made Arnold so anxious to 'save' Christianity from its orthodox apologists was his sense of the immense part religion had played historically in the 'humanization of man in society'. The religious tendency to reverence an 'Eternal not ourselves' was a permanent one, and 'All tendencies of human nature are in themselves vital and profitable' (*On the Study of Celtic Literature* (1867), *Complete Prose Works*, Vol. III, p. 348). The notion that man's development must be many-sided is repeated again and again in Arnold's literary criticism and social writings—it is at the centre of *Culture and Anarchy* (1869)—and is forcibly expressed in the late 'A Liverpool Address':

> Money-making is not enough by itself. Industry is not enough by itself. Seriousness is not enough by itself. I speak now of the kinds of stimulus most in use with people of our race, and above all in business communities . . . Respectable these kinds of stimulus may be, useful they may be, but they are not by themselves sufficient. The need in man for intellect and knowledge, his desire for beauty, his instinct for society, and for pleasurable and graceful forms of society, require to have their stimulus felt also, felt and satisfied.
>
> (*Five Uncollected Essays*, Liverpool, 1953, p. 88)

Political power was passing to the Philistine middle-class, and Arnold's professional experience as an inspector of schools had made him exceptionally aware of the unfitness of members of this class to govern. They had 'a defective type of religion, a narrow range of intellect and knowledge, a stunted sense of beauty, a low standard of manners' (*Mixed Essays* (1879), *Works*, Vol. X, p. 88). Carlyle spoke of the Second Reform Act (1867) as 'the calling in of new supplies of blockheadism', but Arnold knew with whom the future lay. His concern was not narrowly political. As he puts it in 'The Future of Liberalism' (1880), 'the master-thought by which my politics are governed is . . . the thought of the bad civilisation of the English middle class' (*Irish Essays* (1882), *Works*, Vol. XI, p. 135).

This master-thought which inspired Arnold's campaigning for a proper national system of secondary education from the time of his *The Popular Education of France* (1861) [1] until the end of his life, is kept steadily before us in *Culture and Anarchy* (1869) and is satirically illustrated in *Friendship's Garland*

(1871). *Culture and Anarchy*, Arnold's most sustained essay in social criticism, examines the 'bad civilisation of the English middle class' in a framework provided by an analysis of the three classes of English society (the famous division into Barbarians, Philistines and Populace), a discussion of the English love of 'doing as one likes' (a phrase which glances critically at John Stuart Mill's *On Liberty*), and the prescription of culture as 'the great help out of our present difficulties' (*Complete Prose Works*, Vol. V, p. 233). In *Friendship's Garland*, a light-hearted work that Arnold obviously enjoyed writing, the mouthpiece of the author's ideas is an irascible Prussian savant, Arminius Von Thunder-ten-Tronckh, a descendant of the character in Voltaire's *Candide*, and Arnold himself appears ironically as a feeble and harassed but patriotic defender of English institutions and customs living penuriously in a garret in Grub Street. Mr. Bottles, the complacent Philistine manufacturer with the villa at Reigate, is set three-dimensionally before us with all his want of 'sweetness and light', and Arminius barks 'Get Geist' at the English people. The expression 'the two noblest of things, which are sweetness and light' is taken by Arnold for *Culture and Anarchy* from Swift's 'Battle of the Books,' as the terms 'Hebraism' and 'Hellenism' are borrowed from the German poet Heine. Sweetness and light are both connected with Hellenism. All classes in English society lack light, i.e., are inaccessible to ideas, but the Philistines, who are also wanting in sweetness, stand in particular need of hellenization. Hellenism is needed to balance the Hebraism that characterizes the narrow life of that typical Philistine, the strict earnest Dissenter whose horizon is bounded by his home, his office or factory, and his chapel. The Philistines of the middle-class, the inheritors of the Puritan tradition, are 'the best stuff in the nation', Arnold believes, but they must be radically transformed.

> Look at the life imaged in such a newspaper as the Nonconformist,—a life of jealousy of the Establishment, disputes, tea-meetings, openings of chapels, sermons; and then think of it as an ideal of a human life completing itself on all sides and aspiring with all its organs after sweetness, light, and perfection.
>
> (ibid., Vol. V, p. 103)

'Culture' in *Culture and Anarchy* strongly recalls 'criticism' in 'The Function of Criticism at the Present Time', the key essay of *Essays in Criticism* (1865). It is not 'a smattering of the two dead languages of Greek and Latin', as was supposed by John Bright, whose politics Arnold distrusted. It is

> . . . a pursuit of our total perfection by means of getting to know, on all the matters which most concern us, the best which has been thought and said in the world; and through this knowledge, turning a stream of fresh and free thought upon our stock notions and habits.[1]
>
> (ibid., Vol. V, p. 233)

(Cf. 'The Function of Criticism at the Present Time' (1864), 'Its business is . . . simply to know the best that is known and thought in the world, and by in its turn making this known, to create a current of true and fresh ideas' (ibid., Vol. III, p. 270)). Culture, that is to say, acts as a dissolvent. To Arnold human perfection means both 'a *harmonious* perfection, developing all sides of our humanity' and 'a *general* perfection, developing all parts of our society' (ibid., Vol. V, p. 235). The Philistines, who suppose energy and strictness of conduct enough for perfection, are 'incomplete and mutilated men' (ibid., Vol. V, p. 236). What Arnold fears with the decline in aristocratic prestige which must follow the transfer of political power to the middle-class is the Americanization of English society. The aristocratic Barbarians have supported some respect for intellect, have exemplified some amenity in their mode of living. 'America', he writes, 'is just ourselves, with the Barbarians quite left out and the Populace nearly . . . From Maine to Florida and back again, all America Hebraises' (ibid., Vol. V, p. 243).

The nation once Americanized will be in danger of forgetting that there are standards in matters of taste as well as in morals, and that popularity is not commonly a mark of excellence; and Arnold instances the 'unutterable external hideousness' of London (ibid., Vol. V, p. 103) as an example of the depth of English failure already existing. Most Englishmen now believe, he thinks, that 'our greatness and welfare are proved by our being so very rich' and put their faith in machinery, but 'Greatness is a spiritual condition worthy to excite love, interest, and admiration' (ibid., Vol. V, pp. 96, 97), the England of Victoria excites these less in mankind at large than the England of Elizabeth I, and private opulence with us exists beside public need. The Englishman's failure to rise above personal and class interests to an idea of the State as a 'centre of light and authority' is due to his infatuation with a false idea of liberty ('Doing as One Likes'), the fruit of which is the anarchy Arnold discovered in the England of the 1860s. Yet every man has in himself a 'possible Socrates' (ibid., Vol. V, p. 228), a disinterested and classless 'best self', of which the State should be the collective representation. This is, of course, the State conceived as an ideal, and Arnold is aware that the actual number of '*aliens*', as he calls those in each class led, not by their class spirit, but by a general *humane* spirit' (ibid., Vol. V, p. 156), is small. In spite of this he argues that it is only by growth in respect for the idea of the State as a civilizing agent that a divided society will ever attain a 'strict standard of excellence' and a belief in the 'paramount authority of right reason' (ibid., Vol. V, p. 147). Some critics have cocked an ear for Hegelian overtones when Arnold writes about the State, but J. Dover Wilson has replied—rightly, in my opinion—that 'Arnold had no leanings whatever towards the absolute State. His ideal was the service State in a democratical society' (*The Social and Political Ideas of Some Representative Thinkers of the Victorian Age*, ed. F. J. C. Hearnshaw, 1933, p. 186).

Culture speaks 'through *all* the voices of human experience which have been heard upon it, of art, science, poetry, philosophy, history, as well as of religion' (*Culture and Anarchy, Complete Prose Works*, Vol. V, p. 93), but there can hardly be any question that for Arnold it spoke most intimately and persuasively though great literature. His enjoyment of it from a very early stage was accompanied by an active critical play of mind. For example, in his remarkable correspondence with Clough we find him at one time toying with the notion of propriety of form as 'the sole *necessary* of poetry as such' and talking of 'the grand moral effects produced by *style*', at another maintaining that 'modern poetry can only subsist by its *contents*' (*Letters to Clough*, pp. 98, 101, 124). Critical ideas develop. With Arnold we can see them developing from one work to the next. Scholars with a peculiar conception of the kind of consistency to be expected of a serious critic can therefore point to 'inconsistencies', which are sometimes real but more often are, properly speaking, changes of emphasis, related either to the differing objects of the critic's attention or to his judgment of what needs especially to be said at one moment of time. In the preface of *Essays in Criticism* (1865), his first miscellaneous collection of critical essays, Arnold proposes as his aim 'to pull out a few more stops in that powerful but at present somewhat narrow-toned organ, the modern Englishman' (ibid, Vol. III, p. 287). For this purpose, he tells us in 'The Function of Criticism at the Present Time', which I have already described as the key-essay of the collection, the critic must be 'disinterested' and must see Europe

> . . . as being, for intellectual and spiritual purposes, one great confederation, bound to a joint action and working to a common result; and whose members have, for their proper outfit, a knowledge of Greek, Roman, and Eastern antiquity, and of one another.
>
> (ibid., Vol. III, p. 284)

There is little comfort here for Dickens's Mr. Podsnap, who, it will be remembered, thought other countries than England 'a mistake' except for purposes of trade. 'The English critic of literature,' Arnold replies, 'must dwell much on foreign thought . . .' (ibid., Vol. III, pp. 282–3). In the eight essays that follow 'The Function of Criticism at the Present Time' he illustrates this necessity: he writes on 'The Literary Influence of Academies', on French and German authors (Maurice and Eugénie de Guérin, Joubert, Heine), on the philosopher Spinoza's interpretation of the Bible, on 'Pagan and Mediaeval Religious Sentiment', on the Stoic emperor Marcus Aurelius. Not one essay is devoted to an English subject. Arnold brushes aside chauvinistic murmurings blandly with the observation that the critic's duty is to familiarize us with 'the best that is known and thought in the world' and 'much of the best . . . cannot be of English growth, must be foreign; by the nature of things, again, it is just this we are least likely to know' (ibid., Vol. III, pp. 270, 282).

More important than Arnold's assault on English insularity in *Essays in Criticism* (1865) is his explanation of the dignity of the critical vocation. In 'The Function of Criticism at the Present Time' he remarks that modern poetry needs 'a great critical effort behind it; else it must be a comparatively poor, barren, and short-lived affair' (ibid., Vol. III, pp. 261–2). For a creative epoch of literature 'two powers must concur, the power of the man and the power of the moment', an idea Arnold developed from his concept of 'adequacy' in an age's literature in 'On the Modern Element in Literature', his inaugural lecture at Oxford in 1857. The artist's real job is one of 'synthesis and exposition, not of analysis and discovery'. The discovery of ideas is the business of the philosopher; the critic makes ideas current; the artist's gift lies in 'the faculty of being happily inspired by a certain intellectual and spiritual atmosphere' (ibid., Vol. III, p. 261). The critic, then, is much more than a judge. Not only does he interpret the original artist to his age, but he prepares the way for the artist of the next generation by furnishing him with an atmosphere of 'true and fresh ideas'. Literature cannot be in a healthy state without the critic. Arnold's awareness of how subtly literary judgments are formed is impressive and indicates in what respects his mind was more like John Henry Newman's than Dr. Arnold's. He writes:

> . . . judging is often spoken of as the critic's one business, and so in some sense it is; but the judgment which almost insensibly forms itself in a fair and clear mind, along with fresh knowledge, is the valuable one; and thus knowledge, and ever fresh knowledge, must be the critic's great concern for himself. And it is by communicating fresh knowledge, and letting his own judgment pass along with it,—but insensibly, and in the second place, not the first, as a sort of companion and clue, not as an abstract lawgiver,—that the critic will generally do most good to his readers. Sometimes, no doubt, for the sake of establishing an author's place in literature, and his relation to a central standard (and if this is not done, how are we to get at our *best in the world*?) criticism may have to deal with a subject matter so familiar that fresh knowledge is out of the question, and then it must be all judgment . . . Here the great safeguard is never to let oneself become abstract, always to retain an intimate and lively consciousness of the truth of what one is saying, and, the moment this fails us, to be sure that something is wrong. Still, under all circumstances, this mere judgment and application of principles is, in itself, not the most satisfactory work to the critic; like mathematics, it is tautological, and cannot well give us, like fresh learning, the sense of creative activity.
>
> (ibid., Vol. III, p. 283)

This passage should be placed beside an equally impressive passage in *On Translating Homer: Last Words* (1862) on the difficulty and delicacy of the criticism of poetry :-

> To handle these matters properly there is needed a poise so perfect that the least overweight in any direction tends to destroy the balance. Temper destroys it, a crotchet destroys it, even erudition may destroy it. To press to the sense of the thing itself with which one is dealing, not to go off on some collateral issue about the thing, is the hardest matter in the world. The 'thing itself' with which one is here dealing,—the critical perception of poetic truth,—is of all things the most

volatile, elusive, and evanescent; by even pressing too impetuously after it, one runs the risk of losing it. The critic of poetry should have the finest tact, the nicest moderation, the most free, flexible, and elastic spirit imaginable; he should be indeed the 'ondoyant et divers', the *undulating and diverse* being of Montaigne. The less he can deal with his object simply and freely, the more things he has to take into account in dealing with it,—the more, in short, he has to encumber himself,—so much the greater force of spirit he needs to retain his elasticity.

(ibid., Vol. I, p. 174)

In this and the previous long passage quoted Arnold is functioning at the top of his critical powers in looking at the critical act itself. By the extreme care he takes to preserve his balance in walking the critical tightrope (for example, both 'fresh learning' and the need not to be encumbered by it, both absorption in the work under review and similtaneously a withdrawal of one part of the mind to ensure that a self-regarding delight in one's own ingenuity is not taking over) the reader is pre-disposed in favour of the actual judgments on literature that Arnold makes when he discusses translators of Homer or the defects of English Romantic poetry.

To see Arnold at work in practical criticism, as we see T. S. Eliot at it in his analysis of the opening scene of *Hamlet* in *Poetry and Drama* (1951), we must ignore the two series of *Essays in Criticism* to read *On Translating Homer* (1861), in which he offers advice to future translators of the *Iliad* by examining in detail how the translations of Chapman, Pope, Cowper and F. W. Newman have fallen short, or to look at the pages in *On the Study of Celtic Literature* in which by a nice use of quotations he distinguishes the different poetic 'ways of handling nature', and, in doing so, incidentally 're-fines on the meaning given to 'natural magic' in the earlier essay on Maurice de Guérin. Arnold sensibly refuses to define such critical terms, which were to him no more than rough scaffolding found useful in organizing his critical response to particular poets or poems. 'The grand style', he says, 'is the last matter in the world for verbal definition to deal with adequately' (*On Translating Homer: Last Words* (1862), *Complete Prose Works*, Vol. I, p. 188). Instead of defining his terms he offers selected quotations to make their intended meaning plain. 'To be able to quote as Arnold could, 'comments T. S. Eliot, 'is the best evidence of taste' (*The Use of Poetry and the Use of Criticism*, p. 118).

Essays in Criticism, 2nd Series (1888), contains Arnold's most important essays on English literature. 'The Study of Poetry', which opens the volume, was originally written as a general introduction to T. H. Ward's *The English Poets* (1880). It is in this essay that Arnold speaks of poetry as 'a criticism of life under the conditions fixed for such a criticism by the laws of poetic truth and poetic beauty' (*Works*, Vol. IV, p. 4), describes the dangers of the 'personal' and 'historic' estimates of poetry to the real estimate that we need, recommends having 'always in one's mind lines and expressions of the great masters . . . as a touchstone to other poetry' (ibid, Vol. IV, pp. 12–13), and sketches a highly selective survey of the history of English poetry from Chaucer to Burns. From this survey everybody remembers that 'high seriousness' is refused to Chaucer and that Dryden and Pope are dismissed as 'classics of our prose', but when the whole essay is read these judgments appear less eccentric than when thus isolated: there is a sense in which Chaucer is less serious than Villon (yet one wonders if Arnold thought that *any* comedy could have 'high seriousness', or if he had read 'Troilus and Criseyde'); and, although Dryden and Pope are certainly classics of our poetry, Arnold's epigram expresses the sharp drop in the imaginative temperature that is felt as we move from Elizabethan, Jacobean and Caroline poetry at its best to the poetry of the late seventeenth and early eighteenth centuries.

Other essays in *Essays in Criticism* (1888) deal with four of the Romantic poets (Wordsworth, Byron, Keats, Shelley) and with Gray. For Gray Arnold had a fondness founded on a temperamental affinity. 'He is the scantiest and frailest of classics in our poetry, but he is a classic' (ibid., Vol. IV, p. 32). The valuation of Wordsworth as indisputably the greatest of the Romantic poets and the recognition of a Shakespearean felicity in Keats are judgments that modern taste endorses. The essay on Keats, in particular, is full of sound things excellently said, as, for example, the remark that 'Even in his pursuit of "the pleasures of song", however, there is that stamp of high work which is akin to character, which is character passing into intellectual production' (ibid., Vol. IV, p. 83). The essay on Shelley was a review of Dowden's biography of the poet and exhibits Arnold's impatience with the professorial flow of whitewashing sentiment. He intended to supplement this essay with another on Shelley's poetry, but there is no reason to think that, had he lived to write it, he would have changed his view that 'a want of humour and a self-delusion such as

Shelley's' (ibid., Vol. IV, p. 185) must have seriously debilitating effects on a man's poetry. Arnold's judgment of Shelley is disliked by the poet's admirers, but it has legs to stand on.

From this brief account some idea of the range and quality of Arnold's literary perceptions should have emerged. It should not be necessary to say that our valuation of him as a literary critic does not depend on our sharing all his literary tastes, just as it would be very odd if our judgment of him as a social thinker were made to hang on our agreement or disagreement with him over specific social and educational questions. Arnold had a discriminating taste in literature, but we suspect that he was too inclined to identify the serious with the solemn (like other Victorians). He saw clearly much that was wrong in Victorian England, but perhaps he had too much simple faith in the power of education to put things right. What is finally important is the example he sets us of critical integrity by his devotion to the discovery of the truth about any matter in hand, and his candour in avowing the truth—but temperately and with discretion—when he thinks that he has discovered it. There are in Arnold as an older man occasional signs of a stiffening sensibility—for example, in the testiness of a late group of political essays, which was fed by his dislike of Gladstone, and in his unease in his sixties at any freer treatment of sex in French novels and plays than he had been accustomed to as a young man reading the then rather shocking novels of George Sand. It would be inappropriate to lay much stress on these signs. There are fewer of them in Arnold than in most of his great literary contemporaries. To an unusual degree he preserved his flexibility of mind and remained open to new impressions to the end of his life. As a man he conquered 'the haunting, the irresistible self-dissatisfaction of his heart' ('On the Modern Element in Literature,' *Complete Prose Works*, Vol. I, p. 35), made the best of an arduous and not very rewarding professional life, and worked industriously at his books. They are still profitable to read as the productions of a civilized man who cared deeply and intelligently about literature and society.

NOTE

1. The introduction to this book is reprinted as 'Democracy' alongside the later essay 'Equality' in *Mixed Essays* (1879). The two essays are Arnold's most interesting contributions to social thinking apart from *Culture and Anarchy*.

A *Matthew Arnold*

Works of Matthew Arnold, 1903–4. 15 vols. Vols. 1–2 the poems, 3–12 the prose, 13–15 the letters and bibliography. Incomplete, but not yet superseded.

The Poetical Works of Matthew Arnold, ed. C. B. Tinker and H. F. Lowry, 1950. The standard text.

The Poems of Matthew Arnold, ed. K. Allott, 1965. Annotated and contains material omitted from the standard text.

The Complete Prose Works of Matthew Arnold, ed. R. H. Super, Ann Arbor, 1960– . Vols. 1–6 contain Arnold's prose in chronological order down to *Literature and Dogma* (1873). Finely edited, superbly annotated and indexed. The edition will be complete in 11 vols.

Five Uncollected Essays of Matthew Arnold, ed. K. Allott, Liverpool, 1953.

Essays, Letters, and Reviews by Matthew Arnold, ed. F. Neiman, Cambridge, Mass., 1960.

The Notebooks of Matthew Arnold, ed. H. F. Lowry, K. Young and W. H. Dunn, 1952.

Letters of Matthew Arnold, 1848–1888, ed. G. W. E. Russell, 1895. Mainly family letters (with many omissions). Unindexed.

The Letters of Matthew Arnold to Arthur Hugh Clough, ed. H. F. Lowry, 1932. Excellent edition with a useful introduction.

The Portable Matthew Arnold, ed. L. Trilling, New York, 1949. Useful selection of poetry and prose with stimulating introduction.

T. S. Eliot, 'Arnold and Pater', *Selected Essays*, 1932.

L. Trilling, *Matthew Arnold*, 1939. The best book on Arnold.

C. B. Tinker and H. F. Lowry, *The Poetry of Matthew Arnold: A Commentary*, 1940. Still essential for the student, but to be used with caution.

L. Bonnerot, *Matthew Arnold—Poète: Essai de biographie psychologique*, Paris, 1947.

E. K. Brown, *Matthew Arnold: A Study in Conflict*, Chicago, 1948.

J. Holloway, *The Victorian Sage*, 1953.

J. D. Jump, *Matthew Arnold*, 1955.

L. A. Gottfried, *Matthew Arnold and the Romantics*, 1963.

W. D. Anderson, *Matthew Arnold and the Classical Tradition*, Ann Arbor, 1965.

A. D. Culler, *Imaginative Reason*, New Haven, 1966. A study of the poetry.

W. A. Madden, *Matthew Arnold*, Bloomington, Indiana, 1967.

F. R. Leavis, 'Arnold as Critic' (1938), *A Selection from Scrutiny*, Cambridge, 1968.

B *A. H. Clough*

The Poems of A. H. Clough, ed. H. F. Lowry, A. L. P. Norrington
and F. L. Mulhauser, Oxford, 1951. The standard text.
The Correspondence of A. H. Clough, ed. F. L. Mulhauser, 1957.
The Poems and Prose Remains of A. H. Clough, ed. B. Clough, 1869.
Vol. 1 contains the life, selected letters and prose remains.
Selected Prose Works of A. H. Clough, ed. B. Trawick, Alabama,
1964. Badly edited and introduced, but contains new material.

K. Chorley, *A. H. Clough: The Uncommitted Mind*, Oxford, 1962.
An interesting biography.
W. E. Houghton, *The Poetry of Clough*, New Haven, 1963. The best
critical study.
P. Veyriras, *A. H. Clough*, Paris, 1964.

3

DICKENS

ALAN SHELSTON, *University of Manchester*

Dickens has always presented problems for literary criticism. For theorists whose critical presuppositions emphasise intelligence, sensitivity and an author in complete control of his work the cruder aspects of his popular art have often proved an unsurmountable obstacle, while for the formulators of traditions his gigantic idiosyncrasies can never be made to conform. And if difficulties such as these have been overcome by the awareness that Dickens sets his own standards, or rather that the standards that he sets, far from being inimical to great art, are his own expression of it, there remains a further problem : since his own lifetime Dickens has invariably seemed as much an institution as an individual. The institution of the 'Dickens of Christmas', celebrated by Chesterton, but derided by more sophisticated critics ever since, has given way to the Dickens of the academic thesis. The change may perhaps be defined by suggesting that, whereas it was once necessary when advancing the claims of Dickens to insist that he was not an entertainer, it is now becoming increasingly necessary to insist that he was. The invaluable re-assessment of the later novels which has taken place in recent years, emphasizing in particular the social and psychological aspects of their symbolism and structure, has sometimes gone close to producing a Dickens that his contemporaries would have recognized as, at most, only part of the picture. Dickens's art was at once varied and constant; if themes, emphases and preoccupations develop towards the ultimate pessimism of *Little Dorrit* and *Our Mutual Friend*, it is important to remember that Flora Finching and her aunt are cousins, not far removed, of Mrs Bardell and Mrs Gamp, that

74

Pecksniff and Podsnap have much in common, and that the atmosphere of nightmare that is felt so intensely in *Edwin Drood* has been lived through before in Jonas Chuzzlewit's solitary return from the murder of Mr Montague Tigg. Dickens's early success with his public gave him an assurance that led to increased powers of poetic expression and narrative technique, and it gave him also the confidence to assert his thematic priorities to a point where they contradicted the social assumptions of many of his readers, but he never rejected the basic methods which had brought him his initial success. When he collapsed in 1870, having almost completed the sixth instalment of *Edwin Drood*, the manner of his death was peculiarly appropriate: his audience were left in the state of anticipation to which he had accustomed them, but this time there was to be no resolution.

In the nineteenth century the writing of novels emerged from a permitted indulgence to an acceptable career. Fielding and Smollett, Dickens's heroes, did not depend on their novels for a living any more than did Richardson and Jane Austen, whereas for Dickens, Thackeray, Trollope and Henry James, their art ensured not only a means of subsistence but social prestige as well. It is customary to think of Dickens as a critic of much of the Victorian ethos, but whatever reservations the novels may express about self-aggrandizement, no career could demonstrate the ideal of the self-made man more effectively than his own. The boy whose formal education was so abruptly interrupted by his father's financial disasters sent his own eldest son to Eton; the child who had visited his father in the Marshalsea prison was listened to as an adult on the subject of penal reform. The facts of Dickens's early life have been rehearsed frequently enough and there is little need to recount them here other than to emphasize the extent to which Dickens, the chronicler of afflicted children, saw in his own childhood the archetypal experience of the child frustrated by the pressures of an urban and commercialized environment. The account of his childhood employment in the blacking-shop which he gave to his biographer Forster has often been quoted:

The deep remembrance of the sense I had of being utterly neglected and hopeless; of the shame I felt in my position; of the misery it was to my young heart to believe that, day by day, what I had learned, and thought, and delighted in, and raised my fancy and my emulation up by, was passing away from me, never to be brought back any more, cannot be written. My whole nature was so penetrated with the grief and humiliation of such considerations, that even now, famous and caressed and happy, I often forget in my dreams that I have a dear wife and children; even that I am a man; and wander desolately back to that time of my life.

(John Forster, *The Life of Charles Dickens*, Book I, Ch. 2)

Dickens is notoriously self-indulgent in this reflective mood, but the complaint is supported by the facts, and the tone of the passage, especially of its conclusion, was to be transmuted to the tone of *David Copperfield* and *Great Expectations*.

The extent to which the career of Dickens the novelist *was* the life of Dickens the man is best indicated simply by listing his full-length novels with the dates when they appeared. His first publications of any consequence were the *Sketches by Boz* which began to come out in 1836. From that date his novels appeared as follows (the dates are those of their first appearance, in instalment or serial form):

Pickwick Papers (1836–37); *Oliver Twist* (1837–39); *Nicholas Nickleby* (1838–39); *The Old Curiosity Shop* (1840–41); *Barnaby Rudge* (1841); *Martin Chuzzlewit* (1843–44); *Dombey and Son* (1846–48); *David Copperfield* (1849–50); *Bleak House* (1852–53); *Hard Times* (1854); *Little Dorrit* (1855–57); *A Tale of Two Cities* (1859); *Great Expectations* (1860–61); *Our Mutual Friend* (1864–65); *Edwin Drood* (unfinished) (1870).

A man of phenomenal energy, Dickens combined his literary career with a variety of social and theatrical interests. Some of the social concerns are interestingly documented in Philip Collins's two studies, *Dickens and Crime* (1962) and *Dickens and Education* (1963), while the theatrical involvement embraced writing, acting and producing for the stage, and culminated in the famous public readings from his own works. But a glance through the list of the novels shows the extent to which Dickens's life was dominated by the demands of authorship, for apart from the gaps between the last three items there is scarcely an unproductive year. When one considers how each of the novels appeared in either weekly or monthly instalments, and that they were supplemented by short stories and occasional journalism, as well as, from time to time, the duties of an editor, it can fairly be said that Dickens's literary activity over a period of more than thirty years was uninterrupted. (For reasons of space I have confined myself in this study to the novels alone. A full study of Dickens would, of course, pay proper attention to the other aspects of his literary career and in particular to the short stories, some of which throw interesting light on his development.)

The practice of serial publication, a publisher's device to facilitate sales which became an important factor in the development of nineteenth-century fiction, had consequences for Dickens's novels which it is difficult for the modern reader confronted by a set of eight-hundred page volumes to appreciate. Of the novels listed above, nine were originally published in illustrated monthly parts, each consisting of three or four chapters. Of the remaining six, one, *Oliver Twist*, appeared as a monthly serial in the magazine *Bentley's Miscellany*, while the other five, all of them rather shorter, were published in serial form in weekly papers. The effect of such a method of publication on the tone and content of the novels concerned was considerable. In the first place the need to maintain interest by the deployment of an easily identifiable narrative was paramount. Much has been made of the complexity of Dickens's plots but fundamentally a Dickens novel is based on a simple narrative concept like Pickwick's journey, the lives of Oliver Twist, David Copperfield, or Pip, or the hidden secrets of *Bleak House*, *Little Dorrit* or *Our Mutual Friend*. On the other hand, with a basic story established, there is ample opportunity for the multiplicity of character and event for which Dickens is famous; the dual nature of the process is revealed clearly by Dickens's device of two separate narratives in *Bleak House*. The wealth of apparently extraneous detail that is a feature of the novels has sometimes led to the supposition that Dickens wrote without plan, but the information that he gave to Forster, together with his own notes for individual novels, shows very clearly the extent to which, particularly in his later novels, he formulated a basic narrative concept to which he could keep firm hold as his novel progressed.

Serial publication thus posed its own technical problems and to a large extent dictated their solution. It also had the effect of intensifying the relationship between the author and his audience to a degree that can perhaps be compared with the oral narrative poem or the Elizabethan stage. To some novelists, conscious of what they saw as more important obligations, the need to tailor their novels to popular demand was a source of irritation: Mrs Gaskell, for example, had disagreements with Dickens himself over the serialization of her industrial novel *North and South* in his magazine *Household Words*. More than technical issues were at stake, however. In two vital areas audience-demand was a controlling factor over the content of Victorian fiction: the taboo on explicitness in the examination of sexual relationships, and the exploitation of sentiment, which in many ways can be seen as a substitute for a more realistic examination of human emotion.

It should be said straight away that very few major Victorian authors felt these aspects of public taste to be unduly crippling. As Kathleen Tillotson has pointed out, 'With very few exceptions, novelists were contented with such limitations as existed, and moved freely within them, or figure-skated along the edge.' (*Novels of the Eighteen-Forties*, 1954, p. 64) Dickens, however, seems not merely to have accepted these conditions but to have positively endorsed them. Conscious that his instalments were read, as they appeared, at family gatherings, he ensured that they contained nothing that a Victorian family would blush to hear. Furthermore, his manipulation of pathos, evidenced not only by individual incidents like the death of Little Nell and Paul Dombey, but by the total concept of characters like Esther Summerson in *Bleak House* and Amy Dorrit, provides a feature of the novels that to a modern reader can require considerable explanatory apology.

Obviously the emphasis on the pathetic can be attributed to some extent to popular demand: it is well known that at the time of writing *The Old Curiosity Shop* Dickens received numerous letters on the fate of his heroine. What must also be stressed are the powerful elements of sentimentality and morbidity in Dickens's own character which enabled him to respond to this aspect of popular taste. Little Nell was the fictional parallel of Dickens's sister-in-law Mary Hogarth, over whose early death he had grieved inconsolably. She became more than a figure of fiction to her creator, however: approaching the climax of *The Old Curiosity Shop* Dickens told Forster, 'All night I have been pursued by the child; and this morning I am unrefreshed and miserable.' (Forster, op. cit., II. 7) To self-indulgence in the pathetic was added an impulse towards the violent and the macabre. Dickens's readings from his own works show clearly the way in which he wished not only to gratify his own emotional needs in his fiction but also to witness its effect on his audience at first hand. Along with the comic scenes he liked to include in his programmes the most affecting or disturbing passages from the novels – the death of Paul Dombey, the Bob Cratchit scenes from *A Christmas Carol*, the Smike scenes from *Nicholas Nickleby* and, most dramatic of all, the murder of Nancy from *Oliver Twist* – and he measured his success by the degree of emotional response that he could exact from an often weeping audience. In a revealing letter to his wife, describing a private reading, he wrote: 'If you had seen Macready last night, undisguisedly sobbing and crying on the sofa as I read, you would have felt, as I did, what a thing it is to have power.' (quoted E. Johnson, *Charles Dickens: His Tragedy and Triumph*, 1953, p. 532.) The enjoyment of this sense of power over his audience gives us a clue to much that we find disturbing in Dickens's novels: more than any other novelist he needed not merely the applause of his audience but their submission. At the end of his career Dickens wrote in the last pages of *Our Mutual Friend*:

> . . . that I hold the advantages of the mode of publication (i.e. in serial form) to outweigh its disadvantages, may be easily believed of one who revived it in the Pickwick Papers after long disuse, and has pursued it ever since.'
>
> (Postscript)

Even he, however, can hardly have been aware of the full implications of the form for the development of his art.

If the more startling aspects of Dickens's fiction can be traced to traits in his own temperament it must be recorded that his comedy also has its origins in the man himself. Much has been written of his comic technique, but his letters reveal very clearly that the source of his comedy was not a conscious technique, in the literary sense, but a combination of vision and expression that was habitual to him. Writing, for example, of the domestic upheaval caused by some house alterations which he had set in progress he builds up a scene and an atmosphere in much the same way as he does in the novels:

> I am perpetually wandering (in fancy) up and down the house and tumbling over the workmen. When I feel that they are gone to dinner I become low. When I look forward to their total abstinence on Sunday I become wretched. The gravy at dinner has a taste of glue in it. I smell paint in the sea. Phantom lime attends me all the day long. I dream that I am a carpenter and can't partition off the hall.
>
> (quoted Johnson, op. cit., p. 748)

In a similar letter, describing the same events, Catherine, his wife, is 'all over paint, and seems to think it is somehow being immensely useful to get into that condition'. Here we have not only the elaboration of detail in the accumulation of comic disaster that we know so well from the novels, but also that spontaneous inter-relationship of perception and articulation that is the hallmark of Dickens's mode of comic expression. The sentence about his wife, for example, inconsequential though it is, could not have been rendered in any other way and it is typical of countless such observations that appear in the novels, giving to their comedy its inimitable flavour. Character and incident proliferate in Dickens so naturally because they are the product of an imagination that was never still, and of an impulse towards the dramatic evidenced not only by his theatrical activities but by the details of his day-to-day existence. Dickens would never have understood a theory of fiction based on the detachment of the author; the novels, as they stand, are the expression of the man who wrote them.

The origins of Dickens's literary career can be traced to his early employment as a journalist. This work took him first to the Law Courts, including the Court of Chancery, and then to Parliament, and his contempt for these institutions, evinced most powerfully in *Bleak House* but re-appearing consistently throughout his work, is based on the first-hand knowledge of them that he gained at the outset of his career. From reporting he moved on to descriptive journalism of a more imaginative kind and from 1834 to 1835 he wrote a series of sketches which appeared first in the *Monthly Magazine* and then in the *Evening Chronicle*. Some of these, together with some additional sketches written for the occasion, were collected and published in two illustrated volumes under the title *Sketches by Boz* in February 1836. Forster remarks that 'The Sketches were more talked about than the first two or three numbers of *Pickwick*' (op. cit., I. 5.) and certainly they were well received at the time. Their appearance in the *Evening Chronicle* had already attracted the attention of the publishers Edward Chapman and William Hall who invited Dickens to write a series of similar pieces to accompany a set of illustrations that they intended to bring out on sporting themes. From the start the text became more important than the illustrations and *The Posthumous Papers of the Pickwick Club* was born. The work appeared in monthly numbers, running from April 1836 to November in the following year.

Initially the venture seemed to be a failure. The opening numbers sold only four hundred copies and were dismissed by such reviewers as noticed them, but with the fourth number sales began to improve and *Pickwick Papers* suddenly became a triumph, selling 40,000 copies at the height of its success.

Readers of Mrs Gaskell's *Cranford* will remember how Captain Brown was run over by a railway train while engrossed in the latest number of *Pickwick Papers*; his enthusiasm was paralleled with less disastrous consequences throughout the country and at all levels of literate society. Once it had caught on, the book was not just another literary success but a phenomenon and its boisterous and inconsequential spirit came to represent – and indeed to misrepresent – its author for generations to come.

The form that *Pickwick Papers* took was not original. R. S. Surtees had already established himself as a humorous celebrant of sporting life and the sketches which he wrote for *The New Sporting Magazine*, and which were later re-published as *Jorrocks' Jaunts and Jollities* (1838), were the direct source of Dickens's material, most notably of the trial of Bardell *vs.* Pickwick. There was indeed a vogue for this kind of comic realism on familiar topics which had probably attracted the publishers in the first place. But Dickens brought to the form not simply a wish to emulate a successful predecessor but also a comic imagination nurtured on the classics of the picaresque novel. Forster records how Dickens told him that he had, in the happier days of his childhood, 'a little room upstairs. . . . From that blessed little room, *Roderick Random, Peregrine Pickle, Humphry Clinker, Tom Jones, The Vicar of Wakefield, Don Quixote, Gil Blas* and *Robinson Crusoe* came out, a glorious host, to keep me company.' (Forster, op. cit., I. 1) *Pickwick Papers* is in direct line of descent from such a tradition, with Mr Pickwick and Sam Weller as anglicized Quixote and Sancho Panza, journeying in the last days of the stage-coach through pre-industrial England. The story based on the unpredictable adventures of a journey, exploited so successfully by Fielding and Smollett, was rendered obsolete by the coming of the railways, and it is worth remarking that *Pickwick Papers*, the first novel of the greatest urban novelist, was also, in a very real sense, the last major novel of the pre-railway age.

The narrative devices of *Pickwick Papers*, its loosely-connected sequence of events, its interpolated stories and its mildly mock-heroic set-pieces, are techniques that Dickens had learnt from his eighteenth-century predecessors; from them also he inherited the comic amplitude and boisterous humour that is typical of much of the book. Pickwick drinks himself to sleep in Mr Wardle's wheelbarrow and is deposited as a vagabond in the village pound, there to be pelted with rubbish; when Mr Winkle goes shooting, Mr Tupman 'saved the lives of innumerable small birds by receiving a portion of the charge in his left arm.' Pickwick himself comments on the source of much of the comedy:

> 'Does it not, I ask, bespeak the indiscretion . . . of my followers, that, beneath whatever roof they locate, they disturb the peace of mind and happiness of some confiding female?'
>
> (Chapter 18)

Such scenes, however, are always more decorously comic than their counterparts in Fielding and Smollett, and the predominant tone of *Pickwick Papers* is one of benevolence and well-being. Good food, so often a source of comfort in Dickens, is never so effective in resolving disaster as it is in his first novel. The interpolated stories, in which can be seen hints of the violence that was sometimes to predominate in the later novels, are too crude to affect the basic atmosphere more than marginally and even the social realism of the Eatanswill election is presented in such a way that its less pleasant aspects are tempered by the overall sense of inconsequence.

The world of *Pickwick Papers*, however, is not simply the world of Dingley Dell and Eatanswill, neither is its total effect as disjointed as its loosely-constructed technique would perhaps imply. The novel is given shape both by a subtle development in the character of Pickwick himself and by the way in which its thematic concerns, most notably in the sequence of events involving Pickwick and the law, have the common element of an attack on inhumanity and selfishness. The affair with Mrs Bardell begins as a typically Pickwickian episode, but as Pickwick becomes more deeply involved with the legal process, described as an instrument for 'the torture and torment of his Majesty's liege subjects' and 'the comfort and emolument' of its practitioners, there is an increasingly serious edge to the comedy. Ultimately, in the Fleet prison, Pickwick is brought face to face with misery and the effect is not compromised in any way. When the 'Chancery prisoner' dies of consumption, a note is introduced into the novel that its readers have been prepared for over a series of scenes but which its earliest numbers hardly anticipated. In his solicitor's office Pickwick reflects that 'When a man bleeds inwardly it is a dangerous thing for himself; but when he laughs inwardly, it bodes no good to other people' (Chapter 31); the thought has an intensity that indicates the development of Pickwick himself from a myopic comic butt to a figure of wisdom and sensitivity. He himself may not be aware of the development, which was perhaps to some extent sub-conscious on the part of his creator, but it is consistent with a gradual process of unification that is apparent in *Pickwick Papers* as a whole. If we still remember the novel primarily in terms of its superb range of comic incident and character we cannot re-read it and remain unaffected by its social concern and above all by its ultimate affirmation of the pre-eminence of human charity.

Such concerns, of course, are the preoccupations of the novels that followed *Pickwick Papers*, *Oliver Twist* and *Nicholas Nickleby*, both of which take as their central situation the plight of children in the face of institutional cruelty. Undoubtedly Dickens's success with *Pickwick Papers* had given him the confidence to put his own interests at the centre of his fiction, and in practical terms the financial security which it had brought him made it possible to experiment with themes of his own choosing. The change surprised some of the readers of *Pickwick Papers* who, seeing in *Oliver Twist* simply another example of the 'Newgate Novel', objected to its preoccupation with low life. Such reservations were a minority judgement however, and, after all, both *Oliver Twist* and *Nicholas Nickleby* continue to show the imaginative fertility that had brought about Dickens's early triumph.

Of the two novels *Oliver Twist* is the most consistently effective as an attack on social injustice. Far more successfully than *Nicholas Nickleby*, it creates within its comedy the element of evil by which its child-hero is threatened, and the malignancy is rendered more complex by the way in which it is embodied not only in the dramatically criminal figures of Fagin and Bill Sikes but also in the representatives of established authority like the Board of Guardians and the police magistrate Mr. Fang. Here Dickens emphasizes for the first time a quality that was to become a theme of his later work: the innocent are caught between the Scylla of crime and the Charybdis of legalized repression. Mrs. Sowerberry, the undertaker's wife, who had a good deal of taste in the undertaking way', emphasizes the point; the repressive mentality has invaded the family hearth. Compared with this enveloping atmosphere of inhumanity, the cruelties of *Nicholas Nickleby*, for all their vividness, seem parochial; Dotheboys Hall exists not at the centre of the novel but at its perimeter, and once it has been destroyed the novel is given over to issues of romance and to a series of comic portraits which, splendid in themselves, tend to dissipate its thematic interest. Despite the death of Smike, Wackford Squeers is more a figure of fun than the embodiment of inhumanity that Dickens intended, while the wicked Uncle

Ralph and the decadent Sir Mulberry Hawk are scarcely more substantial than those intolerable manifestations of goodness, the Cheeryble twins.

Dickens's next two novels, *The Old Curiosity Shop* and *Barnaby Rudge*, can also usefully be considered as a pair in that they appeared in quick succession in a periodical of his own devising, *Master Humphrey's Clock*. Futhermore, as distinct from the other early novels, they involved a more hectic process of composition, appearing in weekly instead of monthly instalments. The very factor which was responsible for *The Old Curiosity Shop*'s compulsive effect on Dickens's contemporaries, his treatment of the life and death of the heroine Little Nell, has led to its notoriety with succeeding generations and probably no novel of Dickens is now so little read and so much abused. Edward FitzGerald copied out all the parts of the book which involved Little Nell herself : modern opinion would go to the opposite extreme and delete them, leaving an interesting range of incidental characters and some social commentary on industrial England of considerable force. In fact, *The Old Curiosity Shop* deserves more generous consideration than this. Professor K. J. Fielding has commented effectively on its resemblance to allegory (*Charles Dickens*, 1958, pp. 52–54) and like other Dickens children, Little Nell herself assumes symbolic significance when set against the avarice of her persecutors, Quilp and Sampson Brass. However, *Barnaby Rudge*, which met with declining success during the course of its appearance, is now more highly regarded. Based on the Gordon riots, it is in many ways a more stimulating novel on the theme of revolution than the more famous – and more sentimental – *A Tale of Two Cities*. For Dickens, the revolutionary, like the criminal, was a figure of compelling interest; while the behaviour of such characters might be rendered explicable, even sympathetic, by the circumstances in which they found themselves, ultimately they figured as expressions of evil far beyond the powers of rational analysis.

In the five years from 1836 to 1841 Dickens had thus produced five long novels, all of them, to a greater or lesser degree, bestsellers. Unknown seven years earlier, in 1842 he visited America as a literary celebrity. The visit began auspiciously enough, but despite his appreciation of the lavish hospitality of his hosts Dickens could not resist the opportunity to refer repeatedly in his public pronouncements to the vexed issue of international copyright, and in particular to the pirating of English works by American publishers. While undoubtedly in the right, as ever he lacked discretion, and the result was a series of attacks on him in American newspapers for which he, in return, exacted revenge, at first mildly in his *American Notes*, published in 1842, and then more vehemently in the American sections of his next novel, *Martin Chuzzlewit*.

Martin Chuzzlewit, to Dickens's alarm, met with a very luke-warm reception. For Dickens, with his emotional need for the support of his audience, this was particularly distressing, all the more so since he thought the book 'in a hundred points im-measurably the best of my stories.' It has been cogently argued that its comparative failure was due not so much to its own weaknesses as to the limitations of its predecessor, *American Notes*; whatever the reason, it caused its author intolerable anxiety.

Martin Chuzzlewit's lack of contemporary success is par-ticularly surprising when one considers that in some ways it re-invokes the spirit of *Pickwick Papers*. There is, of course, no Mr Pickwick, but Mark Tapley, the pot-boy who becomes the hero's inseparable man-servant, is in the vein of Sam Weller, and the recourse to the familiar aspects of the coaching-inn and the feast are reminiscent of Dickens's first success. *Martin Chuzzlewit*, however, was written to a definitely pre-conceived thematic plan. It has a story devised to demonstrate the eventual triumph of goodness, and the characters also were intended to emphasize the novel's thematic concerns. According to Forster, 'the notion of taking Pecksniff for a type of character was really the origin of the book; the design being to show, more or less by every person introduced, the number and variety of humours that have their root in selfishness.' (op. cit., III. 8) *Martin Chuzzlewit* is thus both a return to the spirit of *Pickwick Papers* and, in technique, a development from it. In that it can perhaps be seen as the culmination of Dickens's early novels it is worth considering in some detail.

Certainly Forster's emphasis on character is borne out by the book itself. Its plot is an amalgam of the improbable and the sentimental, but for what Forster referred to as 'the exuberance of comic invention' its characters are unequalled elsewhere in Dickens. Pecksniff, the hypocritical architect whose moral enun-ciation – ' "Charity, my dear . . . when I take my chamber-candlestick to-night, remind me to be more than usually particular in praying for Mr Anthony Chuzzlewit, who has done me an injustice" ' (Chapter 4) – is superbly parodied by his own drunken declamation at Todgers's boarding-house, Mrs Gamp, the bibulous sick-nurse and layer-out of the dead who regards her clients in the former function in terms of their potential for the latter, and Mrs Harris, a creature not only of Dickens's imagination but Mrs Gamp's as well, are only the more prominent members of the cast of a comedy as expansive as any that Dickens wrote. The inventiveness of the comedy in fact defeats Dickens's moralistic intentions: in a world in which the eventual happiness of the good is scarcely in doubt Pecksniff himself becomes a self-sustaining figure of delight.

Martin Chuzzlewit is not only memorable for its comedy, however. In its variety of scene it achieves considerable atmospheric complexity and in its London scenes in particular it suggests that sense of the density of urban experience that was to become the hallmark of the later novels. When Pecksniff brings his daughters, Mercy and Charity, up to town he brings them to an exciting new world of

> ... steeples, towers belfries, shining vanes, and masts of ships: a very forest. Gables, house-tops, garret-windows, wilderness upon wilderness. Smoke and noise enough for all the world at once.

To the onlooker, however, the scene becomes one of menace:

> The tumult swelled into a roar; the hosts of objects seemed to thicken and expand a hundredfold; and after gazing round him, quite scared, he turned into Todgers's again, much more rapidly than he came out ...
>
> (Chapter 9);

and when Mercy Pecksniff is inveigled into marriage with Jonas Chuzzlewit, who during the course of the novel becomes wife-beater, murderer and suicide, the threat becomes reality. If London is the site of Mrs Todgers' boarding-house, it is also the site of the dwelling-place of Jonas, incarcerated with his aged father and the senile and terrified servant, Chuffey. While the outcome of *Martin Chuzzlewit* confirms its benevolent ethos, Dickens extracts from the sub-plot of Jonas's career a disturbing atmosphere of the macabre. *Martin Chuzzlewit* has its imperfections – amongst them the extended American journey of its hero which Dickens introduced unashamedly in an attempt to stimulate sales, and which, though a sustained *tour-de-force*, can never overcome its digressive effect – but they are the faults of an imagination on the rampage. Dickens may have set out with an end in view, but he found, as he wrote the novel, that, as Forster records, 'it seized him for itself . . . he wept over it, and laughed, and wept again, and excited himself to an extraordinary degree . . . and walked thinking of it fifteen

86

and twenty miles about the black streets of London, many and many a night after all sober folks had gone to bed.' (IV. 4) Such self-absorption was indeed not uncommon to Dickens, but it did not always achieve such fortunate results as it did in this case. From this point his novels were to achieve an often overpowering symbolic and thematic intensity, but they did so to some extent at the cost of the unrestrained comic invention that proliferates in the earlier novels, and to such potent effect in the best scenes of *Martin Chuzzlewit*.

In the novels discussed so far the techniques, both of the fiction itself and of the social criticism embodied within it, are relatively straightforward. The institutions which Dickens attacks, the workhouses in *Oliver Twist* or the Yorkshire schools in *Nicholas Nickleby*, are easily recognizable, and once the abuse has been overcome, the way is open to a happy conclusion. Dickens's conception of character in these novels is similarly uncomplicated: hence the optimism which they imply, which in itself is made more acceptable by the way in which they are distanced in time from the late 1830s and early 1840s when they were written. The stagecoach world of *Pickwick Papers*, *Nicholas Nickleby* and *Martin Chuzzlewit* is fundamentally stable and comforting, and it is only parenthetically that the violence of the changes implicit in the industrialization of society breaks in – as with the London sections of *Oliver Twist* or, more specifically, Little Nell's journey through the Midlands in *The Old Curiosity Shop*. In *Dombey and Son*, however, and in most of the novels which follow it, Dickens locates his action, at least in spirit, in the immediately contemporary world, most emphatically perhaps in *Dombey and Son* itself, with its constant reference to the railway, a symbol of social change of perhaps uncontrollable potential, but also in novels like *Bleak House*, with its descriptions of the squalor of living conditions in the overcrowded city, *Little Dorrit*, like *Dombey and Son*, emphasizing the destructive inter-relationship of economic and moral attitudes, and finally, *Our Mutual Friend*, where the forces of business speculation are seen at work on the raw material of rotting corpses, dunghills – and marriage. As Humphry House has pointed out, the specific abuses attacked in these novels are often things of the past – most obviously so in the case of the Marshalsea prison in *Little Dorrit* – and the physical settings are sometimes a mixture of the contemporary and the recollected past, but the institutions are important not in themselves but as metaphors for a repressive social psychology, in itself the consequence of a predominantly selfish economic ethos, that in its pressure on the helpless individual is identifiably Victorian. The opening of *Little Dorrit* gives the date of the action as the eighteen-twenties, but when Arthur Clennam, its hero, returns to his inheritance the description of the city that greets him in no way evokes the sense of the past:

> It was a Sunday evening in London, gloomy, close, and stale. Maddening church bells of all degrees of dissonance, sharp and flat, cracked and clear, fast and slow, made the brick-and-mortar echoes hideous. Melancholy streets, in a penitential garb of soot, steeped the souls of the people who were condemned to look at them out of windows, in dire despondency. . . . Nothing to see but streets, streets, streets. Nothing to breathe but streets, streets, streets. Nothing to change the brooding mind, or raise it up. Nothing for the spent toiler to do, but to compare the monotony of his seventh day with the monotony of his six days, think what a weary life he led, and make the best of it – or the worst, according to the probabilities.
>
> (Book I, Chapter 3)

Here we are reminded not of anything in fiction but of Blake's *London* in the *Songs of Experience*:

> I wander thro' each charter'd street,
> Near where the charter'd Thames does flow,
> And mark in every face I meet
> Marks of weakness, marks of woe.

The resemblance, of course, is far from coincidental: both Blake and Dickens have at the heart of their work a sense of the threat to the human spirit from the forces of repression, and they locate that threat symbolically in the rapidly developing urban and industrial world around them. The London of *Little Dorrit* though, however specific the dating of the novel, is the London of the tangible present, just as it is in the other later novels (even, in a very special way, in *A Tale of Two Cities*). From the time of *Dombey and Son* Dickens becomes, in the fullest sense, a Victorian novelist.

In the space available here it is scarcely possible to discuss each of the later novels in detail and it must be emphasized that generalizations about them must be qualified, not only by the way in which Dickens presents different aspects of his analysis of society in the novels already mentioned, but also by the diversifying effect of the other novels of this later period, most notably *David Copperfield* and *Great Expectations* with their strongly autobiographical overtones, and *Hard Times* and *A Tale of Two Cities* with their concentration on specific issues. The generalization that I have outlined in the preceding paragraph, however, will, I hope, serve as a context within which discussion of individual novels can take place. For the purposes of this essay I intend to concentrate in some detail on *Dombey and Son* before going on to suggest resemblances and qualifications that may arise from the novels which followed it.

Just as *Martin Chuzzlewit* was written with a pre-conceived moral end in view, so *Dombey and Son* was intended to convey a similar message. Forster records that Dickens told him that the intention in the case of *Dombey and Son* was 'to do with Pride what its predecessor had done with Selfishness' and he goes on to quote a long letter from Dickens outlining the proposed plot in some detail : 'This is what cooks call "the stock of the soup". All kinds of things will be added to it of course.' Dickens's letter emphasizes the central issue of Dombey's pride, expressed in his preoccupation with his son, Paul, and the consequent alienation, on Paul's death, from his daughter, Florence, leading up to 'the decay and downfall of the house, and the bankruptcy of Dombey, and all the rest of it.' (Forster, VI. 2) It makes no mention of Dombey's second marriage, and thus of the way in which the climax of the novel is intensified by Edith Dombey's desertion of her husband, but the novel as it stands is a remarkably consistent development of Dickens's original idea. In particular, his conception of Dombey's character is far more complex than anything he had attempted so far and the relationship of every aspect of the novel to the psychology of its central character is consistently and convincingly handled.

What Dickens's communications with Forster do not stress so emphatically is the way in which Dombey's ruling passion is conceived specifically in economic terms. This is implied, of course, in the ambiguity of the novel's title : 'Dombey and Son' is both a paternal relationship and a commercial concern, and Dombey's tragedy is the result of his inability to distinguish between the two. The point is underlined in the opening chapter of the novel – in contrast with that of *Martin Chuzzlewit*, perhaps the most effective that Dickens ever wrote :

'The house will once again, Mrs Dombey,' said Mr Dombey, 'be not only in name but in fact Dombey and Son; Dom-bey and Son!' ...

... These three words conveyed the one idea in Mr Dombey's life. The earth was made for Dombey and Son to trade in, and the sun and moon were made to give them light. Rivers and seas were formed to float their ships; rainbows gave them promise of fair weather; winds blew for or against their enterprises; stars and planets circled in their orbits, to preserve inviolate a system of which they were the centre. Common abbreviations took new meanings in his eyes, and had sole reference to them: A.D. had no concern with anno Domini, but stood for anno Dombei – and Son.

(Chapter 1)

The first part of the novel is devoted to the stultifying effect of Dombey's inability to see the world except in terms of his own commercial pride: the Dombey children, Paul and Florence, are isolated in a world which denies their natural impulses and affections. Paul, doomed with a precocious world-weariness almost before the novel has begun, dies, and 'Dombey and Son is a Daughter after all'.

The pathetic death of Paul Dombey, more intensely rendered in its way than that of Little Nell, is a reminder that Dickens's new control over his material does not involve any change in his basic fictional techniques. In the confrontation between authority and the child Dickens presents the conflict in much the same way as in the earlier novels, exploiting, for example, the combination of comedy and pathos familiar from *Oliver Twist*. For his education Paul is sent first to Mrs Pipchin, who runs 'an infantine Boarding-House of a very select description' with all the selfish asperity common to Dickensian widows, and then to Dr Blimber's boarding school:

'Ha!' said Dr Blimber. 'Shall we make a man of him?'
'Do you hear, Paul?' added Mr Dombey, Paul being silent.
'Shall we make a man of him?' repeated the Doctor.
'I had rather be a child,' replied Paul.
'Indeed!' said the Doctor. 'Why?'

(Chapter 11)

The comic juxtaposition of uncomprehending adult and un-sophisticated child is reminiscent of Oliver's asking for more, but in *Dombey and Son* scenes like this are integrated into the presentation of Paul Dombey's childhood in a way which qualifies their comedy and emphasizes, by contrast, the completely enveloping nature of the ethos that destroys him.

Dombey's obsession with the power of money lies at the heart of the novel and its repressive consequences are emphasized not only in terms of plot but by the way in which character and location are organized towards a total symbolic effect. It is a common Dickensian technique to identify characters by the life-style of their establishments and he employs it perhaps more purposefully in *Dombey and Son* than in any other of his novels. The business house of Dombey, where fortunes are made and life is destroyed, is contrasted with Sol Gills's shop, where business fails and humanity flourishes; the suffocating institutions presided over by Mrs Pipchin and Dr Blimber can be set against Staggs's Gardens, the home of Paul Dombey's first nurse, and Mrs MacStinger's lodging-house, where if children run wild they at least run naturally. Minor characters, like Miss Tox, Major Bagstock and John and Harriet Carker, are all presented in the homes which they have made for themselves and which express their personalities so precisely. At the centre of the novel Dombey's own house, with its cheerless rooms and staircases, is no home at all : from its windows Florence looks across the street to where she sees a very different household, with a very different head :

> When he had dined, she could see them, through the open windows, go down with their governess or nurse, and cluster round the table; and in the still summer weather the sound of their childish voices and clear laughter would come ringing across the street into the drooping air of the room in which she sat. Then they would climb and clamber up-stairs with him, and romp about him on the sofa, or group themselves at his knee, a very nosegay of little faces, while he seemed to tell them some story. Or they would come running out into the balcony; and then Florence would hide herself quickly, lest it should check them in their joy, to see her in her black dress, sitting there alone.

> (Chapter 18)

For all its considerable qualities of plot it is through effects and contrasts such as these that *Dombey and Son* makes its most telling effect. At the climax of the novel we are again brought back to the Dombey mansion :

> It is a great house still, proof against wind and weather, without breaches in the roof, or shattered windows, or dilapidated walls; but it is a ruin none the less, and the rats fly from it.

> (Chapter 59)

Alone, the ruined Dombey wanders its corridors at night. He

contemplates suicide and is melodramatically saved by the daughter he had spurned, but far more instrumental in the assertion of Dombey's downfall than the events is their setting. The great empty house, which has seen the birth and death of Paul, Florence's solitary growth to womanhood and the hollow triumph of Dombey's re-marriage, is an expression of nemesis far more potent than the events of his career can possibly be.

Running parallel with Dombey's career is that of his unloved daughter : as he moves obdurately towards disaster, she leads a life of emotional starvation from which she is ultimately rescued by her marriage to Dombey's clerk, Walter Gay. Here again the atmospheric contrasts are as important as the narrative events; against the sterility of Florence's environment is set the vitality of the influences which surround Walter Gay. It is worth emphasizing, however, that, just as Dickens's firm hold on the character of Dombey at the centre of the novel gives it coherence and power, so the character of Florence is handled with a sensitivity that gives particular force to her part in the novel. Unlike Esther Summerson in *Bleak House* and Amy Dorrit, Florence Dombey draws from the reader a sympathy consistent with the facts of her situation, largely perhaps because the importance of her role is not specifically emphasized but develops as a consequence of the novel's central theme. This is not to suggest that Dickens deliberately adopted a more naturalistic approach in *Dombey and Son*, which as much as any other Dickens novel, has its high points of melodrama, comedy and pathos. What can be said is that these effects are skilfully controlled towards a unified expression of its central concerns in a way which was new to Dickens, and which was to open up new possibilities for the development of his art. (For a fuller discussion of points mentioned here and of many others see Kathleen Tillotson's excellent chapter on this novel in her *Novels of the Eighteen-Forties*.)

While working on *Dombey and Son* Dickens had confessed to the need he felt to control some aspects of his imagination :

> Invention, thank God, seems the easiest thing in the world; and I seem to have such a preposterous sense of the ridiculous . . . as to be constantly requiring to restrain myself from launching into extravagances in the height of my enjoyment.
> (Forster, op. cit., v. 5)

The admission is an interesting testimony to the way in which Dickens regarded his creative impulse, and in *David Copperfield* he seems to have been able to relax the restraint which he had imposed upon its predecessor. *David Copperfield*'s traditional popularity has always depended to some extent on the 'preposterous sense of the ridiculous' manifested in characters like Micawber and Betsy Trotwood, while the extent of Dickens's 'enjoyment' in the novel is communicated by the particular quality of its reflective tone:

> I never hear the name, or read the name, of Yarmouth, but I am reminded of a certain Sunday morning on the beach, the bells ringing for church, little Em'ly leaning on my shoulder, Ham lazily dropping stones into the water, and the sun, away at sea, just breaking through the heavy mist, and showing us the ships, like their own shadows.
>
> (Chapter 3)

The beautifully realised sense of place, achieved again later in the descriptions of the marsh country in *Great Expectations*, is typical of the best of *David Copperfield*; nostalgia is far too crude a term to define its evocative sensitivity. The attention paid to the other major novels of Dickens's later period by modern critics has led to some neglect of what was once regarded as the representative Dickens novel and it is a neglect that amounts to self-deprivation. But when this is said, it has to be admitted that there is much that is unsatisfactory in *David Copperfield*. In his Introduction to the Everyman edition, written in 1907, Chesterton commented that 'although this is the best of all Dickens's books, it constantly disappoints the critical and intelligent reader.' So much the worse for him, one is tempted to respond, but Chesterton defines the more worrying aspects of *David Copperfield* when he discusses the novel's conclusion: 'I do not like the notion of David Copperfield sitting down comfortably to his tea-table with Agnes, having got rid of all the inconvenient or distressing characters of the story by sending them to Australia.' Dickens was not above getting rid of his more inconvenient or distressing children by sending them to Australia in real life, but the fictional experience is somehow less excusable. The combination of fiction and selective autobiography makes *David Copperfield* a disturbingly self-centred book: its hero is embarrassingly prone to a tendency to self-pity and wishful thinking which he never really outgrows and which is hardly improved by the smugness with which he regards himself at the conclusion of the novel:

> I had advanced in fame and fortune, my domestic joy was perfect, I had been married ten happy years.
>
> (Chapter 63)

The unity which Dickens had had to create in *Dombey and Son* is embodied in *David Copperfield* in its first-person narrative but, in spite of the special circumstances surrounding it, it has important factors in common with the other later novels. Like Florence Dombey, David Copperfield suffers a loveless childhood, emphasized in this case by the physical and psychological violence of his step-father's oppression. In a variety of ways, most obviously in the story of Little Em'ly, this is a Dickensian Song of Experience: the novel has no clearer message than its demonstration of the fragility of childhood innocence. Coupled with this is the sense of isolation, amounting on occasions to desolation, which surrounds David himself as the people to whom he commits himself in his search for security – Steerforth, Dora, even, though through no fault of his own, Peggotty – prove fallible. Given such a demonstration of the instability of existence, how can the marriage to Agnes seem other than a sham? Marriage, in fact, is to seem increasingly a mockery as a means of conclusion in the later novels: what in *Martin Chuzzlewit* is an acceptable convention of comedy becomes in *Little Dorrit*, *Great Expectations* and *Our Mutual Friend* almost a matter for apology.

David Copperfield, for all its variety of character and situation, is, of course, a deeply introspective novel. In the two great novels of the eighteen-fifties which followed it, *Bleak House* and *Little Dorrit*, Dickens turned, more completely than ever before, to an analysis of society. These two novels have attracted so much attention in recent years that it would serve little purpose to attempt a comprehensive account of them here, even were it possible, and instead I intend only to refer to specific issues arising from them: in the case of *Bleak House* the unusual narrative method that Dickens adopted, and its implications for the view of society presented in the novel, and in the case of *Little Dorrit* the organization of the novel towards the expression of an unrelenting social pessimism. (On *Bleak House* see in particular M. D. Zabel's essay in *The Dickens Critics* ed. Ford and Lane. Edgar Johnson's chapter on *Little Dorrit* in his *Charles Dickens* is one of his finest and should be consulted.)

Dickens began work on *Bleak House* at the end of 1851, a year which has often been taken to mark a turning-point in Victorian social history. The Great Exhibition of that year affirmed a commercial and nationalistic pride that could hardly have been predicted from the social unease of the eighteen-thirties and forties: the fifties were the first decade of Victorian self-confidence. The limitations of such an over-simplification have been expertly demonstrated by Professor Asa Briggs (*Victorian People*, Chapter 2) and Dickens himself, no admirer of the Exhibition, was in fact probably more concerned with a speech which he made in the same year on behalf of the Metropolitan Sanitary Association, during the course of which he proclaimed:

> That no man can estimate the amount of mischief grown in dirt, – that no man can say the evil stops here or stops there, either in its moral or physical effects, or can deny that it begins in the cradle and is not at rest in the miserable grave, is as certain as it is that the air from Gin Lane will be carried by an easterly wind into Mayfair, or that the furious pestilence raging in St Giles's no mortal list of Lady patronesses can keep out of Almack's.
>
> (quoted Butt and Tillotson, *Dickens at Work*, 1957, p. 191.)

In *Bleak House* Esther Summerson catches smallpox from the crossing-sweeper, Jo; her aristocratic mother dies at the gate of the poison-infested burying-ground close by Tom All-Alone's. The all-embracing nature of social evil in *Bleak House* is thus made explicit through a symbolism born of Dickens's immediate social concerns. Richard Carstone, the doomed ward of the Court of Chancery, says of that court's operations:

> 'My head ached with wondering how it happened, if men were neither fools nor rascals and my heart ached to think that they could possibly be either....'
>
> (Chapter 5)

The comment applies not just to Chancery itself, but by extension to the social system of which it is presented as the representative institution in the novel.

To emphasize the extent of his social preoccupations in *Bleak House* Dickens deliberately contrived a dual-narrative in which the life-story of his heroine, Esther Summerson, related as a first-person narrative, is interwoven with an extensive range of imaginative social documentation provided by the author himself. The effect is a subtle one – the novel gains stability from the progressive unravelling of Esther's story, while leaving Dickens free to expatiate on various examples of social abuse in the manner of his earlier picaresque method. The evils which he attacks, ranging from slum-dwelling to misguided philanthropy and including every form of exploitation, are indeed related to the main plot, but the fact that the novel is deliberately compartmentalized in this way allows Dickens to extend his social criticism without limitation.

There is, however, a further effect of the narrative method that is vital to an understanding of *Bleak House*. If Dickens supplies his analysis in what might loosely be called the picaresque section of the novel, his remedy is contained in the 'linear' narrative of Esther's life-story, and in particular in its account of her relationship with Jarndyce, the father-figure of the novel, who knows the ways of Chancery and constantly asserts the futility of opposition. Jarndyce's method of allevia-tion is a simple one springing from his inexhaustible bank-account, and, in fact, all that Dickens can offer against the realistic depredations of the social system is charity of im-probably mythic proportions. The inadequacy of such a solution is best demonstrated by the way in which Jarndyce, a descendant of the Cheerybles of *Nicholas Nickleby* and Mr Brownlow in *Oliver Twist* is presented as a figure of semi-divine potential. At the climax of *Bleak House*, when he has made Esther a present of not only her home but also her husband, she describes her reaction:

> I was cold, and I trembled violently; but not a word he uttered was lost. As I sat looking fixedly at him, and the sun's rays descended, softly shining through the leaves upon his bare head, I felt as if the brightness on him must be like the brightness of the Angels.

(Chapter 64)

The unrealistic nature of Jarndyce's role in *Bleak House*, far from providing an answer to the social evil documented in the novel, is, in fact, an expression of pessimism about the prospects of social change as intense as any expressed by the social ana-lysis itself; in that Esther's narrative is ostensibly optimistic, the dual-narrative method can be seen as enabling Dickens to put forward a solution to the problems outlined in the novel which he could scarcely have endorsed in rational terms.

The pessimism implicit in *Bleak House* finds overt expression in *Little Dorrit*, written some five years later. Here Dickens reverts to the world of *Dombey and Son* in that the novel is given a specifically commercial setting: the inter-relationship between financial preoccupations and selfishness is emphasized not only by the thwarted life of the hero Arthur Clennam, a Paul Dombey who managed to survive, but also, in parody, through the social pretensions of William Dorrit, the Father of the Marshalsea, existing in fantasy when he is imprisoned and in fact after his release. The theme is given a fuller social perspective by the career of the financier, Merdle, surrounded by pillars of the establishment until he is exposed as 'the greatest Forger and the greatest Thief that ever cheated the gallows'. (Book II, Chapter 25) The structure of *Little Dorrit* is a simple one compared with the ingenuity of *Bleak House*; the real issue is not, as Dickens himself was forced to enquire in a memorandum, how the Clennams are related to the Dorrits, but how the course of their lives demonstrates the hopelessness of existence in the prison-world that the novel portrays. The prison-symbolism of *Little Dorrit* has received ample comment: one need only remark here on the way in which the actual prisons of the novel and life itself as it is portrayed there become interchangeable. Dorrit released is Dorrit enchained: Clennam imprisoned is Clennam liberated, at least temporarily, from the pressures of the outside world. *Little Dorrit* ends with the marriage of Clennam to the heroine, Amy Dorrit, but the sense of release that this convention had given in the earlier novels is never attempted. The marriage takes place in an atmosphere devoid of festivity and the concluding sentence of the novel describes how, after it,

They went quietly down into the roaring streets, inseparable and blessed; and as they passed in sunshine and shade, the noisy and the eager, and the arrogant and the froward and the vain, fretted and chafed, and made their usual uproar.
(Book II, Chapter 34)

Little Dorrit has its 'good' characters – Amy herself, the Meagleses, Doyce the engineer, and in their own way, the rent-collector Panks and Flora Finching, nursing her senile aunt – but they are all cast in a minor key and their capacity for happiness seems constantly overshadowed by the predominant atmosphere of defeat that the novel suggests. Here the representative institution is the Circumlocution Office, a government department devoted to the frustration of the individual; in *Little Dorrit* Dickens seems to abandon the idea that the individual can assert himself with any hope of success against the pressures of society.

The other novels of the eighteen-fifties, *Hard Times* and *A Tale of Two Cities*, were both written in weekly instalments for Dickens's own periodicals, *Household Words* and *All the Year Round*. Of the novels written in this way only *Great Expectations* really achieves the stature of the major novels although, since its championship by F. R. Leavis in *The Great Tradition*,

Hard Times has come to occupy a special place in Dickens studies. Written soon after the completion of *Bleak House* and after a visit by Dickens to the industrial North, it is, in fact, far more successful as an attack on utilitarianism than as a discussion of specifically industrial issues. The economy of its form has certain advantages in this respect; *Hard Times* makes its points about its chosen target lucidly and forcefully, and certainly Humphry House's assertion that it is 'a sport and an anomaly' (*The Dickens World*, 1941. p. 34) gives a misleading impression. These qualities, however, cannot disguise the fact that its characterization is often unsubtle and its irony often laboured. Amplitude is fundamental to Dickens's art, and the restrictions imposed upon him by the comparative brevity of *Hard Times* are not always successfully overcome.

A *Tale of Two Cities* is more of an anomaly than *Hard Times*, and some critics have related its singular emotional tone to aspects of Dickens's private life, and particularly to his involvement with the young actress, Ellen Ternan. It is probably more to the point to see this novel as an expression of the subconscious fear of revolutionary violence which Dickens had revealed earlier in *Barnaby Rudge* and which he shared with so many of his contemporaries. In the Preface Dickens refers to 'the philosophy of Mr. Carlyle's wonderful book'. Carlyle's *French Revolution* had been published in 1837, at a time when it was easy to see the significance of its theme for contemporary England, but *A Tale of Two Cities*, appearing more than twenty years later, is an interesting reminder that anxiety on the subject of revolution was not confined to the first half of the century. The 'two cities' of the title are, of course, London and Paris, and if the opening chapters express a modernist's contempt for the London of an earlier age, it is not implausible to relate Dickens's account of the fall of the French aristocracy, with its hallmark of gratuitous indifference, to his comments on society in his other late novels. Indeed, some such comparison is suggested in the opening paragraph :

> . . . in short the period was so like the present period, that some of its noisiest authorities insisted on its being received, for good or evil, in the superlative degree of comparison only.
>
> (Chapter 1)

but it is never consistently developed. Inspired by Carlyle, *A Tale of Two Cities* matches Carlyle in its rhetoric and in the vagueness with which its social and emotional themes are explored. For the complexity of tone and analysis that characterizes Dickens's other work of the period are substituted shrill-ness and a pervasive sentimentality epitomized by Sidney Carton's famous last words.

The pessimistic turn taken by Dickens's novels from *Dombey and Son* onwards could scarcely have passed unnoticed by contemporary reviewers. In a long review of *Little Dorrit*, for example, in *Blackwood's Magazine*, entitled 'Remonstrance with Dickens', the writer lamented what he regarded as a distortion of Dickens's natural propensities:

> ... we can't wait for the end of the wilderness of *Little Dorrit* before recording our earnest protest and deep lament; for in that wilderness we sit down and weep when we remember thee, O Pickwick!
> (*Blackwood's Magazine*, April 1857)

The review concludes by begging Dickens not to go on 'building streets of *Bleak Houses*, and creating crowds of *Little Dorrits*'. Pleas for a return to the spirit of the earlier novels were often a way of expressing disapproval of what were felt to be danger-ously radical social attitudes: Lord Macaulay's famous com-ment that *Hard Times* was 'sullen socialism' was not an isolated example. There were other causes for anxiety amongst Dickens's admirers. Aware of his unhappiness in his marriage, which came to a climax with his separation from his wife in 1858, and his removal to his new house at Gad's Hill near Rochester, his friend Angela Burdett-Coutts was afraid that his domestic difficulties had affected his writing. Certainly *Little Dorrit*, in particular, of the later novels seems in many ways to suggest an impasse: the constant atmosphere of failure surrounding its middle-aged hero has psychological as well as social implica-tions.

Settled at Gad's Hill, however, Dickens seems to have found new resources of creative energy. His last completed novels, *Great Expectations* and *Our Mutual Friend*, together with the unfinished *Edwin Drood*, are certainly no more optimistic than the novels which preceded them – *Our Mutual Friend*, especially, suggests a society more positively predatory than anything in *Bleak House* or *Little Dorrit* – but they are marked by new reserves of that fictive inventiveness which is characteristic of Dickens at his greatest, reinforced now by an increasing fascina-tion with the macabre themes of crime and death.

Great Expectations was Dickens's second 'autobiographical' novel – 'autobiographical' in the very general sense that it presents in a first-person narrative the career, and more importantly the psychological development, of its hero. As in *David Copperfield*, Dickens makes skilful use of the narrator's re-collected sense of place. From the opening chapter we are presented through the eyes of the child, Pip, with an evocative picture of the marsh country amongst which he grew up, and to which he is to return, at moments of emotional crisis, throughout the course of the novel:

> Ours was the marsh country, down by the river, within, as the river wound, twenty miles of the sea. My first most vivid and broad impression of the identity of things, seems to me to have been gained on a memorable raw afternoon towards evening. At such a time I found out for certain, that this bleak place overgrown with nettles was the churchyard . . . and that the dark flat wilderness beyond the churchyard, intersected with dykes and mounds and gates, with scattered cattle feeding on it, was the marshes; and that the low leaden line beyond was the river; and that the distant savage lair from which the wind was rushing was the sea. . . .
>
> (Chapter 1)

This kind of atmospheric precision achieves symbolic force and recurs, for example, in Pip's references to the great furnace at the forge where he works with the blacksmith Joe Gargery, and in the descriptions of the decayed sterility of Satis House, the mansion of his supposed benefactress, Miss Havisham.

The theme of *Great Expectations* is that of false pride and again, as in *Dombey and Son*, it is given a specifically monetary perspective: Pip's ambitions to be a gentleman, based on the belief that he is the chosen protégé of Miss Havisham, are shattered when he learns that his sponsor is the convict Magwitch. But *Great Expectations* is, in fact, equivocal about money-values and its real strength lies in the quality of its psychological penetration, revealed not only in its account of Pip's reactions to his situation, but also in features like the mysterious split personality of the criminal lawyer Jaggers and the self-imposed death-in-life of Miss Havisham, the consequence of her having been jilted many years before. Related to, and indeed reinforcing, these psychological concerns is a fascination with crime, emphasized by the role of Magwitch and his involve-ment in the lives of both Pip and the unattainable heroine, Estella. In his notes for the novel Dickens wrote:

Magwitch tried, found guilty, & left for

DEATH

(Butt and Tillotson, op. cit., p. 30)

and at the climax of the novel he includes a highly dramatized account of the death sentence passed on Magwitch at his trial. Preoccupations which had revealed themselves in the early part of Dickens's career, in episodes like Fagin's last night alive, the suicide of Ralph Nickleby and the murder in Martin Chuzzlewit, thus recur in these final novels.

Violence and the mentality of the criminal are even more intensely represented in *Our Mutual Friend* and *Edwin Drood*, and in the latter, with the prominence given to the character of Jasper Drood, choirmaster, opium addict and presumably murderer, Dickens would seem to have intended to concentrate specifically on these issues. Dickens had published Wilkie Collins's *The Moonstone* in *All the Year Round* in 1868 and this may have induced him to write his own detective story, although *Edwin Drood* is a work of potentially far greater power than Collins's novel. Speculation on the subject of Dickens's unfinished novel, however, while fascinating, is not always productive, and I therefore intend to conclude this survey of Dickens's work with a discussion of *Our Mutual Friend*, his last, and arguably his greatest completed novel.

Our Mutual Friend has had a chequered critical career. Its opening numbers were not altogether well received and Dickens endured considerable anxiety about its progress. The young Henry James attacked it violently for its lack of discipline and 'humanity':

> What a world were this world if the world of *Our Mutual Friend* were an honest reflection of it! But a community of eccentrics is impossible. . . . Where in these pages are the depositories of that intelligence without which the movement of life would cease? Who represents nature?
>
> (*The Nation*, I (1865), reprinted in Ford and Lane,
> *The Dickens Critics*, 1961)

and of the early critics only Shaw seems to have anticipated such modern views as those of Edmund Wilson and Edgar Johnson, who rank it with Dickens's greatest achievements rather than considering it as evidence of decline.

The first thing that has to be said about *Our Mutual Friend* is that it is a novel in which Dickens, in a way curiously comparable to Henry James himself in his last novels, takes his fictional techniques to the point of self-parody. The convoluted plot, involving its central character in not two, but three, separate identities, all involving disguise, outdoes anything its author had contrived before; we are asked to accept concealed evidence, simulated behaviour and hidden secrets as part of the day-to-day processes of existence. The characterization offers a range of grotesques like the one-legged Silas Wegg, hired to read the 'Decline-and-Fall-Off-The-Rooshan-Empire' to the equally improbable Golden Dustman Noddy Boffin, Mr Venus Taxidermist and dealer in 'human warious', and Jenny Wren, the deformed dolls' dressmaker, whose love for the good Lizzie Hexam alternates with sadistic fantasies about the fate of her enemies. *Our Mutual Friend* seems at times like a vast and somewhat decaying baroque structure, threatening at any moment to collapse.

The effect of this exaggeration of technique, like that of James's prose in *The Ambassadors*, is one of challenge to the reader, and it is a challenge which, if accepted, intensifies the thematic concerns of the novel. These, crudely, are two-fold and combine the preoccupations which I have outlined in the earlier novels – social constriction, based on obsession with money, and psychological stress, particularly of a violent kind.

Our Mutual Friend is set very firmly in the present : 'In these times of ours, though concerning the exact year there is no need to be precise.' (Book I, Chapter 1) The history of the Harmon inheritance, which consists of a series of dust-heaps containing untold wealth, is introduced at a society-dinner, whose members are presented as typical of the Victorian ruling-class : Veneering, the speculator, who is to become an M.P., Podsnap, the successful businessman, confident in his own incontrovertible and jingoistic morality, and a group of upper-class decadents to whom life is simply a bore. These characters survive at the end of the novel – if Veneering's fraudulent career is about to be exposed, this is mentioned only casually and he will easily be replaced – to conclude the narration of the Harmon story. The implications are obvious : social status may be based on shaky foundations—

> . . . traffic in Shares is the one thing to have to do with in this world. Have no antecedents, no established character, no cultivation, no ideas, no manners; have Shares—
>
> (Book I, Chapter 10)

but the system is immovable. The imagery of speculation is repeated throughout the novel; when the humble Boffins, temporarily enriched by the inheritance, decide to adopt an orphan,

> The suddenness of an orphan's rise in the market was not to be paralleled by the maddest records of the Stock Exchange.

He would be at five thousand per cent. discount . . . at nine in the morning, and (being enquired for) would go up at five thousand per cent. premium before noon.

(Book I, Chapter 16)

Silas Wegg speculates in ingratiation (Book I, Chapter 5), while a pair of confidence-tricksters, the Lammles, speculate in each other in marriage and, disappointed, attempt to entrap another acquaintance, 'Fascination' Fledgeby, the child of a similar mercenary marriage. They

. . . all had a touch of the outlaw, as to their rovings in the merry greenwood of Jobbery Forest, lying in the outskirts of the Share Market and the Stock Exchange.

(Book II, Chapter 5)

In *Bleak House* and *Little Dorrit* Dickens took institutions as metaphors for social malaise : in *Our Mutual Friend* he attacked an economic system, engaging it not on the grounds of theory, but in terms of its effects on human behaviour.

This theme is emphasized by the magnetizing effect of the Harmon inheritance on those who come into contact with it and *Our Mutual Friend* can justly be said to be a fitting culmination to the vein of social criticism which Dickens embarked upon in *Dombey and Son* and pursued through the novels which followed it. Bound into its story also is the interest in the more dramatic aspects of human psychology, which had been hinted at in the early novels and which re-emerged more powerfully towards the end of Dickens's career. The world of *Our Mutual Friend* is a Waste Land in which boredom and criminality flourish. Boredom is seen in the behaviour of the enervated young lawyer, Eugene Wrayburn, who is eventually rescued from his affected nihilism, after a ritualistic immersion in the Thames, by the love of Lizzie Hexam, the waterman's daughter; criminality is revealed through the underworld behaviour of the river-scavengers; and, more specifically, the uncontrollable passion of Wrayburn's rival, the schoolmaster Bradley Headstone, is an extended study in violence on a level which Dickens had scarcely attempted before; inevitably melodramatic, he nevertheless conveys a power born of Dickens's own propensities towards the extremes of emotion.

An account as brief as this can only hint at, and over-simplify, the complexity of a novel like *Our Mutual Friend*. If this novel lacks the thematic coherence of *Dombey and Son*, the range of *Bleak House* or the atmospheric consistency of *Little Dorrit*, it more than compensates for these omissions by the intensity of its satire and by the power of its insights and implications. The eccentricity of its characterization has been cited as evidence of its author's tiredness in the last stages of his demanding career; in fact, *Our Mutual Friend* is an astonishingly inventive, if at times morbid, novel, and far from indicating exhaustion it developed new areas of interest, some of which obviously were to have been explored in *Edwin Drood*.

The reservations expressed by some of the reviewers about the social stance adopted by Dickens in his later novels seem not to have been reflected in his general popularity. He was elated to be able to claim that *Edwin Drood* was meeting with more success than any of its predecessors. His death, like that of Tennyson, the other great Victorian writer to become an institution in his own time, was an occasion for national mourning; a special train conveyed his coffin from Gad's Hill to London for its interment in Westminster Abbey. Like Shakespeare, Dickens worked in a popular medium at a time when it was becoming the predominant literary form and, like Shakespeare, he enriched it through the fertility of his imagination and the extent of his vision. In that that vision, in even the darkest of the novels, remained fundamentally comic, I suspect that, where criticism has found him wanting, it is often because comedy, of its nature, presents particular problems for the moral certitude which criticism tends to embody. This in itself is a measure of Dickens's greatness: like all great artists he forces us to reconsider the attitudes which we bring to art.

BIBLIOGRAPHY

The New Oxford Illustrated Dickens, 21 vols., 1947–59. Original illustrations; brief introductions.

The Oxford Dickens: General editor, Kathleen Tillotson. Potentially the definitive edition. Only one volume, *Oliver Twist*, ed. K. Tillotson, Oxford U.P., 1966, has appeared so far. The text is to be based on a collation of mss., together with other original material.

M. House and G. Storey, edd. *The Letters of Charles Dickens* (The Pilgrim Edition), Oxford U.P., 1965. Twelve projected vols., only two of which (1820–1841) has appeared so far. Meticulous work of scholarship which aims to be completely comprehensive. (Until this edition is complete, the volume devoted to the letters in the 'Nonesuch' edition (1938), while flawed in many points of detail, should be consulted.)

K. J. Fielding, ed., *The Speeches of Charles Dickens*, Oxford U.P., 1960.

J. Forster, *The Life of Charles Dickens*, 1872–74. Authorised biography which draws heavily on the author's personal relationship with Dickens. It remains an invaluable source of information. Latest edition, ed. A. J. Hoppé, 2 vols., 1966.

G. Gissing, *Charles Dickens: A Critical Study*, 1898. The first serious attempt at a full-scale appraisal of Dickens's novels. As a committed realist, Gissing finds Dickens's use of coincidence, exaggeration, etc., disturbing, but his book is a fine examination of one novelist's work by another.

G. K. Chesterton, *Charles Dickens: A Critical Study*, 1906. Energetic discussion, emphasizing extrovert quality of the early novels at the expense, to some extent, of the later work. Idiosyncratic, but certainly not to be neglected.

T. A. Jackson, *Charles Dickens: The Progress of a Radical*, New York, 1938. With Lindsay (see below), the major Marxist orientated study.

H. House, *The Dickens World*, Oxford U.P., 1941. Indispensable study of the relationship between the novels and their social background; a classic of scholarship.

J. Lindsay, *Charles Dickens*, New York, 1950.

E. Johnson, *Charles Dickens: His Tragedy and Triumph*, New York, 1953. Has established itself justifiably as the standard modern biography. Exhaustive detail skilfully deployed, with sound, if somewhat predictable, criticism on each of the novels.

G. Ford, *Dickens and his Readers: Aspects of Novel Criticism*, Princeton, 1955. Valuable account of developments in Dickens's reputation which incidentally suggests useful critical approaches of its own.

J. Butt and K. Tillotson, *Dickens at Work*, 1957. Excellent detailed discussion of conditions under which Dickens worked, serial publication etc. Makes extensive use of Dickens's own notes, number-plans etc.

J. Hillis Miller, *Charles Dickens: The World of his Novels*, Cambridge, Mass., 1958. Spectacular, stimulating on occasions, but too often seems over-concerned with its own existentialist ingenuity.

M. Engel, *The Maturity of Dickens*, Cambridge, Mass., 1959. Discussess novels from *Dombey and Son* onwards.

P. A. W. Collins, *Dickens and Crime*, 1962; *Dickens and Education*, 1963. Well-documented studies of their separate topics; perhaps more interesting biographically than as a contribution to criticism.

S. Marcus, *Dickens: from Pickwick to Dombey*, 1965. First volume of projected two-volume study.

R. Garis, *The Dickens Theatre*, Oxford U.P., 1965. Aims to demonstrate how 'Dickens's moral insight remained for the most part that of the theatrical artist' in an attempt to counteract over-sophisticated critical tendencies of, e.g., Wilson, Hillis Miller, et al.

G. Orwell, 'Charles Dickens', *Inside the Whale*, 1940. Examines contradictions in Dickens's social attitudes, while expressing delight in the singularity of Dickens's fictional techniques.

E. Wilson, 'Dickens: The Two Scrooges', *The Wound and the Bow*, Boston, 1941. Extremely influential account of the novels, relating them to aspects of Dickens's private life and psychology. Brilliant at times, but tends to leap rather easily to its psychological conclusions.

F. R. Leavis, '*Hard Times*: an analytical note', *The Great Tradition*, 1948. The *locus classicus* of Leavis's view of Dickens, which has now, it must be emphasized, been considerably amended.

K. Tillotson, 'Dombey and Son', *Novels of the Eighteen-Forties*, Oxford U.P., 1954. Outstanding discussion of the novel. The book also contains a substantial introduction on the conditions under which the early Victorian novelists worked.

G. H. Ford and L. Lane, edd., *The Dickens Critics*, Cornell, 1961.

J. Gross and G. Pearson, edd., *Dickens and the Twentieth Century*, 1962.

M. Price, ed., *Dickens: A Collection of Critical Essays* (20th Century Views series), New Jersey, 1967.

A. E. Dyson, ed., *Dickens* (Modern Judgements series), 1968.

4

THACKERAY AND TROLLOPE

ARTHUR POLLARD

In his own generation Thackeray was often compared with Dickens. Subsequently he has more usually been placed alongside Trollope, sometimes to the discredit of the latter. There are marked resemblances, but the differences are more obvious. Both are concerned with the life of middle-class and aristocratic society, but Trollope seems nearer both in time and place to his world than Thackeray does to his. Thackeray is much more a story-teller and less of a reporter. He sets up his tales as the showman. There is also a world-weary, mildly sardonic note about his observations, as of a man who has seen and known all and retired from it, a man with the wisdom and experience of age. On the whole, Trollope is not so disillusioned.

   William Makepeace Thackeray (1811–63) was born in Calcutta, the son of an East India Company official who died when the boy was barely five. The child returned to England and was eventually sent to school at the Charterhouse (1822–6). His mother married as her second husband a former lover, Major Carmichael Smythe, whose earlier advances had been frustrated by her parents. Thackeray got on well with his step-father who even helped him to buy a journal after periods at Cambridge and in the study of art and the law had proved vain. The journalistic adventure was no more successful and this together with gambling and investing in an Indian bank dissipated the legacy which Thackeray inherited on attaining his majority. Meanwhile, he met and married Isabella Shawe, who, however, after a brief period of happiness fell ill and became insane. He subsequently derived some comfort from his friendship with Mrs. Brookfield, though this was not without cost to his relations with her husband, William Brookfield.

Although his own attempts at running a journal proved such a failure, Thackeray had at last found a career. He began to contribute to *Fraser's Magazine*, in which he was eventually to publish among others his *Yellowplush Papers* (1837–8; collected 1856), *Catherine* (1839–40), *The Great Hoggarty Diamond* (1841) and *The Luck of Barry Lyndon* (1844; revised as *The Memoirs of Barry Lyndon*, 1856). His work also appeared regularly in *Punch*, to which his most notable contribution was *The Book of Snobs* (1846–7; in book-form 1848; complete, New York, 1852). It was not, however, until the writing of *Vanity Fair* (1848) that the world recognized the appearance of a new novelist of the first rank. By that date Dickens was bringing out his eighth major work, *Dombey and Son*. There followed seven rich years with *Pendennis* (1849–50), *Henry Esmond* (1852), *English Humourists of the Eighteenth Century* (1853) and *The Newcomes* (1854–5). Though he was by no means worked out, Thackeray never again attained the achievement of these years. *The Virginians* (1858–9), the sequel to *Esmond*, cannot really abide comparison with its predecessor, whilst *Lovel the Widower* (1861), *Philip* (1862) and *Dennis Duval* (1864) are sadly repetitive indications of a great talent in decline. All these, together with the charming *Roundabout Papers* (1863), appeared in *The Cornhill Magazine*, of which Thackeray was first editor. He died suddenly on 23 December 1863, a victim of the heart-trouble that had afflicted him for some years and was no doubt largely responsible for the loss of his creative energy.

Thackeray did not possess an inventive imagination. Hence his stories tend to be histories, chronological tales, rather than complex relationships of events and people. Hence also his reliance on areas of life and types of people he himself had known. His own false starts—university, law, art—were useful to him, especially in *Pendennis*, which is often regarded as an 'autobiographical' novel. Many of his characters and places are easily traceable to actual counterparts—Colonel Newcome to Major Carmichael Smythe Major Pendennis to his father-in-law General Shawe, Greyfriars to Charterhouse, to mention but a few (On this subject *in extenso* see G. N. Ray, *The Buried Life*, 1952.) Next to his own experience is that of history, and especially his beloved eighteenth century, which provided material both for lectures (*The English Humourists* and *The Four Georges* (1860)) and for novels (*Esmond* and *The Virginians*).

With the notable exception of Swift, Thackeray was at home with the writers of that era. 'Addison's honoured name' could hardly attract a superlative too extravagant. The whole style of *Esmond*, a measured imitation but in no sense a parody, is a tribute to Addison. Both men enjoyed being spectators and each was a 'preacher without orders' ('Addison and Congreve', *English Humourists*). Thackeray's discursive manner also owes something to Fielding, whose candid portrait of life, and especially of sexual relations, he admired whilst at the same time he regretted that the *mores* of his time forbade him to imitate it. But there were important differences, differences which Bagehot has isolated in his contrast of Fielding's 'bold spirit of bounding happiness' with his successor's more 'anxious temperament'. Bagehot went on to press the sentimental or, rather, 'sensibilitous' comparison with Sterne. Certainly Thackeray shares the faculty of seeing things 'from a *sensitive* aspect', but Sterne's sentimentality seems much more integrated, more essentially part of the man and of the work, than does Thackeray's.

By comparison with the great names of the preceding century Thackeray considered most of his contemporaries insignificant. In 'Novels by Eminent Hands' (originally 'Punch's Prize Novelists', 1847) he satirized Disraeli, Lever, G. P. R. James and Lytton among others. The parody of James begins with the ubiquitous horseman of that author's tales, whilst that of Lever ('Phil Fogarty, a Tale of the Fighting Onety-Oneth') catches this writer's rollicking Irish military narrative brilliantly. The main target, however, was Lytton, who was castigated both as a writer about fashionable life (*Pelham* (1828), for example) and of 'Newgate novels' (*Paul Clifford* (1830), *Eugene Aram* (1833)). Thackeray considered this type of novel dangerous and even Dickens came under his strictures. Both *Catherine* and *Barry Lyndon* were intended as partly ironic, partly direct condemnations of such writings, and in the former we read :-

And here, though we are only in the third chapter of this history, we feel almost sick of the characters who appear in it . . . But how can we help ourselves? The public will hear of nothing but rogues; and the only way in which poor authors, who must live, can act honestly by the public and themselves, is to paint such thieves as they are : not dandy,

poetical rose-water thieves . . . They don't quote Plato, like
Eugene Aram . . . or die white-washed saints like poor 'Biss
Dadsy' in 'Oliver Twist'. No, my dear madam, you and your
daughters have no right to admire and sympathize with any
such person, fictitious or real.

Neither *Catherine* nor *Barry Lyndon* is so superb a piece of
irony as that of Thackeray's master, Fielding, in *Jonathan
Wild*, but *Barry Lyndon* possesses a greater degree of the necessary detachment. These confessions of an Irish rogue have
indeed something of an advantage over *Jonathan Wild* in that
the autobiographical standpoint gives an added level of condemnation through the blatant candour of the narrator ("It
was her estate I made love to"—Chapter 10). Yet Thackeray
has not entirely avoided the error of his contemporaries. Despite all Lyndon's deeds and all the sufferings of others through
those deeds, in the death of his son, the father's grief and the
dying child's plea for his parents' reconciliation, Thackeray
draws our attention to the misdirected worth of his hero and
provides one of those scenes of controlled sentimentality in
which he is unsurpassed.

Barry Lyndon was an eighteenth-century adventurer; his
nineteenth-century successors, climbing the social ladder, had
less spirit and less nobility. They were snobs. Others wrote
about them; there were Lytton's "vulgarly genteel" (*England
and the English* (1833)) and Dickens' succession of them from
Mr. Wititterly (*Nicholas Nickleby*) to the Veneerings (*Our
Mutual Friend*). It was left to Thackeray to give us a whole
Theophrastan gallery of snobs. The species was more easily
recognized than defined. Thackeray has snobs by birth, breeding, profession and environment. There are snobs superior
(even the "Snob Royal") and snobs inferior (or sycophants).
"He who meanly admires mean things" was Thackeray's inadequate attempt at a definition. He shows the condition as
consisting of excessive admiration of rank, irrespective of
worth. Persons of rank despise others, persons with wealth
seek to obtain rank, and persons with neither try to attain
both or to secure the patronage of someone who possesses
them. In this nineteenth-century equivalent of the "rat-race"
social relationships form a labyrinth of greed, hate, flattery
and hypocrisy.

Bunyan's Vanity Fair 'where all such merchandise is sold,
as houses, lands, trades, places, honours, preferments, titles, . . .
[where is] to be seen juggling, cheats, games, plays, fools, apes,

knaves and rogues', comprehensively futile and corrupt, was a perfect symbolic setting for the characters of Thackeray's world. It is a world that reminds one of Ben Jonson where lesser would-be rogues are swallowed up by greater actual rogues. In particular, in Becky Sharp we have a female version of the criminal adventurers Thackeray had condemned. But we admire Becky. We admire her as we admire Volpone—for her sheer resource and success. In a series of episodes she progresses from poor governess to belle of the Waterloo ball. She goes on to even greater triumphs, but after Waterloo there is less luck and more scheming. Her association with the dissolute Lord Steyne and her neglect of her husband and child make her less and less attractive. Her treatment of husband and child offended against the domestic pieties of Victorian England. The book, as a whole, no doubt derived some of its power from the contrast between the raffishness of its Regency setting and the changed manners of three decades later. Thackeray had no love for Evangelicals (what Victorian novelist had?), but they won the day (see, for example, F. K. Brown, *Father of the Victorians, Cambridge*, 1961); it is one of them, Lady Jane Sheepshanks, that he uses to bring about Becky's undoing.

Thackeray sub-titled the work 'A Novel Without A Hero'. It should not be thought that he chose a heroine instead. Becky is not; she is deceived like everyone else. Nor is Amelia Sedley with whom she is so deliberately and extensively contrasted, despite the fact that Amelia is called 'the heroine of this work' with her 'thousand kind words and offices'. These latter are just so much insipidity, like the rest of her character. As Becky increases, Amelia decreases, accepting her lot with a passivity that the Victorians may have thought more noble than later readers have done. She is apparently good, a doll of a character, naïve, trusting—and imperceptive. Dobbin with the nobility of an equally imperceptive character bullies the worthless George Osborne into marrying her; and after his death at Waterloo she rebuffs Dobbin's willingness to marry her by her obstinate, irrational and thoroughly unwarranted fidelity to Osborne's memory. Her sufferings do not dignify her; they serve a better purpose in exposing the various oppressions of husband, father and father-in-law. Dobbin is little better, so properly upright as to be a bore. Was his name indicative of what Thackeray thought about him? The novel loses some of its power in the latter stages, partly because of the change in Becky, partly because the reader is waiting for, but not very interested in, the eventual reunion of Dobbin and Amelia. To Mrs. Liddell's request for such an ending, Thackeray replied, 'Well, he shall [have her], and when he has got her, he will find her not worth having' (L. Stevenson, *The Showman of Vanity Fair*, 1947, p. 172). So much irony for the conventional happy ending! The bad, like Becky, reap a sour harvest, and the good, like Dobbin, do little better.

Vanity Fair is satire in depth, at every level of participation in the novel. In Becky's picaresque progress through the ranks of society, embracing as it does the impoverished gentility of the Miss Pinkertons' school, the houses of the merchants Osborne and Sedley, the country-seat at Queen's Crawley and the acquaintance of aristocracy in Brussels and London, we see the vices Thackeray had condemned among his snobs. We see what money can do and what it makes men do, but at the same time Becky and Rawdon show 'How to Live Well on Nothing A Year' (Title of Chapter 36). We see, too, how Becky's beauty and sexual attractiveness make the men fools and the women jealous. The book is a comprehensive satire, and this being so, the characters are restricted in the directions along which they may develop. Like Jonson's, Thackeray's characters are 'flat', but they are also various in mode of creation and extent of development. It is necessary to mention only the different extraordinarinesses of a Sir Pitt Crawley, come almost straight out of Fielding, or a Jos Sedley, who might have migrated to Dickens.

But Lord Steyne was faithful enough to be recognizable as a version of the Marquis of Hertford, and the setting of the novel is historical. Yet it is also Vanity Fair, in which the puppets move to the master's bidding. The historical circumstances remind us that here is a version of our world; but the 'showman' warns us that there is manipulation to a predetermined end, that *Vanity Fair* is a moral tale. We are also to remember that the 'showman' both is and is not Thackeray. There is a self-authenticating logic about the events. They are what the characters make them, but the characters are also puppets in that they are in the grip of some sort of predestination, usually to wrong-doing. We are not surprised by what happens; our interest is held by anticipation, a waiting for what we feel will eventually happen. The moral therefore does not seem forced; the moralist does not have to coerce his material. The weariness behind the final exclamation is all the stronger :– 'Ah! Vanitas Vanitatum! which of us is happy in this world? Which of us has his desire? or, having it, is satisfied?' Here is the disillusion and resignation that springs from the wisdom of experience. These words are a fitting epitaph to *Vanity Fair*, for in this great sad satire the view Thackeray presents is enough to persuade us that life is like that.

The profundity and sublimity of this novel were never again to be re-captured. The next work, *Pendennis*, was nearly as autobiographical as Dickens' *David Copperfield* which was appearing at the same time. Its central character is an 'irresolute, half-ashamed, sceptical hero, conscious of his own weakness, conscious of his own ignorance . . . governed by tastes and circumstances instead of principles, but clinging firm to old habits, to traditional lessons of truth and honour . . . not very bad, nor very good, nor very anything' (J. Fitzjames Stephen in *Cambridge Essays*, 1855, p. 184). It is a rambling tale, a cumulative characterization, built up from accounts of action and attitude rather than an interpretation developing from the experience of the character himself. It is intimate history with a multifarious background. Thackeray limits his omniscience as narrator and thereby endows Pendennis with a sense of unusual independence. The freedom of the story might almost be a reaction to the control and arrangement in *Vanity Fair*. It also reinforces the sense of Pendennis's own weakness, his tendency to drift at the mercy of events. This appears particularly in his relations with the various women of the novel, one affair after another emphasizing his vacillation and lack of principle, whilst all the time the faithful Laura Bell remains loving, but neglected.

But though Thackeray is less the puppet-master, he is more the preacher. His moralizing commentary is more intrusive, more frequent and usually less piquant than in *Vanity Fair*. The world of *Pendennis* is vicious like that of its predecessors (people like Sir Francis Clavering and Colonel Altamont are nastier than practically anything in *Vanity Fair*), but contrasted with these are Helen Pendennis and Laura Bell in the home from which Pendennis's career begins. They represent a firm moral basis for judging all else. At the same time they are not simple perfection. They seem superior, 'cruel critics' to poor Fanny Bolton, 'a sexual jealousy on the mother's part' towards Blanche Amory. In this way Thackeray tried to meet the perennial difficulty of creating convincingly virtuous characters. He succeeds better with Laura than with Pen's mother, for of

her (Laura) he tells mainly what she does and confines comment to a minimum.

It was in the preface to *Pendennis* that Thackeray made his
famous complaint about Victorian prudery by contrast with
the full-blooded era of Tom Jones. He all but refers to sexual
attraction in plain terms ('This point has been argued . . .'—
Chapter 54) and in *The Virginians* he archly claimed :– 'I shall
not have the least idea of what they have been doing. Have
you, madam? Have you any remembrance of what used to
happen when Mr. Grundy came a-courting?' (Chapter 69; cf.
Chs. 20 and 41). (For an opposite view see the criticism of *Tom
Jones* in *The English Humourists*.) The exclusion of, or confine-
ment to veiled references to, sexual relations gave the Victorians plenty of difficulties, especially with their promiscuous
weak young men. Thackeray chose to meet his problem in his
novel in part by the use of Pen's uncle, Major Pendennis, the
man of the world, a left-over from a more complaisant age,
who knows what young men are made of and what adventures
they get involved in better than their mothers do. His view of
the world and that of Helen Pendennis provide yet another
instance of that recurring conflict in Thackeray, which was
worked out most crucially in just those areas of Victorian
society from which the novelist himself came. Triumphant
Evangelicalism, bringing a new puritanism with it—especially
among the women, was ousting the laxer, but in many ways
more realistic, morals of the Georgian era. Placed in this situation, Major Pendennis is like Amelia, an ambiguous character—
but with this difference that Thackeray seems to have thought
better of him and worse of her than he suspected some of his
readers might.

Like *Pendennis*, *The Newcomes* is 'about all the world and a
respectable family dwelling in it' (Chapter 38). It also draws
extensively on Thackeray's own experience—India, Charterhouse, art studies, even the domineering mother-in-law. The
moral pattern is more obvious than in *Pendennis* :– 'It is not
a sermon, except where it cannot help itself . . . O friend, in
your life and mine don't we light upon such sermons daily?
Here on one side is Self and Ambition and Advancement, and
Right and Love on the other.' (ibid) Again we have in Clive
Newcome, a weak young man as the central character. His
love for Ethel Newcome, his cousin, is frustrated by her family. It is her resistance to domestic pressures that puts her
amongst the most interesting characters of the book. Thackeray was deeply engaged by her situation, in which she was

steered by her grandmother, Lady Kew, especially, first in the direction of one advantageous marriage and then of another. We recall that part of Becky's appeal comes from the manner in which she puts rank and money to confusion. In *The Newcomes* Thackeray fiercely compared the marriage-market to the Indian *suttee* sacrifice :-

> The parents in that fine house are getting ready their daughter for sale, and frightening away her tears with threats, and stupefying her grief with narcotics, praying her and imploring her, and dramming her and coaxing her, and blessing her, and cursing her perhaps, till they have brought her into such a state as shall fit the poor young thing for that deadly couch upon which they are about to thrust her . . . His Grace the Arch-Brahmin will make a highly appropriate speech, just with a faint scent of incense about it as such a speech ought to have, and the young person will slip away unperceived, and take off her veils, wreaths, orange flowers, bangles and finery, and will put on a plain dress more suited for the occasion, and the house-door will open—and there comes the SUTTEE in company of the body.
>
> (Chapter 28)

Refusing to 'believe in elder sons, and a house in town, and a house in the country' (Chapter 45), Ethel shows spirit against the persuasions and cajoleries of her oppressors.

Ethel's brother, Barnes, is the villain of the book—in some ways too much so, for his evil verges at times on the melodramatic. He is snobbish, hypocritical, tyrannical and immoral —and he becomes progressively worse over the novel's history. He exemplifies the novelist's own close moral participation in this book as compared with its predecessor. Thackeray (admittedly through Pendennis, the narrator) acknowledged his danger :- 'A constant desire to throttle Mr. Barnes, to beat him on the nose, and send him flying out of the window, was a sentiment with which this singular young man inspired many persons whom he accosted. A biographer ought to be impartial, yet I own, in a modified degree, to have partaken of this sentiment.' (Chapter 30). And if Barnes is too bad, Clive's father, Colonel Newcome, is in danger of being too good. Set against his half-brothers and their wives (and not least by his spontaneous generosity against the sterile religiosity of the Evangelical Maria), he is too good for the world he lives in and it is obvious, as Thackeray acknowledges, that his trust in the financial security of the Bundelcund Bank will eventually prove misplaced. Adversity does not sour him, and altogether he is Thackeray's most sustained declaration of faith in human nature. In his last words about him Thackeray reminds us that the Colonel retained the goodness and innocence of a child. These words come in the impressive death-scene at Greyfriars where Newcome is now a pensioner where once he had been a schoolboy. Imbued with the pathos of simple statement, the passage is free of censurable sentimentality; the emotion called forth is in no way excessive or factitious :–

> At the usual evening hour the chapel bell began to toll, and Thomas Newcome's hands outside the bed feebly beat time. And just as the last bell struck, a peculiar sweet smile shone over his face, and he lifted up his head a little and quickly said, 'Adsum!' and fell back. It was the word we used at school when names were called; and lo, he whose heart was that of a little child, had answered to his name, and stood in the presence of The Master.
>
> (Chapter 80)

Between the composition of these two domestic novels Thackeray had written the first of his two historical novels, *Esmond*. Despite his admiration for Scott he did not have his predecessor's sense of the colour and adventure of history. Even a fugitive Jesuit like Father Holt does not convey any of that sense of mystery or danger which one associates with Scott's novels. Thackeray's men of history are men of contemplation rather than of action, and in *The Virginians* he takes an early opportunity of moving from the wars of the American frontier to the world of Johnson's London and Tunbridge Wells. In *Esmond* Addison epitomises all that Thackeray admired in the Augustan age (Book II, Chapter 11), whilst at the same time we get a balanced picture of the man, not only sensible and civilized but also self-important and given to somewhat pompous moralizing. In fact, Thackeray sets up a fine contrast between him and Steele with his sentimentality, kindliness and *carpe diem* spirit. I say 'sets up', for Thackeray is arranging his history. Setting of time, place, event and character is more than background, it is the very staple of the novel, but it remains a version of 'facts seen subjectively through the temperament of the writer' (Lord David Cecil, *Early Victorian Novelists*, 1934, p. 88).

The novel is primarily *The History of Henry Esmond . . . Written by Himself*. But though it is written by himself, it is written in the third person. Moreover, it is the memoirs of an old man looking back on a period covering the formative years of childhood, adolescence and early manhood. Here again we have the novelist of memory. The third-person stance gives detachment and perspective, but it loses something in intimacy and vividness. Indeed, given the crises through which he passes, the misunderstanding, suffering and estrangements, Esmond seems all too often all too calm. Impossibly romantic both in politics and in love, he somehow falls short in self-revelation. What Thackeray does achieve is a sense of the child Esmond's loneliness and isolation and something of his helpless attraction towards and ultimate alienation from Beatrix. Even when Esmond discovers that he is the true heir of Castlewood we have an assessment rather than a dramatic realization :-

Should he bring down shame and perplexity upon all those beings to whom he was attached by so many tender ties of affection and gratitude? degrade his father's widow? impeach and sully his father's and kinsman's honour? and for what? For a barren title, to be worn at the expense of an innocent boy, the son of his dearest benefactress. He had debated this matter in his conscience, whilst his poor Lord was making his dying confession. On the one side were ambition, temptation, justice even; but love, gratitude, and fidelity pleaded on the other. And when the struggle was over in Harry's mind, a glow of righteous happiness filled it.

(Book II, Chapter 1)

Only the novel's sure uniformity of tone saves the hero and the author from seeming insufferably priggish. Esmond, indeed, is priggish when the time comes for him to reveal his altruism to Lady Castlewood (Book III, Chapter 2).

She and her daughter Beatrix, the two main female characters, are realized far better. In Lady Castlewood Thackeray portrays a woman of quick and warm emotions, pious, tender, jealous and possessive, 'never sinning and never forgiving'. Esmond's reactions to her at the various stages of his growing-up are one of the book's triumphs. After estrangement, 'as a brother folds a sister to his heart; and as a mother cleaves to her son's breast—so for a few moments Esmond's beloved mistress came to him and blessed him' (Book II, Chapter 6). Some readers have considered Esmond's son-and-lover role as a kind of 'spiritual incest'; though not really surprising, it is difficult to accept. We should not fail, however, to see that this is part of a triangular relationship to which Beatrix contributes. Esmond's infatuation with 'this siren', the delight and despair of numberless suitors, is more readily understandable. We need to note the warnings that Lady Castlewood gives him; they are not disinterested (e.g. Book II, Chapter 8). The degree of Esmond's involvement is to be found in the asperity of some of his comments. Selfish, cruel, ambitious Beatrix may have been, but Esmond does nothing to tone down her faults.

Together these two characters represent a masterly portrayal of the feminine heart and mind. A single passage will illustrate in more detail. Beatrix is speaking to Esmond :–

> 'Hear a last word. I do love you . . . But I think I have no heart; at least, I have never seen the man that could touch it; and, had I found him, I would have followed him in rags had he been a private soldier . . . I am not good, Harry : my mother is gentle and good like an angel . . . Farewell, Cousin : mamma is pacing the next room, racking her little head to know what we have been saying. She is jealous : all women are . . .
> 'Farewell. Farewell, brother.' She gave him her cheek as a brotherly privilege. The cheek was as cold as marble.

> Esmond's mistress showed no signs of jealousy when he returned to the room where she was. She had schooled herself so as to look quite inscrutably, when she had a mind. Amongst her other feminine qualities she had that of being a perfect dissembler.
>
> (Book III, Chapter 8)

There is a pathos about Beatrix's compulsive frigidity which makes Charlotte Brontë's comment that she had 'eventually no heart to touch' seem wide of the mark. The 'brotherly privilege' is also a charged phrase, making the kiss so much less than Esmond wanted and reminding us that the fraternal relationship has meant other things elsewhere (see the quotation in the preceding paragraph). Finally, Thackeray is candid about Lady Castlewood : 'She is jealous,' said Beatrix— she 'showed no signs of jealousy'—she was 'a perfect dissembler'.

The Virginians is the story of Esmond's two American grandsons, George and Harry Warrington, contrasted brothers with a domineering mother. The background is first that of New England with all the grace of colonial life on the eve of the outbreak of the War of Independence, and then of

England itself. It is a spacious novel, not much concerned with a coherent plot but rather with pen-portraits of places and people. There are Washington and Wolfe at length; there is the *ménage* of Colonel Lambert (another Thackerayan character virtuous to the point of stuffiness), set in its upright and kindly goodness against the rascality of Castlewood and the selfish respectability of the English Warringtons; there is the ageing and dissolute Madame Bernstein (Beatrix of the earlier novel), now more leniently handled, a somewhat affectionately labelled 'old Dragon' (Chapter 31) who protects young Harry from scrapes and schemers. There are some effective contrasts, for example, between the rather wild and careless but also warm-hearted Harry and his steadier, more serious brother and between the designing Maria Esmond and the tender, faithful Theo Lambert in their relationships with Harry. *The Virginians* provides a more varied world than that of *Esmond*, but it rambles. It lacks its predecessor's well-defined story (the most clear-cut in Thackeray) and the grace and clarity of that novel's style. The narrator's alternation between third and first-person is also irritating, whilst commentary-intrusions have become yet more frequent than in earlier works. The book as a whole shows a slackening of grip that was ever more confirmed with each remaining novel of the final years.

Thackeray's major novels were long ones—*Vanity Fair* ran to twenty monthly parts and *Pendennis*, *The Newcomes* and *The Virginians* to twenty-four. Only *Esmond* has a tightly-knit structure. The rest are 'large, loose baggy monsters'. 'A novel without a plan', one critic complained of *Vanity Fair* (Robert Bell, quoted G. Tillotson and G. Hawes, *Thackeray, the Critical Heritage*, 1968, p. 66), whilst another, R. S. Rintoul, reviewing *Pendennis*, declared 'Mr. Thackeray either cannot or will not frame a coherent story, of which all the incidents flow naturally one from another, and are so necessarily connected with each other as to form a whole' (ibid., p. 98). Writing by parts may have intensified this lack of coherence, but basically it derives from Thackeray's essentially discursive method. Even then, this general criticism needs to be modified. The unity of *Barry Lyndon* is secured by the simple central idea and the concentration upon the main character, whilst in *Vanity Fair*, *pace* Bell, there is a plan which counterpoints Amelia against Becky, Dobbin against Osborne, the Sedleys against the Osbornes, the various Crawleys against each other, Rawdon against Steyne and so on—in fact, a panorama, a rich fictional world, full to overflowing with scene, incident and character.

Thackeray's discursive method, however, sometimes obscures the inner logic of his dispositions. There seems to be too much sequence and too little consequence. Sometimes the sequence, even, gets blurred in the multiplicity of activity, or the story moves too slowly, or one line of the plot is neglected at the expense of another. This happens to some extent in the later sections of *Vanity Fair*, and even more so in *The Virginians* where our attention is directed to the one brother to the total exclusion of the other for a considerable part of the novel. *Esmond*, as the tale of one man, gained in this regard, but even here there are the lengthy digressions on the age and its characters. *Pendennis* is also basically the tale of one man, but its plot is very lax by comparison with *Esmond* and there are more characters with fuller lives, even to the insertion of a whole additional story in the exploits of the Claverings and Colonel Altamont. The nature of the story in *Esmond* also presumes a definite conclusion, whereas it is no surprise in *Pendennis* to find one of those 'bufferless endings' which occur elsewhere in Thackeray. The phrase is Professor Geoffrey Tillotson's, and it is he who in his indispensable study best sums the matter up when he says: 'Instead of design Thackeray's novels give us continuity.' (*Thackeray the Novelist*, 1963 edn., p. 20).

This continuity is expressed, for instance, in the recurrence of characters and the treatment of successive generations in different novels. The Castlewoods of *The Virginians* resemble in character as well as blood their predecessors in *Esmond* and Madame Bernstein of the later novel is an exactly right development of Beatrix in the earlier. Thackeray believed that 'We alter very little . . . Circumstance only brings out the latent defect or quality' (*Pendennis*, Chapter 59). But critics have complained as Roscoe did in the author's own time that the latent often remains latent in Thackeray's characterization :— 'Even of shallow and worldly Pendennis, how partial and limited, how merely external is our conception' (Tillotson and Hawes, op. cit., p. 269). Thackeray himself could write at different times :- 'I know the people utterly' (*Roundabout Papers*) and 'I declare we know nothing of anybody' (*The Virginians*, Chapter 26). This is not a contradiction. Thackeray is saying that we can know people utterly in social intercourse; we cannot know them at all in their inner beings. There we have to guess. As Roscoe himself put it, 'We don't know our nearest friends; we are always dependent on our imagination.' (op. cit., p. 268). Thackeray did not write the sort of novel that required this sort of imagination. Even in *Esmond* he avoided the direct first-person narration and thus secured a sense of detachment. Pendennis (and his author) are only half-joking in the question 'How can I tell the feelings in a young lady's mind, the thoughts in a young gentleman's bosom?' (*The Newcomes*, Chapter 47). This may be one reason for his preference for narrator *alter egos*; at least they could excuse an absence of omniscience. They are also able to write as historians, relying on experience, that quality in which Thackeray was so strong that G. K. Chesterton could claim, 'He is everybody's past.' He is the novelist of memory and he evokes the emotion of experience. He looks back over lives and this too gives the sense of continuity and succession. His stories read like reliable and mature reminiscence.

But where does the narrator stand in relation to the novel? In fact, we do not take much notice of him except when he becomes actor, as Pendennis does in *The Newcomes*, and then in his dual role he becomes rather irksome. Certainly in the plentiful commentary, whatever may be the pretence, the reader assumes that the voice is the voice of the novelist himself. 'Conceive *The Newcomes* without the presence of Thackeray upon the stage—minus the view it gives us of the working of its author's mind, the glimpses of his philosophy, the touches of his feeling' (W. C. Brownell, *Victorian Prose Masters*, 1902, p. 17).

What then of the author's mind? Was there a division between sceptic and idealist along the lines of the Pendennis-Warrington argument (*Pendennis*, Chapter 62)? Or was there, as some have claimed, a division that made him a sentimental cynic? First, was he sentimental? Consider from areas where this might show—his treatment of women, children, death and the past. In one succession of his women there are Becky, Blanche Amory and Beatrix, in another Amelia, Laura Bell, Lady Castlewood and Ethel Newcome. Their very variety is one measure of Thackeray's judicious assessment of women. None is immaturely or impossibly idealized. Goodness indeed there is, but even of one of the most admirable, Lady Castlewood, he was led to observe :– 'Even the tenderest women are cruel.' Not many children are portrayed in the novels, but of those that are Esmond is shown with deep understanding and in the relationship of Colonel Newcome and his son Thackeray deliberately eschews a fine opportunity for the sentimental :– 'We forbear to describe the reunion of the Colonel and his son.' He did, however, recall the parting seven years before, the small boy's careless and speedy adjustment to the separation and his parents' different response :—

How their hearts followed the careless young ones home across the great ocean! Mothers' prayers go with them. Strong men, alone on their knees, with streaming eyes and broken accents, implore Heaven for those little ones, who were prattling at their sides but a few hours since. Long after they are gone, careless and happy, recollections of the sweet past rise up and smite those who remain—the flowers . . ., the toys . . ., the little vacant cribs they slept in.

(*The Newcomes*, Chapter 5)

This may seem sentimental to us, but the weeping father would not appear so to the Victorians. What is more important is that this account is essentially true to human experience. The passage reminds us of yet another possible area of the sentimental with 'its recollections of the sweet past'. Thackeray continued :— 'Most of us who have passed a couple of score years in the world have had such sights as these to move us.' Again the appeal to the emotion of experience, the nostalgia of happy memory. The difference between Thackeray and some other writers is in his insistence. He does not leave words unspoken.

The nostalgia is a necessary concomitant of *vanitas vanitatum*. We need the happy recollections of the past to face the present and the future, for whatever else there may be, there will be the inevitable sadness of age :— 'That which is snow-white now was glossy black once; . . . that calm weariness, benevolent, resigned, and disappointed, was ambition, fierce and violent, but a few years since.' Age changes a man, but yet he remains the same :— 'Are you not awe-stricken—you, friendly reader . . . to think how you are the same *You*, whom in childhood you remember, before the voyage of life began !' (*Pendennis*, Chapter 60). But this unchanging identity will be changed : the sadness of death will succeed the sadness of life. Whether it be the good making a good end (Colonel Newcome or Helen Pendennis) or the careless coming to a premature dissolution (Lord Castlewood or George Osborne), Thackeray imbues his death-scenes with a more than individual significance. When he tells us that Helen's 'last throb was love and last breath was a benediction' (*Pendennis*, Chapter 58) or that 'Amelia was praying for George, who was lying on his face, dead, with a bullet through his heart' (*Vanity Fair*, Chapter 32), we move beyond the local and particular into an awareness of the shadow of death brooding over all human relationships, an awareness that *vanitas vanitatum* is not unconnected with *memento mori*.

So much for the sentimental. Is Thackeray then a cynic? Is this inevitable in one believing so strongly in *vanitas vanitatum*? The ways of the wicked (a Barnes Newcome or a Becky Sharp) do prosper, but there is no happiness in them, nor ultimate security. The righteous man does suffer and in a wicked world he must inevitably suffer. And mistakes have a habit of exacting long and bitter payment. All this is true, but yet is would be wrong to claim, as Roscoe did, that '*Vanity Fair* is the name, not of one, but of all Mr. Thackeray's works' (op. cit., p. 276). We need to remember the integrity of Henry Esmond, the goodness of Helen Pendennis and Colonel Newcome, the uprightness and kindliness of the Lamberts, the courage of Ethel Newcome, even the faithfulness of Dobbin. As early as the time of *Vanity Fair* he wrote :—

What I mean applies to my own case and that of all of us— who set up as Satirical-Moralists . . . that we may never forget truth and Justice and kindness as the great ends of our profession [which] seems to me as serious as the Parson's own.

(To Mark Lemon, *Letters*, ed. G. N. Ray, 1946, II. 282)

We remember that the preacher of Ecclesiastes, who propounded *vanitas vanitatum* as the doctrine of *taedium vitae*, nevertheless concluded positively with the advice to fear God and keep His commandments. When Thackeray looked around him he saw cause enough for *taedium vitae* :-

Virtue is very often shameful according to the English social constitution, and shame honourable. Truth, if yours happens to differ from your neighbour's, provokes your friend's coldness, your mother's tears, the world's persecution. Love is not to be dealt in, save in restrictions which kill its sweet, healthy, free commerce.

(*The Newcomes*, Chapter 28).

He would not therefore force an ending that contradicted the tenor of his tale. The original conclusion to *Barry Lyndon* is almost violent :-

Justice, forsooth? Does human life exhibit justice after this fashion? Is it the good always who ride in gold coaches, and the wicked who go to the workhouse? . . . Sometimes the contrary occurs, so that fools and wise, bad men and good, are more or less lucky in their turn.

But none of this is cynicism. It is a moral from unflinching realism. There is a lot of evil and some good. Thackeray saw both and it is best to leave him with the description he gave himself—a 'Satirical-Moralist'.

Anthony Trollope (1815–83) shares Thackeray's satirical-moral view of life, his realism, his interest in man in society (especially in the aristocracy and upper middle-classes), his delight in following characters from novel to novel and his indifference to an extensively developed plot. When his *Autobiography* (1883) appeared just after his death, it shocked readers by the candour with which it revealed its author's down-to-earth approach to what he regarded as the business of novel-writing. Trollope was a most prolific writer, producing not only novels but also short stories, biographies, translations and travel books in an unending stream. In the last pages of the *Autobiography* he counselled literary aspirants thus: '*Nulla dies sine linea* . . . Let their work be to them as is his common work to the common labourer.' Trollope's reward was 'something near £70,000' over twenty years of writing.

Yet he was nearly forty before he achieved much success. After school at Harrow and Winchester and Post Office experience in London, which provided material not only for the creation of such young civil servants as Charley Tudor (*The Three Clerks*) and Johnny Eames (*The Small House at Allington*) but also acquaintance with the clubs, duns and other aspects of metropolitan life which occur in the novels, Trollope spent nearly two decades (1841–59) as a postal surveyor in Ireland, broken only by a short period on similar work in the West of England (1851–53). His first two novels, *The Macdermots of Ballycloran* (1847) and *The Kellys and the O'Kellys* (1848), were set in Ireland. Neither was successful, but this did not prevent him from using the same setting later in *Castle Richmond* (1860) and the unfinished *The Landleaguers* (1833). Both these were concerned with political and social problems, the former with the famines of the 1840s (see Cecil Woodham Smith's *The Great Hunger*, 1962) and the latter with the peasantry's rent revolt (the 'boycott') of the late 1870s. In addition, *Phineas Finn* (1869), the story of a young Irish M.P., draws on Trollope's recollections of his residence in Ireland.

But the two years spent in the West Country were more

important for Trollope and for the English novel. There in Salisbury, wandering 'one mid-summer evening round the purlieus of the cathedral [he] conceived the idea of *The Warden*, —from whence came that series of novels of which Barchester, with its bishops, deans, and archdeacon, was the central site' (*Autobiography*, Chapter 5). This work established Trollope's name as a novelist, and over the years there followed its successors in the Barsetshire series—*Barchester Towers* (1857), *Doctor Thorne* (1858), *Framley Parsonage* (1860), *The Small House at Allington* (1864) and *The Last Chronicle of Barset* (1867). So well did he create the place and the people that there were those in 1867 who had had enough of Barsetshire. Such were the two parsons whose particular aversion to Mrs. Proudie drove Trollope to 'kill her before the week [was] over' (ibid., Chapter 15). He regretted the deed, but a few lines later he writes, 'Since her time others have grown up equally dear to me,—Lady Glencora and her husband [Plantagenet Palliser], for instance.' The choice is not surprising, but it serves to remind us that the novelist's next main effort went into the Palliser or political series. These two characters were seen first in *The Small House at Allington* and *Can You Forgive Her?* (1864), but they were to appear again in *Phineas Finn* (1869), *The Eustace Diamonds* (1873), *Phineas Redux* (1876), *The Prime Minister* (1876) and Palliser, Duke of Omnium, alone in *The Duke's Children* (1880). Not all of these novels are predominantly occupied with politics (*The Eustace Diamonds* with its 'thriller' element owes something to the vogue for Wilkie Collins), nor are these the only novels about politics—a notable addition is *Ralph the Heir* (1871), drawing much from Trollope's own experience as unsuccessful Liberal candidate at Beverley in 1868. Together, however, they constitute their author's considered reflection on the political life of the period (see also *Autobiography*, Chapter 16). During the quarter-century which spans the composition of these two main series Trollope also wrote some twenty other novels, prominent amongst which were *Orley Farm* (1862), *The Claverings* (1867), and that mordant magnificent satire of his times, *The Way We Live Now* (1875). From *The Warden* to this last novel marks the breadth of the spectrum through which he viewed life.

The Warden is not the novel Trollope meant to have written; it is all the better for that. He meant it to be satirical, an exposure at once of clerical abuses and of the immoderate newspaper criticism of such abuses (see *Autobiography*, Chapter 5). Some of the attack against the latter remains and there are also the satirical portraits of Carlyle (Dr. Pessimist Anticant) and Dickens (Mr. Sentiment) as well as indirectly through the Grantly sons of the three bishops Charles James (Blomfield of London), Henry (Phillpotts of Exeter) and Samuel, 'dear little Soapy', (Wilberforce of Oxford). But the work outgrew satire in the characterization of the saintly Mr. Harding, the gentle figure exposed to the glare of publicity so uncomfortably and so inculpably. Harding as the suffering centre of the novel concentrates sympathy upon himself and acts as a measure for the criticism of all the other characters.

Another triumph of this novel was the delineation of Harding's son-in-law, the hectoring authoritative archdeacon Grantly. At the end Trollope seems to admit that he is worth better than he has been able to show him, pleading that he 'lacked the opportunity of bringing him forward on his strong ground. That he is a man somewhat too fond of his own way, and not sufficiently scrupulous in his manner of achieving it, his best friends cannot deny . . . Nevertheless, the archdeacon is a gentleman and a man of conscience' (Chapter 20). In his next novel, *Barchester Towers*, Trollope developed this view of Grantly. This work also marks a great advance in his conception of Barsetshire. The cathedral city is fully delineated. We get a panoramic view from the cathedral close. *The Warden* had chosen a topical ecclesiastical scandal as its subject (see R. Arnold, *The Whiston Affair*, 1961). Now Trollope introduces in Proudie one of the new Low-Church bishops of the Palmerston-Shaftesbury epoch after 1855. Ecclesiastical animosities give the book flavour, but the antagonisms of Grantly (aided by Arabin, a Tractarian imported from Oriel) against the bishop's party, which means Mrs. Proudie and the chaplain Slope, are basic human conflicts, seen for the most part from a wry comic angle. This is especially evident in the discomfitures of Archdeacon Grantly, now a much more sympathetic figure. He is baffled and angered by the 'Bishopess' and Slope; we enjoy this. But they are unscrupulous, and so we sympathise with him, and our sympathy adds to our delight when these two are routed. The agent of their distress is one of Trollope's strokes of genius, Signora Vesey-Neroni, daughter of an absentee prebendary, mysteriously married, mysteriously crippled, irresistibly attractive. Trollope also employs her in an unobtrusive way as a shrewd commentator on and stimulator of the action of the novel. Above and beyond his success with individuals, however, is his evocation of the ethos of Barchester, with its sense of a confined society, magnifying small issues as such a community does, suggesting the discrepancies between the ideal (which a cathedral-close in particular should suggest) and the reality, yet despairing of nobody. (Trollope admits that even Slope acted according to his lights.) In this novel, once and for all, Trollope revealed what is perhaps his greatest quality—his unwavering understanding of the behaviour of ordinary men and women.

In the next Barsetshire novel, *Doctor Thorne*, money matters for the first but not by any means the last time in Trollope. Here too, to use the words of Henry James, he 'settled down steadily to the English girl' (*Partial Portraits*, 1888, reprinted in D. Smalley, *Trollope, The Critical Heritage*, 1969, pp. 525–45). The main character is Dr. Thorne, but the novel is about love and money as they affect his niece and ward, Mary Thorne. No less than in Jane Austen's works Trollope's heroines' fates usually depend on finding a 'nice man' and a competence, and these two do not always go together. Trollope was not so bitter as Thackeray about the marriage-market, but he explored with unsurpassed precision that love-hate relationship which subsisted between rank and wealth in his time. The Gresham squirearchy's 'fine old English fortune' has been ruined by a marriage into the aristocracy (Lady Arabella de Courcy), and now, sublimely ignoring the cause of the trouble, she and her family insist that her eldest son, Frank, 'must marry money'. But Frank is in love with Mary who is not only penniless but has no pretensions to birth either. Not that this matters if the money is there, but the de Courcys claim that it does. They ruin Gresham, persecute Frank, scorn the rough-hewn but successful railway-contractor Scatcherd on whose loans the Greshams survive, and despise Dr. Thorne who is the intermediary for the loans. Thorne and Mary are the links in the story. They are also the moral constants, placing everything and everybody in proper perspective. The doctor's moral probity presents the book's central dilemma, for he alone knows that Mary is Scatcherd's niece (as the illegitimate daughter of the latter's sister and his own brother) and as such his likely heiress. She is a proper match for Frank by de Courcy standards. His secret knowledge is the book's central irony, but there is more than Mary's financial eligibility. Nothing can erase her illegitimacy, and both Squire Gresham and Thorne himself are proud of their birth. When Thorne tells Gresham of her fortune, he has to add the wish 'that her birth were equal to her fortune', but he adds also 'as her worth is superior to both' (Chapter 46). It is that which makes the happy ending acceptable. It may seem too good to be true, but it is morally appropriate as a vindication of integrity and constancy.

Trollope's own favourite 'English girl' was Lily Dale in *The Small House at Allington.* Hers is the history of a mistaken choice, the preference of the handsome but superficial and self-seeking Adolphus Crosbie over the devoted Johnny Eames; but when Crosbie deserts her, Trollope does not succumb to the facile solution of marrying Lily to Johnny Eames. Elsewhere he is not so rigorous: Emily Wharton in *The Prime Minister* is permitted after her degrading experience with Lopez to marry Arthur Fletcher and Alice Vavasor in *Can You Forgive Her?*, after hovering between her worthless cousin George Vavasor and the much steadier John Grey, eventually accepts the latter. In this novel also we have the wrong result for Lady Glencora, for choice it can hardly be called in that she had been coerced into a loveless marriage with Plantagenet Palliser, heir to the Duke of Omnium. His dry austerity and commitment to politics contrast with the charm of her former lover, the worthless Burgo Fitzgerald. Only at the last minute is Fitzgerald prevented from eloping with her. There follows a scene unusually strong for Trollope, in which Lady Glencora declares her love for Fitzgerald and asks her husband to let her go. Her passion contrasts violently with his detachment—'If you cannot love me, it is a great misfortune to us both. But we need not therefore be disgraced' (Chapter 48).

The dilemma of choice also informs the action of *The Belton Estate* (1866) where Clara Amedroz has to decide between the somewhat uncouth farmer Will Belton and the polished but self-seeking Aylmer. Money again enters into the story with the Belton Estate's having gone by the death of Clara's brother to Will and her own expected fortune from her aunt Mrs. Winterfield being bequeathed to Aylmer after he had promised to marry Clara. E. A. Baker is right when he says that '*The Claverings* is a variation on the Belton theme with the sex of the rival lovers reversed.' (*History of the English Novel*, Vol. VIII, 1937, p. 151). Harry Clavering is immature. This is one reason why Julia Brabazon rejects him ('She had grown old earlier in life he had done . . .'); Lord Ongar's money was another ('. . . and had taught herself that romance could not be allowed to a woman in her position.') (Chapter 3). With Ongar's early death the book is taken up with Harry's vacillation between his troth to the good-hearted but quite ordinary Florence Burton and the attractions of Julia, wealthy, beautiful and in love with him. Victorian respectability triumphs, above all through Harry's mother, who insists on the marriage to Florence. More than any of Trollope's novels, this one with its story of moral cowardice would seem most likely to provoke the most widely different reactions now and a century ago when it was written.

Inheritance is one of Trollope's favourite devices. One inheritance creates one problem in *The Claverings* and the prospect of another solves another problem. *The Eustace Diamonds* indicates the inheritance in its title, and this novel also presents Frank Greystock with a dilemma of choice not unlike Harry Clavering's. *Lady Anne*, with its tale of the true love of a lady of high rank and a tailor, in some ways resembles *Doctor Thorne*, and as with that novel there is an inheritance at the end to bless the true love. Inheritance has more sombre implications in *Orley Farm*, the plot of which, said Trollope, was 'probably the best I ever made . . . I do not know that there is a dull page in the book' (*Autobiography*, Chapter 9). Like Lady Lovel, the heroine's mother in *Lady Anna*, Lady Mason in *Orley Farm* is a guilt-ridden, ambitious woman. Hers is a tragedy of misdirected maternal love. Her whole position is at risk as a result of a forged codicil to her husband's will, by which she had tried to secure for her own son a small portion of the estate which otherwise would have gone in its entirety to the son of an earlier marriage. The arrangement of characters and their ways of life is such that our whole sympathy rests with Lady Mason. In her and her staunch friend Sir Peregrine Orme Trollope works out the conflicts between personal moral choices and rigid social codes. He shows, too, the divergence between justice and law. Above all, he portrays Lady Mason with all her nobility as she faces her accusers and her apparently inevitable disgrace.

Orley Farm has an intensity rare in Trollope. It is, however, found again in *The Last Chronicle of Barset*, and again he takes a character under the cloud of accusation, this time unjust accusation. Mr. Crawley, the parson of Hogglestock, is a more striking individual than Lady Mason—a man of considerable ability, deeply frustrated, fiercely independent, pathologically gloomy, a character reminiscent of Dostoievsky. But he is without the Dostoievskian proportions: he remains the sort of man we think we might meet. *The Last Chronicle* is extensive in its reference and not always as relevant as it might be. The Johnny Eames episodes in London are something of an excrescence, and so is the death of Mr. Harding. We would willingly lose the first, but not the second. Some of this ex-

traneous narrative was no doubt part of the tidying-up operations as Trollope closed the Barsetshire series. It also serves
another purpose. All that is happening makes the reader realize
that the world passes by whilst an individual suffers. This helps
to intensify the effect of the sympathy of Crawley's friends.
His daughter Grace, in particular, emerges in all her self-sacrific-
ing nobility, worthy of the hand of Major Grantly whose suit
has been jeopardized by her father's possible disgrace and
his father's opposition. The meeting of these two, rich archdeacon and poor curate, at the end deserves quotation, for in
it is embodied the supreme Trollopian recognition :- 'We stand
on the only perfect level on which such men meet each other.
We are both gentlemen' (Chapter 83).

That remark belongs to a world of birth, breeding and status.
It was the supersession of this world by one of wealth, power
and position which provoked Trollope's ire in the darkest of
his novels, *The Way We Live Now*. At its centre is the foreign
financier, Melmotte (most of Trollope's foreigners are of either
dubious or only too obvious morality). Around him is a group
of effete aristocrats. Bogus shares in an American railway and
gaming at the Beargarden (note the name) comprise much of
the book's concern. Over against these characters is the Norfolk squire, Roger Carbury, representative of the old order,
Trollope's mouthpiece in condemning the new, but ineffectual.
The world is a beargarden, and all the individuals in it are
utterly isolated. Even the less repulsive characters like Lady
Carbury indulge in some not very praiseworthy practices. In
its wide-ranging condemnation of society—politics, religion,
family life, law, finance, the squirearchy, London clubs, the
rural poor, even the Americans—this novel is Trollope's *Vanity
Fair*. At times it is even more sombre than Thackeray's novel,
but its very concern to hit out in so many directions is one
means by which it fails in the sustained intensity that marks
its predecessor.

The disillusion that is concentrated in *The Way We Live
Now* is to be found also in the political novels. The personal
and political idealism of Phineas Finn endures many a buffeting
in the two novels about him. Likewise, the world of *The Prime
Minister* and *The Duke's Children* is a place where standards
of behaviour are very relative indeed. Finn, and even more
Sir Thomas Underwood in *Ralph the Heir*, see the chicanery
of electioneering. Finn and Palliser know the nature of political intrigue, the compromise and worse that politics involves.
The central question for both of them is that which Finn asks:

'Could a man be honest in Parliament, and yet abandon all idea of independence?' (*Phineas Finn*, Chapter 58). With both the clerical characters of the Barsetshire series and with his political characters Trollope, as he said at the end of *The Last Chronicle of Barset*, concentrated upon 'the social and not the professional lives'. In fact, he refers to his 'series of semi-political tales' (*Autobiography*, Chapter 17). In the same passage he wrote :– 'If I write politics for my own sake, I must put in love and intrigue, social incidents, with perhaps a dash of sport, for the sake of my readers.' For the most part, this is only too evident, especially in a comparatively unsuccessful work like *Ralph the Heir*. Elsewhere, however, despite the occasional touch of sensationalism (e.g., the Bonteen murder in *Phineas Redux*) there is some powerful 'social' fiction, not least in the Lady Laura Standish sections of *Phineas Finn*. Her husband, the Scottish millionaire, Kennedy, morose to the point of insanity, has all the makings of a Mr. Crawley. Compared with the Finn novels, the later pair based on Palliser (*The Prime Minister* and *The Duke's Children*) show some decline in intensity and concentration.

In all, Trollope wrote some forty-seven novels. Good as they are, the Barsetshire series have attracted a disproportionate amount of praise. Recently the balance has been somewhat redressed, notably by Mr. A. O. J. Cockshut (*Anthony Trollope, A Critical Study*, 1955). The summary of some of the novels given above should show that Trollope's achievement is more various, and sometimes more sombre, than the Barsetshire novels would suggest. And his popularity in his own time took in far more than these. Judged by sales and contract figures, Trollope reached his peak about 1869, whilst his last years from 1876 marked a steep decline in his popularity. Immediately after his death it plummeted almost into oblivion. (On this subject see M. Sadleir, *Trollope, A Commentary*, Revd. edn., 1945, Chapter 10).

In Trollope's world of the upper middle-class and the aristocracy he is concerned for the ideas of the 'gentleman' and of decorum. It is a world where established and accepted ideas and attitudes count for much, Birth, class, rank, property and primogeniture are the several foundations on which the social edifice stands. They need to be secure. Trollope's concern for social wholeness makes him a conservative, and in the rapidly changing ethos of the Victorian age he was almost inevitably something of a sentimental conservative. Without necessarily agreeing entirely with Ronald Knox one can see that he is pointing in the right direction when he says that Trollope 'could not save the old order of things, the world of privilege he so intimately loved, but his sympathies have embalmed the unavailing conflict' (Introduction to the Oxford edition of *The Warden*, 1952, p. xviii). To do this he needed to catch, as he has done, the 'manners' of his society in the sense that Mr. Lionel Trilling has so accurately defined these, 'a culture's hum and buzz of implication . . . the whole evanescent context in which its explicit statements are made . . . that part of a culture which is made up of half-uttered or unuttered or unutterable expressions of value' (*The Liberal Imagination*, 1955, p. 206). In this Trollope has matched Jane Austen, and over a broader canvas. In the society he portrays, 'highly organized, if not complex' (Joseph Conrad—letter to A. N. Monkhouse, 8 February 1924, in Manchester University Library), Trollope suggests the nice gradations between delicacy and coarseness that flourish in a period of flux, but he is especially interested in 'the old order of things' where delicacy is at once the measure and the product of social behaviour. It is sometimes necessary for a character to pit himself against the accepted code, especially in affairs of the heart; personal integrity and loyalty requires it, for example, of a Frank Gresham. Nevertheless, Trollope does not allow us to forget that in Frank's nobility there is more than a touch of the quixotic. Within a society subscribing to a firm set of *mores* there is also plenty of opportunity for tracing the irrevocable nature of the one mistake. Consequences may vary but they are inevitable, whether it be in the history of a Harry Clavering, a Mark Robarts (*Framley Parsonage*) or a Lady Mason.

This reminds us that Trollope's was a moral criticism of life. In the famous twelfth chapter of the *Autobiography* he is emphatic about this. He sees his task under the same image as Thackeray used:– 'The novelist, if he have a conscience, must preach his sermons with the same purpose as the clergyman, and must have his own system of ethics.' Social observation becomes the preliminary to anticipated moral improvement. We should be 'taught to see the men and women among whom we really live,—men and women such as we see ourselves,—in order that we should know what are the exact failings which oppress ourselves, and then to hate, and if possible to avoid in life, the faults of character which in life are hardly visible, but which in portraiture of life can be made to be so transparent' (*Ralph the Heir*, Chapter 56). Trollope was rarely so didactic in statement and almost never so in practice. We do not have the commentaries which Thackeray gives us. In another statement (*The Eustace Diamonds,* Chapter 35) he expresses himself content if a novel's moral impressions produce a limited improvement.

In this relationship of author and reader we need to recognize the importance for Trollope of the ordinary man or woman, 'men and women such as we see ourselves'. In that phrase Trollope links not only author and reader but also the characters of his novels. I can best illustrate the point by quotation from the critics. Trollope, says Michael Sadleir, 'believed that the ordinary man or woman is at heart an honourable, kindly creature' (op. cit., p. 153). He takes persons of this kind or, in Sir Walter Raleigh's words, 'starts off with ordinary people that bore you in life and books and makes an epic of them because he understands affection which the others take for granted or are superior about' (*Letters,* 1926, p. 272). The same regard for the individuality of people inspires both his creation of character and his attitude to his reader. He has what Conrad elsewhere in the letter quoted above called 'his gift of intimate communion with the reader.' Sane, sympathetic, with a confident belief in human nature, these are the qualities that make up his quiet and deep view of life.

Interest and affection produce what James called 'his great, his inestimable merit . . . a complete appreciation of the usual . . . He felt all daily and immediate things' (op. cit., p 527). With typical acuteness James showed how this centred upon character :– 'We care what happens to people only in proportion as we know what people are' (ibid., p. 530). Or, in Trollope's own words :-

> [The author] desires to make his readers so intimately acquainted with his characters that the creatures of his brain should be to them speaking, moving, living, human creatures . . . He must know of them whether they be cold-blooded or passionate, whether true or false, and how far true, and how far false . . . I have lived with my characters, and thence has come whatever success I have obtained.
> (*Autobiography,* Chapter 12)

With ordinary people in fairly ordinary situations ('family feuds, . . . household discomforts and household pleasures . . . small malignities and daily kindnesses'—*The North British Review* XL (May 1864)) he reveals a range of emotions—love and hate, pride and arrogance and envy, ambition, courage and kindness, to name but a few—at work in his characters. He presents these characters fully formed; he does not show them in course of development. He shows them in action; he demonstrates rather than analyses. This is not to say that his characters are either static or predictable. He shows them against a background of changing circumstances which modify their behaviour. He does not seek surprise, but he exploits what a writer in *The North American Review* (XC (1864)) called 'his power of tracing the moral effects of minute circumstances and minute actions'. This can be seen, for instance, in all the consequences that follow upon the inciting of Dockwrath to enquire into the Mason will. Lady Mason has committed the forgery, but Trollope is not mainly interested in what will happen to her or even in her own feelings. What does matter to him is her behaviour, the way in which a woman of her background and character acts (rather than feels) under the different stages of such an accusation. To take a single example :-

> A second bed had been prepared in Lady Mason's room, and into this chamber they both went at once. Mrs. Orme as soon as she had entered, turned round and held out both her hands in order that she might comfort Lady Mason by taking hers; but Lady Mason, when she had closed the door, stood for a moment with her face towards the wall, not knowing how to bear herself. It was but for a moment and then slowly moving round, with her two hands clasped together, she sank on her knees at Mrs. Orme's feet, and hid her face in the skirt of Mrs. Orme's dress.
>
> (*Orley Farm*, Chapter 70)

The scene as a whole moves up to the exclamatory question which is the chapter's title, 'How am I to bear it?' This question has been preceded by the sentence :- 'To Mrs. Orme it was marvellous that the woman should even be alive,—let alone that she should speak and perform the ordinary functions of her daily life.' Mrs. Orme is the expression of the reader's feelings, his presence in the novel. He wonders, like Mrs. Orme, and yet he feels that Trollope is right. People of Lady Mason's position do in her circumstances go on. He is supremely the novelist of outward behaviour, of characters facing the world.

Given this mode of treatment, familiarity is a great asset to him, as can be seen from such extended and developed characters as Grantly, Palliser and Finn. Trollope's own attitude changed towards the first two; the character does not alter, but he himself becomes less critical. Grantly never loses his impetuous and assertive manner, but he is placed in situations where he appears more sympathetic, either because his opponents are unpleasant or because he is the comic victim, humiliated by them, or because he has scope for generosity. Something of the same development takes place with Palliser. On his first appearance in *The Small House at Allington* one reviewer considered him a 'caricature [of] a mathematical formula', and in *Can You Forgive Her?* his most notable quality is frigidity. Later, especially in *The Prime Minister*, we see a concomitant in his unsparing dedication to his work, and by the end of *The Duke's Children* we have completed the sad picture of an essentially austere and lonely man, sad because constitutionally he could be no other than he had been, a man in many ways admirable but incapable of inspiring love.

Love between young people Trollope considered an indispensable element in his stories:– 'A novel can hardly be made interesting or successful without love' (*Autobiography*, Chapter 12). 'Trollope's heroines,' says James, 'have a strong family likeness, . . . it is a wonder how finely he discriminates between them' (op. cit., p. 542). He does, in fact, distinguish neatly in such qualities as scruple, grace, vivacity and beauty. Some of the heroines disappoint somewhat by their lack of positive qualities (Lucy Morris and Florence Burton, for example), but others are strong in the face of unfavourable odds (Mary Thorne, Lily Dale, Lucy Robarts), and there is even a Madeline Stavely to prefer 'mind to matter, which is a great deal to say for a young lady' (*Orley Farm*, Chapter 52). Some of Trollope's older women are even better delineated than his younger ones, perhaps because he can deal in these cases with more firmly defined characters—the dignity, for instance, of Lady Mason or the resource of Lady Carbury, the assertiveness of Mrs Proudie or the unillusioned but not in the least cynical candour of Miss Dunstable.

Trollope was a realist and most of his characters represent quite ordinary people, but the last two mentioned above remind us that he could operate on different levels. We can accept the occasional saint like Mr. Harding or the occasional villain like Melmotte (Lopez in *The Prime Minister* is more doubtful, perhaps because his villainy is not so deeply motivated; he is altogether more shallow), but a Mrs. Proudie shows Trollope moving on the frontiers of caricature, as he does elsewhere in *Barchester Towers* with Slope and in the Barsetshire series generally with more peripheral characters like Fillgrave, the rival doctor to Thorne. There are a number of minimal characters whose names alone are sufficient to characterize them— Neversayedie, Nearthewinde and Closerstil or even the Reverend Mr. Quiverful (with his fourteen children). These names have been criticized as introducing a note inconsistent with the predominant realism. In fact, however, the ordinary view of life includes in its background characters so little known as to be identified only by a single noticeable trait and perhaps even nicknamed by it. And this view of life includes those who look more like caricatures than average beings, 'characters' we often call them. Trollope has some of these; *Orley Farm* is an outstanding example with the lawyer Chaffanbrass (see also *The Three Clerks* and *Phineas Redux*—an interesting example of Trollope's continuity even with a lesser character), Moulder and Kantwise. This trio is reminiscent of Dickens.

Trollope does not rely very much on events. 'The novelist has other aims than the elucidation of his plot' (*Autobiography*, Chapter 12). The 'ravages of love' (to quote James again) served him well—marrying and failing to marry and marrying unhappily. So did everyday affairs of business—signing a bill, filling a place, casting a vote, talk in a club. All contributed to that 'picture of common life enlivened by humour and sweetened by pathos' (*Autobiography*, Chapter 7) which constituted his definition of the novel. Yet, realist though he is, Trollope has provided, in Hugh Sykes Davies's phrase, 'the common reader's most common weakness in his choice of fiction, his liking for some more or less adult fairyland' (*Trollope*, 1960, p. 21). (Likewise, the happy endings may seem too much and too often to be the 'sweetmeats and sugarplums' that *Barchester Towers* said the novel should close with.) This criticism can be levelled against Barsetshire; it is an idyllic addition to England, but we have to remember that the real England is still there, especially London with its troubles. It is more difficult to level it against the later work, and even in Barsetshire it is not escapism. The idyllic emphasizes the realistic; the background is often pleasanter than the characters in front of it. Even the better among them can provoke their creator to acerbity:– 'In her heart of hearts Mrs. Grantly hated Mrs. Proudie—that is, with that sort of hatred one Christian lady allows herself to feel towards another' (*Framley Parsonage*, Chapter 17). Here is another example of Trollope's 'gift of intimate communion with the reader'; he hits exactly the note that his reader would. He thinks and feels plainly and 'with a considerable tone for satire . . . he had as little as possible of the quality of irony' (James, op. cit., pp. 528–9). Trollope's directness and lack of subtlety stimulates the reader's confidence in him.

His style matches his manner. In his own study of *Thackeray* (1879) he required style to be 'easy, lucid and grammatical'. Trollope's is. It is relaxed, too much so at times. 'Every sentence and every word used must tend to the telling of the story' (*Autobiography*, Chapter 12), but sometimes they don't. It is unpretentious and usually efficient; he rarely seeks rhetorical effect. In a characteristic English way he prefers the unadorned and the understatement to the decorative and the dramatic. His tone is that of civilized middle-class conversation, and, as James observed, 'by no means destitute of a certain saving grace of coarseness' (op. cit., p. 528). His particular regard for what dialogue should be (see *Autobiography*, Chapter 12) and his success in making it so has much to do with the establishment of tone. Some of the colloquies are, if anything, too realistic in their laggard pace and even their inadequate significance. Both his stylistic laxity and his verbosity in dialogue may well be attributable to the situation that evoked such feeling in the words :– 'In writing a novel the author soon becomes aware that the burden of many pages is before him' (ibid.).

When he feels the burden most, Trollope is only the 'first-rate plodder' which *The Dublin Review* (LXXI) called him in 1872. More often, however, with his straightforward style and balanced view of life, detached, tolerant, good-humoured, he makes us look afresh at people and events much like those we know. In this sense he gratifies what James, who is still the most perceptive of his critics, called 'the taste for emotions of recognition'. Thereby 'Trollope will remain one of the most trustworthy, though not one of the most eloquent, of the writers who have helped the heart of man to know itself' (op. cit., p. 545).

BIBLIOGRAPHY

A *Thackeray*

Works, 17 vols., 1908. Introductions by George Saintsbury. With original and revised readings and additional material.

Works, 26 vols., 1910–11 (Centenary Edition). Biographical introductions by Anne Thackeray Ritchie, with Leslie Stephen's memoir and many of Thackeray's drawings.

Letters and Private Papers, ed. G. N. Ray, 4 vols., Cambridge, Mass., 1946.

W. Bagehot, 'Sterne and Thackeray', *National Review* 1864 (*Collected Works,* ed. N. St. J. Stevas, Vol. II (1965), pp. 278–312).

A. Trollope, *Thackeray,* 1879. (English Men of Letters Series)

Lord David Cevil, *Early Victorian Novelists,* 1934. A judicious estimate.

J. W. Dodds, *Thackeray, A Critical Portrait,* New York, 1941. 'Criticism with some biographical infiltration.'

J. Y. T. Greig, *Thackeray, A Reconsideration,* Oxford, 1950.

L. Stevenson, *The Showman of Vanity Fair,* 1947.

G. N. Ray, *The Buried Life,* 1952. Suggests originals for many of the characters.

—— *Thackeray,* 2 vols., New York, 1955 and 1958. The standard biography.

G. Tillotson, *Thackeray the Novelist,* 1954. Indispensable critical study.

K. Tillotson, *Novels of The Eighteen-Forties,* 1954. Has a most enlightening chapter on Vanity Fair.

G. Tillotson and D. Hawes (edd.), *Thackeray: The Critical Heritage,* 1968. Extensive anthology of criticism in Thackeray's own time and just afterwards. Good introduction.

B *Trollope*

There is no complete edition. Nine titles are available in the Oxford Illustrated Trollope, but Oxford World's Classics series contains over 30 titles.

Letters, ed. B. A. Booth, 1951.

Henry James, *Partial Portraits,* 1888.

M. Sadleir, *Trollope: A Commentary,* 1927, revised 1945. The standard critical biography.

Lord David Cecil, *Early Victorian Novelists,* 1934 .

L. P. & R. P. Stebbins, *The Trollopes: The Chronicle of a Writing Family,* 1945.

B. C. Brown, *Anthony Trollope,* 1950. A perceptive short study, especially good on Trollope's 'Englishness' and the influence of the Civil Service upon him.

138

A. O. J. Cockshut, *Anthony Trollope: A Critical Study*, 1955. The second part is an attempt to rehabilitate some of the later novels.

R. Helling, *A Century of Trollope Criticism*, Helsingfors, 1956. Surveys the course of Trollope's reputation.

B. A. Booth, *Anthony Trollope: Aspects of His Life and Work*, 1959. Informed critical judgments by a leading Trollope scholar.

H. S. Davies, *Trollope*, 1960. (Writers and Their Work Series)

R. M. Polhemus, *The Changing World of Anthony Trollope*, Berkeley and Los Angeles, 1968. Chronological study of the novels with emphasis on Trollope's changing view of the world. Excellent on 'Love and the Victorians'.

D. Smalley (ed.), *Trollope: The Critical Heritage*, 1969. Companion volume to Tillotson and Hawes' *Thackeray*.

5

THE BRONTËS

WENDY A. CRAIK, *University of Aberdeen*

Although Dr. Leavis found it 'tempting to retort that there is only one Brontë' (*The Great Tradition*, 1948, p. 41), meaning that Emily Brontë was the only genius of the three, most general readers succumb to the same temptation in quite another sense. They assume unconsciously that all three, Emily, Charlotte, and Anne, write novels of the same kind, but in descending order of success. The assumption is a natural and reasonable one, because life offered, or rather, thrust upon them, the same material from which to create, while they themselves, as sisters deeply attached to each other, their home, and the rest of their family, welcomed their fate. For the student and critic the temptation increases, because life rarely offers him the gift of three talents, all major in some degree, all of one blood, and of the same generation, using not only the same form, the novel, but using it in a way that makes the fullest possible use of personal experience. Moreover the experience is not only that of events, people and society encountered together, but also a private spiritual and imaginative life lived for the most formative years in common. In childhood their private fantasy-world belonged to all the children, including Branwell, and although Branwell of necessity, and Charlotte from independence of spirit, fell away, Emily and Anne continued theirs to their lives' end.

While the study of their common ground and the literary uses they found for it is a legitimate and fascinating study, the danger rises when such a study interferes with a just and proper estimate of the quality of what they created from it, when, as is all too easy, one becomes unable to see the literary wood for the biographical trees. Enough valuable and scholarly research has been done on the springs of the Brontë genius and the experience which fed it to render it unnecessary, as well as a practical impossibility, to continue it here. Mrs. Gaskell's excellent *Life of Charlotte Brontë*, written and published only two years after its subject's death in 1855, remains the most valuable single source of biographical information, while Fanny Ratchford's *The Brontës' Web of Childhood* is the authoritative study of the evidence of their inner development.

Only four years separated Charlotte (1816–1855), the eldest surviving member of the children of Patrick Brontë and his wife Maria Branwell, from Anne (1820-1849), the youngest. Although all three of the novelists are vigorously and outspokenly devoted to their Yorkshire West Riding home, they all betray the influence of their parents' origins elsewhere. Their father was an Irishman, born Patrick Prunty, who changed his name by analogy with that of Nelson's title as Duke of Brontë, in the same way as Charlotte wove into her childhood fantasies endless variations on the names and titles of her own hero, the Duke of Wellington. Although spending the greater part of his life as the Anglican incumbent of Haworth, Patrick Brontë had, at Cambridge and after, been under the influence of Wesley and his followers, as had his wife, Maria Branwell, whom he met while in his first curacy. Miss Branwell was a Cornishwoman from Penzance, and on her death in 1821, after nine years of marriage and six children, when Charlotte was five, Emily three, and Anne a year old, the Brontë children were cared for by her unmarried sister Elizabeth, who remained at Haworth until her death over twenty years later. The children of the family were thus turned in upon themselves for society and comfort by an eccentric and solitary father, a strict aunt, the isolation imposed upon them by their own status in Haworth, and the position of the village itself. Their likeness to their parent intensified the effects of his treating them quite unlike children, forcing their unusual intelligence and sensibility into unusually early growth and abnormally developing their intellectual and moral powers. The room which the children occupied during the day was significantly termed, not the nursery, or even the school-room, but the study. From this early stage began the habit of imaginative playing-out of fantasies which is natural to all young children, and the very individual one of blending into it adult matters from real life. They draw constantly upon the politics and political figures of the day, such as Wellington, Napoleon, Wilberforce; upon very adult settings and events—wars, national upheavals and all the internal politics of quite imaginary countries—and upon, in a sense, very adult passions, resulting in rivalry and hatred between kinsfolk, murder, treachery, jealousy and adultery. The consequences of knowing theoretically the outside world, while having personal contact with very few people, together with the consequences of intensely heightening their own imaginations and passions, while having virtually no first-hand knowledge of those of others, are manifest in the novels of all three sisters, and most powerfully used by Emily, the most self-contained of the three. The imaginative epics created by the brother and his three sisters sprang from the personalities they originally assigned to some wooden toy soldiers, but over the years grew into a full-blown fantasy country off the coast of Africa and (later) in the Pacific, whose annals they wrote, whose newspapers they created and whose history they decreed, where necessary by the intervention of supernatural forces (provided by themselves in person). Probably the most significant qualities, besides the remarkable mixture of the real outside world with the personal imagined one, are the force of the passions displayed and the complete acceptance of all kinds of wickedness, provided that the act is the manifestation of passion. The joint world in due course split into Angria, controlled by Charlotte and Branwell, and Gondal, controlled by Emily and Anne; but the surviving evidence of both reveals that in them the moral standards of everyday life are not so much violated, as merely irrelevant, and thus that Emily's novel *Wuthering Heights* is closer to her inner imaginative being than are Charlotte's or Anne's, even though theirs are on the face of it more autobiographical.

Circumstances conspired to force the child Charlotte into facing social and moral responsibility. In 1824 the four eldest girls, Maria, Elizabeth, Charlotte, and Emily were sent away to Cowan Bridge to a school run by the Rev. Carus Wilson for the daughters of poor clergymen. Here Maria and Elizabeth died, leaving Charlotte the eldest in the family. She immortalized her experiences and the school in Jane Eyre's at Lowood Institution, out of Maria's death found wherewith to create Helen Burns's, and exposed her child's-eye view of Carus Wilson in Mr. Brocklehurst. One might well estimate that it was from this period that Charlotte, naturally religious, developed the strong sense of duty to herself and to others and of personal responsibility, which she showed throughout her life. To examine how these conflict with the inner life of the imagination and the passions is the great preoccupation of all her novels; to reconcile them her great achievement.[1]

The Brontë children remained at Haworth for the next five years in a process of self-education, during which most of the surviving juvenilia were produced. In 1831 Charlotte was sent to her second school, run by a Miss Wooler at Roe Head near Halifax. Here she met her three closest lifelong friends, Mary Taylor, Ellen Nussey and Miss Wooler herself, and acquired much of the knowledge and experience out of which she was to create *Shirley*—the West Riding setting, the oral accounts of mill-breakings and the troubles of mill-owners and workers in the Industrial Revolution. She also got to know Mary Taylor's family, whom she re-creates as the Yorkes. Ellen Nussey contributes something to the second heroine Caroline Helstone, but her chief importance to posterity is as the recipient and preserver of the most intimate and personal of Charlotte Brontë's letters. In 1835 Charlotte returned to Roe Head as a teacher, and Emily went as a pupil. Charlotte was a success; but Emily was so unhappy that she went home within three months, and Anne replaced her. A number of Emily's poems date from this absence from home, most of them superficially expressing the longing for the moors which makes it possible, though unenlightening, to diagnose Emily's agony simply as home-sickness.

From 1837 to 1842 the family was broken up, with Anne and Charlotte taking various posts as governesses, while Emily taught for six months in a school at Southowram near Halifax. The spiritual difference between Emily and the others is clear in the use to which they put their experiences and the way they bore them. Charlotte and Anne drew freely upon the places they lived in and the people they met, in *Jane Eyre* and *Agnes Grey*: Emily used only the scenery, for some of the settings in *Wuthering Heights*. Charlotte and Anne, unsuited to teaching small children though they were, survived. Emily succumbed (in Charlotte's words) to 'hard labour from six in the morning to near eleven at night, with only one half-hour of exercise between.' (Letter to Ellen Nussey, October 1837). It has been suggested with great probability that Emily was beaten, not by the physical labour, but by having no chance to live the private spiritual life which was vital to her, which found expression in the Gondal stories and her poems, and which made her, as she herself says, 'comfortable and undes-

ponding' (Birthday Note, 31 July 1845) and wholly self-suffi-
cient in her routine, domesticated and utterly humdrum life
at Haworth. She left home only once more, to stay in Brussels
in 1842 with Charlotte, and learn French and German so as to
be better qualified to set up a school of their own. She was
recalled by their aunt's death, while Charlotte remained as
both pupil and teacher.

Brussels, which had no artistic influence on Emily, had a
shattering one on Charlotte (then aged 26), out of which came
first *The Professor* and later *Villette*. Whether or not one believes, on the evidence of several (certainly impassioned) letters
from Charlotte to M. Héger, the teacher-husband of the Belgian
pension's proprietress, that Charlotte fell in love, there can
be no doubt that out of him, his wife, their school and its
pupils, and Brussels itself, she was able to create first the setting and some of the characters of *The Professor*, and later to
realize Lucy Snow's vision of the city of Villette, the *pension-
nat* and its inmates, and Mme. Beck and Paul Emmanuel .

The other member of the family, Branwell, also had literary
aspirations. Although he has received critical attention,[2] his
only real interest is as an influence on his sisters and as a
contrast to them. His own prose and poetic outpourings demonstrate that the atmosphere of the parsonage, without the
personality and the power to transmute, produced only trash.
His career was one of continuous failure, as a would-be London
art student, as a practising painter in Bradford, as a tutor
and even a railway clerk on the Leeds and Manchester Railway.
He degenerated into a dipsomaniac and drug-addict, making
life for all at Haworth parsonage a dangerous and harrowing
agony until his death in 1848. His contribution to the novels
was partly simply to provide material—all three sisters un-
hesitatingly depicted drunkenness and degradation—but much
more to confirm them in what their private imaginings had
begun, in treating the material of melodrama and of baroque
and Gothic horror as inevitable and essential elements of real
life. Anne alone consciously and deliberately, and very painfully to herself, used Branwell and his fate with a social as
well as literary purpose, when writing *The Tenant of Wildfell
Hall*.[3]

The rest of Charlotte's life, from the return from Brussels in
1844 at the age of 28 to her death in 1855, is a sad record of
deaths and private agonies, little compensated by the sisters'
gradual professional success as novelists. First there was Branwell's decline and death in September 1848; Emily died only

three months later, causing almost as much suffering to her family by her rigid and self-contained refusal even to acknowledge her illness as her brother had by his self-indulgence. Anne died of a pulmonary complaint, like her sister, in the following May. The effect of facing these sorrows, with no support, but only the necessity for giving it to an eccentric and self-absorbed father, darkened Charlotte's already austere view of life, shaded the latter part of *Shirley*—whose composition was interrupted by Emily's death—and coloured the whole of her last novel, *Villette*. Charlotte's marriage to her father's curate Arthur Bell Nicholls in June 1854 can hardly be seen as the blessing Mrs. Gaskell suggests; as Charotte's letters reveal, it caused her considerable anxiety for a long time, as a prospect disagreeable to her father and of doubtful attraction to herself; the pregnancy in which it resulted undoubtedly hastened her death.

The literary progress of the sisters began in 1845, when Charlotte, discovering some poems written by Emily, initiated the project of a joint volume of poems, published under their pseudonyms in 1846 as *Poems by Currer, Ellis, and Acton Bell*. The private publication cost £31, the *Athenæum* reviewed it, and two copies were actually sold. However, a start had been made and as a result Charlotte wrote *The Professor*, Emily *Wuthering Heights*, and Anne *Agnes Grey*. The last two came out together, in three volumes in December 1847, virtually unnoticed. *The Professor* was continuously rejected but, on the encouragement of the publishing house of Smith and Elder, Charlotte offered them her second attempt, *Jane Eyre*, which appeared in October 1847. It was an immediate success. *The Tenant of Wildfell Hall* came out in 1848, to reviews disapproving its subject. *Shirley* appeared in 1849 and marked the virtual end of Charlotte's anonymity: the setting and some of the characters were promptly identified locally, while the attempts of Emily's and Anne's publisher to pass off their work as 'Currer Bell's' forced her into justifying herself to her publishers for what looked like breach of contract. In 1853 came *Villette*.

Charlotte alone made any contact with the literary world of her day, and that scanty. She met Thackeray and made friends, mainly by correspondence, with Mrs Gaskell, Harriet Martineau and the novelist and critic G. H. Lewes. She read widely among her contemporaries, in volumes sent by her publishers, but the only reading which leaves a mark on her own work is that which can be seen in all three sisters, the reading of their youth: the Bible, Shakespeare, Bunyan, the eighteenth-century essayists, Scott, Byron and the political periodicals of the early nineteenth century. The only contemporaries to leave their mark are Thackeray and occasionally Tennyson.

Charlotte Brontë, judged by the esteem of her contemporaries, makes claim to be the major figure of her family; by bulk and variety she is the professional. Whatever the final estimate, her work must be judged by the highest standards, in its own right, and not merely as Dr. Leavis suggests as 'a remarkable talent that enabled her to do something first-hand, and new in the rendering of personal experience, above all in *Villette*'— a talent that he judges to be 'of a minor kind.' (*The Great Tradition*, p. 41).

However, her first attempt, in a public, professional sense, at the novel (putting aside, that is, the private family narratives never intended for outside readers) is undoubtedly minor. *The Professor* is not, within its limits, a failure; it has striking originalities and a few great scenes and passages, but it always remains on a lower level than her other three works. Smith and Elder were wise to reject it, and, since it drove Charlotte Brontë to write *Jane Eyre*, and since, had it been published, she could never have felt free to re-work and transmute its Belgian material and characters in *Villette*, readers must be grateful to them for doing so. *The Professor* must always remain the last read, as it was the last published, of the Brontë novels. Its main importance for the critic, as for its author, is that it enables him to explore what Charlotte Brontë required of a novel, what are its legitimate constituents, and how these constituents are to be used to valid artistic ends. Since the novel is plainly not wholly successful, it is easier to see the originality of its author's starting-point and methods, and the nature of the power that vivifies them, than it is either in a fully achieved masterpiece like *Jane Eyre*, or in a misconceived variant like *Shirley*.

Her own professed aims are surprisingly at odds with the effect she always produces, at her greatest, upon her readers. In her preface to *The Professor* (written when she was hoping, after the success of *Jane Eyre* and *Shirley*, to get it into print) she says:

I had got over any such taste as I might once have had for ornamented and redundant composition, and come to prefer what was plain and homely At the same time I had adopted a set of principles on the subject of incident, etc., such as would be generally approved in theory, but the result of which, when carried into practice, often procures for an author more surprise than pleasure.

I said to myself that my hero should work his way through life as I had seen real living men work theirs—that he should never get a shilling he had not earned—that no sudden turns should lift him in a moment to wealth and high station; that whatever small competency he might gain, should be won by the sweat of his brow; that before he could find so much as an arbour to sit down in, he should master at least half the ascent of 'the Hill of Difficulty'; that he should not even marry a beautiful girl or a lady of rank. As Adam's son he should share Adam's doom, and drain through life a mixed and moderate cup of enjoyment.

Her work, therefore, is to be wholly about real life, drawing on the material of life, with no concessions to fantasy, romance or wish-fulfilment, and, above all, no dependence on previous literary conventions or models. In *The Professor* she keeps almost too rigidly within her self-imposed limits. The career of William Crimsworth begins as a clerk in his manufacturer brother's West Riding factory, continues as a tutor in a Belgian school, is enlivened only by his soon successful love for a fellow-teacher and pupil, and by his employer's unreturned passion for himself, and culminates only in a happy retirement to England again, on the income of several years of successful school-keeping; such a career is inadequate to the power with which Charlotte Brontë endows him of feeling deeply and powerfully and thinking originally, and inadequate also to Charlotte Brontë's own patent power to utilize such thought and feeling in the medium of the novel. But *The Professor* is full of the flavour of things to come. It reveals that its author is developing the autobiographical form in a new way, enabling her to use personal experience to valid artistic ends. (It is significant that her first-person narrator is a means of involvement with the material, but of detachment from the author, since he is, unlike herself, a man.) It possesses the vivid and powerful creation of secondary and unattractive characters done with both scrupulous fairness and with great vigour : Mlle. Reuter here, with the charms of intelligence and health, counteracted by cold-heartedness and deceit, looks forward to Mme. Beck; the vigorously realized Belgian schoolmaster Pelet, and the Englishman Yorke Hunsden, a compound of conscious

Yorkshire bluntness and eccentricity with culture and social polish, point the way to *Shirley* and to *Villette*. Her power to re-create all the moods and passions, transient and cumulative, which attend loneliness, her power to convey their associations with place, time and weather, and to develop her own highly idiosyncratic style in which the heightened, ornate and rhetorical, and the simple and homely co-exist without bathos and may be used with conscious humour as well as for intense drama—all these reveal a writer who knows what she intends, and has the means at her disposal. Her next novel showed her superbly able to use the one and achieve the other.

Though *Shirley* has a wider canvas, and *Villette* a deeper and stranger exploration of the human spirit, both have fallings-off and flaws. *Jane Eyre* is Charlotte Brontë's nearest claim to perfection.

Its achievement rests mainly upon its heroine. More than most first-person narrators, she is the Prince of Denmark of her *Hamlet*, in that everything in the novel bears in some way upon the emotional and spiritual progress which is the essence of the work. Charlotte Brontë's most obvious success is her conscious one, of taking a heroine who is plain, socially insignificant (not even romantically destitute like Oliver Twist), prim to puritanism in her manners, yet utterly unconventional and highly idiosyncratic; she then ensures with never-failing skill that the reader shall care as passionately for her as she herself does about the crises with which life faces her. But Jane Eyre is the means whereby her author achieves greater ends, becoming able to handle material and spiritual states, and to evolve techniques, not hitherto accessible in the novel. Through her heroine Charlotte Brontë embarks for the first time upon the problem of how the vital needs of the individual soul may be reconciled with those of private moral standards, and of the claims of the social world in which the individual must occupy a place. The spiritual needs of Jane Eyre are all too easily summarized as 'love', but the terms in which she declares her passion to Mr. Rochester comprise more than himself:

'I grieve to leave Thornfield: I love Thornfield:– I love it, because I have lived in it a full and delightful life,—momentarily at least. I have not been trampled on. I have not been petrified. I have not been buried with inferior minds, and excluded from every glimpse of communion with what is bright, and energetic, and high. I have talked, face to face,

148

with what I reverence; with what I delight in—with an original, a vigorous, an expanded mind.'

(Chapter 23)

The adjectives here are astonishing ones to apply to the man one loves, even for so idiosyncratic a stylist as Charlotte Brontë. Their use reveals deeper issues and demonstrates the vitality of all those sections of the novels which do not concern the 'love-story'. The events at Gateshead when Jane is a child persecuted and neglected by her aunt and cousins, at Lowood Institution where she is a schoolgirl starved in body, and at Morton where she is a school-teacher tormented in mind and starved in soul, are all part of this deeper examination which is made through Jane. The early episodes, at Gateshead and Lowood, are essential if the reader is to see the sources of the strength whereby Jane rejects Mr. Rochester, and to acknowledge the validity of the principles which compel her to do so. Courage and strength of feeling are what Charlotte Brontë bestows on Jane as given by nature: they enable her to defy her bullying cousins and her harsh aunt. But they are instinctive and amoral. The eleven-year-old Jane who routs her aunt discovers that, unsupported and undirected, they lead to no end:

Something of vengeance I had tasted for the first time; as aromatic wine it seemed, on swallowing, warm and racy: its after-flavour, metallic and corroding, gave me a sensation as if I had been poisoned.

(Chapter 4)

At Lowood she learns of other means of facing life's challenges —those embodied in Helen Burns, who meets hers with a fortitude that takes the form of Christian resignation and meekness under suffering. Although this can never be Jane's way, it enables her to move from her own non-Christian stand:

'You are good to those who are good to you. It is all I ever desire to be ... When we are struck at without a reason, we should strike back again very hard; I am sure we should— so hard as to teach the person who struck us never to do it again.'

(Chapter 6)

Jane sees the force of what Helen says, but sees also, in her reply to Helen's supposition below, a consideration that does not bear on the solitary Helen:

'If all the world hated you, and believed you wicked, while your own conscience approved you, and absolved you from guilt, you would not be without friends.'

'No; I know I should think well of myself; but that is not enough: if others don't love me, I would rather die than live—I cannot bear to be solitary and hated.'

(Chapter 8)

By the climax of her testing at Thornfield, Charlotte Brontë makes us recognize the validity of Jane's position when she is tempted within herself by the ideas that equally tempt the reader:

'Who in the world cares for *you*? or who will be injured by what you do?'

Still indomitable was the reply—'*I* care for myself. The more solitary, the more friendless, the more unsustained I am, the more I will respect myself. I will keep the law given by God; sanctioned by man. I will hold to the principles received by me when I was sane, and not mad—as I am now.'

(Chapter 27)

Her further test at Morton is made by St. John Rivers, who offers her a life devoted to a noble cause, but at the price of complete self-suppression, and what amounts to the killing of her personality. Finally, at Ferndean, enriched by her new knowledge of family life with her three new-found cousins, wiser by her struggle against sterile self-denial, Jane finds, reunited at last with Mr. Rochester, what suits her (in her own words) 'to the finest fibre of [her] nature' (Chapter 37).

Charlotte Brontë's triumph in creating Jane is so complete that it is easy to respond to the careful structure and to overlook it, easy to feel that Jane's character is so complete that it must be her author's. The autobiographical method works so well that the many shifts of narrative viewpoint, which make it succeed, go unnoticed. The great innovation of the method lies in the subtle use of retrospect. Jane is purportedly writing ten years after the final chapter, but within the progress of the action the Jane who experiences constantly pauses to assess her position, to steady herself, whether it is to reverberate mindlessly to Mr. Rochester's near-protestation of love after the fire (Chapter 15), or coldly balance her plain self with the flashing Miss Ingram (Chapter 17). The long chapter in which she goes back to Gateshead for Mrs. Reed's death (Chapter 21) involves reassessments at a greater distance in time, of her childhood eight years before.

The method, of purported autobiography, and this structure, of scenes of passionate involvement controlled and curbed by intervals of constant intellectual reassessment in retrospect, is taken further in *Villette*. Here also the success is so complete that Lucy Snowe has been discussed as if she were her own author, different though she is from Jane Eyre. Lucy is much further than Jane from what most readers think of as a 'normal' personality; the furthest retrospect of herself is greater—she is writing in her old age, when her hair 'lies now, at last white, under a white cap, like snow beneath snow' (Chapter 5)—yet her sufferings, coming from far stranger depths of personality, are as painfully realized as Jane's. The agonies of loneliness, hypersensitivity, melancholy, and introspection, though they cause Lucy moral *problems*, are not shaped by moral *considerations* as Jane's are. Lucy has a harder struggle than Jane, not merely to reconcile the needs of her personality with the rules of society, but to survive as a person at all, in a society whose pressures not only threaten to annihilate her, but actually intensify the conflicts within her own nature. Charlotte Brontë is approaching (from a very different direction) the world of Henry James, in which the standards of judgement must be termed, inadequately, aesthetic. The novel's failures are not because of its strange heroine, nor of her stranger situation (being, like Catherine Earnshaw, in love with two men at once), but because of its divided aims. Lucy, the child of misfortune, is contrasted with Paulina de Bassompierre, in whom Charlotte Brontë intends to portray a nature equally finely balanced, whose destiny is fulfilment and happiness. Unfortunately Charlotte Brontë's powers of characterization are of a kind that catch fire only through a central consciousness. The detachment necessary to such an end cuts her off from her strength; Paulina, and those who concern her, seem unrealized and mechanical as soon as they cease to be of vital concern to Lucy. Charlotte Brontë herself acknowledged the fault, diagnosing that Paulina lacked 'the germ of the real' (Letter to George Smith, Dec. 6, 1852).

Charlotte Brontë's characters other than her heroine have always presented the paradox of seeming to have intense life, yet, when considered separately, of seeming often incredible. After Lucy, one recalls Mme. Beck and Paul Emmanuel as two of the author's finest achievements. Yet of Paul Emmanuel it can be said, as David Cecil said of Mr Rochester, that no flesh-and-blood man could be so exclusively composed of violence and virility and masculine vanity (*Early Victorian Novelists*, 1934). The life the reader responds to in them is not so much their own, but what they have for the heroine through whose eyes, nerves and heart we perceive them. The reader judges them for the way they impress *her* rather than himself. The method explains the power of such unobtrusive triumphs as Bessie Leaven and Mrs. Fairfax in *Jane Eyre* and Mrs. Bretton in *Villette*, as well as of such evident and original triumphs as Mrs. Reed, St John Rivers and Mr. Rochester in *Jane Eyre*, or Mme. Beck and Paul Emmanuel in *Villette*; it explains also the vigour of what have been thought her failures —*Jane Eyre's* Blanche Ingram and her astonishing mother, or *Villette's* Ginevra Fanshawe, Père Silas and Mme. Walravens. The reader, sharing the narrator's experience, feels as she does. However, such feeling never warps judgement. Indeed, Charlotte Brontë constantly forces her reader to make his own assessments of her characters, to check the heroine's conclusions against the facts she provides. One can see how Mr Rochester both understands Jane and misjudges her during their courtship, how he can be the man who realizes that

'If I bid you do what you thought wrong, there would be no light-footed running, no neat-handed alacrity, no lively glance and animated complexion'.

(Chapter 20)

and equally the man who, after she has agreed to marry him, attempts to treat her as a sultan treats a favourite: and how both aspects look forward to his greatest offence against her, in trying to cheat her into wrong-doing and a bigamous marriage. Mme. Beck in *Villette* is an even more complex case, since the narrator's attitude to her changes with time. The qualities which make Mme. Beck morally indefensible but amusing, attractive and in some degree estimable—her cold-hearted composure, the tidiness and desire for propriety which lead her to search, with exquisite neatness and efficiency, the belongings and letters of her employees, the quietly inflexible will, which manipulates (by lying if necessary) any chance event that will give her her own way—all these can seem, to the reader as to Lucy, reprehensible but amusing, when Lucy herself is secure in having no secrets to hide and no desires which cross Mme. Beck's. However, when Lucy, in love with Paul Emmanuel, becomes a threat to Mme. Beck's plans to keep him for herself and her school, Mme. Beck becomes a powerful danger, the more effective in that the reader is never allowed to relax into simple hatred. The virtues of her defects remain unchanged.

When the central narrator is removed, the shaping power it imposes is removed also. Henry James's condemnation of autobiographical novels as 'loose baggy monsters' applies much more to *Shirley*, Charlotte Brontë's only non-autobiographical one, than to the rest. Though her motives in making her second novel quite different from her first are excellent, her intentions were beyond her equipment. A panorama of the West Riding during the Industrial Revolution, to be revealed through the spiritual progress of two young women, one rich, brilliant and fortunate, the other dependent, subdued, and unhappy, who are in their turn to be presented by a detached, Thackerayan, ironic, moralizing narrator—such a project called for too many qualities Charlotte Brontë did not possess and rendered useless some of the best that she did.

The two greatest deficiencies in *Shirley* are an uncertain sense of direction and an unsatisfactory narrative method. The novel has two quite different kinds of theme, interrelated by the action, but demanding, to succeed, two different kinds of narrative. The first centres upon the hero (if the novel can be said to have one), Robert Moore. This theme examines the force of personality and circumstances in shaping a man's fate, as the combined pressures of lack of money, the perils besetting Yorkshire millowners and the clothing industry and the political state of England or Europe and indeed of America all work upon his character to change it and, with it, determine how his life shall go. The other theme is worked out in the eponymous heroine Shirley and in the novel's central perception, Caroline Helstone. Through them the novel explores the dilemma of woman in nineteenth-century middle-class society, forced to find a life for herself, yet deprived (if she does not marry) of the means, not only of fulfilling her emotional needs, but of keeping any sense at all of a purpose in life. The novel aches with the pain of Caroline's question when, knowing that she will not marry Robert and that she is prevented from finding a career for herself, she asks:

'What am I to do to fill the interval of time which spreads between me and the grave?'

(Chapter 10)

The first theme is the one embodied in the plot; but a résumé of that plot would not even suggest the existence of

153

the second. The first is done dramatically, with vigorous action and racy dialogue; the second by long revelations of Caroline's spiritual sufferings, by curious duologues between her and Shirley in strangely heightened language, by curious non-novelistic devices—like Shirley's remarkable 'devoir' on 'La Première Femme Savante'— and finally by a brutal change of narrative method in Louis Moore's journal. Both themes are more successful than such analysis suggests and are interrelated, often enmeshed. Their material often overlaps, particularly as regards the characters taking part. Shirley and Caroline are part of Robert's story, he an important element in theirs; Mr. Yorke the mill owner, Caroline's despotic uncle the Rev. Mr. Helstone, and Robert's sister Hortense concern both stories. The same scenes may advance both.

Even more vitally, both themes are coloured by what almost amounts to a third—Charlotte Brontë's potent and original apprehension of what time passing does to the lives of men. She first learned the use of recent history from Scott, but she adapted it to something quite other than his romantic nostalgia in *Waverley* or even his more serious aims in *Heart of Midlothian*. For probably the first time in the English novel, characters not only feel themselves to be mortal, but feel themselves hemmed in by the pressures on their own fates, not only of the chances of history, but also of precious life slipping away. Whether Robert goes bankrupt or not and whether he can marry Caroline depends upon the movements of nations: the repeal of the Orders in Council, allowing American trade, only barely saves him from financial ruin; while Caroline's question above reverberates through the novel, with its plangent periphrasis for 'life'—'the interval of time which spreads between me and the grave.'

Unfortunately, the narrative method chosen by Charlotte Brontë impedes her. Her Thackerayan stance often suits the first theme, but it is fatal to the second. To be detached, humorous, ironic, would-be urbane (though urbanity does not suit so uncosmopolitan a writer) may suit the delineation of Robert the latter-day Coriolanus, or the trenchant Yorkshire types, or the comic curates; it is fatal to the interior stresses of a Shirley and still more of a Caroline Helstone. Charlotte Brontë's intentions in *Shirley* were excellent—to avoid writing a second *Jane Eyre*, to extend both her own range and that of her form, to examine both society and new and deeper recesses of individual consciousness. But what she produced must be considered, in the final judgement, a noble failure. Her claim

to greatness must rest upon *Jane Eyre* and *Villette*. (A few fragments exist of unfinished novels, notably a fragment concerning
two brothers called *The Moores*, (printed in W. R. Nicoll's
edition of *Jane Eyre*, 1902) recalling *Shirley* only by the name;
and the opening chapters of a work stopped by marriage and
death, called *Emma* (first printed in the *Cornhill Magazine*, April
1860), which treats the sufferings of an unattractive small girl,
thought to be rich and found to be poor, whose stay in a small
school is chronicled by a dispassionate male observer. Neither
is of artistic interest. They are merely outlines too rough to help
much in a study of their author's processes of creation.)

Anne Brontë dwells in the shadow of her two sisters. Though
undeniably less than they, she is no mere pale copy of either.
She is of interest to the student of all three for her original
use of their common material; she is of interest in her own
right for being, apparently quite unwittingly, a startling innovator, not, like Emily, in structure and theme, or like Charlotte, in intention and apprehension, but in materials and morals.
It is impossible to miss the originality of her subject in *The
Tenant of Wildfell Hall*, a controlled, unsparing study of drunkenness, debauchery and degeneration which proceeds inexorably to its conclusion in death, examining on the way the
consequences of sin to the sinner himself, to those in his
private life, and to the society around him. Although the title
suggests Helen Huntingdon (the 'tenant') as the central interest
and although the first quarter of the novel is the autobiography of Gilbert Markham, a young North-country farmer
who connects himself with the main story only by falling in
love with the mysterious Helen, nevertheless the novel's prime
mover, the reason for its existence, the source of its power,
is Arthur Huntingdon, Helen's husband. His career, from marriage to death, is chronicled in the bulk of the novel.
Anne's own statement of her purpose in writing, in her
preface to the second addition, is a naïve one :

I could not be understood to suppose, that the proceedings
of the unhappy scapegrace, with his few profligate companions I have introduced, are a specimen of the common
practices of society : the case is an extreme one, as I trusted
none would fail to perceive; but I knew that such characters
do exist, and if I have warned one rash youth from following
in their steps, or prevented one thoughtless girl from falling

into the very natural error of my heroine, the book has not been written in vain.

Anne Brontë as a novelist is not so naïve. Aware of her moral purpose and competent with the usual tools of the novelist, she is, rather, innocent and candid, unaware only of the startling novelty of her material and the unconventionality of her moral conclusions. Using the unfortunate Branwell (as Emily had used him in *Wuthering Heights*) she chronicles how self-indulgence degrades and ruins Arthur Huntingdon and how Helen Huntingdon, attempting again and again to save him, her love for him, their marriage and the upbringing of their son, finds that such suffering, far from ennobling her, tempts her in desperation to accept a lover as a means of escape:

> then I hate [Huntingdon] tenfold more for having brought me to this!—God pardon me for it—and all my sinful thoughts! Instead of being humbled and purified by my afflictions I feel that they are changing my nature into gall.
>
> (Chapter 35)

Anne Brontë faces all the practical realities of the situation, not least the power of the law, which makes Helen the guilty party if she leaves her husband, and so deprives her of the right to the custody of the son for whose sake she wants to go. Her scenes are fully realized by nicely chosen details; she delineates the full horror of life with drunkards, revealed by a man who scoops out half-dissolved sugar-lumps from his over-sweetened coffee and dumps them back in the sugar-bowl, or by a sober man who has to use a drawing-room candle to burn the hands of a drunkard restraining him (Chapter 31); she faces also the horror of nursing a man dying of alcoholism and gangrene; she may not turn the reader's stomach, she certainly chills his nerves.

Like *Wuthering Heights*, *The Tenant of Wildfell Hall* begins almost at the end, a well-chosen device with some of the same effects. Anne Brontë, working on a subject which threatens both sentimentailty and melodrama, avoids both. To do so, she does away with suspense. By knowing the conclusion, the reader is enabled to concentrate on what is being put before him, without anxiety as to the eventual consequences, which he already knows. Also like *Wuthering Heights*, the novel's ending is a diminuendo; Helen's final, happy marriage to Gilbert Markham, though less interesting than what has gone before, is a necessary part of the novel's themes as well as plot, to show that her sufferings have not wholly dehumanized her: Anne consciously rejected her sister's conclusion in *Shirley*, that

> Sweet wild force following acute suffering, you will find nowhere: to talk of it is delusion. There may be apathetic exhaustion after the rack; if energy remains, it will be rather a dangerous energy—deadly when confronted with injustice.
>
> (Chapter 7)

Agnes Grey is less startling, yet almost equally uncompromising. As a heroine, Agnes herself is colourless, but she is the heroine in only a limited sense. She is Anne Brontë's Fanny Price. The novel concentrates upon the kind of society and standards Agnes encounters during her career as a governess with two provincial middle-class country families, the Bloomfields and the Murrays. Her main role in the novel is as the reader's means of seeing this society and judging it. Faulty standards of education and upbringing are the author's theme here, bodied forth pre-eminently in the brilliant coquette Rosalie Murray, who fulfils her destiny under Agnes's anxious, disapproving, partly affectionate, wholly ineffectual observation. The author follows Rosalie inexorably through the last phases of education, through her coming out into society, flirtations with the local clergy, arranged courtship, marriage for money and rank, to the end of her first year of married life, looking ahead to the prospect of a barren existence whose only bitter comfort is to watch a daughter 'grow up to eclipse me, and enjoy those pleasures I am forever debarred from' (Chapter 23), all without realizing that she is condemning that same daughter to the same dreadful upbringing, frivolous and arid, as has ruined herself.

Agnes Grey, less sombre than the later novel, gives its author opportunities both for humorous irony and delicate description. The irony, far from being kept away from Agnes the narrator, often works at her expense. Naïvely enthusiastic over the charms and satisfactions of teaching small children, deciding that

> the clear remembrance of my own thoughts in early childhood would be a surer guide than the instructions of the most mature adviser.
>
> (Chapter 1)

she reinforces her case by quoting Thomson:

> Delightful task!
> To teach the young idea how to shoot!

a sentiment (and an expression of it) trite even when Jane Austen bestowed it upon Catherine Morland in *Northanger Abbey*, whence, in fact, Anne Brontë may have borrowed it (and its ironic intent) since this, though identical with Jane Austen's version is actually a misquotation of the original lines from Thomson's *Seasons* ('Spring', 1149). If the clue here is missed, the reader soon sees Agnes's ignorance promptly done away with by the atrocious Bloomfield children. Anne Brontë, like her sisters, takes a robust delight in the grotesquely, even horrifyingly comic, as the behaviour of this same Bloomfield family demonstrates. That she intends them to be comic as well as horrifying, her own descriptions prove: Mr. Bloomfield, for instance 'had a large mouth, pale, dingy complexion, milky blue eyes and hair *the colour of a hempen cord*' (Chapter 3 my italics). When occasion offers, descriptions are both delicate and lyrical, as when Agnes, on a visit to her former pupil Rosalie, now Lady Ashby, sits neglected in her room:

> As I was not rich enough to possess a watch, I could not tell how time was passing, except by observing the slowly lengthening shadows from the window; which presented a side view, including a corner of the park, a clump of trees, whose topmost branches had been colonized by an innumerable company of noisy rooks, and a high wall with a massive wooden gate: no doubt communicating with the stable-yard, as a broad carriage-road swept up to it from the park. The shadow of this wall soon took possession of the whole of the ground as far as I could see, forcing the golden sunlight to retreat inch by inch, and at last take refuge in the very tops of the trees. Ere long, even they were left in shadow—the shadow of the distant hills, or of the earth itself; and, in sympathy for the busy citizens of the rookery, I regretted to see their habitation, so lately bathed in glorious light, reduced to the sombre, work-a-day hue of the lower world within. For a moment, such birds as soared above the rest might still receive the lustre of their wings, which imparted to their sable plumage the hue and brilliance of deep red gold; at last that too departed. Twilight came stealing on; the rooks became more quiet; I became more weary, and wished I were going home tomorrow.
>
> (Chapter 20)

Undoubtedly a minor talent, Anne Brontë's is undubitably a considerable one, worth more than the scant attention usually spared from her sisters. The great differences of material, structure, tone and treatment, the extra depth and complexity of her second work, suggest that she had more to say than fate allowed her, and more, and growing, powers as a writer.

The same claims for a great and enlarging future cannot be made for Anne's far greater sister, Emily. *Wuthering Heights* is generally accepted as the Brontë masterpiece; but it stands alone, not only apart from the work of the other members of the family, but from any other novel. It had no precursors and has had no successors worth considering. The only literature close to it is Emily Brontë's own poems, which, great though some of them are, are chiefly valuable for revealing what has gone into the making of the novel. Neither they nor *Wuthering Heights* itself give any hint that anything more could have come out of it. On a literary level, Emily Brontë died fulfilled.

While the greatness of the novel has been owned in steadily increasing enthusiasm ever since its very unsensational publication, opinions vary widely over what constitutes that greatness. The reader who responds to the force of the whole often has reservations about its parts—about the characters of the leading figures, Heathcliff and the elder Catherine, about the remarkable narrative method (by means of two main fictional narrators and several minor ones), about the attitudes to religion which lie behind the events, even about the quality and amount of the supernatural forces introduced.

Emily Brontë is the most self-effacing of writers, but she gives her readers clearer leads than she seems to do. One of the clearest is about her topic. The first chapter introduces the chief character, Heathcliff, whose doings occupy the bulk of the narrator Lockwood's attention for the next three; in the fourth, asking the housekeeper Ellen Dean for 'something of my neighbours,' he goes on to request, specifically, Heathcliff's history; in Ellen's story (the bulk of the novel) he gets precisely what he asked for. The known span and compass of Heathcliff's life at Wuthering Heights is the span and compass of the novel. When he is not there there is no story—as is demonstrated most strikingly by the way Ellen Dean passes over in a few sentences the three years of his absence, even though during them Catherine has her first major illness and experiences the first part of her married life with Edgar Linton. Heathcliff is, therefore, the structure of the novel.

Powerful though Heathcliff is, another is more. There can be few novels in which the heroine dies less than half-way through; there can be few heroines whose passion so permeates all its pages. She is Heathcliff's motive, his hold on life, just as she declares he is hers. Her confession that

'my great thought in living is himself. If all else perished, and *he* remained, *I* should still continue to be, and if all else remained and he were annihilated the universe would turn to a mighty stranger.'

(Chapter 9)

is partnered by his prayer to her at her death :

'Be with me always—take any form—drive me mad! only *do* not leave me in this abyss where I cannot find you! Oh God! it is unutterable! I *cannot* live without my life! *I cannot* live without my soul!'

(Chapter 16)

Through him she lives on for another eighteen years, until he has unconsciously completed his task of restoring the equilibrium of society at the Heights and Thrushcross, which was disrupted by his arrival as a dirty, ragged, black-haired foundling, the cuckoo in the Earnshaw nest, and next by Catherine's self-destroying act when, spiritually bound to him, she gave herself to Linton, thereby splitting her very nature in two.

These two are the life of the novel, its *raison d'être*. The social, spiritual, even supernatural, disturbances are but repercussions of the disturbances in them; the other characters (barring the narrators) exist only in relation to them and are seen by their light. The novel opens with them. Lockwood meets Heathcliff first, at the point in his career when his task of vengeance is virtually completed. Nothing stands in the way of a union between the younger Catherine, the Linton heir (herself half Earnshaw), and Hareton, inheritor of Wuthering Heights. Nothing now therefore prevents Heathcliff from his union with Catherine as he himself dimly perceives in his later confession to Ellen Dean :

'I get levers and mattocks to demolish the two houses, and train myself to be capable of working like Hercules, and when everything is ready and in my power, I find the will to lift a slate off either roof his vanished. My old enemies have not beaten me; now would be the precise time to revenge myself on their representatives: I could do it; and none could hinder me. But where is the use? I don't care for striking; I can't take the trouble to raise my hand.'

(Chapter 33)

Almost immediately after Lockwood meets Heathcliff in the flesh, he meets Catherine also, in the spirit. In the brilliantly-conceived nightmare she is not the woman who died, but a child, who wails that she has been 'a waif for twenty years' (Chapter 3). Lockwood sees, in fact, the only complete Catherine, the child who has not yet separated herself from her more essential self, Heathcliff. When death re-unites them, social order returns, the younger generation are free to be happy at Thrushcross, and Joseph to behave with his old curmudgeonly gusto at the Heights; Ellen, the barometer of disturbance in both places, is happy in the union of her two charges. We are able to accept both Lockwood's faith that no-one could 'imagine unquiet slumbers for the sleepers in that quiet earth' (Chapter 34); and to accept equally that 'they *walk*', that the boy with the sheep has seen 'Heathcliff and a woman, yonder, under t' nab' and that Joseph has seen 'two on 'em, looking out of his [Heathcliff's] chamber window, every night since his death' (ibid); the whole novel has gone to prove that such indeed is their heaven; to be thus is to be at peace, reunited with each other and with the Heights.

While it is underestimating Emily Brontë to suggest that the other characters are mere shadows, yet it is safe to say that their personalities are limited to what they share with those of the protagonists. The range of emotions and responses in *Wuthering Heights* is limited, though the depth of the emotions is far from being so. All characters exhibit courage, meet adversity with defiance, and counter wrong with the urge to vengeance. Isabella, her love for Heathcliff turned to hate, taunts, goads and defies him; Hindley Earnshaw, drunken and bankrupt, protests that he will have pleasure in sending his own soul to perdition to punish its maker (Chapter 9). They never feel that resignation is a virtue, or that they should exercise self-control: all that is required of them is that they accept the full consequences of their acts. Even Edgar Linton, the nearest to a type of Christian virtue, is more willing to die to be with Catherine than to live and take care of his daughter.

Such positions necessarily result in violence, and violence in cruelty. Even so, the novel is neither as violent nor as cruel as it seems. Much of the violence is of expression and interpretation, not action; most of the cruelty is not gratuitous or sadistic, but the inevitable breaking out of overwhelming passions. Emily Brontë takes care that the outward surface of life shall not heave or break too often with all the turbulence beneath: Kenneth the doctor visits the Heights and sees nothing much amiss; the housekeeper Zillah sees little to disturb her even while young Linton Heathcliff is dying. The great scenes of violence are not as memorable as the great scenes of passion: one remembers Catherine's self-revealing delirium (Chapter 12), her last scene with Heathcliff (Chapter 15) or those just before his death (Chapters 33 and 34) more vividly than that in which he almost kills Hindley and Isabella on the night of Catherine's funeral (Chapter 17). Significantly, this last—containing perhaps the most brutal acts Heathcliff, the most brutal character, commits—is not simply an outburst of self-indulgent spite against those who have injured him. He has been goaded past bearing by Isabella's taunting his most vital feelings:

'Heathcliff, if I were you, I'd go stretch myself over her grave and die like a faithful dog. The world is surely not worth living in now, is it? You had distinctly impressed on me the idea that Catherine was the whole joy of your life: I can't imagine how you think of surviving her loss.'

(Chapter 17)

She has hit on the truth; he has indeed meant to die to be with her; but as he tells Ellen later, he has come up again to the Heights in the firm faith that the spirit of Catherine is accompanying him home and that he will see her there:

'Having reached the Heights, I rushed eagerly to the door. It was fastened; and, I remember that accursed Earnshaw and my wife opposed my entrance. I remember stopping to kick the breath out of them, and then hurrying upstairs, to my room and hers.'

(Chapter 29)

He is cruel, not for sadistic self-satisfaction, but out of an over-riding passion; so even is Lockwood when, unable to free himself from the child-phantom

I pulled its wrist on to the broken pane, and rubbed it to and fro till the blood ran down and soaked the bed-clothes.

(Chapter 3)

Again the action is not deliberate cruelty; the doer feels no

162

satisfaction, still less pleasure: indeed he emphasizes that 'the intense horror of nightmare' was upon him and that '*terror* made [him] cruel.'

Paradoxically, speech is often more violent than action, and often negates what it seems to suggest. Heathcliff as a boy talks of 'painting the house-front with Hindley's blood' (Chapter 6), but, secure in his union with Catherine, does nothing. When his actual revenge comes, it consists in simply letting Hindley ruin himself, while the details are not discussed at all. Even more striking are the abounding allusions, in imagery and speech, to heaven, hell, God, the devil, damnation, the supernatural and the more fearsome figures of folklore. It is constantly suggested that Heathcliff may be a fiend, a hob-goblin, or a devil. He and Catherine, and the other characters, talk of their own future life beyond death with the most startling misuse of the conventional Christian terms. The result is to make the reader take nothing on trust, to reject not only the usual connotations of the concepts but the concepts themselves, and so draw gradually to Emily Brontë's own strange non-Christian sense of the universe. The conventional utterances are put in the mouth of Ellen, who sees plainly what is before her but is an inadequate interpreter. By a series of unconscious rejections of her judgments (though not of her statements of facts) the reader comes to accept as truth Heathcliff's outburst to the dying Catherine:

'Because misery and degradation, and death, and nothing that God or Satan could inflict would have parted us, *you,* of your own will, did it.'

(Chapter 15)

God and Satan are synonymous, relevant only for their power over these two; heaven and hell are union and separation, having nothing to do with other people, or with right and wrong, or reward and punishment.

Within her only novel Emily Brontë has created the world in her own image, and peopled it with the powerful impulses of her own nature. Much is omitted; but the power of what it contains is unique.

> The earth that wakes one human heart to feeling
> Can centre both the worlds of heaven and hell.

The difficulties that face the reader of *Wuthering Heights* face even more forbiddingly the reader of her poems. While it is possible to approach the novel without any knowledge of whence it sprang, many of the poems are almost unintelligible if their provenance is unknown. While some few are unmistakably great lyrics, many are interesting mainly as evidence of the mind and private world from which the novel sprang. Thirdly, while it has been proved that most, if not all, of them are dramatic monologues—the outbursts of invented characters in imagined situations—,several of them draw upon states of apprehension known only to the mystic.

The poems have the same limitations as the novel: they are most at home with elemental and exteme emotions—the intensest love, extreme hate, suffering, fortitude or grief. They work by suggestion rather than reason, and depend upon a close union between man and nature; they express themselves in a highly personal mixture of the almost casually idiomatic and the highly rhetorical, through a limited range of powerful images; they are poems of mood, more often preoccupied with coming death and a lost past than with a living and absorbing present; when they do deal with the present, the tone is most often melancholy or brooding. What are perhaps Emily Brontë's two best-known lyrics embody many of her most striking qualities—the lines beginning 'No coward soul is mine' and those beginning 'Cold in the earth'.

The first has been taken as her own creed, especially since Charlotte Brontë erroneously stated that they were 'the last lines my sister Emily ever wrote' (They exist, however, in a manuscript dated January 2, 1846—nearly three years before her death, differing but little from Charlotte's text.) They would, if so, he remarkable for the daughter of a Low-church vicar of the Church of England. There is no theology in them: the deity is defined no more than as the

> God within my breast
> Almighty ever-present Deity !
> Life, that in me has rest
> As I, undying Life, have power in Thee'!

The final stanzas assert that death shall have no dominion, in a way that shows the same sense of man's relation to the universe as that postulated in the novel, though the terms in which it is expressed here are the converse:

> Though earth and moon were gone,
> And suns and universes ceased to be,
> And thou wert left alone,
> Every existence would exist in Thee.

There is not room for Death,
Nor atom that this might could render void,
Thou—THOU art Being and Breath,
And what THOU art may never be destroyed.

This conclusion is the positive expression of Catherine's negative, her cry that 'if all else remained, and [Heathcliff] were annihilated, the universe would turn to a mighty stranger' (Chapter 9).

Although many of Emily Brontë's poems, like 'Cold in the earth',[4] might fairly be termed dramatic monologues, they are far removed from those of that most notable practitioner, Browning. The stance and tone are unusual. There is no place for an auditor and one has no sense that any reader of the poem is being taken into account: the speaker of this one, the woman wailing for her lover dead for 'fifteen wild Decembers', is speaking to the dead alone. Nor does the poem express any trace of the nostalgia or gentle melancholy that would be natural after so long: she 'forgets' him because she dare not remember a still passionate grief it would kill her to indulge; she

Dare not indulge in memory's rapturous pain,
Once drinking deep of that divinest anguish
How could I seek the empty world again?

The passion is the more fierce for being held in check, for being indeed never indulged. The poem is not an indulgence, but an explanation: as in the novel, still waters run deep and strong, but absence of action is not absence of passion.

Emily Brontë's poetic techniques work upon the mind through the senses and by associations. She keeps to essentials:

Cold in the earth, and deep snow piled above thee!
Far, far removed, cold in the dreary grave!
Have I forgot, my only love, to love thee,
Severed at last by time's all-severing wave?

This is the germ of the whole. The cold and the vicious 'severance' are spiritual and metaphorical, as well as actual, suffered by the speaker as well as the dead. Cold, distance and time are taken up and explored as the poem progresses, and produce a mass of tensions, for while cold suggests rigidity, the vocabulary and imagery are all of movement and violence—thoughts *hover* and *rest their wings*, wild Decembers *melt*

into Spring. Again as in *Wuthering Heights* there comes a
point at which the image, impossible in literal terms, comes
to be the 'real' truth, with the speaker's

> burning wish to hasten
> Down to that tomb *already more than mine.*
>
> (my italics)

Although passion is what the reader notices most, a real poetic,
controlling intellect is at work without which the passion
would be of little worth.

Emily Brontë, on the evidence of the poems, has been termed
a mystic. It is true that some of her poems call upon experiences that it is difficult to define in any other way; it is equally
true that they too are the utterances of imaginary characters
in invented situations. Best known among them are perhaps
the lines beginning 'He comes with western winds',[5] probably
one of the most remarkable attempts to define and realize the
indefinable and unrealistic that has ever been made.

The poems of Charlotte and Anne, though they achieve competence, though Anne wrote one or two hymns that are still
used, and though Charlotte was consciously competent in
rhythm and metre where Emily often faltered, are nevertheless the words of Mercury after the songs of Apollo. Had their
authors not been novelists, they would never have been considered as poets. But apologies are unnecessary. The Brontës
stand secure. It is few families that can claim one good novelist,
one great one, and one woman of genius who produced a unique
novel and a handful of immortal verse.

1. Like her father she was Tory in politics and had affinities with Wesleyanism in faith. His example may have inspired his family also in their literary composition—he had himself published both prose and verse—although the private nature of their writings, and the form in which they produced them—miniature imitations of books and newspapers, not in long-hand but in a kind of print—suggest inner compulsion, rather than any desire for fame.

2. Notably from a few earnest defenders: Francis H. Grundy (*Pictures of the Past*, 1897), and Francis A. Leyland (*The Brontë Family: with Special Reference to Patrick Branwell Brontë*, 1886). The myth begun by the latter that Branwell conceived the whole of *Wuthering Heights* and wrote the opening chapters dies hard. A recent, accurate and scholarly study is W. Gérin's *Branwell Brontë*, 1961.

3. Branwell's passion for Mrs. Robinson, the mother of the family at Thorp Green, where he and Anne worked as tutor and governess, has wasted far too much time and attention. Whatever the facts (which are demonstrably fewer than his family and Mrs. Gaskell believed, being mainly Branwell's own invention, whether through drug-induced illusion, or as guilty self-exculpating lies to raise him in the eyes of his family) they had few literary uses for the novelists and produced no more than a passing allusion by Charlotte in *The Professor* to the degrading nature of illicit passion.

4. Emily Brontë's own heading to this lyric is *R. Alcona to J. Brenzaida*, alluding to two great figures of the Gondal epic. J. Brenzaida is the Emperor Julius, who was treacherously slain at his own coronation. Rosina Alcona was his wife, with a spirit as fiery as his own, who had disposed of one husband to marry him, who ruled, and had many lovers, after him. She is the Cleopatra of Emily's epic and has much in common with Catherine Earnshaw.

5. This poem begins two lines earlier in some editions, with the words 'A messenger of hope comes every night to me'; the reason is that the lyric is an extract from a longer, narrative, Gondal poem and that this monologue begins, properly, in the middle of a stanza.

BIBLIOGRAPHY

Life and Works of Charlotte Brontë and Her Sisters, ed. Mrs. Humphry Ward and C. K. Shorter (Haworth Edition), 7 vols., 1899–1900.

Novels and Poems of Charlotte, Emily and Anne Brontë, 7 vols., 1901–7 (Oxford World's Classics).

The Shakespeare Head Brontë, ed. T. J. Wise and J. A. Symington, 20 vols., 1932–8. Definitive edition—Novels in 11 vols.; Life and Letters in 4 vols.; Miscellaneous and Unpublished Writings, 2 vols.; Poems, 2 vols.; Bibliography, 1 vol.

Legends of Angria, ed. F. E. Ratchford and W. C. de Vane, New Haven, 1933. Compiled from early writings of Charlotte Brontë.

Complete Poems of Anne Brontë, ed. C. K. Shorter and C. W. Hatfield, 1923.

Complete Poems of Charlotte Brontë, ed. C. K. Shorter and C. W. Hatfield, 1923.

Complete Poems of Emily Brontë, ed. C. W. Hatfield, New York, 1941.

Gondal's Queen: A Novel in Verse by Emily Brontë, ed. F. E. Ratchford, Texas, 1955. Poems arranged as coherent reconstruction of the Gondal epic.

Mrs. E. C. Gaskell, *Life of Charlotte Brontë*, 2 vols, 1857; 3rd edition "revised and corrected". The standard biography.

Transactions and Publications of the Brontë Society, Bradford (then Haworth), 1895–

C. K. Shorter, *The Brontës and Their Circle*, 1896. A pioneer piece of scholarship.

C. P. S[anger], *The Structure of 'Wuthering Heights'*, 1926. The first and invaluable analysis of structure.

Lord David Cecil, *Early Victorian Novelists*, 1934. Chapters on Charlotte and Emily.

F. E. Ratchford, *The Brontës' Web of Childhood*, New York, 1941. The authoritative study of the juvenilia.

M. Lane, *The Brontë Story: A Reconsideration of Mrs. Gaskell's 'Life of Charlotte Brontë'*, 1953.

M. Visick, *The Genesis of 'Wuthering Heights'*, Hong Kong, 1958; Oxford, 1959. Examines the relationship of the poems to the novel.

W. Gérin, *Anne Brontë*, 1959.
—— *Branwell Brontë*, 1961.
—— *Charlotte Brontë*, 1967.
All three are the fullest biographies to date.

R. B. Martin, *The Accents of Persuasion*, 1966. A critical study of Charlotte Brontë's novels.

I–S. Ewbank, *Their Proper Sphere*, 1966. A study of the Brontë sisters as essentially female novelists of their times.

W. A. Craik, *The Brontë Novels*, 1968.

MRS GASKELL AND GEORGE ELIOT

BARBARA HARDY, Birkbeck College, London.

Although there are two places—Knutsford in Cheshire, and Manchester—which provided sources and images for much of Elizabeth Gaskell's writing, hers was not a life which can be very obviously mined for constructive criticism. We have to observe the background of Unitarianism, on her father's side and her husband's, her domesticity, her social contacts with the industrial world and the literary world, in the North, in London and in Europe. We need to insist on her close and sympathetic knowledge of the lives of the poor. Her letters show how she and her daughters were exhausted and appalled by their relief work in Manchester during the cotton famine of the early sixties, for instance. And there are many points of detail in the novels that can be traced back to a direct or indirect biographical source, like the change of faith of Mr. Hale in *North and South*, which transforms but uses her own father's conscientious resignation from the Unitarian ministry, or the celebrated anecdotes about the cow's flannel coat and the cat who swallowed the lace in *Cranford*. But if there were crises in her emotional and intellectual life, like the crises which mark the lives and the art of Dickens, Thackeray, and George Eliot, they remain invisible. Hers is a remarkable and various body of novels and stories which have to be looked at in and for themselves.

This is of course not to deny that her most important works are very potent social expressions both in their steady and complete presentation of a society in whole and parts, as in *Cranford* and *Wives and Daughters*, and as criticisms and appeals, showing a view of contemporary society, its suffering, irrationality and injustice in that clear but never impersonal mirror which she holds up to her time. Recent criticism, rightly reacting against an older and pretty persistent view of her art as the product of a minor, charming, but slender talent, has emphasized the eloquence of her sociological thinking and feeling, and both Kathleen Tillotson, in *Novels of the 1840s*, and Edgar Wright, in his recent critical study, have examined her didacticism and handling of social facts. Both Wright and Arthur Pollard, the other recent defender of Mrs. Gaskell's powers, have also stressed her importance as a psychological novelist, whose social analysis depends very markedly on a realistic handling of the language, manners and passions of human beings. Looking at her in the large context of the Victorian novel, I am impressed anew by her freedom from simplification and caricature. The great social critics in nineteenth-century English fiction are, I suppose, Jane Austen, Dickens and Thackeray. Theirs is essentially an art of fable, of bold and telling outline, of the conspicuous and critical embodiment of ideas in satiric forms. Mrs. Gaskell is unusual as a social novelist in her avoidance of satire. Not that this avoidance is always a merit in her novels: at times she too is writing a kind of fable, most notably in her first novel, *Mary Barton*. Here the portrait of the manufacturing class and of trade unionism is the worst kind of caricature, crude, very simplified, stereotyped and lacking both the bite of humour and its frank admission of bias and exaggeration. But strengths and weaknesses are often very intimately associated and if we pay for this absence of satire by such embarrassing and implausible crudities, we also gain the particularly intimate, alert and live creations of her sympathy, which manage, almost miraculously, to stay well on this side of sentimentality.

Pollard has truly said that Mrs. Gaskell 'is never a propagandist; or if she is, she is only a propagandist for sympathy'. This seems to point to the heart of her individuality as a novelist, as well as showing the way to reconcile the praise of her sociological imagination with that of her psychological powers. If I had to fix a label to her special contribution to what we conveniently call 'The English novel', I would describe her as essentially a novelist of sensibility. It is a phrase which describes her changing powers throughout her career. Although she wrote only six important novels, one fine *nouvelle*, *Cousin Phillis*, and one of the best Victorian biographies, *The Life of Charlotte Brontë*, (as well as many stories and sketches, some good but many really very undistinguished), her talent is a very various one.

Mrs. Gaskell did not say a great deal about her art but what she did say provides an excellent entry into the imagined world of her novels. That very phrase, 'imagined world', is a commonplace but generally useful critical formula, expressing the novel's inventiveness, unity, and double concern with the individual life and the portrayal of environment. But it seems rather inappropriately used of Mrs. Gaskell. When she talks about her novels, she insists, rather as D. H. Lawrence did, on her own therapeutic relation to her creations. This comes out very noticeably, for instance, when she compares her own writing with that of Charlotte Brontë, whom she knew and responded to so sympathetically. She says this, in a letter of April, 1853:

> The difference between Miss Brontë and me is that she puts all her naughtiness into her books, and I put all my goodness. I am sure that she works off a great deal that is morbid *into* her writing, and *out* of her life; and my books are so far better than I am that I often feel ashamed of having written them and as if I were a hypocrite.

In no way at odds with this comparison, I think, is her suggestion that *Mary Barton* was a novel which perhaps suffered from working off too much that was morbid into the novel out of her life. It is well known that she undertook the novel, at her husband's suggestion, after the death of her ten-month-old son from scarlet fever, and she talks revealingly about its darkness and its origin in what she thinks might be 'a wrong motive for writing . . . sure only to produce a failure'. She saw the novel as an especially effective refuge and calm refreshment for women, but concluded, after a good deal of wounding criticism, not entirely of an aesthetic kind, that she was perhaps in error when she used the composition of the novel as a 'refuge to exclude the memory of painful scenes which would force themselves upon my remembrance'.

To begin then, with *Mary Barton*. Seeing it as a novel of sensibility is essential when we look at its origin in personal suffering, and when we look at her reactions to the criticism of the novel, so different from the confident resentment of insensitivity which can be found, for instance, in George Eliot. In Mrs. Gaskell's self-doubting, honestly explanatory and searching comments on the response (not so much of literary critics as of people in Manchester of whom she knew) can be found

the sense of a wounded nerve of feeling disappointed or frustrated in the very act of heartfelt appeal. She has this to say
in a letter about the possible imbalance or injustice which certain readers felt about the novel:

> I can remember now that the prevailing thought in my mind
> at the time when the tale was silently forming itself and
> impressing me with the force of a reality, was the seeming
> injustice of the inequalities of Fortune. Now, if they oc-
> casionally appeared unjust to the more fortunate, they must
> bewilder an ignorant man full of rude, illogical thought, and
> full also of sympathy for suffering which appealed to him
> through his senses. I fancied I saw how all this might lead
> to a course of action which might appear right for a time to
> the bewildered mind of such a one, but that this course of
> action, violating the eternal laws of God, would bring with
> it its own punishment of an avenging conscience far more
> difficult to bear than any worldly privation. Such thoughts
> I now believe, on looking back, to have been the origin of
> the book. 'John Barton' was the original title of the book.

Mary Barton, as it was eventually called, is a novel which
cuts a deep channel both for the personal bereavement and
her sympathy for the sufferings of the industrial poor. Those
feelings are so merged in their profound and fierce flow that
I would make no attempt to speculate about their causal relation: feelings for children are conspicuous, and highly relevant in the book, but coming invariably out of all such
feelings, from every aspect of this story of family unity, disintegration and pain, is a bewildered and frustrated social questioning. Arthur Pollard quotes her attempt to reason with a
poor man about his bitter hostility to the rich, and his answer,
reasoned in tears, 'Aye, ma'am but have ye ever seen a child
clemmed to death.' *Mary Barton* begins with a revised version
of this question when John Barton asks what the 'gentlefolk'
have ever done for him:

> If my child lies dying (as poor Tom lay, with his white lips
> quivering, for want of better food than I could give him),
> does the rich man bring the wine or broth that will save his
> life?

The novel is punctuated by comments on child-death. Some
are very muted, and no less touching for that, as in the words
'the aged, the feeble, the children, when they die, are scarcely
noted by the world'. Some are more strikingly personal. More-

over, the novel insistently takes us back to the childhood even of the adult characters, and certainly two of the long digressions (sometimes criticized as instances of imperfect grasp of construction) seem to be justified by this insistence. Job Legh's story of how he and his friend brought their granddaughter Margaret, as a small and very helpless baby, from London to Manchester, and Alice Wilson's tales of her childhood (to which she reverts in her happy deathbed) both give new colour to the primary feeling for children. Job's story has a comic, even grotesque, way of loving and pathetic appeal, Alice's has a radiant, innocent, pastoral joy. Not only is there this variety of emotional colour, and the much-needed relief from the horrors and desolations of the child-deaths, but also there is always Mrs. Gaskell's characteristic social and psychological particularity. I would claim that it is this particularity that distinguishes her 'morbidity' from the strong general demands, sentimental and distastefully morbid, of Dickens's Nell and Tiny Tim. Her morbidity is excessive, in a strict aesthetic sense, taking us out of the novel in a way which is both painful and under-distanced, but which also makes it appropriately painful propaganda for the sympathies. It is revelatory fiction such as George Eliot was trying to write in *Scenes of Clerical Life*, but its materials have a horror, pity and passionate hysteria, which find no place in George Eliot.

This hysteria is in the materials. Mrs. Gaskell dramatizes the passions, but controls them and keeps them individual. At times she steps outside the story to reason and explain, to placate her gentle reader and beg a tolerance for the violence of these agitators and assassins, but then she says, 'Let us now return to individuals'. Her sensibility takes in and shows the full range of experience, to take us, as Zola does, from comfort to bleakness, from nourishment to starvation, from some small colour and ornament to bareness and squalor. The interestingness of the novel and its emotional appeal go together. She wants to show the fall from one state to a worse, like any tragedian. She wants also to show, in a sharply argumentative way, the working class culture, its ceremony, sociability, hospitality, song and science. Thus she creates not only a realistic picture of the culture (in a way that Gissing, when he takes us inside the houses and habits of the poor, usually fails to do), but gives animation and richness to what is not just a fable, and shows not the being of two nations, but their becoming. If she simply contrasted the starvation and disease in the poor home with the breakfasting of the rich (as she does at one point in the novel) we would have an effective simplification but as a less complete picture, and, ultimately, a less potent appeal to the heart. Hers is, like George Eliot's, a very conservative imagination, and these novels combine a realistic report with a very modest demand, not for a radical redistribution, but for a minimal nourishment for body and soul.

A similar truthfulness comes out of her knowledge that her two nations are not all that separate in origins: she knows Mrs. Carson, who was working-class, is particularly isolated and barren because she has no resources, and we appreciate also the importance of goods and money, in a novel about the material, not the hereditary, basis of class, about labour and capital, not about blood and rank. I stress this truthfulness because the novel's plotting, as too often in Mrs. Gaskell, is strained and even implausible. She said that John Barton was her hero, the character round whom 'all the others formed themselves . . . the person with whom all my sympathies went, with whom I tried to identify myself at the time, because I believed from personal observation that such men were not uncommon', and his displacement is the novel's great failing. Her publishers apparently persuaded her to call the novel *Mary Barton*, but the chief cause for the change must be the shift in the emotional centre. With John's guilt comes his inevitable absence from the scene, and our lack of access to his inner life. Though the track of Mary's feelings has from the beginning been woven in with his, it too rather thins out in the more heavily plotted final episodes, where the novel turns from sensitive social appeal and psychology to the sensational, highly active, and rather over-optimistic conclusion. It is perhaps because of the powers of feeling in the main body of the novel that the last third is so disappointing.

Like *Mary Barton*, the other novels, whatever their material and themes, have this potency and variety of feeling. Even the stagey villain, Harry Carson, his father, and Esther, the prostitute, lose a little of their staginess in being brought into the mainstream of feeling: we see them too as children and parents, not as divided from the rest of the action in melodramatic stereotype throughout. The only other novel which shares the partial staginess and the over-optimistc ending is *Ruth*, another social novel, separated from *Mary Barton* by *Cranford*, and thus making it impossible for us to talk about Mrs. Gaskell's 'sociological period'.

Mary Barton's powerful topicality (as a novel about Chartism appearing less than ten years after the Charter had been rejected, and at a time of depression, insecurity, and great want) made it a successful and much-discussed novel. *Ruth* had a similar success. It was very widely reviewed, receiving high praise for its truth and moral beauty, as well as hostility and disapproval. Mrs. Gaskell was deeply hurt by the disapproval, but even though the book was banned by fathers of families and even burnt, she believed in its seriousness and fervour. There are perhaps two chief reasons for the antagonism it aroused: its subject, which was seduction and illegitimacy, and its theme, that of Hardy's *Tess*, the moral innocence of the seduced girl.

It is in fact a very narrowly didactic book, which deals with a much more simply saintly woman than Tess, and which is a fable of atonement, by love and death. One might say that Ruth's nobility almost puts her beyond the typical social problem which she is intended to represent. The book has certain flaws: it begins by showing the seduction of a very simple little girl, and eventually shows her as a much more intelligent and complex woman, rather startlingly enlarging her character and creating a resolution which to my mind makes for disunity and implausibility. We may very well understand how the flaw came about. Mrs. Gaskell shows the inner life of Ruth sporadically, so that some of her reactions are available, some rather arbitrarily absent. The necessary sexual reticence of the Victorian novel, even in the forties, meant that our knowledge of Ruth is really very incomplete, and though some aspects of her sensibility are very finely presented —like her reactions to the natural scene and to people in Wales —some of the portraiture is rather external. In the later parts of the novel Ruth's fears and insecurity about her child, especially when her seducer comes back into her life, are movingly and persistently shown, as are the feelings and moral life of the Bensons and the Bradshaws. Live and moving too is the more reticent but decorous treatment of the alienation and reserve of Leonard, the child, after he finds out that he is illegitimate, and the breaking of shame by eloquent pride in the moment when he finds that his mother is a beloved public heroine. But there are ellipses and dead patches in the novel, and the apotheosis by death seems at once inevitable, and unadventurous. Unlike *Mary Barton* and *North and South*, the novel fails to give a complete enough rendering of its characters. What is meant to be another typical plea on behalf of social suffering becomes inappropriately idealized— why plead for saints like Ruth?—and over-simplified—how about the sympathy needed by more ordinary victims of the social traps? But it must be admitted that the idealized portrait has considerable beauty and if the novel is read as a study in saintliness rather than in sin, its humanity and drama will be more impressive.

Mrs. Gaskell's novels always have the interest of particularity. Ruth's idealization never takes off from the solid earth to become stereotyped or lachrymose, like the portraits of Agnes Wickfield or Esther Summerson. In *Ruth* there is the solidity and vividness of the comic-serious relationships of the Bensons and the Bradshaws, the enacted and implied complexity of Jemima Bradshaw, and the unpatronizing beauty and humour of the characterization of the servant, Sally. In *North and South*, the best of the three social novels, there is this kind of solid and varied realism of character and a much freer treatment of the element of fable. Mrs. Gaskell realizes at this stage that fictions are created by people, necessarily but falsely, and that degree of simplification and crudity which escaped her control in *Mary Barton* and *Ruth* seems, in this remarkable novel, to have been assimilated, dramatized, and finally criticized. In *North and South* it is the characters, not only the author, who construct fables. The novel shows the dangerous inadequacy of fables, and its characters are educated out of their fictions and face the complexity of loving, working, serving, and leading. Having said this, I must add that the novel's ability to face complexity and do, as George Eliot said we must, 'without opiates', is in the end limited. Like most Victorian novels, it mends matters with authorial magic, and the problems of love and industrial failure are solved and dismissed by coincidence and that favourite device of the bourgeois novel, the unexpected legacy.

Mrs. Gaskell shares these limitations with Dickens and George Eliot and Charlotte Brontë—with all the great Victorian novelists, perhaps, except the Thackeray of *Vanity Fair's* great, sour, truthful satire. In spite of them, she writes a novel of penetrating psychology. In the previous novels we are moved by the poignancy of feeling, which makes the ever-interesting and effectively appealing narrative medium, but in *North and South* there is a new element, of surprisingly psychological content. We are moved and held not just by the dramatic liveliness, but by what it reveals of human nature.

This revealed depth of content is the fact of human fiction, the fabling about *North* and *South* which forms the central dream of the novel. It is a dream dreamt by the heroine, Margaret Hale, and like many human dreams, it is dreamt as a stabilizing reaction to instability. Intuitively or deliberately, Mrs. Gaskell shows Margaret on the eve of returning to the place and parents she has known only discontinuously during her adolescence. Her return brings her not the pastoral peace and family joy she expects and needs, after the disruptions and oppressive joys of London life, but a father who is about to resign his ministry, and indeed a father and a mother who lean on her, heavily and pathetically. This is the first stage in her waking and dreaming : the pastoral dream and the childhood idyll fail. When the Hales move to the North, the dream returns again in a protective and temporarily restorative fashion. She has been teased in London for the sort of pastoral idealized picture she has of Helstone, the village of her childhood, and in the grim Darkshire where they try the new life, the pastoral dream is first needed, then tried, and, after a long, slow testing in complex experience and varied relations, found wanting.

It is not the only illusion in the novel. Matched with it, in strength, unity and partial plausibility, is Mr. Thornton's unenlightened belief in autonomy, freedom and power of master over worker. This is a dream which, like Margaret's, is dreamt by someone sufficiently sensitive and intelligent to allow intransigent experience to shatter the dream. Both dreams are theoretic, and when Margaret learns what the urban North is like, and when Thornton learns the humanity and limited freedom of his workers, theory collapses before the largeness and complexity of life as it is. As Arthur Pollard is careful to point out, Thornton remains a benevolent master, putting his faith in workers' welfare and good communication. Moreover, he does not succeed in trade but fails. As in the earlier novels, what is impressive is not a confident radicalism but a tentative questioning of the present, not a grasp of economics but a grasp of the individual case. She takes a step beyond *Mary Barton* and *Ruth* in the very muteness of *North and South* : the action is on a smaller, less heroic scale, and there is no trace of the stereotyped fable of *Mary Barton*.

The novel moves insistently from and between its two personal centres of feeling. At last her novel of sensibility is both balanced and complete. We oscillate between Margaret and Thornton, and their range of sensibility prominently includes pride, passion, anger, sensitive sympathy, and moral admiration. These passions largely make up the characters and their affi-

nity. They also unify the action as well as the characters because they are available, most genuinely, in the intimate
personal relationship of sexual and filial love, and in a series
of reactions to society that cut across class divisions. This kind
of emotional continuity and complexity is, in its very nature,
inaccessible to illustration, especially in an essay, and I can
only briefly refer to typically rich and mobile scenes like that
of Thornton's first proposal of marriage to Margaret, the scene
in which she first makes friends with Higgins and Bessy, and
the scene where Thornton first goes to see Higgins in his home.
You will notice the way Mrs. Gaskell always shows or tells—
usually both—what the characters are feeling, and how she
pushes on the emotional development and change variously
and continuously. There are no *lacunae* where you do not
know (and need to know) what the character is feeling, as in
Ruth. You will notice too how often the feelings are not specialized, not kept in separate compartments. Thornton's anger
at Margaret's refusal resembles his anger at Higgins' egalitarian
and rational honesty, and these strong characters can feel
furious and respectful as their pride and anger fight, against
each other's pride and anger, and against themselves. One of
the admirably honourable qualities in the characters of Mrs.
Gaskell is the reasonable passion. If Jane Austen is the first
English novelist to show and be aware of showing a reasonable
sexual love, so Mrs. Gaskell deserves some praise for showing,
with depth and delicacy, a reasonable pride, a reasonable anger,
a reasonable despair. The characters are animated, distinguished,
and, finally, unified by their feelings.

It is this dramatized sensibility, I believe, which takes us
over the weak spots of the action, like the melodramatic and
coincidental business of Frederick's return, Thornton's encounter with Margaret and her brother and the consequent misunderstanding. It is the display and analysis of passions and
intelligence which makes such an effective medium for what I
have called the theme of dreams and fables. Margaret is forced
by reason, respect and sympathy to see that North is not black
to South's white, and Thornton is forced by reason, respect
and sympathy to see that communication between master and
servant is not only possible but honourable, and that violence
and despair have their reasons, as well as their madness.

The novel has many complex moments of feeling that lie
beyond this simple account, and such complexities are present
in all the other novels, which are less conspicuous in their
social criticism. To go back to *Cranford*, her second novel, we

find there not only the charm, pathos, and humour for which it has always been celebrated, but a considerable complexity and subtlety in the presentation of feeling. It is a novel with a displaced personal centre, unlike the others. It is a deliberately handled, almost a Jamesian, displacement. The narrator is Mary Smith, whose sympathy and irony are both more sophisticated and more available than the sensibilities of any of the more involved characters, and with Mary we gradually accumulate a full view of the story. The true active centre is Miss Matty. We piece together, from retrospect, hint, and expressive incident, her timidity, her courage, her spinster's loneliness, her lost love, her family feeling and her suffering. Ultimately, when all is pieced together, it becomes a story of unguessed-at integrity. The bits fit together: Miss Matty's pride, consistency and real dignity when she, unlike the other dear ladies, assumes that they will not accept Mrs. Jamieson's afterthought invitation; her insistence on honouring the Town and County Bank note instead of buying the new dress; and her forbearance when Martha wants to have a follower: all these illustrative incidents create the strong side of Miss Matty, whom we, like Mary, first see as a sweet, eccentric, not very bright, rather dependent old lady. We piece together the story too, first seeing the man she might have married, in the opaque humour of the visit, which allows no tremble of sentiment to get through, and later learning slowly what had happened, through odd bits of gossip, and then in the news of his death. The piecemeal method, like the indirect discovery, is natural, in this most natural-seeming chronicle where naturalness is decorous, and moving, as we accumulate impressions in a continuous process of slight shocks and revisions. Moreover, the rambling and anecdotal form picks up unity in this process. What looked at first like (and was probably started as) a series of episodic sketches, turns out to have a very cunning continuity, quality, and power to move. What looked like insipidity or mere charm turns out to rebuke us for having jumped to interpret it as insipidity or mere charm. Cranford teaches us, by a dynamic process, not to be too easily charmed by quaintness, not to pity precipitately what we may have eventually also to admire. Without wishing to analyse its delicacy out of existence, I should like to praise it for the kind of delicacy which reveals strength. It is an apparently unassuming novel, and its apparent charm and sweetness are as profound and as deceptive as Miss Matty's. It is a novel whose form is perfectly appropriate to its content, so that the two are not separable.

Cousin Phillis, Sylvia's Lovers, and *Wives and Daughters,* coming together, in that order, at the end of Mrs Gaskell's short life, all possess the perfection and subtlety of *Cranford* and add new profundities of vision and feeling. *Cousin Phillis,* her very best piece of short fiction, also has a displaced and detached narrator. Paul Manning is rather like Nelly Dean, in *Wuthering Heights,* not all that detached from the passions he observes and narrates. Again, by a slight delicate shift of a kind usually praised in Henry James, Mrs. Gaskell makes a perfect movement from expectation to surprise. We learn to read Paul as narrator, but in the precipitating event of the story, he becomes a responsible agent, and yet preserves the observer's role, which has encouraged his fault and determines the nature of his punishment. It is also, like *Wives and Daughters,* a perfect instance of control and reserve : its joys and griefs are largely inner and unspoken ones, its very action is contained in the mind and in the heart. It is also, like everything she wrote, full of psychological variety. Mrs. Gaskell really has no minor characters, and both Holdsworth and Holman are as complete, complex, and surprising in their individuality as Phillis herself. The beautiful and bookish country girl, vulnerable, strong, romantic, realistic, loving and sharp, is a brilliant creation who might even, read at the wrong time, bring out a certain softness in Hardy's Tess.

Wives and Daughters, like *Cousin Phillis,* reveals almost unbearable sadness, and shows how human beings bear it. The intensity of grief and the reserve or resolve that makes heartbreak endurable or even mendable, is shown in Molly Gibson, with a patience, pride, and self-aware humour which belongs both to the presentation and to the character. The novel is most remarkably modest, quiet and genial. Molly's passionate feelings are recognized and proffered in a complexity which cannot even be named—does she feel 'anger, dislike, indignation', her author asks, and takes refuge in the intensity and open suggestiveness of an image : 'It was as if the piece of solid ground on which she stood had broken from the shore, and she was drifting out into an infinite sea alone'. Molly's loss of her happy life with her father, then later, the loss of her lover, and later still, the temporary loss of her good name, are all fairly small and fairly private griefs, compared with the deaths and pangs and shames in *Mary Barton, Ruth,* or even *North and South,* but they are real, important, and fully expressive of the problems of moral and social growth and adjustment.

Molly and Sylvia of *Sylvia's Lovers*, in my opinion Mrs. Gaskell's greatest novel, are interesting passive characters, whose lives, like those of many women in and out of fiction, tend to be rather more manipulated than the lives of men. Their passiveness, however, is quite different. Sylvia's life is highly determined, and by social forces: her lover is carried off by the press-gang, her father hanged for violence against the gang, her mother's reason destroyed, and her marriage made by the isolation, desolation and economic dependence brought about by all these incidents. But her feelings, unlike Molly's, are not only strong but have to be expressed: and if she is acted upon, her vitality of feeling becomes an active force. It attacks and exiles her husband in its sheer ferocity. But her passions are complex, and if Philip had learnt to read them as we do, he would have seen her characteristic shift, brought about by sympathy and by reason, from rejection to forgiveness. In *Sylvia's Lovers* and *Wives and Daughters* Mrs. Gaskell seems less interested in the development of sensibility, as in some of the earlier novels, than in its individual pattern, and consequences. She shows, in a way very anticipatory of Hardy, the ironic clash between individual passions. Mrs. Gaskell sets out the kind of vulnerability, innocence, pride, and acceptance, which we will find typical of Molly's adult life, in the early scene where Molly is lost and neglected and let down by her future stepmother. In the varying crises of the novel, the same pattern of feeling and response is provoked, developed, and worked out. Similarly, Sylvia's passionateness, sensuousness, imaginative sympathy, and toughness are shown in the first scene when she goes to buy a cloak and stays to cheer and grieve with the crowd, and are repeated later, many times. The cycle returns most importantly when she refuses to forgive the man responsible for her father's death, but then recoils on her own hardness. This anticipates the revengeful unforgiving passion and recoil to love, with which she meets the discovery of Philip's deception. Philip's track of feeling plays against and with hers, and they are both two of the most moving, emotionally complex and morally tolerant studies of human strength and weakness in the English novel. Sylvia has a marvellous vitality and range of passions which is seldom shown in fiction apart from high intelligence. And the novel's ending, which brings us face to face with inevitable hurt, unnecessary hurt, spent life, new life, strong love, endurance, exhaustion, and the joining of reconciliation with parting, is one of the saddest experiences in the range of Mrs. Gaskell's imaginative achievement.

Mrs. Gaskell wrote to tell George Eliot how much she admired *Scenes of Clerical Life* and *Adam Bede*, and George Eliot replied saying that she had been aware that her attitude to Life and Art 'had some affinity with the feeling which . . . inspired "Cranford" and the earlier chapters of "Mary Barton" ', and had read *Cranford* while writing *Scenes* and *Mary Barton* while writing *Adam Bede*. What she thought about the affinity is a matter for guessing. We know that she also liked *The Life of Charlotte Brontë* and *Sylvia's Lovers* but was critical of the "dramatic effect" and "love of sharp contrasts" ' which she said were obstacles to complete sympathy and typicality in *Ruth*. She rather liked such contrasts herself, though they were perhaps given subtlety and finesse by the greater degree of complexity which they generally possess. There is an affinity between her early work and Mrs. Gaskell's attitude to life and art, in their sympathy, a quality of the imagination not restricted to the creativity of art. It is interesting that George Eliot speaks of the affinity as felt in the early work. In *Scenes* there is not only the deliberate attempt to show ordinariness and average sensibility, but even the convention of a spectator's *persona*. There is also the half-critical but sympathetic reaction to quaintness and humour. But such novelistic affinity was not lasting. The sympathy that showed itself in analysis of average lives and ordinary sensibility created all Mrs. Gaskell's novels, but none of George Eliot's, except for the three stories in *Scenes* and *Silas Marner*, all, significantly, short pieces. She began by wanting to show ordinary life to over-stimulated palates and sensational expectations, but very soon moved from homely realism to what was truly her *métier*, the drama of intellect and sensibility in strong and unusual characters.

We should carefully distinguish the social and the psychological aims here. Both novelists set out, and succeeded, in showing the lower-class sensibility and suffering, after the manner of Dutch painting, as George Eliot says in *Adam Bede*. But Mrs. Gaskell is very much more socially and politically didactic, despite her conservatism, than George Eliot, and one might argue too that she is more sharply sceptical and less complacent than George Eliot in her treatment of labour-relations in *Adam Bede* or of political agitation in *Felix Holt*. George Eliot is much more confident of the rightness of Adam's attitude to his more frivolous fellow-workers, and of the wrong-ness of the mob-violence than Mrs. Gaskell's more troubled questioning ever allows her to be. George Eliot seldom goes into the psychology of the 'wrong' action as sympathetically as Mrs. Gaskell. Indeed, one reason for the revival of interest in Mrs. Gaskell may lie in her appealing lack of moral ab-solutism. George Eliot is much closer to the very unmodern Shavian character who is certain of the difference between right and wrong, both in political and personal morality. She is also more rationally in control of her moral system. When she criticized Mrs. Gaskell for siding so simply with Branwell Brontë, we can perhaps see her rationality set against the more impetuous sympathies of the older novelist. The com-parison is ironic though, since it was Mrs. Gaskell who wrote both to admire the younger woman's novels *and* to wish that she was really Mrs. Lewes. But even George Eliot's social deviation was moral and rational, perhaps a little doctrinaire.

What George Eliot swiftly moves on to do is to depict the social and personal dramas whose protagonist has con-siderable stature. Adam Bede, she says, is not an ordinary man. His rationality, his intelligence, and his creative competence make him the first of her line of extraordinary heroes and heroines. They are always embedded in a 'world' of Amos Bartons, Silas Marners, and Hetty Sorrels, but their mind always provides a complex and articulate stage for inner action. George Eliot's characters have a capacity for moral action and development which seem, pretty clearly, to derive from her own experience, transformed, varied, and inventively re-crea-ted though it was.

Marian Evans, as she was born, had the kind of heavily plotted life of crisis that we find in her novels. Even as a young woman, she was very sensitive to periodicity, discontinuity, and development. What seems to have been a temperamental cyclical quality must have encouraged and in its turn been further provoked by larger crises. George Eliot is very like Wordsworth in the way she seems to need and perhaps to create crises which force a formulation of identity. They shared an acute sense of continuity and discontinuity: of needing and losing a feeling of temporal unity in which past, present, and even future seemed to be linked, and of needing and losing a feeling of a unity of sensibility, in which reason and the passions seemed to be linked. George Eliot can see life as divided into poetry and prose, as a series of movements and losses, of moving from 'the poetry of girlhood' 'the poetry of love and marriage' 'the poetry of maternity' and 'the very poetry of duty' into the world of 'naked prose'. This kind of pattern can be very easily traced in most of her novels, as a process of illusion and vision which takes us from dream to dream until we are—at times by assumption rather than fictional demonstration—'nearer reality'. The whole process is a mid-Victorian evolutionary myth, itself an illusion persuasively grounded on an awareness of the psychological processes of deception, dream and drug.

In her personal life, however, we see a series of crises arranged, naturally enough, in a less evolutionary sequence. There was the first crisis of identity and continuity when, in 1848, she stopped going to church, in an almost sacramental disclosure of her loss of Christian faith. There followed a very troubling sense of dislocation, uprootedness, and subsequently an attempt to restore good relations with her father, in the realization that there was emotional continuity even if belief had been sharply broken. The second crisis, about which we know rather little, in terms of the chronicle of inner life, comes in 1854, when she went to Europe with George Henry Lewes. In her letters to some of her friends, to whom she can admit the truth about their unmarried 'marriage', and in a letter to her brother Isaac, in which she cannot tell the truth, the attempt to hang on the past, and to the personal tradition of family unity, is plain. It is this need for a temporal and personal unity which explains her gratification when, on her marriage to John Cross, Isaac wrote to break the long silence and to forgive.

Her own life was no doubt even more eroded and discontinuous than we know, but these two very conspicuous crises involved a break with the past, choice and conflict between emotional conservatism and intellectual and emotional courage, and provide the model for her art. Characteristic imagery of her novels always reminds us of the importance of a sense of unity: the image of the labyrinth, the snapped thread, the path, and the current, amongst others, all stand as emblems for the dramatic choices and conflicts to be found in her life and in her books.

It is the content as well as the structure of personal experience that creates art from life. Because she rejected Evangelicalism, which at some stages was as anti-life and narrowly puritanical as her aunt's and Dinah's Methodism, in favour of a life-devoted humanism, her novels consistently and persistently make a plea for social love, fellowship, duty to people. If the insistence on human relationship as a duty replaces the Christian ethic, (in her case, as seen in some of her early gloomy letters, an especially uncreative and unattractive ethic), so the sense of collective creation took the place of the Christian immortality. The Positivist hymn, 'O let me join the choir invisible' shows this replacement, and so also does the emphasis placed in the novels on the contribution to society, like Adam Bede's and Caleb Garth's land-improvements, or—twisted ironically—Rosamond Vincy's deceptive legacy from a fine musician's dead touch.

There is the value, too, attached to moral self-determinism, as it is seen in all the novels but most plainly in the wrong moral choices of Tito Melema in *Romola*, set out as a pattern of deterioration, and the right moral choices of Maggie, set out as a rather more complex and unsteady pattern of growth. This gives to the novels something like the systematic, confident, and usually optimistic framework of the Christian Providence novels of Defoe or Charlotte Brontë. It is the kind of firm moral pattern and reference that is both typically Victorian in its humanist substitutions, and typical of George Eliot.

If this kind of pattern were the only moral interest to be found in the novels of George Eliot, the reader would do well to stay with Mrs. Gaskell. But George Eliot's imagination creates characters, events and relationships that have an individual colour and complexity that light up the system, create great novels, make sense to us today, make a picture out of the diagram, *incarnate* (her word) the ideas.

Scenes of Clerical Life show how soon she could look sympathetically at the religious life, whether successful or unsuccessful, and they show too her interest, even within the span of fairly short stories (first serialized as two-part tales in *Blackwood's Edinburgh Magazine*) in the ethic of love. She dramatizes lovingly both the great demands of human intimacy and need, and Wordworth's 'little, nameless, unremembered acts/Of kindness and of love', with their warming or restorative powers. The *Scenes* show, too, her interest in human development, though this is shown in a very simplified pattern, and is sometimes rather said to have happened than shown to have happened. On the whole, the process of growth is not melodramatized but implied in the crucial moment, rather than set out at length. There is the awakening moment, as when Caterina strikes the piano, an incident which very effectively dramatizes and particularizes the metaphor of 'striking a chord' and plausibly restores past feeling after breakdown. There is the temporary growth, which is *not* a final transformation, when Amos Barton throws himself on his wife's grave not only in grief but in the desperate effort to retain grief. Such events show George Eliot's emphasis on the continuity of feeling.

If there are these good moments, there are also the weak ones, such as the assumption or appearance of growth and conversation or change in Janet Dempster, Tryan or Gilfil, where difficulties are passed over and the resounding triumph over the victory of love is scarcely earned. But the *Scenes* have good moments of humour, and at their best an honest, Wordsworthian gaucheness.

George Eliot's psychological powers were no doubt inhibited by the chosen materials. Unlike Mrs. Gaskell, she needed a highly complex intellectual and creative centre in character. Once this is achieved, as in Adam, Maggie, Dorothea, Felix, Esther, Romola, Gwendolen, Deronda, Mordecai, she can then produce marvellously live and sympathetic small studies of the simple soul. Hetty Sorrel's narrow little fantasy-life, with scarcely room in it for more than clothes and faces, is an animated and functional miniature, but the central characters of Adam and Arthur give George Eliot her proper scope. In them she takes time and space to show two very different types of moral character, both changing, both clearly conditioned by position, possessions, and economic morality, both in a way self-regarding and narrow, even though one acts benevolently and the other selfishly. Perhaps we can see here why a novelist who so delighted in antithesis, both of character and event, should criticize the contrasts in Mrs. Gaskell. George Eliot's formalism is always overlaid and qualified by a complex pattern of resemblance, difference, and change. Her contrasts are very mobile, so that when we think we are reading them accurately, we may be caught out, and suddenly forced to see Dinah's limitations of sympathy, as well as Hetty's or Adam's hardness as well as Arthur's.

The novels of George Eliot depend on a constant presence and movement of feeling, like Mrs. Gaskell's, but the more intellectualized subject makes for a cross-hatching of feeling and analysis. Mrs. Gaskell is the kind of novelist whose inner action is filled to the brim by the passions and reflections of the characters. George Eliot's, despite her intellectually elo-quent characters, has a space between the life of the created world and the world of author and reader. There was a time, not so long ago, when it was necessary to explain and justify the insistent presence and commentary of the omniscient author, in the novels of George Eliot, but criticism during the last ten years has shown the mobility, the varying function, and the dramatization of the author's presence, both in lan-guage and imagery. It would be a mistake, however, to insist too strongly on George Eliot's dramatic merits. Henry James, happily and deservedly praising his own creation in the Pre-face to *The Portrait of a Lady*, said that he had tried to achieve —and believed he had achieved—scenes of inner action which had 'the vivacity of picture and the economy of drama'. George Eliot's own commentary has the vivacity, but not the economy. It is an essential part of her individuality as a nove-list that there should be this uneconomical spread, the excess of reflection.

It is this authorial centre from which the feelings of the novel are directed, and I would wish to emphasize its sen-sibility, as well as its intellectual activity. It is very rare to find the author's voice commenting in order simply to explain or analyse: even where explanation and analysis is present, it is presented in the medium of feeling. Because George Eliot tends to have a fairly small spectrum of feeling 'for' and 'about' her characters, the light and shade is chiefly presented in the dramatized actions and language, and in each novel there is a movement to and from this drama and the personal centre. Her voice tends to speak compassionately, sometimes satirically, sometimes in a combination of irony and sympathy, sometimes affectionately, sometimes wryly. It speaks 'for' and 'about' the characters but it also speaks 'for' and 'about' a generalized human nature, using 'we' and 'you' and 'I' in a roughly similar inclusive fashion. When it pities, it pities 'all poor mortals'; when it caresses (which it sometimes does too heavily), it caresses a human object, which, like any human object, needs love; when it praises, it praises the common, not the rare, virtues. For although George Eliot puts in the centre of action characters who are powerful, energetic, crea-tive, and intelligent, she keeps in the highroad of human powers, and even her exceptional characters are representa-tive. Compared with the central characters of Mrs. Gaskell, and for that matter, Thackeray, and Dickens too, her charac-ters have considerable imagination, but in their relation to their environment, in their moral mixture and complexity, and in their passions, they are typical enough. This typicality is very important to George Eliot, in part because she wants, like Wordsworth, to write an unspecialized literature of man speaking to men, *from* and *of* what she constantly calls the 'human lot', in part because it allows her to move naturally and freely from particularity of character and action to the generalization that bridges the experience central in the novel to the unknown but assumed experience of the reader.

In *Scenes* and from time to time in other places too, she miscalculates her tone, reaches too eagerly towards us, is too arch, too intense, too solicitous, too affectionate. In a sense it seems wrong to do what we generally do, and call these artistic faults. When I use the concept of miscalculation, it suggests a control of personality which is usually impossible, for the voice of George Eliot is usually offensive, when it is offensive, not on aesthetic grounds, but as human voices are offensive, distasteful as personality. And at times particularly distasteful, no doubt, because speaking in a voice of unfashionable feeling, vibrating richly and warmly where we like our voices to be cool, expansive where we like dry contraction and laconic understatement, uninhibited where we are inhibited, either from distrust or fear.

In *The Mill on the Floss* George Eliot creates a picture of imaginative richness which has most plainly a reference back to her own experience. It is not indulgent, even in its portrayal of Maggie, in being, as Leavis suggests in *The Great Tradition*, insufficiently critical. It is, on the contrary, very carefully critical of Maggie, both in direct commentary and through the voice of Philip : it criticizes Maggie's shift from one dream to another, it criticizes her religiosity and her lack of self-knowledge. Where it is indulgent—and I think it is 'indulgent' and not 'self-indulgent'—it is in pitying while it criticizes, in pouring over Maggie, or Mr. Tulliver, or Philip, in a constant flowing of love, knowing and maternal. It is also indulgent in the resolution by plot, the restoration of the dream of childhood, relationship, and total understanding in the flood.

George Eliot is a very deliberate artist who builds up the appropriate structure by imagery, casual-seeming *double entendre*—'She'll tumble in one day'—landscape, and folk-tradition. But in spite of the aesthetic unity of the river imagery, in spite of the foreground and background of the great waters, their economic importance and their wild threat, there is no escaping the feeling that George Eliot provided Maggie and Tom with a special Providence which is more damaging than we can suggest by simply calling it unrealistic or melodramatic. It is neither: people are killed by storm and flood, and this flood is given plenty of substance. But it does go right against the grain of the novel's sensibility and argument, which concern themselves with an evolutionary movement away from dream towards waking, from poetry to naked prose. In what seems to me George Eliot's richest and most particularized piece of characterization, Maggie is presented, against her environment, family, education, and religion, as struggling to know and not to escape or to delude herself. At each stage of shedding the dream or the drugging poem, she moves into another, slightly less delusive stage of dream or poetry. We should observe, by the way, that when George Eliot uses the idea of moving from poetry to prose, she is thinking in terms of Romantic poetry. Maggie uses Scott and Byron as escape, Esther Lyon and Mrs. Transome, in *Felix Holt*, use Byron and Chateaubriand. Maggie first makes childish make-believe daydreams, simply cutting out unpleasant friction and shaping the experience anew, to her liking. Later, she finds literature an effective aid to this process, when her intelligence and experience cease to tolerate the cruder forms of wish-fulfilling shape-making. Later still, when the golden gates of childhood close, and she and Tom go home to illness, loss and the frightening responsibility for the once-responsible parents, literature fails too. George Eliot is very good indeed on the desolation which fills Maggie's life between illusions, and her portrayal of ennui, bewilderment, inactivity and misery, all joined together in a feeling defying the power of naming, is painful in its sharpness and truth. But humankind cannot live long without a dream, and Maggie is ripe for religious illusion. Again, George Eliot shows Maggie's conversion with truth and sympathy, observing without harshness, the element of self-indulgence and histrionics. What is perhaps even more remarkable an achievement for such a systematic moralist as George Eliot is the next stage in Maggie's process, which is not given the evolutionary treatment, but shown, very quietly and unfussily, as sliding back into the pre-religious stage of self-gratification. At this stage various dreams merge: Maggie is scarcely carrying out her self-denying intention, but she does retain something of the Thomas à Kempis' altruism. She reverts to Scott, and she is fed, too, by a new source of energizing illusion, the romantic companionship with Philip which is an undemanding form of relationship, a kind of loving which can be refuge and calm repose. Finally, she is forced to discard all the illusions, after a crisis of moral choice and thoroughly miserable and motivated renunciation which seems to reverse George Eliot's own moral choice, in going to live with Lewes, while bringing out plainly the nature of her personal ethic. Maggie refuses to break an unofficial engagement, George Eliot committed adultery; Maggie renounces Stephen on the grounds of feeling and duty, to people, not laws, George Eliot committed herself to Lewes for similar reasons. In the most subtle way the novel disguises, socializes, but also defends George Eliot's own social deviation. In another subtle way Maggie's extreme conversion to religious self-denial and subsequent partial return to her 'habitual self' reverses but uses George Eliot's own conversion from Christianity. The novel is a thoroughly externalized but very personal story. It is also rich, complex, and complete in its rendering of the processes of frustration, exhaustion, and desire. Not only in the figure of Maggie, but also in the characters of Tom, Mr. Tulliver and Philip, George Eliot's ability to show and to analyse reveals itself in very moving and various human materials. The powerful sensibility and imagination of Maggie placed in the centre, George Eliot's ability to substantiate the more average human stuff of Mr. and Mrs. Tulliver is given a subordinate but adequate place. When the wife persuades the husband to work for Wakem, or when Tulliver makes Tom write the vow for vengeance in the family Bible, George Eliot writes a wonderfully individualized version of the stuff of human crisis: the ties of marriage, for instance, are seen as powerfully binding and strangling, against the background of country and family ritual and tradition and in the words of folk-saying, proverb, cliché and the Bible.

It is this kind of richness and honesty which is falsified when George Eliot answers her heroine's final prayer, to spare her further stages of pain and loss. In her other novels, which grow in scale and intellectual analysis, there is always a tension, never quite satisfactorily concluded, between a truthful rendering of people and the meliorist attempt to show at least the possibilities of love, content, harmony. It is a kind of tension not found in Mrs. Gaskell or the Brontës, and it reveals, I think, the imaginative powers and ambitions of George Eliot's greater genius. She was, like Dickens, writing the kind of novel that asked all the questions, and was at least aware of a whole range of possible answers.

She asks about the environment; contemporary society,

ideal society and society localized somewhere in history usually in the early nineteenth century, except in *Romola* and the fully contemporary *Daniel Deronda*. So she handles three periods at once, combining the carefully researched past history (of say, a County town in the 1830s), the present time which is implied or symbolized through historical reference (as the Second Reform Bill is in the First Reform Bill), and the future, in implications for the progress of societies shown through criticism and ideals.

She handles, too, the moral questions of individual conduct: problems of earning a living, of marrying, of staying single, of finding marriage or your job good, bad, indifferent, bearable. She handles a very great range of relationships, all typical and sharply individualized: relationships between brother and sister, brother and brother, sister and sister, parents and children, husband and wife, passionate lovers, romantically sexless lovers, friends, master and servant in a very role-limited relation, master and servant in a free man-to-man relation, rivals, old people and young people, and so on, in a very long list indeed. The list's lengthiness must only be stressed at the same time as we insist on the individuality. All these relationships are dramatized so as to show the social and personal colours of, say, the Lammeter sisters in *Silas Marner*, or Fred Vincy and Rosamond, or Gwendolen Harleth and her mother, or the Princess Alcharisi and her son, but they are also all sufficiently typical, of social and psychological conditions and roles, to make their contribution to the total moral argument.

George Eliot is a very considerable artist, as we see when we shift from the human problems—the actualities and ideals which form the subject, the end of art—to the forms, methods, and style of the novelist. In the last four novels, *Romola*, *Felix Holt*, *Middlemarch*, and *Daniel Deronda* there is a constant experimentation with language and design. Sometimes it is a colossal failure, as with the translated Italian no-language of *Romola* (see Hemingway's *For Whom the Bell Tolls* for another, slightly less disastrous, version of the same answer) or in the poetic style of Mordecai in *Daniel Deronda*, where the imagery and syntax are adapted from the Old Testament and the poetic style of Jehuda Halevy. Sometimes it is a very subdued triumph of impersonation, as in the characteristic languages of *Middlemarch*, where no character lacks his appropriate style. There is always a discrimination, a realism, and an ordering in language. The language belongs to the author, and its irony, movement, and unity rely on a cross-reference from image to image or from phrase to phrase. The characters in Middlemarch, one by one—Dorothea, Rosamond, Fred—all ask, 'What can I do?' in an almost operatic arrangement of words, timbres, and pitch, though that effect is a very muted one. The characters in *Middlemarch* are comparatively described in imagery of water, and the characters in *Daniel Deronda* in the imagery of horses, riders, chariots, control and submission.

The experiment in form is, of course, as in all great art, an experiment in humane analysis and moral argument. The shape of the novel is the shape of the moral vision of experience. George Eliot's characteristic form, present early but fully developed and plain from *Romola* to *Daniel Deronda*, is that of the typical Victorian three-decker novel, the double or multiple action that we find in *Vanity Fair, Bleak House* and *Our Mutual Friend*. George Eliot was using a form typical of her time, shaped and conventionalized by reading habits, costs, serial publication and a demand for expansiveness. But she shapes the form for her purpose, and the form of *Felix Holt, Middlemarch* and *Daniel Deronda* is individual, each novel differing not only from a novel of multiple action by Dickens or Tolstoy, but from each other.

The double plot of *Romola* is the comparison of Romola and Savonarola, the contrast between problems and conflicts of duty and egoism, feeling and reason, in private and public life. The double plot of *Felix Holt*, (a novel which is too unified to be precisely described in this way) compares two Radicals, two kinds of political commitment and action, two classes. The act of contrast and comparison creates the form, but we also have to analyse it in terms of the relationships of the parts in final unity, for the convergence comes about differently, and individually, in each novel. In *Felix Holt* the destinies and actions converge, and what has been ironically a relationship visible to the reader but not to the character, breaks the narrative irony to become junction and discovery. After the tension, the novel's final scenes dissolve the unity, and the double action is felt to diverge, startlingly converge, and diverge again. Each shift in relationship is expressive of the social and personal separations and joinings which form the subject of the novel. In *Daniel Deronda*, which has a more distinct double action, there is a similar narrative irony, though it is much more crucial and terrifying. Once more, there is a social division, though this time roughly between Gentile and Jewish ways of life. But the hero of *each* action is Daniel Deronda and the contrast and comparison made by the structure is made the more powerfully and ironically for this very strong unifying bond, like the bloodstream yoking Siamese twins. That conceit is an appropriate one, for Daniel has to break the bond, and Gwendolen has to bear the pain of its undreamt-of breaking. The reader's double vision has given him a special context for reading both ways of life, as social and personal histories, and has created the felt knowledge of the final break. George Eliot's formal comparisons in these three novels embody stories which generalize and also show the tragic differences and dissociations of the human lot.

Her greatest novel, written between *Felix Holt* and *Daniel Deronda*, is *Middlemarch*. Here the form is one of quadruple action, though once we begin to count the parts we might well feel impelled to enumerate even more divisions. The same kind of social ironies and personal isolations are pointed out as in the other three novels, but there is no special irony of ignorance and junction and separateness, only a series of small ironies, such as Lydgate's thoughts of Dorothea and the reader's silent answering superior knowledge. The multiple form of this novel is perhaps most expressive of two other ideas: the idea of equality of interest and the idea of contingency. The form is the perfect one for proving that George Eliot's 'we' is truly meant, for it creates a rotation which makes us displace each prominent character and move on to another. It creates a model of that illusion of centrality and that fact of typicality which the novel explicitly discusses. 'Why always Dorothea?' asks the novel on one famous occasion. The perfect proof of the question's sincerity is made in a form which refuses to allow central figures to engross our attention. There are a limited number of central figures, true, but the form acts as a model, not a total imitation, and its point seems to be clearly made. The theme of contingency is discovered in the form. It is a novel which sadly but imaginatively sees not the fixity of destiny, which is so limiting and also so morally terrifying in the portrayal of Tito Melema, but its flux, its selection. How free? how determined? asks the novel and shows the variety of possibilities. The very shifts of action, the transformation of minor character in one plot to major character in another, the chanciness, the permutations which come out of contrast and comparison, the generalization, the fast movement which seem at times to blur identity, all these aspects of the structure are expressive. It is a novel as astonishingly broad in social rendering as it is profound in inner analysis and drama. It impresses us passionately with the feeling that these highly differentiated people, these various moral commitments, these richly individualized styles, are made from the same humanity.

George Eliot is perhaps the greatest psychologist in the English novel, and it is important to see her departures from psychological realism. The deviations from her richly various complex norm, like Dinah, Felix, Daniel, Mordecai, are made in the interests of that passionate vision of human societies and moral action which was more important than perfected substance, than writing the good novel. All these characters have a complex enough psyche, but they have a certain fixity, a certain monolithic quality, as of reassuring monumental instances of human virtue, or landmarks needed for George Eliot's hope and faith. Adam progresses from unimaginative rectitude to the pains of loving and knowing beyond himself, Daniel Deronda finds his roots, his identity, his role. They are not characters who are existentially open, who can show new facets, who can surprise themselves, the other characters or the reader, but dramatically imperfect characters who show, like the desperately wish-fulfilling endings, the author's need to idealize, to dream, and to transform.

BIBLIOGRAPHY

A *Mrs. Gaskell*
Works, (Knutsford Edition). 8 vols., 1919–1920.
Letters, ed. J. A. V. Chapple and A. Pollard, Manchester, 1966.

Mrs. E. H. Chadwick, *Mrs. Gaskell: Haunts, Homes and Stories*, 1913.
G. de W. Sanders, *Elizabeth Gaskell*, New Haven, 1929. Includes a detailed bibliography.
E. S. Haldane, *Mrs. Gaskell and her Friends*, 1930.
Y. ffrench, *Mrs. Gaskell*, 1949.
A. B. Hopkins, *Elizabeth Gaskell: Her Life and Work*, 1952.
K. Tillotson, *Novels of the Eighteen-Forties*, 1954. Contains a good discussion of *Mary Barton*.
A. Pollard, *Mrs. Gaskell, Novelist and Biographer*, Manchester, 1965. A good critical discussion, sensitive and straightforward.
E. Wright, *Mrs. Gaskell: The Basis for Reassessment*, 1965. Useful critical discussion, especially good on religious ideas and background.
J. A. V. Chapple, 'North and South : a Reassessment', *Essays in Criticism*, Vol. XVII (October 1967). Good on sensibility and detail.

B *George Eliot*
Works, (Warwick Edition), 12 vols., Edinburgh, 1901–3.
Letters, ed. Gordon S. Haight, vols. I–III, 1954, vols. IV–VII, 1956 (cited as Haight).
Essays, ed. T. Pinney, 1963.

Henry James, 'Daniel Deronda : A Conversation' in *Partial Portraits*, 1888. Reprinted by F. R. Leavis in *The Great Tradition* (see below).
A. T. Kitchel, *George Lewes and George Eliot*, New York, 1933.
J. Bennett, *George Eliot*, 1948. A good readable introduction.
F. R. Leavis, *The Great Tradition*, 1948. A close and searching evaluation of George Eliot, not to be swallowed whole but certainly to be pondered.
B. Willey, *Nineteenth Century Studies*, 1949. Good on the background of religion and philosophy.
B. Hardy, *The Novels of George Eliot*, 1959. Close analysis of structure and narrative modes.
W. J. Harvey, *The Art of George Eliot*, 1961. A more theoretical approach than Hardy's, but similar in conclusion.
J. Beaty, *Middlemarch from Notebook to Novel*, Illinois, 1960. On the genesis and revisions.
G. S. Haight, *George Eliot, a Biography*, 1968. The only exhaustive and full account of the life.

MID-VICTORIAN NOVELISTS
(Disraeli, Kingsley, Reade and Collins)

SHEILA SMITH, University of Nottingham

'Action may not always be happiness,' said the General; 'but there is no happiness without action.' All Disraeli's novels are, to some extent, self-analysis. This advice, offered to Lothair (*Lothair*, Chapter 79), epitomizes Disraeli's own life. He needed the excitement of action, and he soon realized that, for him, the most satisfying activity was politics. Born in 1804 into a family of Sephardim Jews, in comfortable circumstances, he was the eldest son of Isaac D'Israeli, a scholar and writer who achieved fame with his *Curiosities of Literature* (1791–1823), essays and anecdotes about literature and writers. Isaac resigned from the Synagogue in 1817 and, although he himself never became a Christian, he had his children baptized into the Anglican church, so Benjamin's Jewish origins were no hindrance to his political ambitions although many of his opponents sneered at his Jewishness. Contemporary cartoons emphasized his Jewish appearance, and Thackeray's 'Codlingsby' (1847), satirizing *Coningsby* (1844), is strongly anti-Semitic. Disraeli never forgave Thackeray and pilloried him, seventeen years after his death, as the envious social-climber St. Barbe in *Endymion* (1880), a crude and unfair caricature. The powerful intelligence of Jews, such as Sidonia, who makes and breaks kings in *Coningsby*, and the Neuchatels in *Endymion*, and the inspiration of Jerusalem, as in *Tancred* (1847) or *Lothair* (1870), haunt Disraeli's novels. His visit to Jerusalem in 1831 was the climax of his Grand Tour of Spain, Greece and the Near East. These travels and his visits to Italy and Germany formed an important part of his education which was not confined to books ('Nine-tenths of existing books are nonsense, and the clever books are the refutation of that nonsense', says Mr. Gaston Phoebus in *Lothair*), although he read widely in his father's large library. His only formal schooling was a short period at Higham Hall, near Waltham-stow. There was an abortive attempt to make him a lawyer, and he dabbled in journalism, in 1825 attempting unsuccessfully to launch a daily newspaper, *The Representative*. He ran up debts and his first novel, *Vivian Grey* (1826–7), published anonymously, was an attempt to make money. Its hero is an ambitious young man who tries to achieve power by political intrigue, fails, fights a fatal duel, and escapes to the Continent where he meddles in local politics and conducts fruitless love-affairs. The novel ends, abruptly, in the middle of a thunder-storm, obviously because Disraeli could not think what to do with his hero. London society read the book eagerly because so many contemporary public figures appeared in it, thinly disguised. Acclaim changed to mockery, however, when it was discovered that the author was an obscure young man, ignorant of London society or politics. The novel was a continuing embarrassment to Disraeli. Unable to suppress it, he later pruned it for re-publication. Even allowing for its debt to the eighteenth-century picaresque novel, it is a shapeless book, and full of absurdly romantic visions of love and princely luxury. Vivian's exaggerated postures betray Disraeli's enthusiasm for Byron and the Byronic hero:

> He looked up to Heaven with a wild smile, half of despair and half of defiance. It seemed to imply that Fate had now done her worst, and that he had at last the satisfaction of knowing himself to be the most unfortunate and unhappy being that ever existed.
>
> (Book VIII, Chapter 1)

Yet despite the flamboyance of Disraeli's uncontrolled imagination the novel is vigorous, inventive and satirical. One character, Beckendorff, is the first of Disraeli's intelligent, experienced men with the power to influence a kingdom's fate. Speaking to Vivian, he expresses Disraeli's own philosophy of life:

> No conjuncture can possibly occur, however fearful, however tremendous it may appear, from which a man, by his own energy, may not extricate himself, as a mariner by the rattling of his cannon can dissipate the impending water-spout!
>
> (Book VI, Chapter 7)

I have no evidence to prove the efficacy of this method of dealing with water-spouts, but certainly Disraeli's own energy, intelligence and self-confidence, fostered by his friends and particularly by his sister Sarah, helped him to overcome money troubles, bouts of ill-health and failures, and made possible his brilliant political career.

In the 1830s his friendship with Edward Bulwer (whose best-selling novel *Pelham* (1828) owes something to *Vivian Grey*) made him one of the group of writers, artists and politicians who frequented the receptions of Lady Blessington and Count D'Orsay. Bulwer and D'Orsay were both dandies; and Disraeli also took pains to astound London society by his dazzling appearance and wit. One of Lady Blessington's guests described him :

> He was sitting in a window looking on Hyde Park, the last rays of sunlight reflected from the gorgeous gold flowers of a splendidly embroidered waistcoat. Patent leather pumps, a white stick with a black cord and tassel, and a quantity of chains about his neck and pockets, served to make him a conspicuous object. He has one of the most remarkable faces I ever saw . . . His eye is black as Erebus, and has the most mocking, lying in wait sort of expression conceivable . . . His hair is as extraordinary as his taste in waistcoats. A thick, heavy mass of jet black ringlets falls on his ıc͏ᶠᵗ cheek . . . The conversation turned on Beckford. I might as well attempt to gather up the foam of the sea as to convey an idea of the extraordinary language in which he clothed his description. He talked like a racehorse approaching the winningpost, every muscle in action.
>
> (J. A. Froude, *The Earl of Beaconsfield*, 1905 ed., p. 52)

Disraeli had ambitions to be a poet, but had to admit failure. Froude described him reciting his *Revolutionary Epic* at a party given by his admirer, Mrs. Austen. His costume was dandified and Byronic—velvet coat, shirt with the collar open at the throat, embroidered waistcoat, shoes with red rosettes—but the poem was not a success (op. cit., p. 48). His romantic novel, *Contarini Fleming* (1832), also describes his short-lived aspirations to be a poet. During this period he published several novels—*The Young Duke* (1831); *Alroy* (1833), a florid histori-cal romance, with a Jewish hero; *Henrietta Temple* (1837), a semi-autobiographical love story; and *Venetia* (1837), a fictional account of the lives of Shelley and Byron. Apart from *Alroy* these novels are of the kind which Hazlitt called 'silver-fork', purporting to describe accurately the details of fashionable life. The vogue for this kind of novel had been established by Robert Plumer Ward's *Tremaine* (1825). Despite their excesses, Disraeli's early novels have their interest. He was later embarrassed by *The Young Duke*, as he was by *Vivian Grey*, but this improbable tale has a controlling theme important in his later novels—a wealthy young aristocrat's gradual acceptance of responsibility to society. Also it is obvious that Disraeli learnt more from Byron than the cut of a collar. His satirical scrutiny of qualities he had admired or described with conviction is like Byron's treatment of romantic love in, for example, 'Beppo'. Here Disraeli scrutinizes the pose of the fated hero, which he had described with enthusiasm in *Vivian Grey*:

> While he existed, he was one of those men who, because they have been imprudent, think themselves unfortunate, and mistake their diseased mind for an implacable destiny.
> (*The Young Duke*, Book III, Chapter 5)

This amused awareness of the motives behind a grand gesture, which nevertheless attracts him, is of a kind with Byron's insistence on the transitory nature of passion, despite its importance:

> Think you, if Laura had been Petrarch's wife,
> He would have written sonnets all his life?
> (*Don Juan*, Canto III, viii)

One of the characteristics of Byron's later style is also Disraeli's—the ambivalent tone of combined mockery and admiration, in which neither the mockery nor the admiration is lost or destroyed. Byron believes in love, but he can laugh at the follies of men in love. Disraeli enjoys the glamour of aristocracy, but he mocks the aristocrat's follies. Moreover, Disraeli does not simply imitate Byron, he adapts what he borrows to his own purposes. The Duke of St. James comes to trust his own emotions and dare to shape his own destiny, like a true Byronic hero. But the nature of his response to life is original. By the end of the novel the Duke is using his intelligence and perception of society to counter the Utilitarians' arguments and to make a speech on Catholic Emancipation in the House of Lords. Disraeli's flights of romantic fancy were usually related to practical affairs.

His interest in politics increased. If he could not be a poet, he would be a politician and dominate the House of Commons with the power of language skilfully used. At the end of *The*

Young Duke (Book V, Chapter 6) he says how much he enjoys debate and discusses debating styles. He distinguishes between the styles of the Commons and of the Lords, remarking that Byron's Don Juan 'may perhaps be our model' in the Com mons. Disraeli learnt much from the satirical tone of Byron's greatest poem, and the tone of a debater's voice—insistent, witty, controlled—is an important element in his novels.

He published political writings as well as romances during the 1830s, for example, *A Vindication of the English Constitution* (1835), in which he attacked the Whigs and the Utilitarians and declared the Tory party

> . . . the national party; it is the really democratic party of England. It supports the institutions of the country, because they have been established for the common good, and because they secure the equality of civil rights, without which, whatever may be its name, no government can be free, and based upon which principle, every government, however it may be styled, is, in fact, a Democracy
>
> (p. 182)

This conception of Tory politics is very important to an understanding of *Coningsby* and *Sybil* (1845). At the fifth attempt he at last got a seat in the House of Commons, becoming a Tory member for Maidstone in 1837. For some years the world of practical politics left him no time for writing novels. But as he formulated his political ideas and, from being a laughing-stock in the House, came to be regarded as a formidable speaker, he began to think of publishing his political manifesto. He chose the novel to do this because there was the chance it would reach a wide audience. He was resentful when Peel gave him no office when he became Prime Minister in 1841, but it gave him the time to write.

Novels in the 1830s were beginning to reflect the growing seriousness of the time. In *Sartor Resartus* (1833–4) Carlyle mocked society's follies and false values and devastated the novel of high fashion. His satire was echoed by Dickens in *Nicholas Nickleby* (1838–9) in his extract from the novel enjoyed by Mrs. Wititterly. Dickens, the most popular novelist of the time, had directed the public's attention from high society to ordinary life. 'He has made washerwomen as interesting as duchesses', as Mrs. Oliphant later remarked ('Sensation Novels', *Blackwood's Magazine*, (1862), pp. 564–84). Dickens's exuberant comedy was always based on a penetrating observation of his own society. Even the romantic tales of criminals and their escapades—of the kind of Ainsworth's *Rookwood* (1834), with dashing Dick Turpin as hero—could be moral or philosophical, as in Bulwer's *Eugene Aram* (1832) or *Paul Clifford* (1830), and Dickens in his preface to *Oliver Twist* (1837–8) repudiated the false glamour of the fictional criminal and claimed he was substituting the squalid, insecure life of the real criminal; while Thackeray produced his satirical version of the criminal novel in *Catherine* (1839–40).

The 1830s and 1840s were a period when writers and reformers attempted to inform the middle-class public and influence opinion concerning the social miseries brought about by the Industrial Revolution. It was the age of Royal Commissions and Blue Books examining labour conditions in factories, the health of towns, sanitation, destitution in town and country. And the literary counterparts of these enquiries were the novels written to expose and examine social problems, novels 'with a purpose'. For example, Anthony Trollope's mother, Frances, published *Michael Armstrong* (1840), a melodramatic account of child labour in the factories; and in *Jessie Phillips* (1843) she attacked the 1834 Poor Law, as did Dickens in *Oliver Twist*. In *Helen Fleetwood* (1841) Charlotte Elizabeth Tonna exposed the miseries of the rural poor who came to the industrial town to look for work.

Disraeli's *Coningsby* was also written with a purpose. In this novel he comments upon contemporary society, but from a practising politician's viewpoint. In Disraeli's words, the novel was intended 'to vindicate the just claims of the Tory party to be the popular political confederation of the country'. His purpose gives the book direction and he writes with a new power. He takes the old literary convention of the young aristocrat's education through a series of encounters and adventures and uses it to explore the contemporary situation. He expresses his increasing opposition to Peel :

> The Tamworth Manifesto of 1834 was an attempt to construct a party without principles—its basis therefore was necessarily Latitudinarianism, and its inevitable consequence has been Political Infidelity . . . There was indeed a considerable shouting about what they called Conservative principles; but the awkward question naturally arose, what will you conserve?
>
> (Book II, Chapter 5)

The novel is an attempt to answer this question, to propound the principles of a Tory party responsive to the needs of contemporary society. Coningsby, thoughtful and idealistic, questions the old-style Toryism of his grandfather, Lord Monmouth (modelled on the Marquess of Hertford, who was also to be Thackeray's Lord Steyne in *Vanity Fair*). To Monmouth, the mighty aristocrat, politics are simply a matter of self-aggrandizement and place-seeking. Coningsby believes in a different kind of Toryism which has obligations to society and is based on an ideal union of Church, Monarch and People—in fact, Young England, the creed of a small group of friends, all Tory M.P.s looking to Disraeli for leadership. They appear in *Coningsby*. Coningsby himself is George Smythe, Lord Henry Sydney is Lord John Manners, Buckhurst is Alexander Baillie-Cochrane. Young England was not a political party, rather a group of friends sharing political views. They were active for a very short period from 1842 to 1846. They attacked the Utilitarians and looked back with nostalgia to an idealized feudal system in which Church and aristocracy combined to protect the rights of the people. They criticized the 1834 Poor Law, attempted to improve working-class housing conditions, emphasized the importance of holidays for the working people and supported Lord Ashley's factory reforms. They also argued that the Church had a responsibility for men's bodies as well as for their souls. (For a full account of Young England and Disraeli's part in it, see R. Blake, *Disraeli*, 1966, pp. 167–89.) Like the Oxford Movement and the later Pre-Raphaelite Brotherhood, Young England was a romantic protest against the scientific, Utilitarian economics and politics of the time. They were guilty of many follies, including an uncritical adulation of the Stuarts, particularly Charles I, and their dream of uniting aristocrat and worker was sometimes expressed in cricket matches and social functions of which the embarrassment is plain even in contemporary newspaper reports. But they genuinely desired reform, and Lord John Manners's journals show his determination to fulfil the responsibilities which he felt wealth and aristocratic position bring.

Like many Victorian novels, *Coningsby* popularizes current ideas rather than expresses new ones. They are not confined to politics. Like Carlyle, who also loathed the Utilitarians and favoured a feudal hierarchy in society, Disraeli emphasizes the wonder of the Industrial Revolution, part of the 'romance of reality' to which novelists were beginning to turn for material. 'Rightly understood, Manchester is as great a human exploit as Athens' (Book IV, Chapter 1). He also stresses the importance of an intelligent, responsible and energetic leader in this new sociey. 'In all things we trace the irresistible influence of the individual' (Book V, Chapter 4). Sidonia is the romantic, powerful individual in *Coningsby*, and he inspires Coningsby with his ideals.

The marriage between Coningsby and Edith Millbank, daughter of the humanitarian factory-owner, symbolizes the alliance between the traditional aristocracy, invigorated by an awareness of their responsibilities, and the new aristocracy, the great industrialists. Disraeli's adaptation of the conventional romantic plot shows perception of how the centres of power in the evolving English society were to be formed; it is a good example of his use of romance to express practical political alignment.

Coningsby is a challenge to the youth of the nation expressed not so much in the hero, who is rather a pallid character, as in the persuasive tones of Disraeli's oratory, which makes a powerful effect in the book, despite his habit of holding up the action while he debates various political themes. Apart from Disraeli himself, the great character of the novel is Lord Monmouth with his princely way of life—here in his exposition of the old Toryism Disraeli finds new purpose for his scenes of high fashion. Part of Monmouth's entourage is his creature and politician Rigby, a brilliant satirical portrait. In fact, the strength of the novel is its ability to express political activity and the minutiae of politics, not least their intrigue in which Tadpole and Taper play their part. Sidonia is an exotic, incredible dream-figure; Tadpole and Taper are all too real.

In the General Preface to the collected edition of his novels (1870) Disraeli explains:

> The derivation and character of political parties; the condition of the people which had been the consequence of them; the duties of the Church as a main remedial agency in our present state, were the three principal topics which I intended to treat, but I found they were too vast for the space I had allotted to myself. These were all launched in *Coningsby*; but the origin and condition of political parties, the first portion of the theme, was the only one completely handled in that work.

Next year, in *Sybil*, I considered the condition of the people.

Using his own experiences in a tour of the northern industrial cities, but also relying on Blue Book information, Disraeli in *Sybil* explores another current idea—that of the Two Nations, the Rich and the Poor, living side by side in England yet knowing nothing of each other. Egremont, the younger son of a noble family, learns something of working-class life through his friendship with Walter Gerard, the Chartist leader, Sybil, Gerard's daughter and Stephen Morley, the Chartist journalist. Disraeli crams into the novel a bewildering number of topics—Chartist mobs, the iniquity of the truck system, the appalling conditions in which women and children worked in coal-mines, the growth of trades unions, the plight of the handloom weavers, the agricultural depression, the insanitary squalor of the agricultural labourers' existence. No wonder that the novel is disorganized, and that some of the Blue Book facts are undigested. Disraeli's imagination was not like Mrs. Gaskell's; he could not enter sympathetically into the actual conditions of the poor. The handloom weaver's speech is stilted and the attempts at dialect produce only bastard Cockney. But *Sybil* is not a domestic novel, but discursive, rhetorical:

> Even now, in the quiet times in which we live, when public robbery is out of fashion and takes the milder title of a commission of inquiry, and when there is no treason except voting against a minister, who, though he may have changed all the policy which you have been elected to support, expects your vote and confidence all the same; even in the age of mean passions and petty risks, it is something to step aside from Palace Yard, and instead of listening to a dull debate, where facts are only a repetition of the blue books you have already read, and the fancy an ingenious appeal to the recrimination of Hansard, to enter the old Abbey and listen to an anthem!

(Book IV, Chapter 6)

Disraeli adapts the tone of parliamentary debate to serve the purposes of his novel—it can be quietly sarcastic and abusive, as in this quotation, or fiercely attacking, or challenging, or exhilarating. By means of this rhetoric he can refer the reader from scene to scene, using them as the points in his debate, directing the reader's attention to a panoramic view of English society. The debater's voice, and the intelligence and perception implied by the voice, hold the fragments together. The plot is both improbable and impossible, the love-scenes melodramatic and absurd, yet the novel reveals a tough intellect. For example, Disraeli approves of Trafford's mill and the amenities he provides for his workers, but he is aware that some people would feel oppressed by such paternalistic concern for their well-being and gives the words of a mill-hand who says as much. He describes the horrors of Devilsdust's childhood, and realizes that, harsh as life in the factory is, it provides him with a refuge and a place, however humble, in society. He represents 'Bishop' Hatton, the master locksmith, as a coarse brute, but shows that Hatton's mastery of his craft gives him an authority which England's effete aristocracy have forfeited. Disraeli is one of the few English novelists concerned with maintaining a flow of ideas in a novel. He appeals to his readers' intelligence as well as to their imagination. You may not agree with his ideas, but you cannot ignore them.

Sybil is anti-democratic. It would be surprising if, written at this date and by a man in Disraeli's circumstances, it were not. His attitude to Chartism is the same as that expressed in his speeches in the House of Commons in 1839 when Attwood supported the National Petition. He voted against Attwood's motion but sympathized with the Chartists' demands for social justice. The people themselves were not to have political power, but their leaders were to improve the people's condition. Fear of revolution, violence, disorder—a fear also found in the novels of Mrs. Gaskell, Kingsley and Dickens—is evident in the riot scenes at the end of *Sybil*. The nation was to entrust itself to responsible leaders who would wield their power for the people's good; and Disraeli was determined to be one of them.

Tancred does not substantiate Disraeli's claim that it is to demonstrate 'the duties of the Church as a main remedial agency in our present state'. Tancred, a young English nobleman, renounces English society and discovers that the source of spiritual power is Jerusalem. As Robert Blake remarks of Disraeli's odd ideas about race and religion at this time, 'To him the Jew is a proto-Christian and Christianity is completed Judaism' (op. cit., 1966, p. 204). The best part of the novel is the early section describing contemporary aristocratic society. The improbable incidents of Tancred's spiritual odyssey recall the rhetorical excesses of *Vivian Grey* and *Contarini Fleming*. As in his first novel, Disraeli ends the book obviously because his invention fails him. After all, any descent from Mount Sinai is bound to be anti-climax!

The little group known as Young England drifted apart. Disraeli wanted higher position than the leadership of a rogue group in the Tory party. In 1852 he became Chancellor of the Exchequer; and in 1868 for a few months he realized his ambition to be Prime Minister. During the years 1847–69 he had no time to write novels. But when he lost office he began to write *Lothair,* which I consider his best. It was again prompted by contemporary events: Garibaldi's abortive campaign to liberate Italy in 1867 and the wealthy Marquess of Bute's conversion to Roman Catholicism in 1868.

Lothair is an aristocrat who will possess immense wealth and estates when he comes of age. His parents are dead, and one of his guardians is Cardinal Grandison (a composite portrait of Manning and Wiseman) who was appointed to his position of trust before his conversion to the Roman Catholic Church. Brought up by his other guardian, an austere Scots Earl, Lothair does not meet the Cardinal until he is nearing his majority. Supported by the wealthy Catholic family the St. Jeromes, who have a beautiful niece Clare Arundel, the Cardinal attempts to convert Lothair and secure his great wealth and position for the Roman Catholic Church. At first Roman Catholicism's graciousness and ideal spirituality attract Lothair, and he dreams of building a cathedral, although he cannot make up his mind whether it is to be Anglican or Catholic. Then by chance he meets Theodora, the inspiration of the revolutionary societies of Europe, and joins her in the attempt to free Rome from Papal and French rule. They fail and Theodora is killed. Lothair is taken wounded into Rome where he is nursed by Clare Arundel. The Roman Catholics spread the news that he was fighting on the Papal side and that the woman who rescued him was the Virgin Mary. Lothair takes part in a great thanksgiving festival commemorating this miracle but does not realize that he has condoned a lie until next day he reads an account of the thanksgiving in a Roman Catholic journal.

In the novel's central scene the Cardinal, in gentle, reasonable words, tries to persuade him that he is mistaken, that he was in fact fighting for the Papacy. It is the climax of the long subtle campaign to possess Lothair, and at last he sees it as such. It is the most masterly scene Disraeli wrote. His ability to suggest tones of voice is at its greatest here. For a comparable fictional embodiment of brainwashing techniques, particularly the brainwasher's insidious tenderness and concern for his victim forming part of the undermining attack, English readers had to wait for Arthur Koestler's *Darkness at Noon* (1940) or Orwell's *1984* (1949). To appreciate the delicacy of Disraeli's touch in handling the contemporary fear of increasing Roman Catholic power in England one has only to compare the crude melodrama of the priest who also tries to ensnare a wealthy aristocrat in Wilkie Collins's *The Black*

Robe (1881). Disraeli's attitude to the Roman Catholic Church had greatly changed since *Sybil* in which he yearned for the beauty and social security of the pre-Reformation Church as he saw it. In *Lothair* its grace and apparent concern are part of its snare. Lothair escapes the Cardinal and finally marries his former sweetheart who comes of a good Anglican family, so he and his wealth remain within the Church of England. A well-written scene is Lothair's final meeting with the Cardinal in England, when Grandison, far from showing resentment or anger at his defeat, is all sweet graciousness and urbane goodwill. *Lothair* is the most controlled and best shaped of Disraeli's novels. He had at last achieved his greatest ambition and no longer needed to strain for effect or to persuade the public that he had a substantial political programme. He was still given to sudden lapses of style. He never had the great literary artist's ear for nuances of language. Queen Victoria was understandably a little amazed at his prose. 'Mr. Disraeli (*alias* Dizzy) writes very curious reports to me of the House of Commons proceedings—much in the style of his books', she wrote to the King of the Belgians in 1852. In *Lothair* he occasionally produces sentences which read like excerpts from Daisy Ashford's *The Young Visiters*. This is the description of the Cardinal at a fashionable reception :

> After all, the Mikado himself was not more remarkable than this Prince of the Church in a Tyburnian drawing-room, habited in his pink cassock and cape, and waving, as he spoke, with careless grace his pink barrette.
>
> (Chapter 8)

But, generally speaking, the style is assured and flexible, the tone that of a confident, controlled voice enlivening civilized conversation with illuminating wit. For example, the description of the wealthy and nonchalant Lord St. Aldegonde's red republicanism :

> He was opposed to all privileges, and indeed to all orders of men, except dukes, who were a necessity. He was also strongly in favour of the equal division of all property, except land. Liberty depended on land, and the greater the landowners, the greater the liberty of a country.
>
> (Chapter 21)

This extract illustrates the fascinating ambivalence of Disraeli's attitude towards the aristocracy—his pleasure in their elegance and his mockery at their decadence; it also demonstrates his power of self-parody.

There are also instances of Disraeli's penetrating intelligence producing ideas which his imagination represents in scenes and dialogues. For example, Lothair takes Theodora and her husband to Blenheim where his friendship with the owner allows them the privilege of walking in the private gardens. Theodora responds to their beauty but they express for her a principle of exclusion which she finds depressing—' "The manners of your country are founded on exclusion".' She dislikes the ' "artificial loneliness" ' of the great parks surrounding aristocratic houses. She goes on :

> 'I admire nature, but I require the presence of humanity. Life in great cities is too exhausting; but in my village there should be air, streams, and beautiful trees, a picturesque scene, but enough of my fellow-creatures to ensure constant duty.'
> 'But the fulfilment of duty and society founded on what you call the principle of exclusion, are not incompatible,' said Lothair.
> 'No, but difficult. What should be natural becomes an art; and in every art it is only the few who can be first-rate.'
>
> (Chapter 25)

There is acute perception in that final epigram. In these few sentences Sir Willoughby Patterne's grace, weakness and menace are summed up. Disraeli was not always prolix and diffuse; he could discipline his prose to great effect.

His last complete novel, *Endymion*, was half written by 1874, the year in which he again became Prime Minister, this time for six years. It was published in 1880. It is the fairy tale of a young man, Endymion, who by dint of intelligence, hard work, and good luck rises from obscurity to become Prime Minister. The book has a nostalgic charm, and gives a retrospective if somewhat romantic survey of political events in the 1830–50 period. But the tone is tired and the flashes of wit are rare. The novel's romantic idealism can be gauged by the description of Lord Eglinton's medieval tournament in 1839. In *Endymion* the extravagant attempt to re-live the triumph and excitement of a medieval joust is a miraculous pageant of splendour and beauty. In fact, the event was a fiasco, ruined by the relentless rain of Ayrshire in August. The novel is monotonously optimistic and all comes right.

When Disraeli died in 1881 he left unfinished nine chapters

of a novel describing the career of Joseph Toplady Falconet who was to have been Disraeli's satirical portrait of Gladstone.

Disraeli is an exotic among English novelists. His novels, judged by the standards of 'pure literature', are hopeless. They make much more sense if seen in the context of the eighteenth-century discursive novel, Byron's satiric narratives and Thomas Love Peacock's witty conversation pieces. He did not have a solid and secure position in the middle classes, as many Victorian novelists had, nor did he so closely direct his appeal to the middle-class public or accept their mores. His early books were directed at the fashionable and political society of London. And, although my researches into the public's response to *Sybil* (*Mr. Disraeli's Readers*, 1966) have shown that readers from all classes of society wrote to Disraeli about the book, none of his novels claimed the great middle-class response accorded to Dickens and Trollope. *Coningsby* went through three editions in 1844, but his first great success was *Lothair*. As Robert Blake points out, it was natural that everybody should want to read a novel written by an ex-Prime Minister. There are no insipid, middle-class ladies, adoring and submissive, in his novels, but women like Theodora, who could have been melodramatic but is, in fact, impressive, or Endymion's determined and ambitious sister, Myra. Nor do Disraeli's novels express the middle-class idea of heaven — marriage, a competence and a little house. The claustrophobic refuges provided at the end of *Oliver Twist*, *Nicholas Nickleby* and *Martin Chuzzlewit* are not found in his romances. His two great themes are aristocratic life and the business of politics, and I can think of no other English novelist who can describe them so well. The middle-class Victorian writers were, generally speaking, weak on aristocrats. The reviewer of 'Recent Novels' for *Fraser's*, April 1849, remarks on the 'tawdry lies' of the novelists purporting to describe the 'fashionable world'. As for politics, when Trollope's Duke of Omnium becomes Prime Minister he does nothing, because Trollope obviously does not know what Prime Ministers do. But Disraeli did. The speech and actions of the 'gentleman in Downing Street' in *Sybil* are entirely convincing:

'You must summon a council for four o'clock. I have some deputations to receive, which I will throw over; but to Windsor I must go. Nothing has yet occurred to render any notice of the state of the country necessary in the speech from the Throne.'

'Not yet,' said his companion; 'but what will tomorrow bring forth?'

'After all it is only a turn-out. I cannot recast her Majesty's speech and bring in rebellion and closed mills, instead of loyalty and a good harvest.'

(Book VI, Chapter 1)

And Disraeli's view of both aristocracy and politics is comprehensive not rigid—he loves them and yet laughs at them, and at its best his ironic style well expresses this ambivalence.

Disraeli is not a great novelist, but he is a good one. His achievement is uneven but ultimately the interest of the novels is the interest of his own colourful personality. His energy, intelligence and flamboyant imagination inform their rhetoric, their incidents, their dialogue. 'May one not lament the degradation of a promising novelist into a Prime Minister?' asked Leslie Stephen ('Mr. Disraeli's Novels', *Hours in a Library*, 1876). But in truth Disraeli the novelist and Disraeli the politician cannot be separated.

Charles Kingsley's novels are also characterized by the writer's powerful personality, evident in style and tone. His first novel was *Yeast* (1848), published anonymously. Inspired by his brother-in-law Sidney Godolphin Osborne, Rector of Durweston, who worked to improve the living conditions of the Dorset agricultural labourers, Kingsley used the novel to shatter the notion that dirt and disease existed only in industrial towns and that life in the country was healthy and idyllic. Disraeli had made the same point in his description of Marney in *Sybil*, but *Yeast* is the first novel devoted to the subject. Like so many novels of the 1840s, *Yeast* has a serious purpose and Kingsley wants to confront his readers with reality:

Of all the species of lovely scenery which England holds, none, perhaps, is more exquisite than the banks of the chalk-rivers—the perfect limpidity of the water, the gay and luxuriant vegetation of the banks and ditches, the masses of noble wood embosoming the villages, the unique beauty of the water meadows, living sheets of emerald and silver, tinkling and sparkling, cool under the fiercest sun, brilliant under the blackest clouds.—There, if anywhere, one would have expected to find Arcadia among fertility, loveliness, industry, and wealth. But, alas for the sad reality! the cool

breath of those glittering water-meadows too often floats
laden with poisonous miasma. Those picturesque villages are
generally the perennial hot beds of fever and ague, of squalid
penury, sottish profligacy, dull discontent too stale for
words. There is luxury in the park, wealth in the huge farm-
steadings, knowledge in the parsonage : but the poor? those
by whose dull labour all that luxury and wealth, ay, even
that knowledge, is made possible—what are they? We shall
see, please God, ere the story's end.

(Chapter 3)

Like Disraeli's, Kingsley's style depends on oratory, but it is
the oratory of the pulpit, not of the House of Commons. Here
the appeal is to God, and the novel's concern is moral. In his
preface to the 1851 edition Kingsley says that he wrote it
because he was afraid that society was losing 'the living spirit
of Christianity' and he felt that most people were clinging 'to
the outward letter of it, whether High Church or Evangelical;
unconscious, all the while, that they are sinking out of real
living belief, into that dead self-deceiving belief-in-believing,
which has been always heretofore, and is becoming in England
now, the parent of the most blind, dishonest, and pitiless
bigotry.'
Relying partly on what he had seen of Sidney Godolphin
Osborne's parish in Dorset, partly on S. G. O.'s evidence included in the *Reports of Special Assistant Poor Law Commissioners on the Employment of Women and Children in Agricul-
ture* (1843) and partly on his experience of his own Hampshire
parish, Kingsley described the agricultural labourers' crowded
and insanitary cottages, the typhus they bred and the squire's
indifference. Alone among the social-problem novelists of his
time Kingsley gives some idea of the sexual squalor of the
poor. This is one of the themes of 'A Rough Rhyme on a Rough
Matter', a poem supposedly written by Tregarva, the game-
keeper, for which he is dismissed the squire's service. Frederic
Harrison thought Kingsley's ballads the best things he wrote
and, although it is over-explicit and too long, 'A Rough Rhyme'
with its direct attack and haunting rhythm, epitomises much
of what he says in the novel. I can quote only a few verses
here. A poacher's widow is speaking :

'A labourer in Christian England,
Where they cant of a Saviour's name,
And yet waste men's lives like the vermin's
For a few more brace of game . . .

211

'You have sold the labouring man, squire,
Body and soul to shame,
To pay for your seat in the House, squire,
And to pay for the feed of your game.

'You made him a poacher yourself, squire,
When you'd give neither work nor meat;
And your barley-fed hares robbed the garden
At our starving children's feet . . .

'Our daughters with base-born babies
Have wandered away in their shame;
If your misses had slept, squire, where they did,
Your misses might do the same . . .'

It is a courageous novel; and it frightened the publisher of
Fraser's Magazine, where it first appeared.

It is true that Kingsley wrote the book because he desperately
wanted money, but he also wanted to propagate the ideas of
Christian Socialism, which taught the social responsibility of
the Church and agreed with Lord Ashley's insistence that
improved morals among the working classes were largely dependent upon improved living conditions. Kingsley was anti-
intellectual. He had no patience with philosophy or theological
niceties. He felt that the Evangelicals were too concerned with
the next world to pay sufficient attention to man's happiness in
this, and that the Tractarians and High Church thinkers were
too idealistic and preoccupied with the past rather than with
the present. In *Yeast* the hero, Lancelot Smith, a rich merchant's
son, is gradually awakened to the miserable existence of the
agricultural labourers largely by the efforts of Tregarva who
speaks very like Carlyle. Tregarva takes Lancelot to a village
fair. On the way Tregarva criticizes the Young England aristocrat, Lord Vieuxbois:

'Look at that Lord Vieuxbois, sir, as sweet a gentleman as
ever God made . . . He spends his whole life and time about
the poor, I hear. But sir, as sure as you live he's making his
people slaves and humbugs. He doesn't see, sir, that they
want to be raised bodily out of this miserable hand-to-mouth
state, to be brought nearer up to him, and set on a footing
where they can shift for themselves. Without meaning it,
sir, all his boundless charities are keeping the people down,
and telling them they must stay down, and not help themselves, but wait for what he gives them. He fats prize-

labourers, sir, just as Lord Minchampstead fats prize-oxen and pigs.'

Lancelot could not help thinking of that amusingly inconsistent, however well-meant, scene in *Coningsby*, in which Mr. Lyle is represented as trying to restore 'the independent order of peasantry,' by making them the receivers of public alms at his own gate, as if they had been middle-age serfs or vagabonds, and not citizens of modern England.

'It may suit the Mr. Lyle's of his age,' hought Lancelot, 'to make the people constantly and visibly comprehend that property is their protector and friend, but I question whether it will suit the people themselves, unless they can make property understand that it owes them something more definite than protection.'

(Chapter 13)

A telling point. Kingsley, although often befogged with prejudice, was not without ideas; but from this extract we must not argue that he believed in democracy. In his novels, as in Disraeli's, the independence of the lower orders must be achieved within the existing class-structure. Tregarva is careful to call Lancelot 'sir'. And of his next novel, *Alton Locke* (1850), which is concerned mainly with Chartism and working-class misery in London but also touches upon agricultural distress, Kingsley wrote:

The moral of my book is, that the working man who tries to get on, to desert his class and rise above it, enters into a lie, and leaves God's path for his own—with consequences . . . I think the cry 'Rise in Life,' has been excited by the very increasing impossibility of being anything but brutes while they struggle below.
(To an unnamed country rector, 13 Jan 1851, quoted by F. E. Kingsley, *Charles Kingsley: His letters and Memories of his Life*, 1877, p. 247)

Kingsley was twenty-nine when *Yeast* began to appear, and Rector of Eversley (Hampshire), the living he held until his death in 1875. His father had, like so many Victorian clergymen, taken holy orders because this was one of the few dignified professions open to impecunious gentlemen. The family lived for several years at Barnack, in the Fens, near Stamford. Charles loved the Fen country and later described it in his historical novel, *Hereward the Wake* (1866). They also lived at Clovelly in Devonshire, where he became interested in the sea-shore and marine life. Clovelly appears as the fishing-village Penalva in *Two Years Ago* (1854) and is described at length in *Westward Ho!* (1855). Referring to his excitement at the Crimean War but his inability to write about it because he had not experienced it, Kingsley wrote to William Cox Bennett '. . . I am essentially a Pre-Raphaelite in poetry, and can only imagine what I have seen.' This is also true of his novels. One of their strengths is his description of landscapes he knew and loved; and he can hold the reader's attention with his descriptions of the wonderful creatures Tom Thurnall, the doctor in *Two Years Ago*, finds in the rock-pools. Kingsley's accurate observation and imaginative re-creation of marine life is best seen in his book for children, *Glaucus, or the Wonders of the Sea Shore* (1855). This began as a review of books by his friend Philip Gosse, Edmund Gosse's father. Unlike Gosse, Kingsley did not find contemporary scientific discoveries a challenge to his faith in God. For him the material world was a manifestation of God's love, and scientific discovery simply a further revelation of the wonder of God's universe.

In 1836 the Kingsleys came to live in Chelsea, where Kingsley's father had the living of St. Luke's. The Carlyles were near neighbours. Charles became friendly with Carlyle and was greatly influenced by his writings and ideas. Kingsley's hard-hitting style echoes his, and Mackaye in *Alton Locke* and Tregarva are obviously modelled on his friend. Carlyle had the habit of claiming God's support for his dogmatic pronouncements. In 1850 John Stuart Mill queried his right to quote God's authority for his assertion that the white races are innately superior to the black. Kingsley also assumes that the Almighty shares his prejudices and lays about him with the wrath of Jehovah when he is attacking the Roman Catholics in *Yeast* and *Westward Ho!* or Evangelical preachers and the 'unmanly' poet Vavasour who lives for art in *Two Years Ago*. Gerard Manley Hopkins who, as a Jesuit, could not be expected to sympathize with Kingsley's views, once complained in a letter that Browning

> . . . has got a great deal of what came in with Kingsley and the Broad Church school, a way of talking (and making his people talk) with the air and spirit of a man bouncing up from table with his mouth full of bread and cheese and

saying that he meant to stand no blasted nonsense. There is a whole volume of Kingsley's essays which is all a munch and a not standing of any blasted nonsense from cover to cover.

*(Correspondence of G. M. Hopkins and R. W. Dixon,
ed. C. C. Abbott, 1935, p. 74)*

There is a great deal of 'munch and not standing of any blasted nonsense' in Kingsley's novels. His moralizing lecturing can be exhausting and a sign of prejudice rather than of thought, as his sorry public debate with Newman showed. It also reflects the increasing and unattractive 'earnestness' of the period which was later to be savaged by Samuel Butler in *The Way of all Flesh* and, more flippantly, by Wilde in *The Importance of Being Earnest*. Kingsley's ideal of the practical, 'manly' Christian, the sturdy huntsman and fisherman who would help anybody and not bother about theological speculations, later dubbed 'muscular Christianity' (a phrase Kingsley hated), is exemplified also in Thomas Hughes's hero Tom Brown, and in Thomas Arnold's ideal public school boy, who had healthy limbs and pure thoughts.

Hughes became one of the group of Christian Socialists when he heard F. D. Maurice preach in the chapel of Lincoln's Inn. Maurice had a great influence on Kingsley, who called him 'the Master'. He had read Maurice's books at Cambridge, but he did not meet him until 1844. They became close friends. Maurice owed a considerable debt to Coleridge's thought on the social ethic implicit in the Church's teaching. He was concerned with social reform, but he believed that it could come only by religious means. A moral change of heart in individuals was to bring about the social revolution. He was a shy man, but humane and compassionate, believing that the Church should be for mankind and opposed to sectarian bigotry and exclusiveness. His appointment as Professor of Theology at King's College, London, was terminated when he published his *Theological Essays* in 1853. In this book he dared to suggest that after death God did not punish sinners for eternity. This was regarded as dangerous unorthodoxy. On 14 July 1853 Kingsley wrote to Maurice about the *Essays* remarking that they have given him courage to speak more boldly and that the book's theme will frighten people,

. . . especially such an expression of it as that in §3. P 144. As I read it, I shuddered, to think how here was *the* truth the cardinal truth of my own heart, to preach wh [which]

215

I wish to live and die—And yet so new a truth to me, that till I began to read your books, I never had had an inkling of it.

(British Museum MS 41,287)

The paragraph in question occurs in Essay VII 'On the Atonement' and ends describing Christ:

> One who appears as the actual representative of Humanity, cannot be a formal substitute for it. We deny Him in the first character, by claiming the second for Him.

Christ as 'the actual representative of Humanity.' This was at the heart of Maurice's teaching and why he inspired the Christian Socialists. It was why Kingsley resented Young England's patronage of the poor because this denied the dignity of a human being made in God's image. As Maurice himself wrote late in the century in *Christian Socialism* (1893), 'Our Church must apply herself to the task of raising the poor into men; she cannot go on . . . treating them merely as poor.' In terms of theology Maurice was as anti-Utilitarian and as anti-Benthamite as Disraeli was in the sphere of politics, and he had considerable influence on Christian social thought in the nineteenth century, even though his assumption that working men would readily become Christians and accept the Christian teaching and ethic caused the failure of some of his practical schemes for reform. As K. S. Inglis wrote,

> What was most important in Maurice, as an influence on Christian social attitudes, was not the particular method he recommended for achieving a harmonious society but the fact that he had given a theological justification for trying to replace the spirit of competition in society by the spirit of co-operation.
>
> (*Churches and the Working Classes in Victorian England*, 1963, p. 267)

The principle of Christian brotherhood was embodied in the Christian Socialists' establishment of Working Men's Associations for Co-operative Production, for example, the Working Tailors' Association in London in 1850. This kind of association they saw as an alternative to Chartism and the hope for the betterment of the working classes after the fiasco of the Chartists' Third Petition in 1848. This is the main theme of Kingsley's *Alton Locke*.

The hard core of Christian Socialism was represented by Maurice, Kingsley and John Ludlow, who was much influenced by Buchez, who had established workers' associations in France. In May–August 1848 the group produced a penny weekly *Politics for the People*, in which Kingsley wrote under the name 'Parson Lot'. It had no practical schemes for reform, but appealed to the working classes to realize the futility of merely political reform and emphasized the need for individual moral reform and an acceptance of Christianity. The Christian Socialists appealed to the upper classes to resist the Utilitarian philosophy and to participate in brotherly co-operation with the classes below them. Kingsley got the reputation for being a fire-brand, and when in *Yeast* he attacked the Game Laws and implied that the landowners exploited both the land and the labourers, the publisher of *Fraser's Magazine*, in which the novel was appearing, insisted that the tale be brought to a close because readers were offended. The ending of the book is very confused and shows Kingsley's harassed state and mental fatigue.

Politics for the People was followed by *The Christian Socialist* (1850–1) and the *Journal of Association* (1851). The style and attack of Kingsley's social-problem novels are those of the polemic articles which he contributed to these journals. Kingsley saw them partly as extended tracts, which helps to account for their crudity. In fact, *Alton Locke* is a fictional version of Kingsley's *Cheap Clothes and Nasty*, a revelation of sweatshop practices in the tailoring trade based on Henry Mayhew's researches. It appeared in January 1850 as one of the 'Tracts by Christian Socialists', while he was still engaged upon the novel.

Christian Socialism as an organized movement lasted from 1848 to 1854, when the Society for Promoting Working Men's Associations (founded 1850) was wound up. Its practical achievement was the sponsorship of the Industrial and Provident Societies' Act (1852), which gave Co-operative Societies recognized legal status and a reasonably satisfactory measure of protection for their funds, the impetus Ludlow in particular gave to the Co-operative movement, and the interest in working men's education which resulted in the foundation of the London Working Men's College (1853–4). Kingsley was particularly interested in education; some of the most powerful scenes in *Alton Locke* are those in which Alton denies himself food and sleep in order to read his books; his desperate struggle against poverty, squalor and bigotry and his search for the means of achieving a better life are well done. Kingsley turns to real life for his horrors, and the most compelling descriptions are those of scenes he himself had witnessed—the slums of Jacob's Island or the miserable little boys in the fields trying, with their frozen hands, to turn the turnip cutter. While he wrote he was again over-worked and ill, and the novel is hurried and disorganized, particularly at the end. Its main fault is one common to propaganda novels—the propaganda becomes more important than the novel. Kingsley is so eager to plead the cause of Christian Socialism that he virtually abandons Alton, who has told his own story in desperate, indignant, passionate words, and allows Eleanor to preach him, passive and convalescent, a series of sermons. To allow him to be convinced by Eleanor, Kingsley makes Alton's character totally inconsistent with what it has been. At the beginning Alton has a lively and enquiring mind. At the end he accepts Eleanor's illogical statements with scarcely a murmur. Kingsley described Alton's poetry becoming poorer as he deserts his own kind and tries, for love of Lillian, to ape the upper classes. He is blind to his character's degeneration into a cipher as soon as he accepts Christian Socialism. Carlyle's panacea, emigration, takes Alton to America at the end of the novel. He dies before he can get there and put Christian Socialism into practice.

Kingsley was always given to 'spasms of sympathy' and his interest in Christian Socialism began to cool after 1852. Also his prefaces to the later editions of *Alton Locke* show that he felt that many of the abuses he had criticized had been rectified. But he always believed that moral regeneration was dependent on improved living conditions, and all his life he preached sanitary reform. The best scenes in the long-winded novel, *Two Years Ago*, are those in which Tom Thurnall tries to teach Devonshire villagers that cholera is not a visitation from God to be passively accepted, but the result of insanitary conditions which can be changed.

Yeast and *Alton Locke* are Kingsley's best novels. *Hypatia* (1852–3), describing the struggle between Christianity and paganism in fifth century Alexandria, is, as G. H. Lewes wrote, 'ambitious, but somewhat wearisome'. *Westward Ho!* (1855) was a best-seller because it expressed the patriotic enthusiasm for war aroused by the Crimean War (it can be compared with the ending of Tennyson's *Maud*), mirrored the confidence of the English nation and voiced the contemporary fear of increasing Roman Catholic power in England. Copies of the novel were sent to the soldiers fighting the Crimean War; it is to be hoped that it consoled them for the inefficiency with which the campaign was conducted. Kingsley stopped thundering against the aristocracy and began to move in exalted company. In 1859 he became Queen Victoria's Chaplain and was later Chaplain to the Prince of Wales. In 1860 he became Regius Professor of Modern History at Cambridge, where he was remarkable for his enthusiasm and his friendly attitude towards undergraduates rather than for his scholarship.

His most attractive book is *The Water Babies* (1862–3). In this fairy tale he describes moral evolution in physical terms, illustrating his central belief that the physical is an expression of the spiritual, but without distorting the narrative or resorting to preaching. Kingsley tells his story with humour and gaiety —qualities obvious in his letters to his children and in Edmund Gosse's memories of him, but not greatly evident in his novels.

Kingsley's imagination was not subtle or powerful, and the moralist in him distrusted art; to the practical parson and the vigorous sportsman art was 'unmanly'. He had none of the great novelist's joy in creation. Dickens hates and fears Chadband in *Bleak House*, but the artist delights to create an entertaining fiction to express that hatred and fear. Kingsley dislikes the stupid, frivolous apothecary's daughter in *Two Years Ago*, so he turns from her with an impatient 'Bah!' and then harangues the reader on this example of middle-class stupidity. Kingsley had something of the Philistinism criticized by Arnold in *Culture and Anarchy* (1869), and also of Hebraism, the Victorian delight in activity without sufficient thought as to the purpose and significance of that activity. Yet he was an influential writer, and particularly he stirred young people's imaginations. William Morris, writing in 1883 of his time at Oxford in the 1850s, said 'I was . . . a good deal influenced by the works of Charles Kingsley, and got into my head therefrom some socio-political ideas which would have developed probably but for the attractions of art and poetry.' (*Letters of Morris to his Family and Friends*, ed. P. Henderson, 1950, p. 185) 'He woke them up in all sorts of ways, about all sorts of things', wrote Frederic Harrison (*Charles Kingsley's Place in Literature*, 1895, p. 561). His energy and enthusiasm were both his strength and his weakness as a writer. They tempted him to harangue the reader, but they also gave fire to his observations and to the causes for which he fought. He dared to write about urgent problems in three of his novels, and he described with passion what he had seen of the London slums and the rural hovels, creating realistic settings of considerable power. *Alton Locke* is interesting reading because of its bitter cry against the frustrations caused by class-distinctions, even though the novel's plot stifles this protest.

'The greatest benefit we owe to the artist, whether painter, poet, or novelist, is the extension of our sympathies', wrote George Eliot ('The Natural History of German Life', *Westminster Review* (1856) pp. 51–79). The novel in the Victorian period developed in style and subject-matter by extending the areas of human experience which it explored, by making its readers more aware of themselves and of society as neither drama nor poetry did. Charles Kingsley is a minor novelist, but in *Yeast, Alton Locke* and *Two Years Ago* he helped to extend the novel's subject matter, and to make it more serious, more concerned with reality. He saw God, Heaven and Hell in human terms. This was an asset to him as a novelist, and gave substance to his novels.

Ten years ago the world in general had come to a singular crisis in its existence. The age was lost in self-admiration . . . We were about inaugurating the reign of universal peace in a world too deeply connected by links of universal interest ever to commit the folly of war again—we had invented everything that was most unlikely, and had nothing before us but to go on perfecting our inventions . . .

So writes Mrs. Oliphant, discussing 'Sensation Novels' in *Blackwood's Magazine* (May 1862). Her words help to explain the optimistic tones of Kingsley's prefaces to the later editions of *Alton Locke* when he was turning away from Christian Socialism because he felt its mission had been accomplished. But Mrs. Oliphant described how this complacent mood was shattered by war (the Crimean War was fought 1854–6; the American Civil War began in 1861)—upheavals sufficiently distanced to be regarded in England as exciting. She tries to explain the popularity of the sensation drama and the sensation novel because of the public's craving for excitement:

. . . it is only natural that art and literature should, in an age which has turned to be one of events, attempt a kindred depth of effect and shock of incident. In the little reflected worlds of the novel and the drama the stimulant has acted strongly, and the result in both has been a significant and remarkable quickening of public interest. Shakespeare, even in the excitement of a new interpretation, has not crowded the waning playhouse, as has the sensation drama with its mock catastrophes; and Sir Walter himself never deprived his readers of their lawful rest to a greater extent with one novel than Mr. Wilkie Collins has succeeded in doing with his 'Woman in White'.

Wilkie Collins's *The Woman in White*, his first resounding success, was published in 1859 in Dickens's new magazine *All the Year Round* and sent the sales soaring. The book hit the popular taste and set the fashion for sensation novels. (Others were Ellen Price Wood's *East Lynne* (1861) and Mary Elizabeth Braddon's *Lady Audley's Secret* (1862).) The solemn *Edinburgh Review* might insist on the novelist's moral appeal—'To an inquisitive youth, novels are a series of lectures upon life, in which the professor addresses his pupils as his equals and as men of the world' (July 1857)—but one of the novels reviewed in this article was Charles Reade's *It is Never Too Late to Mend* (1856), which was a popular success partly because it dealt with the recent scandal at Birmingham Gaol (where a young prisoner committed suicide; enquiry was made into the management of the prison, and the governor William Austin was tried and imprisoned for three months), but also because the book was full of exciting incident—punishments in the prison, suicide, the adventures of a ticket-of-leave man in Australia, escapades in the Australian gold fields. The public liked a strong story-line and had come to expect a moral interest. *It is Never Too Late to Mend*, which criticized the contemporary prison system, gave it both. Browning, for example, was not popular because he was obscure and given to philosophizing. When *Men and Women* appeared in 1855, the *Saturday Review* complained 'It is really high time that this sort of thing should, if possible, be stopped. Here is another book of madness and mysticism . . .' George Eliot's meditative novels, with their concern for motive and the slow shaping of character, and George Meredith's philosophical romances, were a new departure in English fiction (*Adam Bede* was published in 1856 and *The Ordeal of Richard Feverel* in 1859, the same year as *The Woman in White*). By the time Anthony Trollope wrote his autobiography (1875–6) he could survey the literary scene and conclude :–

Among English novels of the present day, and among English novelists, a great division is made. There are sensational novels and anti-sensational, sensational novelists and anti-sensational; sensational readers and anti-sensational. The novelists who are considered to be anti-sensational are generally called realistic. I am realistic. My friend Wilkie Collins is generally supposed to be sensational. The readers who prefer the one are supposed to take delight in the elucidation of character. They who hold by the other are charmed by the construction and gradual development of a plot. All this is, I think, a mistake,—which mistake arises from the inability of the imperfect artist to be at the same time realistic and sensational. A good novel should be both . . .

(Chapter 12)

The argument, which Trollope thought so wrong-headed, began in the fifties (Trollope's *The Warden* was published in 1855). But the kind of sensation achieved in *The Woman in White* was different from the sensation of, for example, *It is Never Too Late to Mend*. As Mrs. Oliphant points out, Collins's sensation is not usually dependent upon extraordinary happenings—murders, suicides, seductions—but 'the simplest expedients of life'. Unlike Dickens, he rarely resorts to the supernatural. He can get his effect from the appearance of a woman at night on a quiet suburban road:

> I . . . was strolling along the lonely highroad—idly wondering, I remember, what the Cumberland young ladies would look like—when, in one moment, every drop of blood in my body was brought to a stop by the touch of a hand laid lightly and suddenly on my shoulder from behind me. I turned on the instant, with my fingers tightening round the handle of my stick.
> There, in the middle of the broad, bright highroad . . . stood the figure of a solitary Woman, dressed from head to foot in white garments . . .
>
> (*The Woman in White*, The Story begun by Walter
Hartright, Section IV)

Count Fosco, the impressive villain of the piece and Collins's most successful character, is no exaggerated melodramatic Italian. He makes his effect precisely because of the contrast between the comfortable solid reality of his appearance—he is fat, fond of pastry, vain, likes to keep pets—and the malice of his intentions.

In all his novels Collins is well able to suggest the externals of mid-Victorian society, particularly its bricks and mortar. He does not make poetry of them as Dickens does—Collins's chimneys never mop and mow as do the jeering stacks near Todgers's in *Martin Chuzzlewit*—but Valentine Blyth's house among the growing suburbs in North London places his way of life exactly in *Hide and Seek* (1854); Miss Gwilt's tireless spirit has a perfect foil in the dreary lodging set in a waste of cheap new houses, some of them still unfinished, in *Armadale* (1877); and the extraordinary legless man, Dexter, in *The Law and the Lady* (1875) is made almost convincing by his setting —the big, gloomy, old house in its grounds, defying the advance of the speculative builders and remaining aloof while the cheap little villas go up all around it. The new manor house Thorpe-Ambrose, in *Armadale*, is an epitome of high Victorian civilization:

> It was a purely conventional country-house—the product of the classical idea filtered judiciously through the commercial English mind. Viewed on the outer side, it presented the spectacle of a modern manufactory trying to look like an ancient temple. Viewed on the inner side, it was a marvel of luxurious comfort in every part of it, from basement to roof.

> (Book II, Chapter 2)

For the period 1850–70 was not only a period of great events in which people might be supposed to respond to exciting incident in novel and drama, it was also the age of flourishing commercial venture and middle-class comfort. Harriet Beecher Stowe, visiting England in 1853, remarked 'the matter of coziness and home comfort has been so studied, and matured, and reduced to system, that they really have it in their power to effect more, towards making their guests comfortable, than perhaps any other people' (*Sunny Memories of Foreign Lands*, 1854, p. 13). But such comfort could be stifling. There is an extraordinary outburst at the end of *Armadale* when the Sanatorium, where Miss Gwilt hopes to commit her murder, is thrown open to visitors. A lot of ladies arrive:

> In the miserable monotony of the lives led by a large section of the middle classes of England, anything is welcome to the women which offers them any sort of harmless refuge from the established tyranny of the principle that all human happiness begins and ends at home. While the imperious needs of a commercial country limited the representatives of the male sex, among the doctor's visitors, to one feeble

223

old man and one sleepy little boy, the women, poor souls, to the number of no less than sixteen . . . had seized the golden opportunity of a plunge into public life.

(Book V, Chapter 3)

The commercially successful mid-Victorian period was, to the middle-classes, oppressive both physically and morally. Both Reade and Collins campaigned against the deadening concept of Respectability. Their friendship really began when Collins defended Reade against the critics who described his novel *Griffith Gaunt* (1866) as immoral and indecent. (It is Reade's best novel. It is spoilt by a conventional ending, but it is Reade's subtlest study of human relationships. It was decried because Griffith is a bigamist and because Reade described happiness in an illicit sexual relationship.) It seems to me that the sensation novel and the sensation drama were popular in such a period because they offered release in excitement. Collins's particular kind of sensation was popular because he suggested the extraordinary in the context of the monotonous lives lived by ordinary people. In *Armadale* he describes the treachery of the Norfolk Broads :

Firm as it looked, the garden-ground in front of the reed-cutter's cottage was floating ground, that rose and fell and oozed into puddles under the pressure of the foot.

(Book II, Chapter 9)

Collins's best novels are powerful, because in his neutral, prosaic style, often using a variety of narrators, each adding a vital piece to the mosaic, he evokes a solid, commercial society and discloses the pressures and horrors behind the façade, 'firm as it looked'. Sir Percival Glyde commits forgery to make it appear that his parents were married so that he could claim an estate, and plans to incarcerate his wife in a lunatic asylum to enjoy her fortune; Magdalen Vanstone in *No Name* schemes for a loveless marriage so that she can possess her dead father's money; to avert financial ruin Mr. Ablewhite, the eminently respectable philanthropist, steals a priceless diamond; Miss Gwilt, like a chess-player meditating her moves, plans murder to get a title and an estate. Unconventional himself—he had two mistresses and three illegitimate children—Wilkie Collins's sensation novels have worn better than Reade's, because they expose the dark places of a commercial society, realistically portrayed.

Reade also described the horrors in contemporary society—in *Hard Cash* (1863), as in *The Woman in White*, greed for money causes a sane person to be imprisoned in a lunatic asylum; in *It is Never Too Late to Mend* he exposes the cruelties inherent in well-intentioned schemes of penal reform; in *Foul Play* (1868, written with Dion Boucicault, the Irish sensation-dramatist) the practice of risking men's lives in unseaworthy ships for the sake of the insurance; in *Put Yourself in His Place* (1870) outrages committed by trades unionists. But, unlike Collins, he cannot suggest the substantial reality of that society, partly because he is too anxious to obtrude himself and his opinions upon the reader, partly because he piles incident upon incident in his narrative until the reader is dizzy and incredulous, partly because he had, surprisingly enough, an interest in the psychology of the characters involved in his startling scenes and some of his best writing describes their inner feelings rather than outward appearances—for example, Gerard's escape from the haunted tower in *The Cloister and the Hearth* (1861) is almost cinematic. His perilous climb down the rope is described from his viewpoint; the stones of the tower passing near his face, whilst below his friends look up at him and he is aware of their raised hands, their eyes, their teeth. Similarly subjective are Robinson's experiences in the punishment cell in *It is Never Too Late to Mend*, or Alfred Hardie's anguish as he realizes that all his actions will be interpreted as those of a maniac. Both Reade and Collins shared with Dickens the view that the novel should be dramatic. They both loved the theatre and Reade wanted to make his name as a dramatist but wrote novels in order to live. He wrote over thirty plays, including translations, adaptations and collaborations. He loved the immediate response of an audience and mistrusted the power of the printed word to convey to a reader the effects he wanted; so he resorted to all kinds of typographical devices to embody his dialogue and situations—capitals for shouts, small print for whispers, drawings of objects important to the plot like the knife bearing grains of gold in *It is Never Too Late to Mend*. Both novelists turned their own plays into novels, to the detriment of the novels which become stagey with the 'tableaux' of the contemporary sensation drama, its violent action, its exaggerated gestures. Reade used his play *Gold* (1853) for the Australian scenes of *It is Never Too Late to Mend*; the early play he wrote with Tom Taylor, *Masks and Faces* (1852), became the novel *Peg Woffington* (1852). Collins wrote *The Fro-*

zen Deep (1856) for Dickens's theatricals at Tavistock House and later turned it into a novel; *Man and Wife* (1870), which marks the decline of Collins's work as a novelist, was first conceived as a play, and *The New Magdalen* (1873) was written simultaneously with the play which Collins kept just one stage ahead of the novel. In the sensation dramas which Reade wrote from many of his novels startling effects are often achieved by the use of real water or real explosives on the stage, or real objects are used to set the scene. *Free Labour*, the play he made from the novel *Put Yourself in His Place*, had a scene 'in the course of which the audience has the pleasure of seeing Mr. Neville actually forge *real* edge tools, on a *real* anvil, with a *real* hammer—and uncommonly well he does it' (*The Times*, 31 May 1870).

This belief in fact as a source of art is evident in Reade's social-problem novels. When they were adversely criticized he referred his critics to the newspapers and Blue Books from which he had got his material. Unlike Collins, he lacked invention, and because he relied so heavily on facts, he defended himself by preaching the fallacious theory that factual reality in a play or novel ensures artistic reality. Moreover, he was so accustomed to looking at life in terms of the sensation drama (as Quiller-Couch rather unkindly pointed out, Reade for years lived with a second-rate actress, Mrs. Seymour) that he exaggerated his facts into melodrama. This is true of *It is Never Too Late to Mend*, *Hard Cash* and *Put Yourself in His Place*.

It is interesting to compare these novels with *Sybil* or *Yeast* or *Alton Locke*. These earlier novels are concerned with commenting upon the nature of a whole society, and they are optimistic, looking forward to the possibilities of the future. Reade comments on specific abuses which have become apparent in society—its failure to deal with criminals, for example—and he aims not so much at society's regeneration as at public opinion which will force a small specialized group of men—like prison governors and chaplains—to act more responsibly. Reade's social-problem novels, in fact, are closely related to his journalism and publicise events and personalities as newspapers do. It was through his journalism—he was a very active journalist—that he freed a sane, wealthy man from a lunatic asylum in the Fletcher v. Fletcher case, the germ of *Hard Cash*.

His 'stage eye' and his delight in startling facts and newspaper cases help to give Reade's novels the strong tones and over-emphasis which the modern reader dislikes. There was a close relationship between novelist and reader in the Victorian period, and Reade exploited it vigorously. Collins's best novels have a subtler appeal to the reader's pleasure in solving a puzzle and each stage leads him a step nearer the solution. Reade was serious and sincere in his desire for reform, but his work shows the danger of propaganda in the novel, that character and subtle human relationships are lost in the broad effects necessary to catch public attention. Also it needs a great artist to make a temporary situation universal, otherwise the novel ceases to be interesting when the reform has been accomplished. Despite a melodramatic plot, Marcus Clarke's *For the Term of his Natural Life* (1874), on the Australian penal settlements, is a more impressive book than *It is Never Too Late to Mend*, because Clarke succeeds in making the criminals' battle with the Australian bush and the sea an image of man's insignificance and heroism.

Unfortunately, Reade influenced Collins to plead for specific reform in his later novels, for example, *Man and Wife*, based on the Report of the Royal Commissioners on the Laws of Marriage, 1868, or *Heart and Science* (1883), which attacks the vivisectionists. Collins could absorb incidental social comment into his novels, but a plot controlled by a specific social abuse narrowed his vision and his indignation disturbed the calm detachment of his style.

From the 1860s he suffered increasing pain and illness, so that he was forced to take large doses of opium. He was always a careful craftsman and he worked steadily at his fiction, but undoubtedly his art became more mechanical as his health deteriorated. But although the critics commented adversely, his popularity remained immense. When in 1884 the *Pall Mall Gazette* held a ballot to determine the most popular writer, Collins topped the poll.

Reade's first love was the theatre and, when short of money, he was not above writing a worthless pot-boiler novel like *White Lies* (1857), but both he and Collins helped to make fiction a serious craft by their unremitting labour and their theorizings on the art. Reade's energy seems to us to have been largely mis-spent, although George Eliot took him seriously as a writer and the young Henry James praised him. The Victorians were used to broad effects in their fiction and drama and they approved of sincere moral intention; his exaggerated writing did not seem so jarring to them as it does to us. But he created his sensation from solid subject-matter, as did Collins.

Both are minor novelists, but Collins's subtler art has worn better, and his original treatment of the sensation novel produced the modern detective novel. Both are, above all, narrators. 'Everyone writes novels nowadays but nobody tells stories', Collins complained (quoted by K. Robinson, *Wilkie Collins*, 1951, p. 328). It is fashionable today to despise the art of narrative but, as E. M. Forster remarks in *Aspects of the Novel*, it is the novelist's basic art and, he implies, the simplest. On the contrary, it is a very difficult art. Perhaps the best narratives in the English language are the traditional ballads, and they are effective because they are economical and implicit:

> O laith, laith were our gude Scots lords
> To wet their cork-heel'd shoon;
> But lang or a' the play was play'd
> They wat their hats aboon.

This one verse of 'Sir Patrick Spens' evokes an aristocratic society, the dramatic encounter between such fastidious elegance and the elements and its inevitable outcome. The shoes and the hats particularize the action, and the poet's wry humour emphasizes the grim disaster without exaggerating it. Just enough details are given for the listener's imagination to work upon.

Charles Reade is a lesser narrator than Wilkie Collins because he is too explicit—he directs his reader too obviously. To a lesser degree, Collins is also guilty of this:

> The construction is most minute and most wonderful. But I can never lose the taste of the construction. The author seems always to be warning me to remember that something happened at exactly half-past two o'clock on Tuesday morning; or that a woman disappeared from the road just fifteen yards beyond the fourth milestone. One is constrained by mysteries and hemmed in by difficulties, knowing, however, that the mysteries will be made clear, and the difficulties overcome at the end of the third volume.
>
> (Anthony Trollope, *Autobiography*, Chapter 13)

It is a just criticism; yet there is a pleasure in tracking the mystery to its solution. A minor pleasure, perhaps, but a real one.

BIBLIOGRAPHY

A *Disraeli*
Novels and Tales, ed. P. Guedalla, 12 vols., 1926–7.

L. Stephen, 'Mr. Disraeli's Novels', *Hours in a Library*, 2nd Series, 1876.

F. Harrison, *Disraeli's Place in Literature*, 1894.

J. A. Froude, *The Earl of Beaconsfield*, 1905; first published 1890. Lively if adulatory biography by one of the Great Victorians. The emphasis is on Disraeli's personality and on his achievements as Prime Minister. There is a good chapter on *Lothair*.

M. E. Speare, *The Political Novel*, Oxford, 1924. Argues that Disraeli created the political novel which he considers to be dominated by ideas rather than emotions. Some questionable generalizations but a useful comparison of Disraeli's thought with that of Carlyle.

V. S. Pritchett, 'Disraeli', *The Living Novel*, 1946.

B. R. Jerman, *The Young Disraeli*, Princeton, 1960.

S. M. Smith (ed.), *Mr. Disraeli's Readers*, Nottingham, 1966. Letters written to Disraeli and his wife by readers of *Sybil*. Introduction and commentary.

R. Blake, *Disraeli*, 1966. Important and detailed biography of Disraeli. It closely follows his political career but there are full references to the novels and some illuminating details of their composition, publication and reception.

B *Kingsley*
Life and Works, 19 vols., 1901–03.

F. Harrison, *Charles Kingsley's Place in Literature*, 1895.

C. E. Raven, *Christian Socialism 1848–1854*, 1920.

W. H. Brown, *Charles Kingsley. The Work and Influence of Parson Lot*, Manchester, 1924. Style occasionally florid, and the book uncritical and rather complacent, but the writer knew Ludlow and gives some useful facts of the Co-operative Movement's debt to the Christian Socialists.

G. Kendall, *Charles Kingsley and his Ideas*, 1947.

A. R. Vidler, *The Theology of F. D. Maurice*, 1948. Systematic study of Maurice as theologian and of Christian Socialism as the manifestation of his theology at one period of his life. Useful bibliography of Maurice's writings.

R. B. Martin, *The Dust of Combat, A Life of Charles Kingsley*, 1959. Fairly detailed biography with some literary criticism; a good bibliography of critical works on Kingsley. Sometimes inaccurate.

Sheila M. Smith, 'Truth and Propaganda in the Victorian Social Problem Novel', *Renaissance and Modern Studies*, VIII, 1964. References to Kingsley, Disraeli, Reade.

P. R. Allen, 'F. D. Maurice and J. M. Ludlow: A Reassessment of the Leaders of Christian Socialism', *Victorian Studies*, XI, 1968.

C *Collins*
There is no readily available collected edition of Collins's novels. His major novels were published in Tauchnitz's *Collection of British Authors*, 1856–66, and by Chatto and Windus, 1875–1905.
Dorothy Sayers, Introduction to *Great Short Stories of Mystery, Detection and Horror*, 1928.
S. M. Ellis, *Wilkie Collins, Le Fanu and Others*, 1931.
T. S. Eliot, 'Wilkie Collins and Dickens', *Selected Essays*, 1932. Includes illuminating discussion of the nature of melodrama.
R. Ashley, 'Wilkie Collins and the Detective Story', *Nineteenth Century Fiction*, VI, 1951.
B. A. Booth, 'Wilkie Collins and the Art of Fiction', *Nineteenth Century Fiction*, VI, 1951.
K. Robinson, *Wilkie Collins, A Biography*, 1951. A substantial biography with some sound literary criticism; particularly good on the relationship between Collins and Dickens.
N. P. Davis, *The Life of Wilkie Collins*, Urbana, Ill., 1956. Some extravagant claims for Collins as a novelist, but a detailed and well-documented biography.

D *Reade*
Novels, 17 vols., 1895.
W. C. Phillips, *Dickens, Reade and Collins, Sensation Novelists*, New York, 1919. Does not sufficiently relate the vogue for 'sensation' to the society in which it arose, but includes an interesting account of nineteenth-century methods of publishing and selling novels to meet the demands of an increasingly varied range of readers, and the effect of these demands on the novels produced.
E. W. Hornung, 'Charles Reade', *The London Mercury*, IV, 1921.
E. G. Sutcliffe, 'The Stage in Reade's Novels' and 'Charles Reade's Notebooks', *Studies in Philology*, XXVII 1930.
M. Elwin, *Charles Reade, A Biography*, 1931. A full and detailed biography; not much literary criticism. A sensible discussion of the relationship between the events of Reade's life and his literary, dramatic and journalistic work.
A. M. Turner, *The Making of The Cloister and the Hearth*, Chicago, 1938. Exhaustive study of the sources of the novel, but little critical evaluation.
Léone Rives, *Charles Reade, Sa Vie, Ses Romans*, Toulouse, 1940. Over-estimates Reade's importance as a writer, but a useful biography.
W. Burns, 'The Sheffield Flood: a Critical Study of Charles Reade's Fiction', *Publications of the Modern Language Association of America*, LXIII, 1948.
Sheila M. Smith, 'Propaganda and Hard Facts in Charles Reade's Didactic Novels', *Renaissance and Modern Studies*, IV, 1960.

8

MEREDITH, HARDY AND GISSING

PATRICK M. YARKER, *King's College, London*

Pessimism. A History and a Criticism, by James Sully, published in 1877, was an acknowledgement of a mood that had been growing for a generation, and was now almost general. It was no more than a mood, because few in England were prepared to be outright pessimists with all that that involved Only one or two, such as James Thomson, whose *The City of Dreadful Night* (1874) reflected the teaching of Leopardi, were prepared to accept the full Continental doctrine. Yet scarcely any in the latter half of the century escaped its influence completely, and as the period wore on into the Decadence of the nineties it became more widespread. Sully suggested that it came partly from cynicism engendered by religious scepticism, and partly from 'a sense of the hollowness of the last century optimism'. Undoubtedly the collapse of religious authority and the discrediting of the optimistic monisms of the eighteenth century, with their Utilitarian offshoots, combined with the dead weight of scientific determinism to produce impossible tensions in those who tried to reconcile old habits of thought with the new circumstances. Yet, however blank the intellectual outlook, the belief prevailed that right and order would survive, and that man himself would supply the moral guidance evidently lacking elsewhere in the Universe. 'Meliorism', defined by Sully as 'the faith which affirms not merely our power of lessening evil—this nobody questions—but also our ability to increase the amount of positive good', was, with agnosticism, the characteristic doctrine of the period. The word is attributed to George Eliot, and the idea, with its onus of human responsibility, appealed to novelists. Even

Hardy borrowed the name, though the possibility of improvement can be seen only far down the perspective of his thought.

George Meredith (1828–1900) appears at first sight to have little to do with pessimism. He had a fundamental vigour and zest for life, and might have said with Browning's David 'How good is man's life, the mere living!'. He has been called a temperamental optimist. But his optimism was really only a determination to see the bright side of things; it was not a systematic view of life. For if there is a bright side, there must also be a darker one, and of this Meredith was fully aware. His novels, for all their high spirits, take a gloomy view of human nature. The only thing is that he presents this as a form of comic warning, implying that we are at liberty to take notice and do better. No more is implied, for to Meredith the 'shapeliness' of our life on earth is all that need concern us:

> We do not get to any heaven by renouncing the Mother we spring from; and where there is an eternal secret for us, it is best to believe that Earth knows, to keep near her, even in our utmost aspirations.
>
> (*Lord Ormont*, Chapter 14)

But to say 'it is best to believe . . .' implies that belief is a matter of arbitrary choice, and throws an air of sham over the whole thing. Meredith's earthbound optimism is something of an expedient, even, perhaps, a desperate clinging to the known in face of the unknown. He was called the reconciler of Wordsworth and Darwin, but this is hardly so. To Wordsworth Nature was the visible manifestation of a spiritual order of being, and his great power as a poet was his capacity to suggest both aspects in his words. In Meredith's poetry, however, Earth and Nature are realities, existing for themselves alone; even man appears only as a figure in the landscape. In his poem 'A Faith on Trial', or in 'The Woods of Westermain', and others in the volume of *Poems and Lyrics of the Joy of Earth* (1883), he set out a creed that makes no attempt to minimize the anomalies and frustrations of human life, and its final extinction. The well-known 'Dirge in Woods' (1870) has an Arnoldian cadence:

> Overhead, overhead
> Rushes life in a race,
> As the clouds the clouds chase;
> And we go,

And we drop like the fruits of the tree,
　　Even we,
　　Even so.

On the Darwinian side, however, the picture was a little
brighter. He believed that the emergence of consciousness
marked the limit of Natural Selection, and that thereafter man
must himself take a hand in the agonizing process of his creation. This prospect filled Meredith with exhilaration, for it
restored the sense of man's co-operation with Nature. Imperfect and evolving, he must strive to follow his higher consciousness. For the older biological factors of evolution remain active. The predatory element, the 'scaly Dragon-fowl',
is still apparent in man's nature as 'egoism', or the wilful assertion of the self in crass unawareness of the personalities and
rights of others. Each man's task is to quell this primitive
egoism which alienates him from the rest of creation and to
cultivate awareness of life as a whole. The task is hard, but
his efforts are not unaided. Even the bitterness of life can be a
guide, administering a 'celestial hail of thwacks'. But above
all, the universal harmony, manifesting itself in common
sense and having as its instrument of correction the Spirit of
Comedy, serves to maintain the essential balance between
blood, brain, and spirit, by which harmony is achieved.

This is the theme of Meredith's novels: the regulation of
human behaviour by the operation of the Comic Spirit. Wherever there is an aberration or want of proportion the Comic
Spirit seeks to correct it. The novels all deal, in various ways,
with this corrective process. In them egoism is shown in countless forms, though reduced in Meredith's comic world to a
series of grotesque posturings and expedients, having in various
degrees painful, even tragic, consequences, although remaining basically ridiculous. Seen in one light it is hardly an optimistic picture. The Comic Spirit presides over it with the
'sunny malice of a faun', waiting with suppressed glee for the
next absurdity, which always comes. In 1877 Meredith gave
his famous lecture *On the Idea of Comedy and of the Uses of the
Comic Spirit*, explaining its function:

Men's future on earth does not attract it; their honesty and
shapeliness in the present does: and whenever they wax
out of proportion, overblown, affected, pretentious, bombas-
tical, hypocritical, pedantic, fantastically delicate; whenever
it sees them self-deceived or hoodwinked, given to run riot
in idolatries, drifting into vanities, congregating in absurdi-

ties, planning shortsightedly, plotting dementedly; whenever they are at variance with their professions, and violate the unwritten but perceptible laws binding them in consideration one to another; whenever they offend sound reason, fair justice; are false in humility or mined with conceit, individually, or in bulk—the Spirit overhead will look humanely malign and cast an oblique light on them, followed by volleys of silvery laughter.

(An Essay on Comedy, 1897, pp. 89–90)

This detached view of life, uncommon among Victorians, perhaps owes something to Meredith's unusual upbringing. The Merediths were of Welsh extraction, but the family history really begins with his grandfather, Melchizedek Meredith (1763–1814), a well-known tailor and naval outfitter in Portsmouth. His portrait as 'the Great Mel' in *Evan Harrington* is no doubt authentic, and the novel reflects, with varying fidelity, much of the family background. George Meredith's father was the youngest of the Great Mel's seven children. When he was seventeen the Great Mel died, much in debt, leaving him, like Evan Harrington himself, to carry on the business, for which he had no inclination. Unlike Evan, however, he did not wed an heiress, but married the daughter of a local innkeeper. It was a successful match, and George Meredith, their only child, was born on 12 February 1828.

It is a curiosity of Meredith's life that these simple facts of his birth and parentage remained virtually unknown until after his death in 1909. Indeed, he took active steps to conceal them, and allowed romantic rumours concerning his origin to proliferate. But even more remarkable is the fact that in the Countess de Saldar in *Evan Harrington* (she was a portrait of his aunt Louisa, whose husband became a friend of the king of Portugal) he showed, with rich comedy, the absurdity of one whose extravagant horror of her tailoring origin led her into impossible shifts to conceal it. Whatever the explanation of this paradox, Meredith was clearly uneasy about his connection with trade and sought to sever it as soon as he could. It is possible that this inner uncertainty explained the 'faked' social values that E. M. Forster detected in his novels (*Aspects of the Novel*, 1949 edn., p. 86).

The second factor from his childhood that influenced his later life was his two years at the Moravian school at Neuwied on the Rhine. This school, dedicated to the principle of individual freedom, had a wide reputation, and boys from all over Europe were to be met there. Thus from the provincial milieu of the high-class tailoring business in Portsmouth Meredith was translated to a cosmopolitan centre alive with European liberalism. For in 1842, when he went there, the ferment that seethed up in 1848 was already active, and Meredith was greatly affected by it. It was said that he lived perpetually in the spirit of 1848. He returned to England with a taste for German literature that led him to Carlyle, and a zeal for revolutionary politics that soon gained him many friends of similar outlook.

Among these were Edward Peacock, son of Thomas Love Peacock, and his sister, Mary Nicolls, whose sailor husband had been drowned shortly after their marriage. Meredith, then twenty-three, fell passionately in love with this tragic and beautiful daughter of the legendary friend of Shelley. She was seven years older than he, but after a furious courtship they were married, and the disastrous story partly recorded in *Modern Love* began. They lived at first with Peacock at Lower Halliford, but when their son Arthur was born, this further invasion proved too much, and they had to go. Peacock exerted a lasting influence on Meredith, to be seen not only in some of his more crotchety characters, but also in certain dialogue-scenes, such as the 'Animated Conversation at a Luncheon-Table' in *The Egoist*, which might almost belong to one of Peacock's books.

His first essay in narrative fiction, however, was in a different genre. *The Shaving of Shagpat* (1856) was an oriental tale, owing something to *Vathek* and to Southey's *Thalaba the Destroyer*, as well as to *The Arabian Nights*, but having elements of comedy that were Meredith's own. He denied intentional allegory, but this tale of a hirsute enchanter who holds a city in superstitious subjection by means of a single hair, and of the efforts of Shibli Bagarag, the barber, to shave him, and so become 'Master of the Event', doubtless reflects his ideas of rationality and freedom. It was followed by *Farina. A Legend of Cologne* (1857), a less successful parody of the Gothic tale of terror.

In the meantime his marriage was becoming impossible. Both were highly-strung and uncompromising, and a series of domestic disasters and difficulties with lodgings made things worse. In 1858 Meredith's wife ran away with Henry Wallis, the Pre-Raphaelite painter, for whose *Death of Chatterton* Meredith had posed. They went to Wales, where she bore Wallis a son, and then on to Capri. Arthur Meredith remained with his father, and though she returned the following year, Meredith never saw his wife again. She died friendless in 1861, and in the next year Meredith published *Modern Love*, a sequence of fifty sixteen-line 'sonnets', in which he probed the anatomy of an unhappy marriage with skill and experience. He concludes that there was no avoidable blame:

> The wrong is mixed. In tragic life, God wot,
> No villain need be. Passions spin the plot:
> We are betrayed by what is false within.
>
> (No. 43)

The effect of the disaster had already appeared, however, in *The Ordeal of Richard Feverel* (1859), a book in which Meredith's bitterness is clearly visible beneath the surface. For, though treated as a comedy, the book ends in disaster for the innocent, and has an undercurrent of resentment, springing from the fact that Sir Austin Feverel's wife has run off with a poet. This warps his nature so that he resolves to bring up his son without knowledge of sexual love until he himself should choose him a partner. But Richard falls in love with Lucy, a farmer's niece, abducts and marries her. His father, however, so plays on his filial affection that, torn between this and his love for Lucy, he causes her much needless suffering and a tragic death. The book has many shortcomings, chiefly a lack of unity and motivation, but it contains the elements of much of Meredith's later work. Sir Austin is the first of his egoists, and his egoism destroys the natural harmony, with disastrous consequences. The irony, sustained throughout, is some of the harshest that Meredith ever developed. It was, for example, Sir Austin's own half-hearted affair with Lady Blandish that frustrated his 'System' by awakening romantic notions in Richard; his success in separating Richard from Lucy brought about what he most feared for his son (though advocating for others) 'to drag him through the sinks of the town'; in the end he realizes that Lucy is an admirable daughter-in-law, but it is then too late. Lucy dies, and Richard is left to endure the full agony of realization.

Meredith's irony depends on his attitude to his characters; it is not irony of situation, representing the grimness of human fate, but irony of folly, comic irony (though sometimes grim enough). For this reason Meredith never shrank from comment in his own person, or through the medium of an imaginary arbiter such as 'the Philosopher'. This is sometimes tedious, and he erred, too, in placing too great a reliance on the tone.

The result is that his novels exist at several removes from life, and their effect is mainly intellectual. Although the movement towards realism was getting under way when he wrote, he had no bent for it. As W. E. Henley put it, his characters are not human beings but 'compendiums of humanity' (*The Academy*, Vol. xvi (1879), p. 369), so that his comic world, though far from ordinary life, is, in its own way, true.

The next novel, *Evan Harrington* (1861), is far more in the spirit of comedy than its predecessor. The Countess Louisa, for example, is in the broad tradition of matronly humour, though her social snobbery was a more recent emergence. In her assumption of a foreign manner that leads her to address her sisters as 'You English' she is of the order of pretenders who almost deceive themselves. 'We must honour Papa, even though we cannot, of course, acknowledge him' is the measure of her candour and family affection. She maintains her impossible position, both in her own and others' eyes, with immense resource and powers of generalship that proclaim Meredith's respect for the formidable capacity of women, even at a time when he still smarted from its effects. His books contain many masterful women—Rhoda Fleming, Vittoria, Diana Warwick, Carinthia Fleetwood; even the less forceful, such as Clara Middleton in *The Egoist*, have a determination not to be brooked, and one recognizes the force of Sir Willoughby Patterne's complaint, 'I am favoured by fortune from my birth until I enter into relations with women!' (Chapter 40). For the women have an egoism of their own before which the male kind, otherwise rampant, is rebuked. The Countess Louisa is, in her many-sidedness, one of the best of Meredith's women characters, though her position is different from those of the others. There is little else in *Evan Harrington* to approach her. The book was published serially in *Once a Week*, with illustrations by Charles Keene, and was given by the reviewer in *The Saturday Review* 'a front place in literature that is . . . not destined to endure' (Vol. xi (1861), p. 77).

Meredith was now on intimate terms with Swinburne and the Rossettis and rented a room from them at 15 Cheyne Walk. He had formed two other friendships that influenced his novels. The first was with Janet Duff-Gordon, who inspired his more sympathetic heroines such as Rose in *Evan Harrington*, and the second was with Frederick Maxse, a naval officer who had distinguished himself in the Crimea. He was to be the model for the hero of *Beauchamp's Career*. About this time Meredith became literary adviser to Chapman and Hall, in which position he had some influence on younger novelists.

The next novel, *Emilia in England* (1864), afterwards called *Sandra Belloni*, repeated some of the comic features of *Evan Harrington* in the three Pole sisters, daughters of a merchant, who aspire to 'Fine Shades' of 'Nice Feeling'—perhaps owing something, too, to Ruskin's ideal view of the merchant in *Unto This Last*. They are contrasted with the simple ardour of Emilia, daughter of an itinerant Italian musician and possessor of a fine natural voice. *Rhoda Fleming* (1865), however, was a departure from Meredith's earlier vein. This story of a girl seduced by a young egoist has been said to give 'a curious impression of having been written in collaboration with Hardy' (S. Sassoon, *Meredith*, 1948, p. 73); but Dahlia Fleming is unlike Tess. Her sister Rhoda is the one to carry on the 'Woman's Battle' of the original title. However, Meredith's approach to the theme, critical of the marriage custom, ironical about the need for the girl to be made an honest woman at all costs, is certainly more that of the late rather than the mid Victorian period. *Vittoria* (1866), sequel to *Sandra Belloni*, is Meredith's tribute to Mazzini and the 'Spirit of 1848'. Emilia, now a trained singer, gives her voice to the cause of freedom by singing a revolutionary song in the Opera House at Milan as a signal for the revolt against Austria.

In 1864 Meredith had married Marie Vulliamy, daughter of a neighbour, and this second marriage was to be as happy as the first had been wretched. The only shadow was the growing estrangement from Arthur, who was sent away to the Pestalozzi school in Switzerland for his health and seldom saw his father thereafter. A son, William Maxse, was born, and the Merediths moved to Flint Cottage, Box Hill, where the novelist spent most of his remaining years.

The Adventures of Harry Richmond (1871) was his first production at Flint Cottage and was serialized in *The Cornhill Magazine* with illustrations by George du Maurier. Written in the first person, as Harry's narrative of the struggle between his father and grandfather, each trying to save him from the other, the book owes much to Dickens, but develops, though it does not sustain, an exuberance of its own. Richmond Roy, the father, reputedly the son of a Royal Duke, a charlatan and poseur of egregious audacity, captivates Harry, and finally gains his understanding and loyalty. Though full of comment on contemporary questions, the book does not develop a pur-

pose in the manner of the earlier novels. 'Uncurbed by philosophical reservations, George Meredith had been able to allow
his imagination free scope', said an admirer. It may be, though,
that Meredith's genius needed such a curb. *Beauchamp's Career*
(1876), which he told John Morley was 'philosophical-political,
with no powerful stream of adventure', certainly provided one.
In 1867 Maxse retired from the Navy and stood as Radical
candidate for Southampton, and thereafter uttered a series of
reforming pamphlets. Meredith helped in his election campaign which failed, and produced his own pamphlet in the
'Up at Midnight' dialogues in *The Graphic*. It was the time of
the Paris Commune, which Meredith greeted with an Ode.
These activities were the background of the novel, which is
diversified by uncertain but passionate amours, and such scenes
as that (as E. M. Forster put it) 'of one old man whipping
another from the highest motives' (*Aspects of the Novel*, 1949
edn., p. 87). It is Meredith's best-constructed novel.

But narrative was not his main interest. His eye was on
the drama of the big scene, and his stories too often repeat the
same features—the jealous influence of an older man on a
younger, the blighting of true love by wrong-headedness, the
impossible passion for an ideal beauty. These elements serve
only to connect the set pieces. His essay on Comedy is largely
an account of the comic drama, with the emphasis on Molière
and Congreve, and the success of his next book, *The Egoist*
(1879), rightly regarded as his masterpiece, has something to
do with its organization on the lines of a play. The narrative
is far simpler than in earlier books and is developed in a series
of dialogues. The characters are fewer than usual, and are
grouped around the central figure, Sir Willoughby Patterne,
gaining depth when, like Clara Middleton, they stand in open
conflict with him, losing it as they move towards the circum-
ference. Sir Willoughby is essential egoism. His monomania is
no mere crotchet, like that of Sir Arthur Feverel and others. In
them there is always a spark of genuine feeling, a heart capable
of being touched. But Willoughby has no heart; he has nothing
at the centre at all. Outward appearances, the cutting of an
appropriate figure, are all that he understands. He sees others
only in terms of his own reputation.

'Egoism', a word dating from the late eighteenth century,
was one of the key terms of the nineteenth. It bred an antonym,
'altruism', first used by Comte to provide an alternative to the
principle of self-interest, long thought the chief motive in human
affairs. Under Comte's influence a new ethic developed, in

which egoism was the negative and altruism the positive morality. Meredith, however, does not present egoism in these terms in the book. Willoughby's self-centred assumptions about Clara are exasperating, but comically so, for we see that he injured no-one but himself. Egoism, we understand, is the alienating principle, and if an individual chooses it, he must bear his resulting isolation. It was Meredith's most optimistic novel, and this, perhaps, was what he referred to when he told Stevenson, 'it is a Comedy with only half of me in it, unlikely therefore to take either the public or my friends' (*Letters*, ed. W. M. Meredith, 1912, Vol. I, p. 297). He was mistaken, but there was point in his remark. In another sense it may have been what he put in unnecessarily, rather than what he left out, that was rejected. W. E. Henley, friend of both Meredith and Stevenson, reviewed the book in terms that might apply to Meredith generally :

> His pages so teem with fine sayings, and magniloquent epigrams and gorgeous images, and fantastic locutions, that the mind would welcome dulness as a glad relief. He is tediously amusing; he is brilliant to the point of being obscure; his helpfulness is so extravagant as to worry and confound. His ingenuity and intelligence are always misleading him into treating mere episodes as solemnly and elaborately as a main incident; he is ever ready to discuss, to ramble, to theorize, to dogmatize, to indulge himself in a little irony, or a little reflection, or a little artistic misdemeanour of some sort.
>
> (*The Athenæum*, 1 November 1879, p. 555)

The Egoist is freer from these faults than are most of the novels, but the indictment stands, and in some of the later books these faults were seriously aggravated.

The Tragic Comedians (1880) was based on the affair between Ferdinand Lassalle, the German socialist, and Helene von Donniges, as a result of which Lassalle fell in a duel. *Diana of the Crossways* (1885) also relied to some extent on historical personages, in this case Lady Caroline Norton and Lord Melbourne. Its theme, however, that of a married woman estranged from her husband, was becoming increasingly important with the triumph of feminism, and was to be the main concern of novels in the nineties. Meredith's last three works, *One of Our Conquerors* (1891), *Lord Ormont and His Aminta* (1894) and *The Amazing Marriage* (1895, but begun in 1879) all approach it in different ways. His son Arthur died in 1891, estranged from him as his mother had been. This perhaps revived something of Meredith's former outlook, for these novels all deal with broken marriages, now, 'n accord with the new spirit, carried to the full length of desertion and adultery. But the target of his attack was less personal than social, for each shows that modern society fosters egoism, with consequent wretchedness to the individual, and, in spite of the continued comic treatment, a gloomy outlook for mankind.

When Meredith died in 1909, his fame was at its height. Wilde, who had included a number of epigrams on Meredith in *The Decay of Lying*, also said :-

One incomparable novelist we now have in England, Mr. George Meredith. There are better artists in France, but France has no one whose view of life is so large, so varied, so imaginatively true. There are tellers of stories in Russia who have a more vivid sense of what pain in fiction may be. But to him belongs philosophy in fiction. His people not merely live, but they live in thought.

(The Soul of Man Under Socialism)

It is true that Henry James complained bitterly about *Lord Ormont*, possibly because in it a Jamesian situation is handled in an unJamesian manner (*Letters*, ed. P. Lubbock, 1920, Vol. I, p. 224). But he also praised Meredith's 'big strong whiffs of manly tone and clear judgment' (quoted by J. Lindsay, *George Meredith*, 1956, p. 372), and these qualities also appealed to R. L. Stevenson, who first met him in 1878, and ever thereafter 'served under his colours'. Stevenson loved his romance, his broad and active view of life, and admired his brilliant insight and analysis of character. Meredith's poetry made him 'drunk like wine', and he was fascinated by his style and poetic approach to reality.

Hardy reflected different aspects of the master's work. He received from him the myth-making element, the presentation of ideas in terms of life. More, he drew from Meredith his cosmic view of human life, presided over by eternal Spirits, who, without participating, manipulate events. Glimpses of the 'squatting imps' that Meredith described in the Prelude to *The Egoist*, waiting and watching, with 'ears at full cock, for the commencement of the comic drama of the suicide', are continually caught in Hardy's novels. But the difference is that, whereas in Meredith the activities of these imps of the Comic Spirit work for Harmony, and therefore the eventual good of mankind, Hardy's watchers are malignant, or, at best, indifferent to the good or suffering of men. Hardy's irony, therefore, is a tragic irony of events or destiny, rather than a comic irony of character and folly. Meredith's egoist is not a universal figure. We may all be egoists in our way; but we are all capable of chastening by the celestial thwacks. But to Hardy the ills from which men suffer are irremediable.

For Hardy absorbed far more of the pessimistic doctrine than did Meredith. He was the reverse of gloomy by nature, but he had a shrewder understanding than had Meredith of the negative aspects of Victorian expansion. His origins were no more lowly than were Meredith's, but his roots were far deeper in the soil. The son of a builder, he was born in 1840 at Lower Bockhampton, a small hamlet on the edge of what he came to call Egdon Heath. There were generations of farming tradition behind him. He had an instinctive feel for the immemorial way of life, regulated by the seasons, punctuated by secular or ecclesiastical festivals, and maintained by 'practices which had suffered no mutilation at the hands of time'. Moreover, in those ancient regions evidence is plentiful of occupation and husbandry since prehistoric times. Hardy's sense of the past was fostered by the propinquity of these earlier inhabitants, who had never really vanished from the scene.

But now he saw this long continuity interrupted. Unlike Meredith, Hardy felt the loss of religious faith; but it would be wrong to regard him as a nineteenth-century philosophical sceptic, or convert to agnosticism. His view of religion was not unconnected with his sense of the continuity of Dorset life since pagan times. The Church had come, and given the familiar pattern of Christian worship to the land, but it had not altered the fundamental beliefs, chthonic and fatalistic, that governed the lives of the people. Hardy's position was that of a further stage of sophistication, analogous, perhaps, to the legacy of the Enlightenment within the Church itself, the rational aspect slowly obliterating the sacramental. He remained, as he said 'churchy; not in an intellectual sense but in so far as instincts and emotions ruled' (F. E. Hardy, *The Later Years of Thomas Hardy*, 1930, p. 176). He thought of taking Orders when he was twenty-five; but he was already aware of a distance from his fellow-worshippers in Westminster Abbey. He felt increasingly wistful, longing for what he could no longer share. When he left school in Dorchester, he was articled to a local architect and restorer of churches, and he remained in this profession until the success of *Far from the Madding Crowd* released him in 1874. This active concern with the fabric of churches, decayed but extant, has an appropriate quality.

So, too, have the stories of gruesome but incongruous contents of coffins and other instances of macabre comedy that his profession afforded. For whereas Meredith was enabled by his Epicurean outlook to see life as a comedy with overtones of pathos, Hardy was impelled to the opposite view. He saw life as tragic, but with aspects of comedy. His sense of humour was irrepressible, but it was always inclined to the sepulchral. It became increasingly grotesque, and eventually did not relieve the pessimism of his novels but emphasized it, giving his work the 'twilight' quality that Meredith deplored. His self-acquired love of the classics fostered his belief in fate. His reading of the philosophers, of J. S. Mill and of Herbert Spencer's *First Principles* with its emphasis on force and causality, or of Schopenhauer and von Hartmann who proclaimed the doctrine of the unconscious Will, merely formulated what he already instinctively believed. Whereas mankind has consciousness, the force that controls him has not. Blindly, this unconscious Will frustrates and confounds man's noblest endeavours and passes on, unaware of the havoc caused. The imps that Meredith saw attendant on the Comic Spirit were to Hardy the agents of this alien force.

Hardy's novels present this sombre pageant from below, in the setting of his native Dorset, or Wessex, as he called it. The 'regional novel' was well established in English fiction by 1870, but Hardy brought an intensity to both landscape and figures that gave them something of the quality of myth. The literary heritage of his rustics has often been noted. They have affinity with Shakespeare's 'rude mechanicals'; their stoicism is reminiscent of Wordsworth, their earthiness of Scott. William Barnes, the Dorset poet, contributed much to their speech and activities. But Hardy also knew them well. In 1883 he published an essay on 'The Dorsetshire Labourer', giving an unsentimental picture of

> a number of dissimilar fellow-creatures, men of many minds;
> infinite in difference; some happy, many serene, a few depressed; some clever even to genius, some stupid, some wanton, some austere . . . each of whom walks his own way the road to dusty death.

From all these elements he fashioned something like a chorus to his drama. They act and are acted upon; but they live their lives according to the conditions that engulf them. Among themselves they are honest, kindly, tolerant; steeped in superstition, they have an instinctive sense of the workings of fate that preserves them from *hubris*. They find an earthy happiness in their limited aspirations, commenting shrewdly on their betters who fail to do so. Over them the Comic Spirit may be said to preside and their unconscious humour epitomizes the comic irony of life.

Like Meredith, Hardy was much concerned with class-distinctions, and his first novel, *The Poor Man and the Lady* (written 1867, but never published, and now lost) was on this theme. Meredith read it for Chapman and Hall and advised Hardy to concentrate on greater complication of plot. This advice was followed in *Desperate Remedies* (1871), the ramifications of whose action are reminiscent of Wilkie Collins. It is a novel of dark passages and 'moral obliquity'. It was attacked as immoral, but the country scenes were praised; so in his next novel, *Under the Greenwood Tree* (1872), moral issues were evaded, and the rustics of the Mellstock Quire have the scene almost to themselves, as they campaign against their replacement by an organ. The tale of Dick Dewey's courtship of Fancy Day is a slight one. It has a happy ending, but it lay in Fancy's power to give matters a different turn, and she all but did so. Love, to Hardy, was an additional affliction laid on already suffering humanity. Edmund Blunden drew attention to Swinburne's address to Aphrodite in *Atalanta in Calydon*, which Hardy had read with 'glad surprize' :-

> Was there not evil enough,
>   Mother, and anguish on earth
>   Born with man at his birth
> That thou, having wings as a dove,
> Being girt with desire for a girth,
>   That thou must come after these,
> That thou must lay on him love?

This was Hardy's view. Love, more than any other human attribute, puts man at the disposal of the tragic powers. *A Pair of Blue Eyes* (1873) develops this theme. It is set in Cornwall, whither Hardy had been sent by his employer to design a new tower for St Juliot's church, near Tintagel. While there he fell in love with Emma Gifford, the Rector's sister-in-law, and was idyllically happy for his whole stay in Cornwall, as one of his most famous poems relates :

When I came back from Lyonesse
With magic in my eyes . . .

In the novel the love story follows a very different course.
Leslie Stephen, the editor of *The Cornhill Magazine*, had liked *Under the Greenwood Tree*, and asked Hardy to write a serial novel for his magazine. The result was *Far From the Madding Crowd* (1874), Hardy's first financial success, and on the strength of it he and Emma Gifford married. The novel marks a stage, for it was his first attempt to develop Wordsworth's view that in rural life 'the essential passions of the heart find a better soil in which they can attain their maturity'. It is a vigorous account of the conflict of individuals with each other and with circumstances. The main characters, Gabriel Oak, Boldwood, Serjeant Troy, and Bathsheba Everdene, are drawn with bold strokes, emphasizing their independence, and setting them starkly against fate. Bathsheba is the first of his passionate women, capricious, wilful and proud. Her three lovers reflect different aspects of her nature. Troy has the romance of martial legend implied by his name. His scarlet is like the note of a trumpet; he woos her with his sword. But by this time the other face of romance was all too familiar. Troy is not heartless, but he is shallow, and, for all his swordsmanship, weak. He deserts Fanny Robin, who dies bearing his child, and, after his marriage to Bathsheba, deserts her too. Farmer Boldwood, outwardly stolid, shows in the end the destructiveness of passion. Oak is like his name, too, and his marriage to the widowed Bathsheba, when all passion is spent, is an acceptable triumph for 'that love . . . beside which the passion usually called by the name is as evanescent as a stream'. But this was Hardy's concession to the public; he originally meant Bathsheba's awakening to come too late. The malignant power of fate is palpable in the novel—and at one point visible, too. In a moment of repentance Troy plants Fanny's grave with flowers. Above it, the gutter of the church-tower ends in a gargoyle, with 'short, erect ears, eyes staring from their sockets, and its fingers and hands were seizing the corners of its mouth which they thus seemed to pull open to give free passage to the water it vomited'. That night it rained, and the spout from this grotesque orifice washed away the tokens of Troy's remorse. This charade, one of many in the novels, epitomizes much of Hardy's attitude to life and of his method of expressing it.
His imagination was keenly visual, and by startling images

he brings the living scene before the reader with astonishing suddenness. In contrast, his prose comments are often laboured and self-conscious. He gave his own explanation of this:

> It is, of course, simply a carrying into prose the knowledge I have acquired in poetry—that inexact rhymes and rhythms now and then are far more pleasing than correct ones.
>
> (*The Early Life of Thomas Hardy*, p. 138)

But the effect is often less pleasing than he supposed, and critics have complained of the 'inartistic knottiness' of his prose.

He wrote a further novel for Leslie Stephen, *The Hand of Ethelberta* (1876), 'a somewhat frivolous narrative', according to Hardy's preface, on the Meredithian theme of a butler's daughter who conceals her lowly origin for matrimonial ends. Very different was the next novel, *The Return of the Native* (1878), whose great protagonist is, of course, Egdon Heath. Hardy's descriptions of 'Haggard Egdon', instinct with a life alien to the social ways of men, are triumphs of his method. Egdon dominates the lives of all who live on its fringes. Not all are able to come to terms with its sombre presence; to some it is actively hostile. Only the rustics accept it without question. It is at once a symbol and a manifestation of the 'unwitting Will', blind, non-human, timeless. Its appeal is to an instinct deep in man's nature but, so Hardy believed, beginning to stir anew, for Clym Yeobright, who 'indirectly bore evidence that ideal physical beauty is incompatible with emotional development' can understand its grandeur, so inimical to 'the sort of beauty called charming and fair'. Curiously, Hardy chose to match this romantic concept with a classical form, giving the novel unity of place and action. Critics disliked it, however, and he was obliged to mitigate some of its gloom before it could be published.

His next novel was accordingly much lighter, taking some of its inspiration from comedy rather than from tragedy. *The Trumpet Major* (1880) is Hardy's most genial novel, having, in spite of its martial background, more affinity with *Under the Greenwood Tree* than with any other. It reflects his lifelong fascination with the Napoleonic Wars, which reached its climax in *The Dynasts*. The Hardys, who had been living at Sturminster, near Poole, had moved to London in 1878, taking a house near Wandsworth Common. In the winter of 1880 Hardy fell ill and remained incapacitated for some months, during which he dictated a novel to his wife. This was *A Laodicean* (1881), his least successful book. When he recovered, Hardy moved again to Dorset, settling in Wimborne. Here, in the year of a comet, he wrote *Two on a Tower* (1882), in which he sought 'to set the emotional history of two infinitesimal lives against the stupendous background of the stellar universe', as he said in the Preface. This theme had been in his mind for some years, and had already appeared in some of his lyrics, notably 'A Lunar Eclipse' and 'In Vision I Roamed' (1866). But, though possible in a short lyric, the theme is unsuited to a novel, where all the interest is naturally on the infinitesimal lives. But the loneliness of man haunted his imagination, and he turned increasingly to the epic theme of an individual against fate. *Far from the Madding Crowd* and *The Return of the Native* had been concerned with groups of people who act and react to the impulse of their natures. Now he began to consider the problem of one who tries to combat his nature, to overcome the passions and reverse their effect; the efforts, in other words, of the individual will to assert itself. But, in Hardy's view, the individual will is a figment; it is no more than a manifestation of the general Will in the individual life. Such efforts, therefore, are doomed. So long as they do not conflict with the general Will, the illusion of the individual will may persist and even appear triumphant. But in the end the reality will assert itself.

This is developed in *The Mayor of Casterbridge* (1886), Hardy's version of the theme of crime and punishment. Michael Henchard is an epic figure, standing among his fellows 'like a great tree in a wind'. He is also an attempt by Hardy to create a complex character, at odds with himself. The causes of both his rise and fall are to be found in his own nature to an extent not seen before in the novels. Chance, as always in Hardy, plays a large part in the plot. But from the first episode, in which he sells his wife and child, the defects of his character are clear. Later, his good qualities are equally apparent, but his fortitude and determination to overcome his faults, his honesty and courage, cannot wipe out the consequences of his action. Nevertheless, his strength and ruggedness are apt to a certain phase of development, and Henchard has twenty years of triumph. But they must needs give way before the new order, represented by Farfrae, with his modern methods. Thereafter, transformed to stubbornness and rigidity, they cause Henchard's ruin. There is thus a secular pattern in the novel, which increases the Lear-like aspect some have found in it.

The location of the book reflects Hardy's move to Dorchester in 1883, first into a house in the town itself and, finally, in 1885, to Max Gate, the house he designed for himself on the outskirts, which was to be his home for the rest of his life. The first book he wrote at Max Gate was *The Woodlanders* (1887), a transitional work that looks back to *Far From the Madding Crowd* (and even earlier) in its plot, but reflects Hardy's new preoccupations in its theme. The doctrine of the Unfulfilled Intention marks a variation of his thought and is explicit in his description of Hintock Wood:

> Here, as everywhere, the Unfulfilled Intention, which makes life what it is, was as obvious as it could be among the depraved crowds of a city slum. The leaf was deformed, the curve was crippled, the taper was interrupted; the lichen ate the vigour of the stalk, and the ivy slowly strangled to death the promising sapling.
>
> *(The Woodlanders,* Chapter 7)

Another new preoccupation, which had already appeared in *The Return of the Native*, and was to be of great importance in *Jude the Obscure*, was with 'modern nerves' and their incompatibility with 'primitive feeling'. In this respect Grace Melbury is a forerunner of Sue Bridehead.

The next novel was *Tess of the d'Urbervilles* (1891), in which he returned to his epic theme. The doctrine of the Unfulfilled Intention here takes on a more bitter aspect as Hardy questions the process by which 'so often the coarse appropriates the finer thus, the wrong man the woman, the wrong woman the man'. This, he says, 'many thousand years of analytical philosophy have failed to explain to our sense of order'. *Tess* differs from the earlier novels in that it was motivated by a social purpose, which he showed by his defiant caption to the title, 'A Pure Woman'. Not only the dispensations of fate, or the depravities of mankind, but the polite conventions of society were the objects of his scorn. Frankness in fiction was, during the eighties and nineties, an issue of growing importance and concern. In writing of Tess's seduction and its consequences Hardy cannot be said to have made a new departure, for the theme was much exploited, and had been treated with greater freedom by earlier writers. But by making her the heroine, and showing everyone else up in a poor light beside her, he deliberately challenged the view, more Malthusian than Christian, that a girl who has an illegitimate child, though she may be pitied, cannot be forgiven. It was a view that had been under fire since the House of Lords Select Committee in 1881, but it was not yet routed, and Hardy suffered for his temerity.

He had never been thoroughly reconciled to novel-writing, though he had become resigned to it as 'a trade'. Poetry had always been his preoccupation; he returned to fiction only to earn a living. If, however, his novels were not acceptable to the public he saw no point in writing any more. After reading a review of *Tess* he wrote in his journal

> Well, if this sort of thing continues no more novel-writing for me. A man must be a fool to deliberately stand up to be shot at.
>
> (*The Later Years of Thomas Hardy*, p. 7)

However, adverse criticism was not general, and it was understood that the book was a masterpiece. Hardy did not hesitate to expose himself as a target once more, and *Jude the Obscure* came out in November 1895. Although the protagonists are very different, it was in some ways a re-writing of *Tess*, with Tess's position between Alec d'Urberville and Angel Clare repeated in considerable detail by Jude's relations with Arabella and Sue. But the book is in a very different key. The 'modern nerves' that Hardy wrote of in *The Woodlanders* take possession of it; the concomitant 'primitive passions' are debilitated and fretful. 'We are horribly sensitive, that's what's wrong with us', cries Jude, and it is the keynote of the book, objectified in the gruesome figure of Little Father Time. Sue Bridehead has all the instability of Hardy's earlier women expressed in terms of nervous exhaustion. Henry James complained to Stevenson that, in *Tess*, 'the pretence of sexuality is only equalled by the absence of it' (*Letters*, Vol. I, p. 194), but in *Jude* both sides of the equation are revised. Hardy wrote that he meant the book to convey 'the contrast between the ideal life a man wished to lead and the squalid real life he was fated to lead'. He referred to Jude's aspiration to scholarship; but the wider reference is made clear by Jude's grotesque symbolic initiation when he is hit on the cheek by a hog's pizzle, thrown by Arabella. Like Meredith's novels of the nineties, *Jude* deals with what Hardy called the 'marriage question'. It does so not in terms of primitive passions, nor of a man's struggle, like Henchard's, against fate, but in terms of social conventions. 'It is no use fighting against God!' cries Sue; but Jude corrects her: 'It is only against men and senseless circumstances'. In their 'irregular' life together they are continually obliged to keep up appearances, and avert the suspicion of landladies. It was properly the realm of the Comic Spirit; when presented as tragedy the effect is lugubrious.

Hardy wrote no more novels after *Jude*, not because of the Press reviews, but because he had exhausted a form that was never congenial to him. In 1898 he published *Wessex Poems*, some of which had been written thirty years before. Poetry was his natural medium; 'I am only a learner in the art of novel-writing' he said after *Tess*, his thirteenth novel. Since 1870, when he visited Peninsular veterans at Chelsea, the idea of an epic on the Napoleonic Wars had been in his mind.

The Dynasts came out in three parts, in 1903, 1906, and 1908. In its Shelleyan complex of non-human Spirits it embodies the ideas of the unconscious Will that lie behind the novels. It looks at man's life from above, as the novels survey it from below. In *The Dynasts* men, even the greatest, are seen to be puppets, activated by strings. Only the Spirits have life.

Hardy's first wife died in 1912. For years she had entertained the delusion that her husband was her inferior, and the effect of this is apparent in *Jude*. Yet after her death he wrote a number of poems recalling their early days together in Cornwall and other memories of her. In 1914 he married his amanuensis, Florence Emily Dugdale, whose two volumes of his Journals and other biographical material are the main source of our knowedge of Hardy's personal life and thought. Hardy died in January 1928.

He is often called a poetic novelist, and the reference is not so much to his images as to his whole attitude to prose fiction. At a time when ideas of verisimilitude and psychological realism were in the ascendant, Hardy was as apt as Dickens to ignore the limitations of every day. 'It is not improbabilities of incident but improbabilities of character that matter', he wrote in 1886. But even if that were true, Hardy's characters have a quality of their own, and inhabit a world in which the elements have been brought into a new relationship, with meaningful conjunctions of events in a landscape vibrant with purpose.

Hardy took Matthew Arnold's phrase 'the imaginative reason' to define his approach to reality, suggesting the capacity to see 'into the heart of a thing'. A very different approach was adopted by George Gissing, whose novels, though they owed much to Meredith, are unlike those of either Meredith or Hardy. Gissing has always been known as a 'realistic' writer;

yet his view of realism was qualified by a belief that objectivity is impossible, for the observer necessarily imposes his own personality on what he sees. Writing of Dickens's practice of 'modifying circumstances' he said

> Our 'realist' will hear of no such paltering with truth. Heedless of Pilate's question, he takes for granted that truth can be got at, and that it is his plain duty to set it down without compromise; or, if less crude in his perceptions, he holds that truth, for the artist, is the impression produced on him, and that to convey this impression with entire sincerity is his sole reason for existing.
>
> (*Charles Dickens*, p. 73)

This view is close to Pater, and it is central to Gissing's approach to the novel. He agreed that the artist must modify his material; but he argued that this modification must be at the behest of his artistic conscience, and not to conform with a separately conceived moral theory or view of life. For this reason he rejected 'naturalism', such as that of Zola, which George Moore was following in England in *A Mummer's Wife* (1882). For the principle of naturalism was scientific, and, said Gissing, 'there is no science in fiction'. Similarly, his pessimism was not a positive belief, such as Hardy's, but an attitude forced on him by experience.

The theme of failure haunted the novels of the later nineteenth century. Meredith treated it in *The Ordeal of Richard Feverel*; Hardy brought it to a nadir in *Jude*, and saw in it the pattern of the future, for Little Father Time was 'the beginning of the coming wish not to live'. Gissing embraced this mood, consciously or unconsciously, until it seemed the ruling spirit of his life. 'Poor Gissing struck me as quite particularly marked out for what is called in his and my profession an unhappy ending', said Henry James. Gissing spoke almost exultantly of his 'futile work' and his 'futile life', and his most autobiographical novel, *New Grub Street*, has failure and loneliness as its theme. Unlike Reardon in that novel, however, he was not a failure; but he felt himself an alien in society and would not adopt its values. His life was marked by appalling errors of judgment whose consequences made him wretched. He existed in garrets and cellars, working incredibly long hours at his novels, always miserably poor, and came to regard such privations as a necessary part of a writer's apprenticeship. 'Has he starved? he would ask, when introduced to a new author's work. Such was the nature of the times that poverty was not only an experience essential to a writer's development but was also, so it seemed to him, a guarantee that he had not compromised his artistic conscience by surrender to the commercial spirit which it was his duty to condemn. His attitude was greatly influenced by Dostoyevsky, who, he said,

> a poor and suffering man, gives us with immense power his own view of penury and wretchedness.
>
> *(Charles Dickens,* p. 222)

But it was an attitude ultimately derived from his own experience. Once, after walking in the slums, he wrote to Frederic Harrison:

> I have involuntarily stood still and asked myself—what then is the meaning of those strange words, Morality, Decency, Intelligence, which I have somewhere heard? . . . here they mean nothing, nay their presence would be an intrusion of an utterly incongruous element.
>
> (23 July 1880—quoted by Korg, *George Gissing: A Critical Biography,* 1963, p. 44)

This was the total alienation of life in the slums, to understand which it was necessary to experience it. Others also despaired of reform. W. Hale White, whose novels, except for their nonconformist background, have much in common with Gissing's, wrote of Drury Lane and the Seven Dials in 1885:

> The preaching of Jesus would have been powerless here; in fact no known stimulus, nothing ever held up before men to stir the soul to activity, can do anything in the back streets of great cities, so long as they are the cesspools which they are now.
>
> *(Mark Rutherford's Deliverance,* Chapter 2)

Gissing agreed. His first novel, *Workers in the Dawn* (1880), was an attempt to test contemporary theories, notably Positivism, against this touchstone. As they were all optimistic in some degree, they all failed leaving only the belief in art and human dignity.

Gissing was born in Wakefield in 1857, the son of a chemist who kept a small shop. He was a brilliant boy at school and in 1872 won a scholarship to Owens College, Manchester. There his brilliance continued and he seemed destined for academic distinction in classics when the first of his acts of folly occurred. He met a young prostitute, pitied her plight and resolved to reclaim her. He sold all his available possessions, but it was not enough, because, unknown to him, her main need was for gin and she had gone on the streets on its account. Eventually, to get money for her, he rifled the Common Room at College, was caught, convicted and sent to gaol. This unhappy story says something of the loneliness and desperation, as well as of the failure of judgment, that led him again and again to similar self-destructive courses. However, he was not friendless and was given a passage to America, where his experiences matched those of Whelpdale in *New Grub Street*. Returning in 1877, he settled in London, ekeing out a living for himself and his brothers and sisters by tutoring, working late into the night at his first novel. No-one would publish it, but at twenty-one he inherited some money from his father's shop and published the book at his own expense. He sent a copy to Frederic Harrison, who was interested in the Comtist element in it and resolved to help the author. He engaged Gissing as tutor to his two sons and gave him many introductions. Although the legacy soon went, Gissing was assured of an income from tutoring. However, he had sent for the girl from Manchester and married her, thereby more than cancelling his advantage. Henceforth his domestic life was a succession of mean lodgings, made unbearable by the irredeemable character, increasing illness and ultimate insanity of his wife.

In these circumstances he wrote his next novel, *The Unclassed* (1884). Meredith read it for Chapman and Hall and recommended its acceptance. As the title suggests, it deals with a number of people, notably Osmond Waymark and his friend Julian Casti, who wish to reject the conventions of society, but find that they cannot. Waymark's circumstances closely follow Gissing's own, and his views are undoubtedly Gissing's:

> the novel of every-day life is getting worn out. We must dig deeper, get to untouched social strata . . . Not *virginibus puerisque* will be my book, I assure you, but for men and women who like to look beneath the surface, and who understand that only as artistic material has human life any significance.

(Chapter 15)

It was a view held by an increasing number. George Moore's pamphlet *Literature at Nurse* (1885) bitterly complained of the limitations imposed on British authors, largely by Mudie's Library which could condemn a book to financial failure by banning it. In 1888 Henry Vizetelly was gaoled for publishing translations of Zola. Hardy found himself in trouble over *Tess* and *Jude* in the 1890s. Gissing himself was constantly obliged to bowdlerize his work in order to get it published at all. Yet the compulsion to depict the darker aspects of urban life as they were, in all their squalor and hopelessness, remained dominant.

Gissing's wife had become so impossible that he was obliged to put her in a nursing home. He never saw her again alive, although she continued a source of anxiety to him until she died in 1888. He now began a more settled life in a flat near Baker Street Station and his output of novels increased. Three were finished in 1885–6: *Isabel Clarendon*, *A Life's Morning* and *Demos*. The first two were a complete break from the subject of the slums, and are psychological studies involving intellectual and moral problems. *Demos*, however, was a return to his previous field, but with a significant difference. In *Workers in the Dawn* and *The Unclassed* his sympathies had been with the poor and his concern was to ameliorate their conditions. Now, however, he proposed to write 'a savage satire on working-class aims and capacities'. In particular, he attacked the socialist reformers, who seemed to him to demand from the working class a degree of responsibility that they were unable to attain. Generations of drudgery, deprivation, and squalor had bred in them a narrow, grasping mentality which no mere improvement of circumstances could alter and which, if it were given responsibility and power, would produce a far worse state than the present. It was a view similar to that expressed by Hyacinth in Henry James's *The Princess Casamassima* also in 1886. Gissing demonstrated it by endowing Richard Mutimer, a superior and independent workman, ardent for the socialist cause, with an unexpected fortune and property in the north of England. He plans a model settlement on the principles of Robert Owen, but his inherent defects of character bring him to ruin and disaster. *Thyrza* (1887) deals with the same theme in the context of education. It is, however, a more sympathetic novel. Thyrza herself contradicts his theory of working-class incapacity, and there are many instances in the novel of the 'kindly sympathy' that elsewhere he failed to observe in the slums.

Early in 1888 Gissing got a telegram saying his wife was dead. He found her lying in a wretched room, almost devoid of furniture and bedding, with the various 'pledges' she had signed, to keep off drink, pinned round the wall. The experience could not fail to plunge him to the depths and his next novel, *The Nether World* (1889), is his most savage indictment of the slums and their inhabitants and of the age that had brought them into being. Palliatives and reforms are pointless in this turbulent abyss, for the people remain wedded to their own damnation. All must be swept away, and a new start made by means of the 'Orphean magic' of 'music the civilizer'. However, the novel contains some of Gissing's most spirited accounts of lower-class life, and the Bank-holiday scene at the Crystal Palace is, with George Moore's Derby Day scene in *Esther Waters*, among the most animated and circumstantial descriptions of popular high-spirits since Dickens.

When *The Nether World* was written, Gissing visited Italy and Greece. As Virginia Woolf said, he 'never ceased to educate himself', and as his horizon broadened, the scope of his novels changed. *The Emancipated* (1890) is partly set in Italy, and deals to some extent with the contrast between the drab outlook of provincial England and the brighter, freer atmosphere of the Mediterranean. More than this was involved in the change, however. The book was the first of a series of novels of middle-class life, dealing with the impact of contemporary life on the individual consciousness—particularly that of sensitive people whose development was stultified by existing conditions and convention. This, in turn, meant that Gissing came to rely less on the realistic presentation of a contrived plot, and began to develop his story from the characters, whose motives he subtly analysed in a manner learned in part from George Meredith.

New Grub Street (1891) is the best-known of these novels, and in some respects is his finest work. It is strongly auto-biographical, and is, perhaps, a little specialized in its account of those who haunt 'the valley of the shadow of books', the British Museum Reading Room. No single character represents Gissing. Reardon, martyred to his artistic conscience, deserted by his talent, agonizing over the poverty to which he has reduced his wife, who deserts him in his distress, is a projection of Gissing's own worst fears. Biffen shows his idealization of the artist. Biffen lives in a garret, taking pupils for a few shillings a week, and works at his realistic novel for its own sake, careless of reward, yet risking his life to rescue the manuscript from a fire. Courteous, cheerful and starving, he is a romantic expression of the artist's isolation from the commercial nineteenth century. His act of straightening a book on his shelves before committing suicide suggests Schopenhauer's view that suicide is an affirmation, not a denial, of the active will. On the other hand, Milivain, ever-practical

opportunist, is an ironic comment on the temporizing shrewdness necessary for survival, which Gissing, being incapable of
it, sometimes almost envied. Milvain owes something to Sir
Willoughby Patterne. Amy, Reardon's wife, illustrates Gissing's
insight into feminine motives; he was, said V. S. Pritchett,
'unusual among English male novelists in discerning the
mental life of women' (*The Working Novelists*, 1963, p.
62). Marian Yule is an equally perceptive study, though
her role is more passive. Like many of the novels, *New Grub
Street* abounds in minor characters, sketched in a few strokes.
Gissing's regular technique of presenting the simultaneous
action of several groups of characters, the narrative switching
from one to another, successfully evokes the composite life of
the metropolis. The struggle against poverty, having a demoral-
izing effect on all the characters, provides a unifying theme.

Born in Exile (1892) also deals with the efforts of an exceptional individual to find his true place in nineteenth-century
society; but his difficulty is not primarily economic, but social.
Godwin Peak, a man of humble origins but outstanding ability,
observes that only parsons are exempt from the prohibition
of the class-barrier in matrimony. Although, therefore, his
scientific education and personal conviction make him an
uncompromising atheist, he hides from his enlightened friends,
and establishes himself in Exeter as a candidate for Orders. He
is accepted as such in a cultured and well-to-do household,
falls in love with one of the daughters and almost succeeds
in gaining her acceptance. But he cannot subdue his conscience
and detests the part he is forced to play. Eventually he is un-
masked. This novel, and others among his later works preoccupied with the theme of hypocrisy and charlatanism, questioned the fundamental standards of society.

Whether an intellectual but poor man should marry from
the class of society to which he aspires, and so reduce his wife
to a poverty she is unprepared for, or whether he should marry
from the lower classes and sacrifice companionship in order
to gain a practical partner, is a question met in nearly all Gissing's novels. He was well aware of the perils of the latter
course, which, indeed, Biffen expounds convincingly to Reardon
in *New Grub Street*. Yet he could not overcome his dread of the
former. About 1890 he met several women who interested him,
among them Edith Sichel, George Eliot's disciple. But fear of his
poverty kept him aloof from them, and eventually in that year,
desperate with loneliness, he repeated his former mistake, and
married a woman he had met casually in the street. This

second marriage was, if anything, more dreadful than the first, for there were two children, boys, whose presence increased the nightmare of their domestic life. Perhaps because he was deprived, or deprived himself, of the company of educated women, they began to occupy a growing place in his imagination. *The Emancipated* was concerned with the development of two such women – Cecily Doran, who chose a superficial cleverness, and Miriam Baske who, though beginning far deeper in bigotry and provincialism, possesses a genuine sensibility which comes to life under the guidance of Ross Mallard, an artist with something of Gissing's own outlook. The difficulties of intelligent women play an important part in *Born in Exile*. Now three books were written dealing specifically with women's role in society. *The Odd Women* (1893) deals in part with an institution founded on charitable principles to train women and girls for clerical work, to enable them to live independently. It was followed by *In the Year of Jubilee* (1894) and *The Whirlpool* (1897).

Dickens posed important critical problems for the later nineteenth century. His greatness was assured and all novelists owed him an immense debt; yet none could deny that his novels lacked the qualities of realism and moral toughness that had come to be so highly thought of. Gissing was devoted to Dickens, to whom he owed more than to any other single writer; but he was well aware of Dickens's distortions, and of the enfeebled morality that lay behind his stories and characters. Although these offended his conscience as a novelist, nevertheless he saw that it was wrong to condemn Dickens on their account. In his book *Charles Dickens:A Critical Study* (1898) he insisted that Dickens must be seen in the context of his time. The need to appeal to a middle-class audience had led him to 'idealize' his characters, so that Sarah Gamp, for example, was 'the Platonic *idea* of London's hired nurses early in Victoria's reign'. However, the humorous treatment made her acceptable, for

> Humour . . . is inseparable from charity. Not only did it enable him to see this coarse creature as an amusing person; it inspired him with that large tolerance which . . . preserves a modesty, a humility, in human judgment.
>
> (*Charles Dickens*, p. 92)

This comment suggests Gissing's own sparse use of humour. Biffen, for example, is a humorous character; he is also an ideal one. The more realistic persons in *New Grub Street*, Yule, for instance, are presented with no humour at all.

Gissing finished the monograph on Dickens during a second visit to Italy, and followed it with a series of prefaces on Dickens's novels. Now separated from his wife, he at last found congenial company. His early friends, Morley Roberts and Eduard Bertz, had remained, and in 1896 he met H. G. Wells who was to be a close friend until Gissing's death. He also found at last, in Gabrielle Fleury, a young Frenchwoman who wrote for permission to translate *New Grub Street*, a woman companion. With her he settled at St Jean de Luz. Although far from wealthy, he was better off than he had been. *New Grub Street* brought him something of a popular reputation, and a number of shorter books, notably *The Town Traveller* (1898), sold well. *The Crown of Life* (1899), partly set in Russia, reflects the teaching of Tolstoy, to whom a copy was sent. *Our Friend the Charlatan* (1901) re-tells the story of Godwin Peak, but in an objective and unsympathetic manner.

Gissing was now in poor health, but there still remained to be written one of his best-known works, *The Private Papers of Henry Ryecroft* (1903). In its air of retirement and reflection it is different from any of its predecessors. It is partly auto-biographical, making use once more of Gissing's early privations, yet Ryecroft is not Gissing; nor is he, like Reardon, a projection of Gissing's hopes and fears. His thoughts are his author's, yet he has a detachment and resignation that Gissing hardly attained. The book is presented in oblique form, as a series of papers edited from Ryecroft's literary remains, and this adds to the distance, and gives a reflective authority to the ideas, and a tolerant nostalgia to the account of the early hardships. Ryecroft does not, like Gissing, consider his life futile; he believes that wisdom comes with meditation, and that, beyond man's view, there is a 'Reason for all'. Gissing's own pronouncement was that *Ryecroft* was 'more an aspiration than a memory'.

The second visit to Italy in 1897 had produced *By the Ionian Sea* (1901), a pleasant account of his visit to Calabria. In it he mentions a deterioration in his health, and this soon accelerated. He was working on *Veranilda*, a not very successful historical novel of the sixth century, at his home in France when at Christmas 1903 he caught a cold which rapidly turned to pneumonia. He died on December 28, Wells, who had been brought from England, being with him.

In perspective, Gissing can be seen as very much a transitional novelist. On the one hand, his attitude to contemporary conditions and his developing introspection, particularly his understanding of the unconscious motives that control every-day actions, suggest a twentieth-century sensibility. George Orwell wrote that he

> was interested in individual human beings, and the fact that he can deal sympathetically with several different sets of motives, and make a credible story out of the collision be-tween them, makes him exceptional among English writers.
> *(The London Magazine,* June 1930, p. 36)

Orwell regretted that he had never read *Born in Exile,* but as Gissing's most inward novel it provides some of the best illustra-tions of this point, for example, the account of Peak's first meeting with the man whom he hopes to impress:

> Though his sympathy was genuine enough, Godwin struggled against an uneasy sense of manifesting excessive apprecia-tion. Never oblivious of himself he could not utter the sim-plest phrase of admiration without criticizing its justice, its tone. And at present it behoved him to bear in mind that he was conversing with no half-bred sciolist. Mr Warricombe obviously had his share of human weakness, but he was at once a gentleman and a student of well-stored mind; insincer-ity must be very careful if it would not jar upon his refined ear. So Godwin often checked himself in the utterance of what might sound too much like flattery.
> *(Born in Exile,* Part II, Chapter IV)

The ambivalent attitude of Godwin Peak, a man so introspec-tive that perpetual self-analysis has dissipated his integrity, and the reaction of others to his broken personality form the substance of the novel.

Technically, on the other hand, Gissing's affinities were with an earlier period. His narrative method was straightforward, with occasional confidences to the reader and no concessions to point of view or efforts at verisimilitude. His prose is mainly that of plain statement. His loyalty to the three-volume form meant that he was often needlessly expansive. Yet he was capable of great economy, sometimes implying a great deal of comment in a short passage of observation. A street-scene described makes a complete indictment of the social order. A chance remark yields an insight into both an individual per-sonality and the twists of conventional attitudes. In *Born in*

Exile, for example, an 'advanced' woman is embarrassed to have imparted an item from a Church newspaper:

> 'Please don't think,' cried Mrs Morton . . .' that I read such papers. We never have such a thing in our house, Mr Peak. I have only been told about it.'
>
> (Born in Exile, Part II, Chapter I)

Gissing's irony exists on many levels, and permeates the novels throughout. His indictment was always indirect. In the early novels he let the dreadful facts speak for themselves, setting them out in a dispassionate account that was ironic in itself. Later, he investigated the effect of these facts of life, both visible and invisible, on sensitive natures, and his irony became more overt and outspoken. It is bitter because he sees no hope of change; his characters must endure the burden of their circumstances. 'Realism', he said, 'is a matter of degree and the author's temperament', and his own pessimistic temperament led him to observe that the burden falls most heavily on those whose keener sensibilities make them most vulnerable. His books owe their peculiar grimness, said Virginia Woolf,

> to the fact that the people who suffer most are capable of making their suffering part of a reasoned view of life. The thought endures when the feeling has gone. Their unhappiness represents something more lasting than a personal reverse; it becomes part of a view of life. Hence when we have finished one of Gissing's novels we have taken away not a character, nor an incident, but the comment of a thoughtful man upon life as life seemed to him.
>
> (The Common Reader, Second Series, 1932, p. 223)

BIBLIOGRAPHY

A *Meredith*
Works (Memorial Edition) 29 vols., 1909–12.
Poetical Works, ed. G. M. Trevelyan, 1912.
Letters, ed. W. M. Meredith, 2 vols., 1912.

G. M. Trevelyan, *The Poetry and Philosophy of George Meredith*, 1907. Still an interesting study.

H. Buxton Forman (ed.), *George Meredith. Some Early Appreciations*, 1909. A useful collection of contemporary reviews.

S. M. Ellis, *George Meredith: His Life and Friends*, 1919. An informative biography.

J. B. Priestley, *George Meredith*, 1926. Informative on Meredith's ideas, but little criticism of the novels.

S. Sassoon, *Meredith*, 1948. A sensitive and sympathetic study.

J. Lindsay, *George Meredith. His Life and Work*, 1956. This very full biography is marred by a heavy ideological bias, but contains many interesting details.

N. Kelvin, *A Troubled Eden. Nature and Society in the Works of George Meredith*, Edinburgh, 1961. A systematic study of Meredith's beliefs.

J. W. Beach, *The Comic Spirit in George Meredith. An Interpretation*, New York, 1967. An interesting and informative study of the novels from the aspect of Meredith's ideas.

B *Hardy*
Works (Wessex Edition, 22 vols., 1912–22.
Works (Mellstock Edition), 37 vols., 1921–2.
Collected Poems, 1919.

Florence Hardy, *The Early Life of Thomas Hardy: 1840–1891*.
——*The Later Years of Thomas Hardy: 1892–1928*, 1928 and 1930. Mainly edited from Hardy's journals and notebooks, these volumes are invaluable to students of his work.

S. C. Chew, *Thomas Hardy, Poet and Novelist*, New York, 1921. (revised 1928, reissued 1964). A good general study.

D. H. Lawrence, 'A Study of Thomas Hardy' in *Phoenix. The Posthumous Papers of D. H. Lawrence*, 1936. A brilliant essay, though incomplete.

E. Blunden, *Thomas Hardy*, 1942. This sympathetic study of Hardy's imagination and sensibility also contains many interesting facts.

D. Cecil, *Hardy the Novelist*, 1943. These Clark Lectures illuminate many points in the novels.

Evelyn Hardy, *Thomas Hardy. A Critical Biography*, 1954. This very full study is extremely useful both for the facts it contains and the criticism it advances of the novels.

M. E. Chase, *Thomas Hardy, from Serial to Novel*, New York, 1964.
The serial versions of four, novels related to their later editions.

C *Gissing*

There is no collected edition of Gissing's novels. A few have been
    reprinted in modern editions, however, of which the following
    is a selection :
A Life's Morning, Introduction by William Plomer, 1947.
New Grub Street, Introduction by G. W. Stonier, 1958.
New Grub Street, Introduction by Bernard Bergonzi, 1968.
The Odd Women, 1968.
In the Year of the Jubilee, Introduction by William Plomer, 1947.
The Whirlpool, Introduction by William Plomer, 1947.
The Town Traveller, 1956.
By the Ionian Sea, Introduction by Virginia Woolf, 1933.
By the Ionian Sea, Introduction by Frank Swinnerton, 1956.
Letters to Members of his Family, ed. A. and E. Gissing, 1927.
*George Gissing and H. G. Wells: Their Friendship and Correspond-
    ence*, ed. R. A. Gettmann, Urbana, Ill., 1961.
Letters to Eduard Bertz, 1887–1903, ed. A. C. Young, New Bruns-
    wick, N. J., 1961.
Gissing's Commonplace Book, ed. Jacob Korg, New York, 1962.

J. Korg, *George Gissing: A Critical Biography*, Seattle, 1963.
Frank Swinnerton, *George Gissing, A Critical Study*, 1912. This early
    biography is somewhat biased against its subject.
Morley Roberts, *The Private Life of Henry Maitland*, 1912. A fictional
    biography by Gissing's close friend.
May Yates, *George Gissing, An Appreciation*, Manchester, 1922.
Pierre Coustillas, ed., *Collected Articles on George Gissing*, 1968.

TENNYSON AND FITZGERALD

JOHN KILLHAM, *University of Keele*

In a poem called 'Poets and Critics' (1892, but written long before), Tennyson wrote:

> What is true at last will tell:
> Few at first will place thee well;
> Some too low would have thee shine,
> Some too high—no fault of thine ...

When the lines were published three weeks after his death in October 1892 at the age of eighty-three, his own reputation was extremely high; but by 1922 Thomas Hardy in *Late Lyrics and Earlier* was recording a melancholy truth when he wrote in 'An Ancient to Ancients':

> The bower we shrined to Tennyson,
>> Gentlemen,
> Is roof-wrecked; damps there drip upon
> Sagged seats, the creeper-nails are rust,
> The spider is sole denizen; ...

Part of the mood of the years following the first World War is expressed by W. H. Auden and Christopher Isherwood in their play, *The Ascent of F6* (1936). Ransom is reading from Dante the famous lines the sense of which Tennyson incorporates in his poem 'Ulysses': 'Consider your origin: ye were not formed to live like brutes, but to follow virtue and knowledge.' His comment upon them is: 'Virtue and knowledge! One can picture Ulysses's audience: a crook speaking to crooks ... Who was Dante, to speak of Virtue and Knowledge? It was not Virtue those lips, which involuntary privation made so bitter, could pray for; it was not Knowledge; it was Power.

Power to exact for every snub, every headache, every unfallen beauty, an absolute revenge . . .' For many of the post-War generation, idealism had become suspect and patriotism a sham. Virginia Woolf's portrait of Mr Ramsay in *To the Light-house* (1927), marching about the garden reciting 'The Charge of the Light Brigade' is meant to illustrate a case of hyper-trophy of the will, while that of Sir William Bradshaw in *Mrs Dalloway* (1925) is a condemnation of the English disease of wanting to dominate people in the name of order, discipline, duty—ideals which certainly commended themselves to Tenny-son. In the circumstances it is hardly surprising that a good deal of his poetry should have struck readers of the between-Wars period as being out of touch with reality and betraying a lack of self-knowledge. In the thirties Pound parodied his most popular poems in sharp satires upon Big Business sup-posedly by Alfred Venison, a barrow-poet. Joyce brings him into *Ulysses* (1922) as Alfred Lawn Tennyson 'gentleman poet', and most amusingly deflates Enoch Arden and King Arthur by showing 'the eternal question of the life connubial' in a very realistic light, quite opposed to Tennyson's exalted dream-pictures of love and marriage. And Faulkner has Hightower in *Light in August* (1933), a man who has ruined his life and deserted his responsibilities, find solace in reading Tennyson :

> Soon the fine galloping language, the gutless swooning full of sapless trees and dehydrated lusts begins to swim smooth and swift and peaceful. It is better than praying without having to bother to think aloud. It is like listening in a cathedral to a eunuch chanting in a language which he does not even need to not understand.

Hightower's state at the time is one of withdrawal, an abdica-tion from ordinary living brought about by constant pre-occupation with a dead heroic past.

These modern views of Tennyson are not just, but their exaggeration does draw attention to the curious juxtaposition in much of his poetry of an exalted, dreamy idealism and of violence, suggestive perhaps of the urgency with which the ideal is sustained in face of real-life materialism. 'Maud' (1855) and the two 'Locksley Hall' poems (1842 and 1886), not to speak of the *Idylls of the King*, will illustrate the point. In the poem 'Merlin and the Gleam' (1889) Tennyson allegorically represents his lifelong concern with an ideal of conduct as a 'Gleam' which he followed despite its nearly disappearing in face of death. The 'Gleam' stood for 'the higher poetic imagination', by which he meant the employment of art in the service of ideals. Although he was not alone in believing that artists had a responsibility to inspire and sustain the public in an age when values were in doubt, he himself underwent so much mental anguish in arriving at the religious faith he thought necessary as a basis for morals that whatever we may think of some of his poetry as poetry, it is always interesting if only because it expresses so copiously and variously the Victorian sense of the relaxation in the hold over men's minds of the Christian faith, and the consequent need to elevate its moral behests to the status of an ideal. Nowadays we can hardly subscribe to the opinion that he was one of the greatest poets in the language, but many readers of his best things will echo Disraeli's opinion that 'if not a great poet', he is 'a real one'.

In 'Poets and their Bibliographies' (1885) Tennyson apostrophizes Virgil, Horace and Catullus, concluding:

You should be jubilant that you flourish'd here
Before the Love of Letters, overdone,
Had swampt the sacred poets with themselves.

This must be every true poet's sentiment, even if it could be shown that scholars wished only to further the proper appreciation of his self-approved work. With Tennyson there is particular reason for expressing it because having published under his own name *Poems, Chiefly Lyrical* (1830) and *Poems* (1833)— he had appeared anonymously in 1827 in *Poems by Two Brothers*—he felt that they suffered from mawkishness and metrical irregularity. As a consequence he printed very little until 1842, when two volumes of *Poems* were published, the first consisting largely of poems from the 1830 and 1833 volumes, but considerably revised. (A third was never republished in an authorized edition at all, though some that were not republished in 1842 re-appeared in later collections.) A long poem, 'The Lover's Tale', which Tennyson proposed to include in the 1833 volume but withdrew on grounds of its faultiness was revised in 1868 but was again withheld from publication. Eventually he was driven to publish it in 1879. This sort of diffidence and uncertainty has made Tennyson's work particularly need the services of a bibliographer, and it is now best, as so much that he did not mean to be published has been, that a comprehensive edition should appear.

Tennyson's poetical career began early, among his ten brothers and sisters at home in the crowded rectory at Somersby in Lincolnshire (see *Unpublished Early Poems by Alfred Tennyson*, 1932 and *The Devil and the Lady*, ed. C.

Tennyson, 1930). But it was at Trinity College, Cambridge, that he entered a circle of friends who encouraged him by admiration for his talent and their enthusiastic concern with liberal politics and religious problems. The attachment between the poet and Arthur Henry Hallam, son of the historian, was particularly close. They planned to join forces in writing a volume of poems, but Hallam eventually contented himself with encouraging his friend in the publishing of *Poems, Chiefly Lyrical* and enthusiastically reviewing them. They were both members of the Apostles, or 'The Cambridge Conversazione Society'; together they travelled in the long vacation of 1830 to the Pyrenees to aid General Torrijos's expedition: and in 1832 Hallam became engaged to Tennyson's sister, Emily. Hallam had all the qualities of intelligence and sensibility which were bound to win the admiration of the moody young Tennyson: and they were accompanied by an optimism and fortitude which he particularly needed in face of the criticism (not all of it harsh by any means) his early volumes received. The completely unexpected death of Hallam in 1833 left him to strive against an innate pessimism and doubt, and the 'ten years' silence', until the *Poems* of 1842, was spent not merely in polishing his already published work, but in coming to terms with grief, loneliness and indigence, a process resulting in a great deal of new and varied verse. Some of this went into the second 1842 volume: but many lyrics in a single verse-form dealing with the feelings and reflexions occasioned by Hallam's death lay in manuscript until they were ordered and expanded to form *In Memoriam A.H.H.*, published in 1850.

The early poems to be read in collected editions of Tennyson's works are arranged under titles (not always the same) which are not those of the original separate volumes. In general, *Juvenilia* covers the 1830 poems and *The Lady of Shalott and Other Poems* covers those of 1833, as revised in 1842 or later: *English Idyls and Other Poems* covers the 1842 new poems, but with additions interpolated from the later editions, of which there were eight up to 1853. The arrangement is not as misleading as Wordsworth's, but small irregularities, combined with the fact that the two first categories are heavily revised, make general criticism in an historical context a delicate matter.

This early work shows two impulses operating, one subjective and 'aesthetic', the other seeking identification with the larger life of common men. Paradoxically it was Arthur Hallam, whom Tennyson saw as one admirably fitted for public

life, who probably encouraged the first tendency. In a review
of Tennyson's volume of 1830 (*The Englishman's Magazine*,
1831; in *Tennyson: The Critical Heritage*, ed. J. D. Jump, 1967,
pp 34–49), Hallam very clear-sightedly attributed the difference
between the greatest masters of poetry (Homer, Dante, Shakespeare) and Keats or Shelley to developments in civilization
which had forever extinguished the 'unreservedness of communion' between poets and readers:

> Those different powers of poetic disposition, the energies
> of Sensitive [sensuous], of Reflective, of Passionate Emotion,
> which in former times were intermingled, and derived from
> mutual support an extensive empire over the feelings of
> men, were now restrained within separate spheres of agency
> . . . Hence the melancholy, which so evidently characterizes
> the spirit of modern poetry; hence that return of the mind
> upon itself, and the habit of seeking relief in idiosyncrasies
> rather than community of interest.

The modern poet of sensation, Hallam stated, cannot be expected to exercise authority over public opinion; he must
try to maintain art as a preserve in which feeling can survive
out of reach of those who wish to expel it in favour of their
utilitarian ends.

Many of Tennyson's early poems show that Hallam understood very well one side of his temperament. 'The Poet's Mind'
(1830:1842)[1] shows a fine contempt for the dull Philistine.
Poem after poem celebrates in melodious if occasionally rather
free rhythms, the exquisite pleasure (to the sensitive mind) of
mourning a dying swan, or Oriana killed by a glancing arrow,
or even the dying year:

> The air is damp, and hush'd, and close,
> As a sick man's room when he taketh repose
>   An hour before death;
> My very heart faints and my whole soul grieves
> At the moist rich smell of the rotting leaves,
>   And the breath
>   Of the fading edges of box beneath,
> And the year's last rose.
> Heavily hangs the broad sunflower
>   Over its grave i' the earth so chilly;
> Heavily hangs the hollyhock,
>   Heavily hangs the tiger-lily.

('Song: A Spirit Haunts the Year's Last Hours', 1830: 1842.)

Another series of poems treats of the opposite pleasure of love, both cool ('The Sea-Fairies', 1830: 1853) and warm ('Fatima', 1833: 1842). Yet another combines them, and we have, as J. S. Mill observed, 'not mere pictures, but states of emotion, embodied in sensuous imagery'; 'The Lady of Shalott' is one of these, and the near-symbolist 'Mariana' is another. All these poems show Tennyson's satisfaction with the role of music-maker, the artist of song. His parade of feeling inevitably affronted critics like 'Christopher North' and J. W. Croker, but there were others than Hallam to praise even his precious word-pictures of 'Victorian' young ladies.

But Hallam does not tell all the story. 'The Poet' (1830: 1842) advances a quite different notion of the artist's function. It is to use the 'vagrant melodies' of his song to carry 'the winged shafts of truth', to create a sunrise in which Freedom's glance will melt rites and forms like snow. Pretentious this doubt-less is, and premature the claim that the poet saw through life and death and his own soul to the meaning of the eternal will; but it shows that Tennyson was quite accessible to the call, first uttered by W. J. Fox when discussing the 1830 poems in *The Westminster Review*, to go beyond a 'facility of imper-sonation' and put his art to use. At the same time, poems like 'Supposed Confessions of a Second-rate Sensitive Mind' (1830: 1884) and 'The Palace of Art' (1833:1842) hardly supported any pretension on Tennyson's part to solve the metaphysical problems of the age. The dreadful conclusion of 'The Palace of Art', a poem which displays Tennyson's skill in word-painting, is that withdrawal from real life into an aesthetic preserve is the greatest sin of which the artist can be guilty. 'Oenone' (1833:1842) takes the rejection of mere beauty into classical myth, associating it with sensuality and a fearful outcome in (the Trojan) war; it thus anticipates the *Idylls of the King* which also makes the erotic the type of sin and weakness by which social decline is brought about.

Some of Tennyson's early poems like 'Recollections of the Arabian Nights' (1830:1842) and 'A Dream of Fair Women' (1833:1842) strongly suggest that he sometimes did not rely on his verbal artifice merely, but drew upon private fantasies. The 'Ode to Memory' (1830:1842) suggests that he well knew that his strength lay in his ability to re-enter the world of his childhood, which was blessed with colour and excitement afforded by books and a sense of freedom in the security of a home which was in reality far from serene. If this is correct, then it is not difficult to imagine how disturbing must have been the realization that the way of the pure artist might be sinful; 'The Palace of Art' presents the sense of guilt and isolation :

> A spot of dull stagnation, without light
>   Or power of movement, seem'd my soul,
> 'Mid onward-sloping motions infinite
>   Making for one sure goal.
>
> A still salt pool, lock'd in with bars of sand,
>   Left on the shore; that hears all night
> The plunging seas draw backward from the land
>   Their moon-led waters white.

'The Lady of Shalott' (1833 : 1842), on the other hand, although it may show in allegory the possible fate of the artist who cannot bear too much reality, lavishes so much artistry on the pathetic figure of the Lady that one may connect it with the impulse to compose lyrics (like 'Mariana' (1830 : 1842) for instance) achieving an inspired blend of pathos, colour, symbolic landscape and musical refrain to produce rare effects of feeling or mood rather than any detachable meaning. At this time Tennyson's poetic encompassment of reality may be measured by 'The May Queen', 'The Miller's Daughter' (1833 : 1842) and 'The Gardener's Daughter' (1842 but an earlier version was written by 1833), the last being two idyls of courtship and marriage, admirably suited to the Victorian taste for sentiment and pastoral.

The death of Hallam was a severe blow, not merely because their friendship sustained Tennyson in his loneliness and melancholy, but also because he had intellectual strength with which to meet the religious doubts which at that time Tennyson was experiencing. In 'Supposed Confessions' he had already written :

> How sweet to have a common faith !
> To hold a common scorn of death !
> And at a burial to hear
> The creaking cords which wound and eat
> Into my human heart, whene'er
> Earth goes to earth, with grief, not fear,
> With hopeful grief, were passing sweet !

Now he seriously asked himself whether life was worth living. Being a poet he began very quickly to put his feelings into poems, some of which appeared first in the second volume of *Poems*, 1842. One, 'The Two Voices', deals directly with the thought of suicide, which is rejected because life speaks within him of hope :

> Moreover, something is or seems,
> That touches me with mystic gleams,
> Like glimpses of forgotten dreams ...

The conclusion is confident, and pre-figures the confidence of some of the poems Tennyson wrote much later in life; but there was still a long way to go. Other poems written or revised after Hallam's death are not so positive. Thus he revised 'The Lotos-Eaters' of 1833 to make escape into indolent dreaming to have its justification in the sufferings of mankind, sufferings to which the gods are indifferent. Tennyson's talent for luxurious description now found its perfect outlet, and the poem is deservedly famous. It is an excellent example of a favourite Victorian poetic form, the dramatic monologue, in which very often (as in Browning), a saving irony plays over the supposed speaker's sentiments. In 'The Lotos-Eaters' Tennyson could securely express his own yearnings for release from suffering, confident that his readers would recognize the Homeric and Lucretian parallels and exempt him from the charge of escapism. He resorts to the same device in 'Tithonus' (begun in or before 1833 but not published until 1860), which dramatizes the myth of the mortal to whom Aurora gave immortality, but not immunity from the sufferings of old age. The loss of youth is the respect that makes calamity of so long life. Tithonus begs Aurora for release; pleading that all living things enjoy the boon of death :

> The woods decay, the woods decay and fall,
> The vapours weep their burthen to the ground,
> Man comes and tills the field and lies beneath,
> And after many a summer dies the swan.

At first sight 'Ulysses' might seem, as Tennyson himself asserted, to express a contrary belief, the need for going forward into life despite the pains of age and the inevitability of death, just as in 'The Two Voices' he had written :

> 'Tis life, whereof our nerves are scant,
> Oh life, not death, for which we pant;
> More life, and fuller, that I want.

But we cannot help noticing that Ulysses resembles the lotos-eaters in his willingness to give up thoughts of wife and son, together with his ordinary duties as governor of the isle; nor can we ignore the valedictory associations of the great deep upon which he means to sail:

> The long day wanes: the slow moon climbs: the deep
> Moans round with many voices. Come, my friends,
> 'Tis not too late to seek a newer world.

The concern is as much with death as in the 'Morte d'Arthur': the hungry heart of Ulysses is bent upon the gleam of an un-travelled world, and the restless pursuit of experience will never end until it arrives there and gains a peace that passes understanding. Arthur too finds a sort of death by water, but his passing to the idyllic island-valley of Avilion is described in more portentous imagery, for which the modern 'frame' serves as apology. The 'Morte d'Arthur' does not reach the level of the classical monologues. Its colour and glitter are splendid in their way, but the poem is too contrived and pictorial to involve our deeper feelings. The conclusion suggesting that Arthur re-appears in 'the modern gentleman' is an example of Tennyson's remarkable lack of a sense of bathos, evident in a number of poems. But it shows that his apprehension that the ideals he aspired to could not survive under the conditions of the modern world was, at this point in his career, restrained by hope that in the end they would re-assert themselves in new forms. (Tennyson's interest in the Arthurian story also appears in a stanza of 'The Palace of Art'; and in the two poems 'Sir Galahad' and 'Sir Launcelot and Queen Guinevere', first published in 1842, but very probably written, like 'The Lady of Shalott', at Cambridge or soon after). 'Locksley Hall' expresses anxiety and revulsion at the signs of the times, and hope that all will be well: the moving irony of 'Ulysses' is replaced by another sort altogether, one dependent upon attri-buting yearning for withdrawal and peace (between nations this time) to a character whose near-hysterical utterances in face of disappointment are meant to betray to the reader their inadequacy. Unfortunately the final resolve to enter fully into the modern age sounds equally hollow:

> Not in vain the distance beacons. Forward, forward let us
> range,
> Let the great world spin for ever down the ringing grooves
> of change.

In 'The Golden Year' (1846) Tennyson later shows his consciousness of the fact that he was naturally disposed to handle the long-ago or the far future; contemporary problems relating to the condition of England in an age of industrialism and unbanization glanced at in 'Locksley Hall' were really outside his range. Characteristically he put his hope in gradualism (see, for example, 'You ask me why . . .', 'Of old sat Freedom on the heights', 'Love thou thy land'); his poetry on modern subjects written when the pain of his loss had quietened took the form of 'idyls' like 'Audley Court' and 'Walking to the Mail', or *vers de société* like 'The Talking Oak', 'Amphion' and 'The Day Dream'. Clearly Tennyson was searching for a new manner, perhaps in the hope of achieving popularity. 'Dora' affects an austere plainness; 'Will Waterproof's Lyrical Monologue' and 'The Vision of Sin' display an unexpected flair for facetious rhyming. In all this variety of work there is nothing very impressive, save for 'Break, break, break' which with 'Tears, idle tears' from *The Princess*, eloquently expresses his passion for the past, the past of his youth before experience of death or the past immortalized in the literature which described a golden age. It is as if he were deliberately avoiding the serious vein (which all the while was being released in the future *In Memoriam*) and cultivating the pretty, the charming, the sentimental. Poems like 'Godiva', 'The Lord of Burleigh' and 'Lady Clare' were perfectly adapted to the popular taste. 'Will Waterproof's Lyrical Monologue' may supply a clue to the reason for it in its hints of a fear of the critics and an 'eternal want of pence'.

The most ambitious of the poems in this new, lighter vein is the one which follows *Poems, The Princess*, first published in 1847, but revised in subsequent editions. This must strike the modern reader as a most curious undertaking for the poet of 'Ulysses' and 'Tithonus'. But it has for subject that very question which in his review of the 1830 volume W. J. Fox had wished Tennyson might think worthy of his powers if he truly aspired to the role he had outlined in 'The Poet', namely, the education of women. True to his resolve to cultivate the lightness of touch which he admired in older poets and apparently felt necessary as a counter to his natural seriousness, he embarked upon a tale of the absurd lengths a headstrong princess went to preserve her university of women from the interference of men. The story is much more fantastic than *Love's Labour's Lost*, and freely combines medieval and modern, a state of affairs justified by the pretence that it is told by a succession of undergraduate narrators to amuse themselves and some ladies on a picnic. (The 'modern' note is struck by the holiday amusements of the Mechanics Institute, particularly the 'strange experiments' wherein sport 'went hand in hand with Science' : but it is harmonized with elements drawn from distant times and places, so that a strange air of unreality is lent to the scene, an effect reproduced in the tale itself by the 'weird seizures' of the Prince.) What begins as genial satire turns into sympathy for the Princess's cause. Although the prince who had tried to overset her scheme is defeated, she tends him and is won over to marriage. Was ever woman in this humour woo'd? The 'strange diagonal' the story takes shows clearly that Tennyson believed that in marriage the sexes fulfil not only one another's needs, but also nature's evolutionary plan : if marriage is to be meaningful, women must be freed from the restrictions they have suffered under in the past. There is in Tennyson a feminine streak which both makes him sympathetic to the women's cause and also underlies that dependency, even inadequacy, out of which his best poems come to be written. The lyrics 'Tears, idle tears', 'Now sleeps the crimson petal', 'Come down, O maid', which find a place in *The Princess*, all express in different ways his need and his characteristic inactivity, his submissiveness. He does not act, he waits, and his best poems are those which express expectancy or resignation.

In Memoriam, published in 1850, also ends with a marriage and the anticipated birth of a child which will prove 'a closer link/Betwixt us and the crowning race' which, 'no longer half-akin to brute', will in the far future supplant the humanity whose present ignorance of the meaning of life brings the agonizings over death recorded in the earlier 131 sections of the poem. Those sections, seen from the concluding standpoint of 'colossal calm', appeared

> As echoes out of weaker times,
> As half but idle brawling rhymes,
> The sport of random sun and shade.
> (Concluding stanzas)

The confident conclusion occurs 'some thrice three years' after the dark day of Hallam's death; the passage of three Christmases is marked by poems in the series (XXX, LXXVIII and CV); but in fact nearly seventeen years had passed between that day and the publication of the poem, and for many of the poems the date of composition is a matter of speculation. But some were written right through the period in which Tennyson was producing the light-hearted work just described.

The poem finds its unity in the stanza form, from which Tennyson summons constant variations of effect, and in its subject, death. But it lacks the sort of structure found in 'Lycidas' or 'Adonais' or 'Thyrsis', all of which in various ways find, through an act of imagination, a means of moving away from the mere fact of death into a deeper sense of how to live. Critics have found pastoral elements in *In Memoriam* and have claimed for it the status of an elegy; but although many of the individual poems record the beauty of English landscape and season and relate to one another on occasion (through subject or imagery), they remain 'brief lays' and 'short swallow-flights of song'. They move away from sorrow over the death of Hallam to general speculations on what death may bring, and then return to Hallam again. But they never transcend the preoccupation with time and mortality, which takes ever-new forms as thoughts occur to the poet. The conclusion is itself a new departure. T. S. Eliot's comparison with a diary is just, for the poems are poignant personal responses to new grounds for hope or despair offered by particular occasions—anniversaries, books read, visits made. There is no total transformation wherein the doubts are swept away by a sudden recognition that it is life, not death, that counts. Tennyson's conclusion puts hope in lives yet to come, not in life here and now.

Although *In Memoriam* has no organic development, but only a switch from despair to an evolutionary hope, individual poems have an imaginative power very unlike anything else that Tennyson wrote. The narrow limits of the octosyllabic lines, arranged in rhyming quatrains, force him into a disciplining of his usual largeness, occasionally even slackness, of utterance; but he is not cramped by the restrictions of his stanza. Occasionally he sustains a thought through a long period:

> Till now the doubtful dusk reveal'd
>   The knolls once more where, couch'd at ease,
>   The white kine glimmer'd and the trees
> Laid their dark arms about the field:
>
> And suck'd from out the distant gloom
>   A breeze began to tremble o'er
>   The large leaves of the sycamore,
> And fluctuate all the still perfume,

274

And gathering freshlier overhead,
  Rock'd the full-foliaged elms, and swung
  The heavy-folded rose, and flung
The lilies to and fro, and said

'The dawn, the dawn', and died away;
  And East and West, without a breath,
  Mixt their dim lights, like life and death,
To broaden into boundless day.
                                    (XCV)

Some of the poems have an air of conscious pastiche:

When rosy plumelets tuft the larch,
  And rarely pipes the mounted thrush . . .
                                    (XCI)

But while all of them show conscious artistry and rely upon
musical phrasing, many succeed in conveying powerful impressions of despair, grief, resignation and hope. They are often
occasioned by a scene, a visit, a departure, and Tennyson fuses
the feeling with the objects that prompt it. It is this which
gives the poems merit, rather than any consistent conclusion
on the problem with which the poet is beset. For although
at times he felt life to be so intolerable that death would be a
relief, at others he was filled with dread at the thought that
his life would end. *In Memoriam* exhibits his fear and doubt in
the way it considers any possibility whatever that might bear
on the meaning of death. Although he can occasionally feel
that his intuition that he can never die is sufficient, he tries to
find evidence to support him in the science which is opposed
to intuition. Inevitably, the poem shifts from position to position, and even the introductory stanzas are less expressive of
faith in the Christian revelation than a prayer for enlightenment by way of more scientific knowledge of a sort which will
permit mind and soul to be reconciled; and this despite the
fact that

We have but faith : we cannot know;
  For knowledge is of things we see . . .
                          (Introductory stanzas)

Tennyson differs fundamentally from Arnold, whose *Empedocles on Etna* shows that the logical consequence of seeing
man to be free, free that is from any natural or divine restriction on his actions, could be to impose upon him an intolerable
burden. Arnold went on to consider ways in which men could

guide their actions by taking thought on their own nature, and ensuring that all its sides were developed harmoniously. Tennyson, on the other hand, broods upon the ways in which man may develop his nature in conformity with an ideal which has the same inner sanction as the belief that death cannot be the last word and that life is therefore purposive. His ideal conforms to what Nietzsche termed the Aryan myth, as opposed to the Hellenic one of Prometheus, and involves the idea of sin and the repression of some human drives to the end that others may develop. *In Memoriam* illustrates afresh what was implicit in 'The Palace of Art'.

> Arise and fly
> The reeling Faun, the sensual feast;
> Move upward, working out the beast,
> And let the ape and tiger die.
>
> (CXVIII)
>
> Let him, the wiser man who springs
> Hereafter, up from childhood shape
> His action like the greater ape,
> But I was *born* to other things.
>
> (CXX)

After *In Memoriam* Tennyson becomes more and more concerned with an ideal of conduct which is to raise the spirit of man to its high destiny, and incidentally, more and more critical of lapses from it.

Tennyson was appointed Poet Laureate in 1850. The 'Ode on the Death of the Duke of Wellington' (1852) was a convenient means not only of gratifying his dislike of France and Louis Napoleon, expressed in a number of poems of this time, but also for praising one who embodied his ideal of selflessness and duty. It illustrates Tennyson's habit of surprising his readers by some new development, this time in composing a splendid occasional poem in the 'Pindaric' form. In *Maud* (1855) he surprised them even more. Here was the Laureate apparently attacking the morality of the nation of shopkeepers through the transparent mask of a frenzied young man whose father had committed suicide on being ruined by his fraudulent partner. (Fraud was also the subject of 'Sea Dreams'.) Gladstone was at a loss to understand why Tennyson should imagine that the Crimean War could be regarded as a means of achieving 'the effectual renovation of society'. Later he came to see that the words of a withdrawn man restored by love to 'oneness with his kind' were not to be attributed to the poet himself; but there are so many poems expressing dislike of the age that it is hard to believe that Tennyson did not have to invent too much. *Maud* is one of Tennyson's most carefully contrived poems, even though built around 'O, that 'twere possible', a lyric composed not long after Hallam's death : and the censorious passage is well fitted to its context. Self-obsession is, Tennyson suggests, a disease which conduces to a particular sensitivity to the inadequacies of society, though sufferers only hug it to themselves and do nothing. The cure comes with action, even if it takes the form it does. The main interest in the poem is, however, the development through an extraordinary range of lyric-forms of changing feelings as scepticism is followed by love, temporary collapse and recovery. *Maud* is something of a *tour de force*, combining the wildness of 'Locksley Hall' with the melancholy of 'Mariana', but also advancing the narrative, setting scenes and suggesting character. It is extravagant, admittedly, and seems more so when particular poems are taken out of context. Nevertheless, it is one of Tennyson's most successful long poems and is his particular representation of the effect upon a susceptible mind of the workings of a society which made money and position its principal concern. Not that realism is the important thing, at least in the usual sense; psychological realism there certainly is. The story part of the poem has its weaknesses from the standpoint of a political criticism, but it served Tennyson well in affording him situations of despair and exaltation which he was specially well-equipped to handle lyrically. It contrasts very forcibly with the narratives of 'Enoch Arden' and 'Aylmer's Field' (1864), which instead of a first person, lyric treatment, have the stately march of Tennysonian blank verse not dissimilar to that used in a specimen translation of the *Iliad* made about the same time. Although the incidents described in both poems are said to have taken place many years before, they are really no less modern and ordinary than those in *Maud*. 'Aylmer's Field', in fact, is more explicitly Victorian in its condemnation of the pride of wealth and family than *Maud*, and the date 1793 which stands at the beginning is clearly meant as an admonishment to the likes of Sir Aylmer who might read the poem in 1864. Both poems have passages which are conventionally Christian in their standpoint, but Tennyson is really appealing for recognition that true nobility may be found at social levels below that which claims that virtue as a right of birth. 'Lady Clara Vere de Vere' anticipates 'Aylmer's Field' :

> Kind hearts are more than coronets,
> And simple faith than Norman blood.

'Enoch Arden' surrounds the self-sacrifice of a sailor who finds his wife and family happy with a second (and richer) husband and father with the exalted music appropriate to the heroic poem. Alone and unrecognized, death dawns upon him; but he keeps his counsel

> For thro' that dawning gleam'd a kindlier hope
> On Enoch thinking 'after I am gone,
> Then may she learn I lov'd her to the last.'

Enoch follows his gleam as faithfully as Ulysses, and the light of the ideal is made to fall upon the simple annals of the poor. The modern ear catches ironies where none were intended, for it will not suffice to transfer a modern tale into the place properly occupied by the heroes of myth. Tennyson was trying to impose his vision upon his characters, instead of entering imaginatively into their lives in the manner of a novelist. Mrs. Gaskell had told a very similar story of a returned lover's sacrifice only a year before (in *Sylvia's Lovers*); and a novelist could have handled the action of 'Aylmer's Field' much more convincingly by spending more time on the characterization, and consequently the motivation. Only by turning to dialect could Tennyson honestly represent the very unidealistic attitudes to life of working people, and in a series of poems realise the grim humour and doggedness of real countrymen. How to give practical expression to his ideal in regular poems remained a problem to the end of his life.

His most ambitious attempt was *Idylls of the King*, twelve books of a long poem dealing with incidents from the Arthurian cycle. His interest in the legends given such wide currency by Caxton's edition of Sir Thomas Malory's *Morte Darthur* is evident from his own 'Morte d'Arthur' of 1842 (adapted to the new poem as 'The Passing of Arthur'), and several lyrics. His plan for a long poem on the subject was made as early as 1833, and it seems that he planned to turn it into an allegory of the intellectual tendencies of the nineteenth century. But in the end the poem, parts of which were published separately over the years between 1859 and 1885, had only a 'parabolic drift'; much of it followed the main lines of Malory's account, although, as the title suggests, only selected incidents were given. The love of Lancelot and Guinevere which led to the downfall of the Round Table, and which Malory could yet not feel it in him to condemn, is made by Tennyson the rift within the lute which progressively destroys the harmony upon which the Round Table depends. The Idylls vary considerably in treatment. 'Lancelot and Elaine' is a rapid and plain narrative of the incidents leading up to the death from unrequited love which formed the subject of 'The Lady of Shalott'. But other Idylls depart from this plainness of style and subject in several ways as Tennyson feels that simplicity or grandeur are involved. Simplicity he often renders by an attention to homely detail which makes his characters most unromantically present to the reader's eye, as if they were actors in costume. (G. M. Hopkins called the Idylls 'Charades from the Middle Ages'.) The Earl Doorm episode in 'Geraint and Enid' is typical:

> He spoke: the brawny spearman let his cheek
> Bulge with the unswallow'd piece, and turning stared...

Grandeur, on the other hand, is frequently sought in mist and vapour, darkness and glaring lights ('The Coming of Arthur', 'Guinevere', 'The Passing of Arthur').

The sinfulness of Lancelot's relationship with Guinevere is brought home to the reader not only by the encouragement it lends to thoroughly wicked women like Vivien and Ettare and the sorrows of innocent ones like Enid and Elaine, but also by Arthur's reaction once their guilt is known:

> I hold that man the worst of public foes
> Who either for his own or children's sake,
> To save his blood from scandal, lets the wife
> Whom he knows false, abide and rule the house: ...
> I cannot take thy hand; that too is flesh,
> And in the flesh thou hast sinn'd; and mine own flesh,
> Here looking down on thine polluted, cries
> 'I loathe thee ...'
>
> ('Guinevere')

Although Swinburne may have been wrong to insist that Arthur himself ought to have been shown as equally guilty of sexual impropriety (because the accounts vary), he voiced a feeling shared by other readers that Tennyson had deliberately removed all tragic interest from the fatal love of Lancelot and Guinevere. (The same can be said of his account of Tristan and Isolt.) To make matters worse, the Dedication speaks of Prince Albert as 'Scarce other than my king's ideal knight'; and the epilogue to Queen Victoria connects the faith and loyalty, the lack of which led to the last battle in the West in which Arthur was wounded and conducted out of life, with the faith and loyalty to the crown on which the imperial greatness of England depended:

> The loyal to their crown
> Are loyal to their own far sons, who love
> Our ocean-empire with her boundless homes
> For ever-broadening England, and her throne
> In our vast Orient ...

The 'parabolic drift' of the poem is certainly not in doubt, for Tennyson makes plain that Camelot, Arthur and the Round Table have an ideal and even supernatural status. Yet they are not spiritual and timeless: they are sometimes very real and substantial, and their overthrow demands that we think of them as under the dominance of passing time, of Mutability, the condition of real existence to which the Victorians were exceptionally sensitive. The resultant 'drift' is therefore accurately termed not allegorical, but parable-like: and it may strike some readers that the parable really amounts to an admonition to the nation to remember that 'the old order changeth, yielding place to new': that if Arthur could refuse tribute to Rome because it had become weak, others could do the same if Britain allowed irreverence and disloyalty to sap her faith in herself.

The hints that Arthur is akin to Christ and that the doubtfulness of his title should not diminish faith in his right to rule suggest that Tennyson was not unwilling to surround the idea of nationhood with an aura of holiness. Arthur's disapproval of the quest for the Holy Grail, which Galahad attains only at the cost of never returning to the practical duties of the Round Table, suggests that for the majority true religion is shown more by unity in practical purposes than in the private pursuit of a beatific vision which in the springtime of Christendom was the highest reward of faith. (Compare the early 'St Simeon Stylites', published in 1842.) The *Idylls*, read symbolically, connect private life with national life; animality, sin, is a threat to the commonweal. It is not difficult to see why Kipling should have received Tennyson's praise as that of a general to a private, nor why in our own century Virginia Woolf and others should have associated him with their suspicion that Proportion has a formidable sister whose name is Conversion. (The pitch at which his fluent blank verse holds the reader in contemplation of the pure and illicit loves of Arthur's court may explain Faulkner's reaction.)

But to bring a charge of jingoism against Tennyson, citing his later poems like 'The Revenge' and 'The Defence of Lucknow', as well as 'Riflemen, form', 'The Charge of the Light Brigade' and *Maud* as additional evidence, would not really be just. (See Tennyson's own answer in the epilogue to 'The Charge of the Heavy Brigade at Balaclava'.) He is certainly a patriotic poet: the conclusion of *The Princess* illustrates his life-long prejudice against the French. Several of the plays he wrote in the seventies and eighties (*Queen Mary, Harold* and *Beckett*, for example) after completing the bulk of the Idylls ('Balin and Balan' had yet to appear, in 1885) deal with English historical subjects. Nevertheless, taking the *Idylls* in conjunction with other late poems, one can see that Tennyson, still beset with doubts and difficulties over religious faith, was attempting in the *Idylls* to associate religion and the aspirations of society in such a way that each supported the other. His idealism could not rest in either alone since his doubts, if not about the existence of a divine power, then about its proper claims upon its believers, were still great, and what he saw of the reality of English life filled him with deep concern. His last volumes of poems (*The Holy Grail and Other Poems*, 1869; *Ballads and Other Poems*, 1880; *Tiresias and Other Poems*, 1885; *Locksley Hall Sixty Years After, etc.*, 1886; *Demeter and Other Poems*, 1889; *The Death of Oenone, Akbar's Dream and Other Poems*, 1892), varied as they are, contain a good number dealing with religious faith and with social conditions: some are full of foreboding, like the epilogue to the *Idylls*.

'The Higher Pantheism' (1869), read at the first meeting of the Metaphysical Society, has a ring of desperation about it, its ugly rhythms and trite sentiment fully meriting Swinburne's parody. 'Lucretius' (1863), a return to the dramatic monologue, is inferior to the early ones, but like 'Tiresias' (1885) and 'Demeter and Persephone' (1889), is an example of the skill with which the old poet could combine scholarship with his own leading ideas. 'Lucretius', though careful in its use of Epicurean doctrine, makes the erotic fantasies of the Roman poet express something of Tennyson's own strong belief in the reality of sin, its association with the animal part of man's nature, and the need of faith to overcome it. 'Tiresias' is an obvious counterpart to Tennyson's view of himself as a prophet earnestly trying to persuade men to a life of self-sacrifice in the interest of national survival. 'The Ancient Sage' (1885) expresses Tennyson's own religious doctrine in the person of

Lao-tse. It shows, as does 'The Higher Pantheism', into how simple a form that doctrine had developed (or declined) since *In Memoriam*. Comparisons have been made between *In Memoriam* and the Christian existentialism of Kierkegaard, and between 'The Higher Pantheism' and the neo-Platonism of Plotinus: some resemblance between his belief and German transcendentalism certainly exists, but 'The Ancient Sage' shares Tennyson's faith that we have within us occasional gleams from the wholly spiritual world, or the Nameless: the physical world in time is but a shadow. This intuition is what Tennyson had always fallen back on and no other source for it is really necessary. In 'The Ancient Sage' it is asserted confidently, even jubilantly; and the young sybarite who feels that all is vanity is advised to

> leave the hot swamp of voluptuousness
> A cloud between the Nameless and thyself
> And lay thine uphill shoulder to the wheel ...

But another late poem, 'Vastness' (1889), tells a very different story—

> What the philosophies, all the sciences, poesy, varying voices
>   of prayer?
> All that is noblest, all that is basest, all that is filthy with all
>   that is fair?
> What is it all, if we all of us end but in being our own corpse-
>   coffins at last,
> Swallow'd in Vastness, lost in Silence, drown'd in the deeps
>   of a meaningless Past?

The faith that death is not final is uttered in a single faint line at the end. 'Locksley Hall Sixty Years After' (1886) is equally despondent: although it is a dramatic monologue, it must surely register some part of Tennyson's own conviction that there is very little reason to think that the best is yet to be. Progress is now only to be feared: science has no charms for a people who have lost the sense of wonder with which their grandfathers greeted its successes of sixty years before. The poem is as rhetorical as its predecessor and is not likely to win its way by its charm of numbers, but detestation of mass-building, the popular press and lying politicians is put across with crude effectiveness. Other poems in the late volumes show Tennyson's sense of the cruelty and indifference of much that men say and do ('Rizpah', 'Romney's Remorse', 'Despair', 'St Telemachus', 'The Dead Prophet').

Not everything in the last volumes is gloomy. Poems like 'To

Vergil', and 'Frater Ave atque Vale' (in memory of his poet-brother, Charles) are free from the chill recollection that art and life are both brief, now that astronomy and geology have become 'terrible muses' ('Parnassus'). There is room for humour and hope—and finally for the poem 'Crossing the Bar', which so faithfully represents the conclusion of Tennyson's struggle to achieve a faith that would conquer death.

Tennyson's verses 'To E. FitzGerald' were meant to accompany the poem 'Tiresias' as a gift to commemorate his friend's seventy-fifth birthday: but as the 'postscript' says, they never met FitzGerald's eyes, for the poet of the 'golden Eastern lay' died on 14 June 1883, nine months before the birthday in question. It is very probable that if he had lived, FitzGerald would have been embarrassed by them, although Tennyson had been his friend since 1835 at least. It is not simply that FitzGerald was averse to his personal life being made public, as Tennyson, like some other Victorians, was (See his poems 'To———, after reading a Life and Letters' and 'The Dead Prophet'). The recollections included in the complimentary lines of 'old Fitz' surrounded—and surmounted—by pigeons as he sat in the garden of his house called Little Grange outside Woodbridge, Suffolk, of his spare diet and Tennyson's one-time trial of it and its consequences, of the admiration his *Rubáiyát of Omar Khayyám* had earned 'from our best/In modern letters', all these are innocent enough and are as charmingly expressed as any of the occasional verses in which Tennyson is so effective. Rather it is that Edward FitzGerald was singularly averse to putting himself forward as a poet or writer worthy of the sort of esteem which he thought belonged to original artists. Throughout his whole literary life he was utterly self-effacing. It was only by chance that his authorship of the *Rubáiyát* became known. Tennyson had something of this, too (*In Memoriam* was first published anonymously), but it is entirely characteristic of FitzGerald that he should have heaped praise upon Tennyson in his 'Euphranor', and have persuaded him to publish again in 1842, after a virtual silence of ten years: while he, for his part, though ready to print at his own expense, and glad to have the praise of friends and well-wishers, consistently avoided the limelight, refusing to allow any 'puffing' by his 'publisher', Quaritch, and even keeping his name from the title-page of all his works save the *Six Dramas of Calderon Freely Translated*.

Tennyson's verse-letter throws light upon both men. It is entirely characteristic, for instance, that Tennyson should take the occasion of FitzGerald's death to speak again of his pre-occupation with personal survival, his trust that death was not the 'deeper night' :—

> The deeper night? A clearer day
> Than our poor twilight dawn on earth—
> If night, what barren toil to be!
> What life, so maim'd by night, were worth
> Our living out? Not mine to me
> Remembering all the golden hours
> Now silent, and so many dead,
> And him the last.

It reveals, too, that Tennyson knew why FitzGerald would not in all likelihood approve the gift of 'Tiresias', an old poem in MS especially re-furbished to serve the occasion; but only accept it

> Less for its own than for the sake
> Of one recalling gracious times,
> When, in our younger London days,
> You found some merit in my rhymes,
> And I more pleasure in your praise.

In the postscript he tells us that

> I fancied that my friend
> For this brief idyll would require
> A less diffuse and opulent end,
> And would defend his judgement well,
> If I should deem it over nice . . .

Even before the 'younger London days' FitzGerald had shown signs of restiveness before Tennyson's diffuseness and opulence —both men were extraordinarily consistent through their lives. Of four stanzas (later deleted) which introduced 'A Dream of Fair Women' he wrote in 1833: 'This is in his best style: no fretful epithet, nor a word too much.' Later that year he mentions that Tennyson 'is chiefly meditating on the purging and subliming of what he has already done, and repents that he has published at all yet. It is fine to see how in each succeeding poem the smaller ornaments and fancies drop away, and leave the grand ideas single.' But even when the 1842 volumes appeared, FitzGerald saw much of 'his great fault of being too full and complicated', and wished he had published the new work separately. 'The other will drag it down.' Still, 'with all his faults' (and he was equally severe on another thing he thought Tennyson had no talent for, namely, trifling and badinage), 'he will publish such a volume as has not been published since the time of Keats: and which, once published, will never be suffered to die.' He thought it 'The last of old Alfred's best': believing that criticism between friends should be above all things critical, he found objection to much of the work published after 1842, save perhaps for *Maud*, which though in the vein of Browning, was far superior to that poet's detestable productions in the 'gurgoyle' manner. *In Memoriam*, though full of the finest things is, he thought, 'monotonous, and has the air of being evolved by a Poetical Machine of the highest order.' He thought the Idylls 'pure, noble and holy', but it was the dialect poem 'Northern Farmer: New Style' with its coarse yet humorous portrayal of human self-interest which moved him. These were FitzGerald's 'crotchets', but they seem less eccentric today.

Towards the end of his life many people thought him eccentric, and in the matter of his dress he may have been. All his life he had an assured income, for although he was the seventh child (among eight), his family, which descended on his mother's side from the fourth Earl of Kildare, was wealthy. From the age of nine, Edward, born Purcell, bore his mother's name. At the university, or soon after, he adopted the plain style of living Tennyson refers to. He offered financial assistance to both Thackeray and Tennyson, the last of whom in the forties suffered that eternal want of pence that the son of a disinherited Lincolnshire rector might expect to enjoy, particularly if he took up no occupation other than writing poetry. Fitz-Gerald avoided the extravagant way of life between Brighton and Portland Place which his mother found natural to her aristocratic taste. Although he visited London frequently and stayed with friends a good deal, he spent most of his life in various lodgings at no great distance from his birthplace, near Woodbridge in Suffolk: only for the last nine years of his life had he a permanent home of his own. He studied the ways and speech of countrymen and seamen, and avoided the gentry. It is not surprising that a man of such tastes should prefer his friend's Lincolnshire farmer to his Round Table, and should attribute his decline from poignant lyric into ideal 'epic' to wealth, adulation, a wife, lack of occupation and separation from common life at one or other of his retreats at Farringford or Aldworth.

FitzGerald regarded himself not as a genius like Tennyson, but as a man of taste, one who lived by cultivated feelings which found their gratification in friendship, music, painting—and literature, not much of which was appearing in modern times. He was decidedly not a recluse. When his friends (and among them he counted Thackeray and Carlyle) could not be in his company, he wrote letters which served as substitutes for conversation : and he was sometimes fearful that his friends, when they met him again, would find the real thing inferior to the surrogate. His letters form a valuable part of his production. Nor was he a scholar, in the narrow sense. In his extensive reading his attitude can perhaps be best described as that of a gentleman; he read to please his own taste. He was deeply suspicious of German aesthetics, because he thought books ought to serve right thinking and acting. He kept a commonplace book, and in it noted good things read and heard alike : though when he came to publish his *Polonius: a Collection of Wise Saws and Modern Instances* (1852) he could not always identify the quotations. His *Euphranor: A Dialogue on Youth* (1851, revised 1855 and 1882) gives an excellent impression of his mind : it pictures young men at their pleasures in Cambridge, and thereby distils the doctrine that the aim of education should be to breed men of sense, taught to be practical and energetic as well as sufficiently read in books to be able to carry on good conversation. FitzGerald carried this spirit into his reading. Like Dr Johnson, he did not always care to read a book through; if parts of it were flat or redundant, he would (literally) cut them out, thus reducing the call on shelf-space, doubtless a convenience to so unsettled a man. His reading in ancient authors did not cease after his time up at Cambridge. He read enthusiastically wherever the fancy took him—and eventually it took him outside Greek and Latin and into Italian, German, Spanish and Persian. He made, and had printed, his own translations of the *Agamemnon* (1869), a conflation of the Oedipus plays (1880, 1881), and published translations of six plays of Calderon (1853) : two more were privately printed in 1865.

In all this work he sought to do for others what he regularly did for himself—to transfuse the spirit of the original. His *Agamemnon*—a 'per-version', as he called it, a tragedy 'taken from Aeschylus'—attempted to free the drama from all that impeded its 'accelerating interest from beginning to end', and to 'make the Poet free of the language which reigns over that half of the world never dreamt of in his philosophy'. He was under no delusion that such a taste could be truly achieved by other than 'some Poet, worthy of that name, and of congenial Genius with the Greek.' He felt that meantime he could best introduce an English reader to the play by what Dryden called 'metaphrase', that is, by transfusing its soul at the expense of the exact form of its body. So, he confesses, he used great licence only that he might be more faithful.

It is entirely characteristic of FitzGerald that he should have had printed a retrenched version of Crabbe's *Tales of the Hall*, the most genial of that poet's verse-tales, in which he saw qualities akin to Jane Austen's, and that he had it in mind to publish an edition of Dryden's Prefaces. He delighted in the thews and sinews of the language, in humour and good sense : Tennyson was almost certainly right in his rueful anticipations about the reception 'the diffuse and opulent end' of his 'Tiresias' would have had.

FitzGerald is known today principally for his *Rubáiyát of Omar Khayyám*, although he himself preferred his version of *Salámán and Absál, An Allegory, Translated from the Persian of Jámí*. (His other translation from Persian, Attar's *Mantik uttair*, entitled *The Bird Parliament*, was not published in his lifetime. Like *Salámán*, it was written before the *Rubáiyát*. The *Rubáiyát*, or quatrains, of FitzGerald's Omar are commonly thought of as exotic, but the unaffectedness of the language (and the humour) should not be lost sight of :

Ah, make the most of what we yet may spend,
Before we too into the Dust descend;
    Dust into Dust, and under Dust to lie
Sans Wine, sans Song, sans Singer, and—sans End!

Of course, the allusions to tavern and temple, to 'Kaikobád the Great, or Kaikhosrú' and the rest, not to speak of the close-gathered stanza with its triple, occasionally quadruple, rhymes in imitation of the original, do cast a powerful Eastern spell, just as the Bible occasionally does: the stanzas on the Potter and the pot have obvious biblical associations not likely to be lost on Victorian readers, and certainly not on Browning (whose 'Rabbi Ben Ezra' has the same metaphor, used in a contrary sense). Although nominally a translation, it is really an English poem in its own right, and could nowadays be quite aptly called an 'imitation' in Robert Lowell's sense. It made a great impression on Ruskin (who addressed a letter to its anonymous author, begging for more, which took ten years to reach him), on Rossetti and Swinburne (who bought the brown-paper wrapped copies from a remainder-box) and on the many others who bought the next three editions.

The first edition has only 75 quatrains, while the fourth has 101, which is nine less than the second. Between 1859 and 1879, between the first and fourth editions, FitzGerald made considerable changes in the wording of the stanzas, and in the order in which they occur. This alone would suffice to show that he followed his usual practice of allowing himself considerable freedom in his adaptation of the originals, which consisted of an MS in the Bodleian Library, a copy sent him by his friend and mentor, E. B. Cowell, from Calcutta, and for the second edition (1868) an edition published in Paris in 1867 by J. B. Nicholas. He omitted many amatory and vinous stanzas, 'mashed' others together, and gave a sort of progression, imperfect though it is, from morning to evening. It is therefore vain to charge him with inaccuracy. He *was* an amateur and he did make mistakes, but the translations which have followed his achieve what interest they have because they throw light on FitzGerald's poem. By that light one sees that he is surprisingly close to many of the original quatrains, yet has managed to replace their abruptness by lines which, with a few exceptions in which the syntax is tortured, run very easily. The phrasing is carefully managed to bring pauses *within* the lines. This avoids the monotony which end-stopped lines with recurring rhymes are prone to suffer from, and strengthens the impression of a speaking voice which the colloquialisms supply. Really, the *Rubáiyát* is a dramatic monologue, and its swerves in thought or 'argument' both serve and are served by the metre. (FitzGerald's metrical skill is also evident in 'The Bird Parliament', which shows a command of the eighteenth-century manner in the heroic couplet.) Some inversions and archaisms occur, but they contribute to the impression of antiquity, while the imagery is as Persian as anyone could wish, even though FitzGerald did not care to mention a leg of mutton among the sufficiencies of life in stanza XII (Fourth edition).

FitzGerald's poem achieved its success because it appealed to a public perplexed in the extreme by the constantly-debated problems of faith and conduct which deepened every year after 1859 (in which *The Origin of the Species* was also published). FitzGerald himself had passed through a period of religious doubt and felt the power of modern science (particularly geology) to throw down old beliefs. He was quite aware of the 'wickedness' of the *Rubáiyát* (even *Fraser's Magazine* would not publish the least 'wicked' of them), but believed

Omar's doubts to be shared by most reflective people in his day, even if, like him, they were still Christians. 'Omar' does not question the existence of God, only his inscrutability and his neglect of man's urgent need of illumination: so he remonstrates, appeals, even chides. He does not follow his own recommendation to leave thought about life and death alone, and his resort to the pleasure of the moment does not derive from natural sensuality but from bafflement of the intellect. Still, the poem does look forward to Pater and Swinburne; yet the enthusiasm for the poem in the nineties does not alter the fact that it offers very little in the way of self-indulgent delights, and from a present-day standpoint compares more interestingly with Tennyson, Arnold and Browning than with, say, the early Yeats, Dowson or Wilde. Its humour and lightness of touch in dealing with such serious issues contrasts strikingly with the later work of Tennyson, whose poem 'The Ancient Sage', with its emphasis on sin, individual experience, private intuition and renunciation, shows another sort of response to the decline of Christian faith.

NOTE

1. The date of first publication in the 1830 and 1833 volumes is followed by that of first re-publication. This does not mean that no further changes in the texts were made.

BIBLIOGRAPHY

A *Tennyson*

Works with Notes by the Author, ed. (with Memoir) Hallam, Lord
   Tennyson, 1913.
   A single volume printing of the Eversley Edition, 9 vols., 1907–8.
Poetical Works, Including the Plays, 1953. (Oxford Standard Authors)
   Has an appendix of suppressed poems.
The Devil and the Lady, by Alfred Tennyson, ed. C. B. L. Tennyson,
   1930.
Unpublished Early poems, ed. C. B. L. Tennyson, 1932.
None of the editions listed above contains Tennyson's contributions
   to *Poems by Two Brothers*.
Poems, ed. C. B. Ricks, 1969. Comprehensive, annotated.

R. Jones, *The growth of the Idylls of the King*, Philadelphia, 1895.
Hallam, Lord Tennyson, *Alfred Lord Tennyson: a Memoir, by his
   Son*, 2 vols., 1897. Comparison with *Materials for a Biography
   of AT*, 4 vol. privately printed by Hallam, Lord Tennyson for
   his children shows how freely the *Memoir* was adapted from
   the poet's surviving papers.
Hallam, Lord Tennyson, *Tennyson and his Friends*, 1911.
[Sir] Harold Nicolson, *Tennyson: Aspects of his Life, Character and
   Poetry*, 1923.
D. Bush, *Mythology and the Romantic Tradition in English Poetry*,
   Cambridge, Mass., 1937.
W. D. Paden, *Tennyson in Egypt; a Study of the Imagery in his
   Earlier Work*, Lawrence, Kansas, 1942.
[Sir] Charles [C.B.L.] Tennyson, *Alfred Tennyson*, London and New
   York, 1949. The standard biography.
E. B. Mattes, *In Memoriam: the Way of a Soul*, New York, 1951.
E. D. H. Johnson, *The Alien Vision of Victorian Poetry*, Princeton,
   1952.
J. Killham, *Tennyson and 'The Princess'*, 1958.
J. Killham (ed.), *Critical Essays on the Poetry of Tennyson*, 1960.
J. H. Buckley, *Tennyson: the Growth of a Poet*, Cambridge, Mass.,
   1961. Uses the Tennyson materials at Harvard.
J. Richardson, *Pre-Eminent Victorian*, 1962.
V. Pitt, *Tennyson Laureate*, 1962.
R. W. Rader, *Tennyson's 'Maud': The Bibliographical Genesis*, Berke-
   ley, California, 1963.
J. D. Jump (ed.), *Tennyson: the Critical Heritage*, 1967.

B *FitzGerald*

Letters and Literary Remains, ed. W. A. Wright, 7 vols., 1903 (containing *More Letters* and *Letters to Fanny Kemble*, ed. Wright,
   1895 and 1901).

Variorum and Definitive Edition of the Poetical and Prose Writings,
ed. G. Bentham, New York, 1903. No letters, but includes items
omitted in Wright.
Some New Letters . . . to Bernard Barton, ed. F. R. Barton, 1923.
(Published as *Edward FitzGerald and Bernard Barton,* New
York, 1924).
Letters from Edward FitzGerald to Bernard Quaritch, ed. C. Quar-
itch, 1926.
A FitzGerald Friendship, ed. C. B. Johnson and N. C. Hannay, 1932.

E. H. Allen, *Edward FitzGerald's Rubáiyát of Omar Khayyám.*
1899. Gives Persian original, literally translated.
A. Y. Campbell, 'Edward FitzGerald' in *The Great Victorians,* ed.
H. J. and E. Massingham, 1932.
A. McK. Terhune, *The Life of Edward FitzGerald,* New Haven, 1947.
Includes a list of FitzGerald's major works and editions in
which they appear.
A. J. Arberry, *Omar Khayyám; a New Version Based upon Recent
Discoveries,* New Haven, 1952.
—— *The Romance of the Rubáiyát,* 1959.
R. Graves and Omar Ali-Shah, *The Rubáiyyát of Omar Khayyám,*
1967. A new translation from 'a twelfth-century manuscript
of uncontradictable authority.' Revives the claim that Khayyám
was a Sufi mystic, and the charge of inaccuracy in 'translation'.

THE BROWNINGS

ISOBEL ARMSTRONG, *University College, London*

The Brownings were eccentrics, both in their art and in their personal lives. Their marriage has come to seem one of the most romantic happenings of mid-Victorian literary life and yet it was remarkable for its oddity: it was the marriage, at forty, of an aggressive blue-stocking and pampered gentleman's daughter—egocentric, prejudiced, perceptive and clever—to a rather raw and unsuccessful poet some years younger than herself and socially very much her inferior. Robert Browning was the son of a bank clerk, a respectable but humble origin. He had flirted with the radical politics and unitarian thinking of W. J. Fox and his circle, had then moved into the theatrical world (thus making his social position more dubious than ever), writing plays which were not popular successes, even if they were not quite complete artistic failures. It was a rakish affair, indeed, and one can only admire the resilience and adventurousness of this pair as they freed one another. Elizabeth Barrett escaped from the restrictions of an oppressive father and an at least partly self-induced neurotic sickness; Browning escaped from the narrowness of life as the only son of unwisely admiring parents. Both of them, though in late life, made a bid for an existence which was emotionally mature, productive and balanced. But in order to achieve this they chose the life of the exile or the expatriate, in virtually permanent residence in Italy, creating for themselves the conditions in which artistic eccentricity could thrive because they were necessarily cut off from the language, the social pressures and commitments of their country and therefore of the readers for whom they continued to write. Neither became a European writer—although

Mrs Browning, in unread poems such as *Casa Guidi Windows*, perhaps attempted to be one; and yet neither is as centrally Victorian as, say, Carlyle or Tennyson. Their necessary lack of involvement is beautifully suggested by Mrs Browning in *Aurora Leigh* in a passage which says a good deal about the strange dissociation of living in a foreign land, a dissociation which crept into both poets' work :-

> It's sublime,
> This perfect solitude of foreign lands!
> To be, as if you had not been till then,
> And were then, simply that you chose to be :
> To spring up, not be brought forth from the ground,
> Like grasshoppers from Athens, and skip thrice
> Before a woman makes a pounce on you
> And plants you in her hair!—possess, yourself,
> A new world all alive with creatures new,
> New sun, new moon, new flowers, new people—ah,
> And be possessed by none of them! no right
> In one, to call your name, inquire your where ...
> —Such most surprising riddance of one's life
> Comes next one's death; it's disembodiment
> Without the pang.

This 'riddance' of English life in 1846 had by far the greatest effect on the poetry of Robert Browning. And this is to be expected, for he is, of course, undeniably a poet of major importance. Though all her work is artistically ambitious and bears the mark of her extraordinary precocity, her learnedness and outspoken intelligence, Elizabeth Barrett's poetry mostly reads as a Victorian period-piece. Her poetic techniques, her language, her thinking, all seem rather conventional now and very much of her time. The first part of the fifth book of *Aurora Leigh*, for instance, is a miniature Victorian *ars poetica* and must be read now for its historical interest alone. Many of the thoughts in this book are also expressed in her husband's poem, 'Fra Lippo Lippi'—'Let poets give it voice/ With human meanings ...'—but we do not read *Fra Lippo Lippi* for historical reasons, and this is the measure of Browning's stature. For all her violence and intelligent passion ('How arrogant men are!'; 'Since when was genius found respectable?'), Mrs Browning lacks the daring of the real eccentric. Poor Marian Erle, like all respectable Victorian fallen women, is *drugged* as well as

seduced in order to show just how respectable she really is—
and this happens in what was intended to be Mrs Browning's
most outspoken work, Aurora Leigh, which is a strange blend
of real open-mindedness and thoroughly reactionary thinking.
Browning is never caught inadvertently making such concessions to his time.

Yet the idiosyncratic freedom and independence of Browning's poetic experiments creates special difficulties for a critic:
it is difficult to discover a centre to his work or any driving
preoccupations. It seems all Gothic frolic with minor historical figures, the poetry of an antiquarian with surprising streaks
of energy, violence and intellectual sophistication. What
unifying drive can one discover among such diverse works as
a poem about a medieval quack philosopher (Paracelsus, 1835),
or about an extremely minor poet caught up in the political
struggles of pre-Dantean Italy (Sordello, 1840), a series of plays
which are anything from the austere studies in political loyalty
in Strafford (1837) to the overheated love-story unexpectedly
embodied in a play with all the conventions of Victorian melodrama (A Blot in the Scutcheon, 1843), monologues spoken by
mad dukes, Italian Renaissance painters, characters from
Shakespeare and biblical characters? For want of any better
we still use the nineteenth-century descriptions and categories
evolved to discuss Browning's poetry in terms mainly of its
'philosophy': we talk of Browning's fascination with a sort
of metaphysical tetrad—Love, Art, Beauty, Evil—categories
which can be traced back to such works as Mrs Sutherland
Orr's Handbook to the poetry of Browning. Studies of this kind
were admirable enough in their day but the rigorous concentration on prose meaning makes the fact that Browning wrote
poetry almost irrelevant. Again, we use Browning's own categories, subjective and objective poetry, which he introduced
in his essay on Shelley. Or again, we talk about Browning's
dramatic power and psychological insight as if they were the
most important things about his poetry, while it is arguable
that Browning was often remarkably deficient in both. In any
case, such an approach ignores the shading of the monologues
from dramatic particularity to straightforward philosophical
debate to the expression of undaunted, impersonal lyric feeling and throws a misleading emphasis on the lyrics and love
poems as dramatic expressions of feeling.

What is needed is a way of looking at Browning which will
get further into the poetry than the nineteenth-century cate-

gories I have mentioned and be more inclusive than discussions of his dramatic power. A wonderfully perceptive remark by Matthew Arnold, perceptive because it was written in 1848, well before Browning had produced the poems most people regard as typical of him, suggests what kind of poet he really is. Comparing him with Keats, Arnold puts Browning firmly in the mainstream of Romantic poetry :–

> As Browning is a man with a moderate gift passionately desiring movement and fulness, and obtaining but a confused multitudinousness, so Keats with a very high gift is yet also consumed by this desire . . . neither understand that they must begin with an Idea of the world in order not to be prevailed over by the world's multitudinousness.
>
> (*Letters . . . to Arthur Hugh Clough*, ed. H. F. Lowry, Oxford, 1932, p. 97)

Arnold's remark, I suspect with more insight than he knew, suggests so much—the greedy, swamping physicality of Browning's poetry and the lava-like quality of the language and structure of the poems—and without assenting to his cool evaluation it is possible to see that it suggests also the intellectual or philosophical stresses and distresses behind Browning's work. For Browning began life as a Romantic poet with aesthetic, political and philosophical preoccupations similar in kind to those of the earlier Romantics before him, passionately desiring the world's multitudinousness indeed, but passionately believing also in the possibility of discovering a *unifying* Idea of the world. He wrote three poems before 1840 in this high Romantic mode, diffuse and confused indeed, but two of which (*Pauline* and *Sordello*) compare favourably with the mature work of Keats and of Shelley. What follows is a gradual retreat from Romantic form and Romantic philosophy, and the rest of Browning's poetry is a toughly ardent criticism of Romantic idealism, particularly of Romantic views of freedom, the imagination, and the belief in feeling as a necessarily energizing power. A high Romantic optimism gives way to a guarded and occasionally raucously ironical scepticism. What Arnold does not suggest is Browning's self-consciousness about his artistic difficulties—how to express a rich assent to the world's confused multitudinousness which was not itself confused : how not to be prevailed over, invaded by the 'movement and fulness' but to find an Idea of the world which was nevertheless moving and full. To '*begin*' with an 'Idea of the world' would have been anathema to him. In fact, what Browning does in his post-Romantic phase is to find more and more precise ways of expressing the psychological perplexities of the *pursuit* of order and meaning amid the moving fulness of the world's multitudinousness. There is no nihilistic acceptance of chaos in his poetry as some people have claimed, but he proclaims no discoveries. Abt Vogler's momentary discovery of harmony and unity is the most provisional and fleeting of orders, created as it is out of extemporized notes. Browning's palace of sound is evanescent and fragments almost as soon as it is created. The pleasure domes of the unifying imagination in *Kubla Khan* are positively solid by comparison with it.

In the poems written after his departure to Italy in 1846 Browning can be seen restricting and delimiting the areas of experience explored in his poems. The huge, inclusive metaphysical constructs of the earlier work disappear and everything he wrote was on a smaller scale and took a wayward and eccentric form—lyrics so fragmented by fits and starts and spurts of feeling that they seem to break apart, monologues embodying strange situations and full of obliquities of meaning. Yet such poems as 'By the Fire-side', 'Childe Roland', 'Andrea Del Sarto' and 'Fra Lippo Lippi' are Browning's major work. The restriction of his material is a way of concentrating and clarifying his meaning; the eccentric form is actually a liberation, a way of exposing Romantic values by testing them out in extreme and curious contexts. In this account of Browning's work I shall discuss mainly the achievement of *Men and Women* (1855). But in order better to place these achievements it is necessary to look at some of the early poems and that transitional drama, *Pippa Passes* (1841).

Browning's early poems have dark elements, obsessed as they are with disintegration, betrayal, guilt and failure, but they still offer a positive Idea of the world in the face of these things, an Idea which is seen as applicable to the life of the whole society. *Pauline*, discovering as it does the imagery of schizophrenia, is best called an expressionist poem, Browning's *Ewartung*. It is a study of disintegration. The speaker describes an orgiastic grasping of experience, physical, emotional and intellectual, without any attempt to establish a creative order. He is simply invaded by the world's multitudinousness and all experience takes on a destructive life of its own—'I seemed the fate from which I fled'.

I am made up of an intensest life,
Of a most clear idea of consciousness
Of self . . .
And to a principle of restlessness
Which would be all, have, see, know, taste, feel, all—
This is myself.

But *Pauline* is also an account of recovery, a gradual and in-explicable mending symbolically suggested by a passage at the centre of the poem describing a woodland walk descending into a dead undergrowth and then following a path upwards into liberating sunlight. The speaker emerges whole, with his flagrantly utopian beliefs in freedom and perfectibility almost unscathed.

Sun-treader, I believe in God and truth
And love.

This is an address to Shelley and in it Browning re-affirms all his hopes of 'perfecting mankind', hopes abandoned in the earlier part of the poem. Browning's early passion for Shelley, whose beliefs he interpreted in the most optimistic way and whose vegetarianism and atheism he embraced with pedantic enthusiasm, manifests itself in this poem in Shelleyan imagery and a symbolic mode which seems very like Shelley's *Alastor*. But *Pauline* is Shelley psychologized and Browning's interest in the boundless possibilities of 'the unshaped images which lie/Within my mind's cave' is always in the complexity and subtlety of psychological processes, processes which he later tried to build into the very structure of his poems.

With *Paracelsus* and *Sordello* the attempt to convey the world's multitudinousness is made on a grander and grander scale so that with *Sordello* it includes the political and artistic life of a whole society, virtually of a whole culture. And yet as the scale becomes larger, there is an increasing recognition of randomness and disorder in all our affairs and of the dif-ficulties of seeing the world as a meaningful whole. Although in Paracelsus the ordering powers of the creating mind are celebrated with passion—

'Truth is within ourselves; it takes no rise
From outward things, . . .
There is an inmost centre in us all,
Where truth abides in fulness . . .'

297

Paracelsus fails to establish any kind of meaningful relationship between the various aspects of his personality and dies fragmented and incomplete: the gradual corruption of the intellect has come about because he has not been able to acknowledge and reconcile with it his need for a life of passion and feeling. In *Sordello* (a much better poem than the mechanical *Paracelsus*), as the young poet reaches out for a more inclusive existence, the more he tries to relate himself to a larger whole, his society, and the more he tries to act meaningfully, to make moral choices, the more broken and fragmented he becomes. He leaves the promiscuous imaginative life of Goito, self-enclosed and disordered (beautifully realized in the language of the poem which suggests the rich swamping messiness of his created world), in search of a productive relationship with an audience. This in turn forces him to consider his social and political responsibilities. His loyalties are all with the humanitarian Guelfs, but by a cruel twist of fate he is actually heir to the Ghibelline leadership. This unexpected relationship is precisely the opposite of the purposeful, retributive fate of tragic action and suggests, like Pippa's hidden relationship to her Monsignor, the way in which chance, sheer randomness, is as much a factor to be weighed in our moral choices as any other and diminishes our freedom as much as any conflict of loyalty. What *Sordello* is concerned with, as Michael Mason has pointed out, is the multitudinous complexity of the circumstances behind any moral choice and consequently of action. (In *The Major Victorian Poets: Reconsiderations*, ed. I. Armstrong, 1969). It is a thoroughly political poem, intensely concerned with the realities of belief and action.

Pippa Passes is Browning's last attempt to explore the problems of meaningful order and action on a large scale. Pippa, the poor factory girl, moves past four tenuously related groups of people at crucial moments of moral decision and seemingly affects the course of their lives by her lyrical songs. She breaks into the stagy eroticism of Ottima and Sebald who have murdered Ottima's husband only to find that they are freed neither from hate ('Now he is dead I hate him worse') nor from the growing staleness of their relations with one another, into the deliberations of the artist, Jules, who has been tricked into marrying the daughter of a prostitute, into those of the would-be political assassin, into the conversation of prostitutes, into a scheme for her own moral corruption being concocted by a servant of the Monsignor. The incidents seem arbitrarily chosen and randomly put together, the disorganized product of Browning's imagination overflowing as a froth of poetry and prose, much as Pippa describes the sun boiling over and spurting its light into the new day at the beginning of the poem. But here is the world's (or society's) multitudinousness, public and private—love and art, church and state. The 'formless' structure seems to me deliberate, for it asks the question of the poem—*is* there order, *is* there pattern, in human actions? How meaningfully does Pippa impinge upon the decisions of others, and how far can we assent to her own conviction of pre-ordained pattern and determined action?—'With God, whose puppets, best and worst,/Are we'. Can we indeed derive an Idea of the world from the scattered events of the poem? The answers are left ambiguous and complex: Pippa's song pushes Sebald into action but it does not alter his egocentric longing for purity, his desire to be free of the *guilt* of his crime rather than the crime itself; Jules decides to marry Phene but only because he decides to treat her like one of his own sculptures and he retreats into isolation and into the sterile freedom of his own idealized art. Every character acts on an intuitive response to Pippa's songs, but in every episode the quality of the feeling behind the impulse is suspect. The certainties, the positives of *Pauline* and even of *Paracelsus* have disappeared.

After the philosophical strenuousness of the early poetry it could look as if Browning simply gave up in his later work and accepted the arbitrary chaos of the world's multitudinousness, celebrating the life of feeling and impulse, the extreme of randomness. This is not true. In the lyrics written after his departure for Italy Browning evolved a form and a language which could enact a haunting, exasperated pursuit of pattern and meaning. In the monologues he found a form where he could explore the human need to create and rehearse an image of the world and of the self. Direct treatment of political and social issues and institutions disappears, just as Browning gives up exploring directly the problems of freedom and choice (It is the first two episodes of *Pippa* which carry over into Browning's later poetry. In the Ottima and Sebald episode we recognize the macabre, overloaded feeling of poems such as 'The Laboratory' (1844) or 'In a Gondola' (1842) or the emotions of Guido in *The Ring and the Book*. The Jules and Phene episode looks forward to poems about the artist such as 'Andrea del

Sarto' (1855), 'Fra Lippo Lippi' (1855) and 'Abt Vogler' (1864). These things now emerge indirectly, subsumed under Browning's preoccupation with art and with the life of the emotions, particularly with situations where feeling has turned in on itself and become corrosive. Browning became a psychological poet, not in the sense that he understood character, but in the sense that he explored the processes of perception and introspection.

To give some sense of the achievements of Browning's maturity I shall look at three well-known poems from *Men and Women:*—'Childe Roland', 'Two in the Campagna' and 'Fra Lippo Lippi', and then briefly at 'The Ring and the Book', his last important work.

The crude, violent symbolism of 'Childe Roland' is typical of Browning only in its grotesquerie, for Browning did not often use the indeterminateness of symbol in his work. Nevertheless, its preoccupations are central to his poetry and it is rightly seen as an important poem. Created out of a hint from *King Lear* it is Childe Roland's account of a last desperate quest for the mysterious dark tower. It is like a more terrible and concentrated *Pauline*, another description of disintegration conveyed through hysterical imagery of overwrought physical horror.

> —It may have been a water-rat I speared,
> But, ugh! it sounded like a baby's shriek.

Confused multitudinousness, indeed, but not so confused as to be a meaningless invasion of horror. It is a miasmic poem of continually dissolving certainties and contradictions. As soon as the quest begins the knight is convinced that the leering old man's directions are false, and yet he leaves the 'safe way' for the 'ominous tract' which, *'all agree'*, hides the dark tower. He sees the whole quest as a progress, a series of definite steps and achievements, in linear terms. If you like, he has an 'Idea of the world' which he attempts to impose on his experience, but his experience constantly resists this formulation, constantly breaks out against such a notion with a raw violence. For what the knight does is to walk a psychological treadmill, repeating the same experience in a multitude of different and ever more violent ways. The imagery is all circular, even though it may look superficially as though some progress has been made. A river is crossed but the knight's experience is no better on the other side—'Now for a better country. Vain presage!' A landscape changes but things are the same—'And just as far as ever from the end!' An appalling conflict, a 'mad brewage', has taken place, but penned in a hollow where no footsteps can be seen leading out of or into the fight.

> Whose savage trample thus could pad the dank
> Soil to a plash? Toads in a poisoned tank,
>   Or wild cats in a red-hot iron cage.
>
> The fight must so have seemed in that fell cirque.
>   What penned them there, with all the plain to chose?
>   No footprint leading to that horrid mews,
> None out of it.

Toads in a poisoned tank, wild-cats in a red-hot cage, these are the tortured images of a person who is trapped in his own anguished fears and fantasies, the self-created prison of his own identity. The knight sees his quest in terms of an escape from the self, the search for some revelation from without. But he is forced to confront himself and to go deeper and deeper into the dark regions of his being, the caves of the mind celebrated in *Pauline*. Revelation of a kind is granted the knight when he recognizes the true nature of his 'quest'. The plain dissolves into a bowl of mountains (another circular image of the cage of the mind) and he realizes that 'progress' is impossible—'you're inside the den'. A truer, living and moving idea of his quest is discovered. With this acceptance (and it follows that the knight must accept the irrational violence and hate of the poem as his violence and hate. 'Den' is a thoroughly appropriate image for the self here—dens and violence go together) comes the realization that he is upon the dark tower without having recognized it, so different is it from his preconceptions. The discovery of meaningfulness never happens as it is expected to happen.

But what is the dark tower? Some people see it as a kind of milestone marking the knight's end and they see the whole poem as a symbolic account of a man facing death. But the dark tower, ugly ('round and squat', at any rate unprepossessing), opaque and mysterious ('blind as the fool's heart') and yet unique, stands surely for that core of the self which each person blindly assumes to exist in order to see himself as a living, active entity at all. It is that irreducible nub of being which we irrationally intuit and which enables us to feel that we are uniquely 'I'. It must be the organizing centre of our world, the synthesizing and unifying agency of our lives. Childe Roland's discovery is that some kind of redeeming centre can be found in the self in spite of the world's multitudinousness. The blast on the horn is an act of celebration and of defiant fear, celebration because a unifying power has been discovered, fear because chaos can always come again. The dark tower corresponds to the 'intensest life' of *Pauline* and 'inmost centre' from which truth can be derived in *Paracelsus*, but the easy confidence in the creating mind has darkened. The world's multitudinousness is threatening and inchoate, no longer a source of unqualified delight, and high Romantic optimism is soberly qualified in this mature poem.

Most of Browning's love-lyrics are puzzled and puzzling, agnostic about the experience of loving. A poem like 'Meeting at Night' (1845), with its rhythms of mounting orgasmic excitement and swift, thrusting, *achieved* sexual passion is a rarity among these lyrics. 'Meeting at Night' is a celebration of sheer physical feeling—

> As I gain the cove with pushing prow,
> And quench its speed i' the slushy sand ...
>
> And blue spurt of a lighted match,
> And a voice less loud, thro' its joys and fears,
> Than the two hearts beating each to each!

—but Browning's lyrics generally combine the passionately cerebral with an intense physicality. The happy ease in eagerness of 'Meeting at Night' (like 'Childe Roland', an account of a journey, but this time a journey full of certainty), appears, when it does appear in the other poems, shot through with disappointment or scepticism. The blue spurt of the match (like Abt Vogler's palace of sound), a sudden illumination, incandescent but transitory, could be an image for love as it is seen in other lyrics. There is the rejection of love in 'A Woman's Last Word' (1855) where the refusal to quarrel is seen as a rejection of love because it is a refusal to communicate at all. There is 'A Lover's Quarrel' (1855), which turns upon a subtle reversal of the implications of spring and winter imagery. In the 'blocked-up' snow of winter the lovers existed in happy isolation, literally playing games—they pretend to be sailors, the man paints a charcoal moustache on the woman's face—and now they have quarrelled and now that it is spring the man simply feels that he must 'bear with it', rejecting change and with it the 'living and moving' for fantasies of fulfilment in the frozen past. As he imagines a meeting in a crypt beneath the snow, he is 'blocked-up' indeed, incarcerated in memory. The Shelleyan cave of the mind, like the den of 'Childe Roland', has modulated to an eerier place, a crypt. This lyric, with its combination of the domestic and the macabre, intellectuality and a sort of ravenousness for the sensuous is characteristic of Browning's mature love-poems. So is the use of contradiction between metre and rhythm to express a complexity of mood— the rhythms of exasperation and pain drive across the playful, tripping metre.

'Two in the Campagna' is another poem about failure or incompleteness in love. It is an attempt to define an elusive and subtle feeling which seems the key to the whole meaning of the relationship between two lovers, a feeling which constantly evades definition, the meaning and pattern which the speaker attempts to impose upon it—'Where does the fault lie?' All that he can do is to write a poem about a feeling about a feeling which mimes the attempt to catch at the 'living and moving' reality of experience. Ultimately the search brings him no further discovery, no 'Idea of the world', only a reinforced knowledge of the teasing incompleteness of love and of his own inability to define it.

> Just when I seemed about to learn!
> Where is the thread now? Off again?
> The old trick! Only I discern—
> Infinite passion, and the pain
> Of finite hearts that yearn.

But a kind of secondary knowledge has been gained: he knows about incompleteness and about the necessity to seek for structure in the 'world's multitudinousness', to be 'off again'.

In this poem Browning's language marvellously renders the fluidity of experience. His way of missing out grammatical connectives of all kinds, of breaking up sentences, of jerking from tense to tense, of letting adjectives clot together with the raw immediacy of a sensation becomes highly expressive here. The first stanza, for instance, catches the reader in an intricate web of tenses which open up all kinds of doubts, possibilities, and uncertainties, particularly as the whole of the stanza is framed as a question and the poem opens on a passionately complex, doubting note.

303

> I wonder do you feel today
> As I have felt since, hand in hand,
> We sat down on the grass, to stray
> In spirit better through the land,
> This morn of Rome and May?

It is a comparison of past and present, but the clauses determining past and present have such an uncertain grammatical and logical status that the comparison becomes complicated. The woman and the speaker are repeating the experience of a May-time walk, pausing to reflect upon the things ahead of them (straying in spirit), but by asking 'do you feel today/ As I *have felt since . . ?*' Browning adds a further straying in spirit, introspection about that past event *felt in the past* and possibly to begin again with the impetus of the repeated experience. We seem to have come in on the poem in the middle of a continuous striving with introspection. The last line of the stanza returns to present time, but with a trailing subordinate phrase, so that the perplexities introduced after the first line seem still governing the present—everything is still open.

'For me, I touched a thought . . .' The introspection does begin again and what follows is one of Browning's most brilliant renderings of a random but intense associative thought-process in terms not of the content of the thought but of what it feels like to think. Linked indissolubly with the visual straying in spirit the process is seen in sharply physical terms. To *touch* a thought gives the thought the force of a sensation and in another image, comparing the process with the random complexities of the spider's web, Browning suggests how the mind spins its own perplexities and throws out its own threads of feeling and thought to escape from the very complexities it creates, thus creating further involutions of uncertainty— 'yonder weed/Took up the floating weft'. The thread of thought strays arbitrarily outwards from blind green beetles in an orange flower to the quiet Campagna; and the poet's speculation strays outwards, too, to the large questions of love and freedom and spontaneity and will, but he is led insistently back to the same painful sense of loss and incompleteness and faced at the end of the process with the same endless process of definition. When 'the good minute goes' the self is left still spinning at the centre of the web. In a letter to Ruskin Browning spoke irritably of his failure to 'make out' his thoughts with his language and explained that the difficulty arose because his poetry was 'a putting of the infinite within the finite' (*The Life and Work of John Ruskin*, ed. W. G. Collingwood, 1893, Vol. I, p. 200). If 'the infinite' here means the suggestion of endless, random experience with endless possibilities, Browning has expressed it in this poem both through language and form. The perplexity of the poem is created as much by what it does not say—in the gaps and leaps of the syntax and the associative process—as by what it says. Like so many of Browning's lyrics this poem is circular and returns to its beginning, an unbroken continuum of experience.

I have emphasized the achievement of Browning's lyrics (and I think they are the most interesting, if not the best things he wrote) because it is usual for the dramatic monologues to be given the greater share of critical attention. Perhaps this is because in them he is most clearly an innovator but it may be that the monologues are the easiest of all his poems to understand. Some of the monologues, of course, are more dramatic than others: some of them, like 'A Death in the Desert' (1864), simply put theological ideas in a dramatic setting, or, like 'Bishop Blougram's Apology' (1855) and 'Mr Sludge, "The Medium"' (1864) they sport with ideas, looking at the strange possibilities inherent in what by then were familiar Romantic notions. The dazzling intelligence of these monologues lies in the choice of a dramatic situation which will amplify and multiply the implications of the idea—a trick medium claims the prerogatives of the Romantic poet, the created world of the imagination: a time-serving bishop rests his weary conservatism on an assent to intuitional feeling. Some of the monologues re-create in a condensed form the obsessions of Browning's early work. There is the mad duke of 'My Last Duchess' (1842) who cannot love without so possessing and destroying the identity of his wife that he literally kills her and lives with her dead substitute, a work of art. This recalls Jules in *Pippa Passes*. The Bishop ordering his tomb at St Praxed's (1845) still grasps insatiably, to 'have, see, know, taste and feel, all' at the very edge of death, taking to a lurid extreme the violent need to possess the world's multitudinousness expressed in *Pauline*. Some of the best monologues are those where Browning returns to his restless preoccupation with the need to impose a shape on experience, a need so great that the speakers continue to see their lives as meaningful wholes, even if the explanation they offer is patently the wrong one. 'Andrea Del Sarto', with its Chekhovian ironies, 'Fra Lippo Lippi' and 'Caliban Upon Setebos' are monologues of this kind. In 'Fra Lippo Lippi', in particular, Browning's early worries about the artist's audience, the feeling that creation is not completed until it is shared, expressed in *Paracelsus* and *Sordello*, re-appears. Indeed, the monologue form allowed Browning to demonstrate the processes of communication in their essence, for the silent listener to whom the monologue is addressed as silently governs the way the nature of an experience is formulated. The most interesting achievement of the monologue-form is its way of being a study in the subtle reciprocal action and interaction between speaker and listener so that any Idea of the world which emerges depends on the two people encapsulated in the poem. It is as if Browning's large, baffled preoccupation with the freedom of the individual, poet or not, to act and by his actions to affect or relate to the external world and to society is expressed indirectly and with wonderful simplicity and concentration through the conditions imposed by the form of the monologue itself. In the monologues he found a model for expressing the problems he explored in so many ramifications in the early poems.

'Fra Lippo Lippi' seems like a robust defence of the aesthetic and emotional freedom of the artist but when his listeners are taken into account the painter's manner seems more like robust defensiveness. He is defending a splendidly celebratory view of art as a re-animating power, art which is thoroughly democratic, based as it is on the portrayal of the actual, not an ideal world :–

> you've seen the world
> —The beauty and the wonder and the power
> The shapes of things, their colours, lights and shades,
> Changes, surprises,—and God made it all!
> —For what? ...
>
> ... Art was given for that;
> God uses us to help each other so,
> Lending our minds out.

But the tone of his celebration and its passionate praise of the living and moving world is significantly different from the aggressive bravado of the rest of the poem. Fra Lippo Lippi cannot sustain the quality of this feeling and presents himself blusteringly as the typical bohemian artist, or rather, the popular view of the bohemian artist—promiscuous, hedonistic and flagrantly against all orthodoxies. The reason for this is the presence of the watch, sceptically listening to his explanations. Lippi passionately believes himself to be a popular artist and is one, but when faced with an element of his audience, he loses confidence, distrusting their belief in him and ingratiates himself his listener—

Yes, I'm the painter ...
What, brother Lippo's doings, up and down,
You know them and they take you? like enough!
I saw the proper twinkle in your eyes—
Tell you, I liked your looks at very first.

He projects a defensive image of himself and yet this is superimposed on another image of the painter he would like to be. On the other hand, the painter he would like to be is conditioned always by the painter he acts.

The poems of *Men and Women* and of *Dramatis Personae* (1864) will always be the poems people read but they have more meaning when they are related to their raw material, Browning's early work, and that, too, grows in stature. But what of the later work? Apart from a strange renewal of power in *Parleyings With Certain People of Importance in Their Day* (1887) the pattern is one of unsteady but definite decline after *The Ring and the Book* (1868). There are erratic flashes of strange intensity in poems such as *Fifine at the Fair* (1872), but in general Browning lost his agnostic puzzlement and became dogmatic—and boring.

Some people end Browning's effective poetic achievement with *Dramatis Personae*, but *The Ring and the Book* can claim to be his last important work. This vast collection of monologues is a sustained and dazzling exploration of the overwhelming question which is asked in different ways in so many of Browning's poems: if we accept that 'truth is within ourselves' and rely on the simple experiential validity of the *feeling* of rightness, how can we know that feeling does not mislead us? This time it is asked on a huge scale and involves the beliefs and institutions of a whole society. Debating the Roman murder case of 1698 when Guido Franceschini stabbed his wife, Pompilia, every speaker—citizens, Pope, lawyers, participants—rests his interpretation of the events on pure feeling, pure intuition. But as each monologue qualifies another, defining and re-defining the nature of intuition as the basis of judgment, feeling becomes anything but pure. In the last monologue of the poem, the violent despairing speech of Guido before his execution, destructive or diseased feeling is the cause of evil and the inmost centre of the self is invaded by it.

> Nor is it in me to unhate my hates,—
> I use up my last strength to strike once more
> Old Pietro . . .
> . . . and I grow one gorge
> To loathingly reject Pompilia's pale
> Poison my hasty hunger took for food.

The metaphysical scale of the early poems has returned, but with all the concentration and intensity learned in the intervening time.

I have tried to show that Browning is a major poet rather than to take up and demolish the familiar case against his poetry—his vulgarity, coarseness and violence. Whatever the immediate impact of his poetry, one cannot fail to recognize in it a controlling intelligence, often exasperating but more often performing with a virtuosity both brilliant and profound. One person at least recognized his power when his contemporaries failed to acknowledge it—his wife. 'My cricket chirps against thy mandolin', she wrote in *Sonnets from the Portuguese* (IV). These sonnets, with their rather bookish Shelleyan imagery ('Straightway I was 'ware,/So weeping, how a mystic Shape did move/Behind me . . .'), their diffuse emotionalism, or perhaps 'emotionalosity', are all that Elizabeth Barrett Browning is now remembered by. They compare badly wih the arresting intensities and intricacies of Browning's love poems (for instance with that tiny essay in adoration, 'Song'), and yet occasionally one feels in them the pressure of real bewilderment, uncertainty and wonder, particularly in Sonnets X, XX, XXII, XXIX, XXX, XL. And occasionally she will discover a grandly bizarre image to match the extravagance of her feeling.

> and distort
> Thy worthiest love with worthless counterfeit;
> As if a shipwrecked Pagan safe in port,
> His guardian sea-god to commemorate,
> Should set a sculptured porpoise, gills a-snort,
> And vibrant tail, within the temple-gate.

One reads these poems, I think, for a curiously pervasive femaleness. And this is so with her only other work which survives as a readable poem, *Aurora Leigh*. Its femaleness rather than its feminism is its most interesting quality now. The memor-

able parts of *Aurora Leigh* are the accounts of the quietly rebellious girl living under the restraints of rigorous gentility
or its female cattiness about men, as in this description of
masculine embarrassment at a risqué remark about the revealing clothes of Lady Waldemar.

> The student flinched,
> Sir Blaise, the same; then both, drawing back their chairs
> As if they spied black-beetles on the floor,
> Pursued their talk . . .
>
> (Book V)

'Who loves *me*?' Aurora Leigh cries with passionate self-pity.
Elizabeth Browning understood what it was like to be a woman
who made violent emotional demands on the world and yet
despised the 'luxury of emotion', and she is particularly perceptive about Aurora's proud, exacting sensibility. Happily
for Aurora her youthful, arrogant dismissal of Romney Leigh
because he could not respect the claims of art is not final and
the two are united when Marian Erle, the working-class girl
once engaged to Romney, releases him.

Elizabeth Barrett Browning expounds almost without question the Romantic beliefs in spontaneity and the autonomy of
the artist which her husband accepted with such urgent scepticism. Her ability to make these beliefs the foundation for an
irrational hatred of social reform is perverse, as is her loathing
of the working classes.

> . . . Romney Leigh, who lives by diagrams,
> And crosses out the spontaneities
> Of all his individual, personal life,
> With formal universals. As if man
> Were set upon a high stool at a desk,
> To keep God's books for Him, in red and black,
> And feel by millions!
>
> (Book III)

This perverseness seems to have hardened with the departure
to Italy, whereas for Browning the break with England allowed
a new imaginative freedom and originality—as if he were able
to take stock of the possibilities of this early poetry and gained
the confidence to experiment. But if his art gains in concentration and in the more daring play with concepts and passions,
there is also present the sense of a man struggling with a living
emotional situation. The virtuoso intelligence is up against
a flesh-and-blood reality. Marriage and Elizabeth Barrett, as

well as the departure for Italy, 'blooded' and shaped the perceptions of the early poems. The self-important public figure of Browning's later years, the extraordinarily conventional man who was, puzzlingly, such a great artist (portrayed in Henry James's *The Private Life*) seems to have given up the enthusiasms and eccentricities which were the life of his early work and of *Men and Women*. It was a creative as well as a personal loss that his later years were free of 'the living and moving' pressures of his marriage.

BIBLIOGRAPHY

A *Robert Browning*

Works, ed. F. G. Kenyon, 10 vols., 1912.
The Complete Works, ed. Roma A. King *et al*, Ohio, 1968– .
The Letters of Robert Browning and Elizabeth Barrett Browning, 2 vols., 1899.
Letters, ed. T. L. Hood, New Haven, 1933.

Mrs. Sutherland Orr, *A Handbook to the Works of Robert Browning*, 1886.
W. H. Griffin and H. C. Minchin, *The Life of Robert Browning*, 1911, revd., 1938.
W. O. Raymond, *The Infinite Movement*, Toronto, 1950.
Betty Miller, *Robert Browning, A Portrait*, 1952.
W. C. DeVane, *A Browning Handbook* revd., New York, 1955.
P. Drew (ed.), *Robert Browning*, 1966.
Maisie Ward, *Robert Browning and His World*, 1968.

B *Elizabeth Barrett Browning*

Poetical Works, 1904 (Oxford Standard Authors).
Letters, ed. F. G. Kenyon, 2 vols., 1897.

G. B. Taplin, *The Life of Elizabeth Barrett Browning*, New Haven, 1957.
Alethea Hayter, *Mrs. Browning*, 1962.

HOPKINS

NORMAN H. MACKENZIE, *Queen's University, Ontario*

During the life-time of Gerard Manley Hopkins (1844-89) only a handful of special friends so much as knew that he was an active poet. Even within this closed circle there were some who turned with distaste from his work as freakish or disrespectfully headstrong. When Robert Bridges sent the popular Victorian poet, Coventry Patmore, his beautifully transcribed album of Hopkins's verse, starting with 'Pied Beauty', and including now-celebrated poems such as 'The Windhover', 'The Wreck of the Deutschland', 'The Leaden Echo and the Golden Echo', 'Binsey Poplars', and 'God's Grandeur', Hopkins received a completely negative, dispiriting response from his fellow Catholic:

> My Dear Mr. Hopkins,—I have read your poems—most of them several times—and find my first impression confirmed with each reading. It seems to me that the thought and feeling of these poems, if expressed without any obscuring novelty of mode, are such as often to require the whole attention to apprehend and digest them; and are therefore of a kind to appeal only to the few. But to the already sufficiently arduous character of such poetry you seem to me to have added the difficulty of following *several* entirely novel and simultaneous experiments in versification and construction, together with an altogether unprecedented system of alliteration and compound words;—any one of which novelties would be startling and productive of distraction from the poetic matter to be expressed.
>
> (Hopkins: *Further Letters*, 2nd Edn., 1956, p. 352)

Fortunately for us, Hopkins continued to evolve his rhythm, structure and diction from his own concepts of first principles instead of discreetly modifying prevailing fashion. Only a few of his poems were published during the nineteenth century. Even the first edition of 1918 sold with unenthusiastic leisureliness, but since 1930 Hopkins has come into his own: his intense perceptiveness, the fibrous strength of his textures, his success in 'breaking the feet' of the traditional English iambic— all these lent impetus to modern poets confronting a rather different world from his own. Hopkins remains unique, without obvious predecessors or followers who could be described as belonging to his 'school'. He was godfather rather than parent to many of the vigorous poets of the first half of this century. The growth of his reputation has been marked by the progressively fuller and more careful editions of his works, which now run to six large volumes: the *Poems* (which includes original compositions and translations in Welsh, Latin and Greek); three volumes of his *Letters*, lively with debates on poetic form and astute judgments of contemporary writers; a volume of his *Sermons and Devotional Writings*, strangely different from the pulpit literature of his age, different too from the Thomism of most Catholics because he preferred the individualistic philosophy of Duns Scotus; and finally the splendidly edited *Journals and Papers*. (See bibliography p. 332, for details and the short titles by which they are cited.) Embedded in his first diary are not only his earliest attempts at verse, set in revealing contexts, but also his Ruskinesque drawings. Knowing the Rossettis and Holman Hunt, he seriously considered becoming an artist himself. (For his sketches, see *Journals*, pp. 453–5 and the plates which follow.) In music, lack of training prevented his attaining any fluency in performance or composition, but from the tunes which he wrote for various poems, mostly by his friends, experts can deduce a melodic inventiveness. (See *Journals*, pp. 457–497 for reproductions of his music, and commentary by Dr John Stevens.)

Hopkins's journals extend from the year he entered Oxford up to February 1875. The earliest diaries record his perceptive speculations about the affinities between words of similar sound, both within English (standard and provincial) and in related languages. His own original hypotheses were based upon a sense of a word's innermost 'scape': he tended to follow the lead of those etymologists whose proposed derivations lent most vitality to a term. Philology in the mid-Victorian age, if less scientific, was more exhilarating than in later years. Many scholars believed that particular consonant clusters preserved basic Sanskrit roots, each of which had resulted in whole family-trees of descendants. Thus English words beginning with *fl*—were thought to preserve a root meaning to fly or flow. (W. Fowler, *The English Language*, 1857, p. 109.) Hopkins offers conjectures about some twenty words beginning with *fl*—, differentiating subtly the gradations represented by *flick*, *fleck* and *flake*, and tentatively coupling with them *flitch*. When therefore we encounter 'flitches of fern' in his 'Inversnaid' (1881) we might well associate the phrase with the 'flake-leaves light' of 'Epithalamion' rather than invoke a crude kitchen image. Moreover, in English dialect use, another word 'flitch' was a variant of the verb 'to flit', while a third homophone, used around Oxford, was a variant of the adjective 'flick' meaning pert, lively, quick. All these associations tend to colour the term in 'Inversnaid'. Hopkins's philological interests continued throughout his life (see for example, *Letters* III, pp. 280–6), and once he had found something to say, his knowledge of the ancestry of words helped him to concentrate a great density of meaning into a short space.

More profoundly shaping his work came the concept for which he invented the word *inscape*. Many streams of thought contributed to its evolution. Ruskin, for example, in his *Modern Painters* continually searched for the scientific 'Law' or inner organization which accounted for a specific appearance in a certain type of cloud or landscape or tree. (See N. H. Mac-Kenzie: *Hopkins Among the Victorians*, pp. 159–165.) Philosophers from Plato to the Schoolmen of the Middle Ages had theorized about the *potential* and the *actual*, about *form* and *matter*. Hopkins uses the word *inscape* in his *Journals* with some flexibility. Less precisely applied, it may merely point to the recurring outward pattern shared by all members of a species, or repeated in man-made things such as the successive tie-beams of a barn roof. But in more typical passages Hopkins is referring to the sum of the special qualities within an object which give a sensitive observer an insight into its distinctive nature. After he discovered, with strange exhilaration, the *Opus Oxoniense* of Duns Scotus (to whom he shows moving gratitude in his sonnet 'Duns Scotus's Oxford'), he looked more and more for the moment of vision, of interior perception into an object's being (the result of the *instress* or pressure pulsing from its individual or specific qualities), as opposed to the superficial, confused knowledge with which most people rest content. All his best poems seem the product of such vision: they try to reconstruct in the intricacy of intermingling phrases the *inscape* which he has discovered. (See W. A. M. Peters: *Gerard Manley Hopkins*, 1948, Chapter I for an excellent treatment of *inscape* and *instress*.)

While an undergraduate at Oxford Hopkins fell first under the spell of the Tractarians (or Puseyites), who represented the ritualistic fringe of the High Anglican Church. Deeply in earnest himself, exacting in every matter of conduct or conscience, he began to question the authenticity of the English Church, like many another student in the years following the publication of Dr Newman's *Apologia Pro Vita Sua* (1864). At length, after much mental turmoil (reflected both in his diaries and current poems), he decided in 1866 to enter the Church of Rome. His conversion created a dissonance between himself and his family, still apparent in a sonnet written in Ireland nearly twenty years after this event: 'To seem the stranger lies my lot' (*Poems*, p. 101). The tension was increased when he decided to abandon all thought of art or poetry as a career, perhaps even as a relaxation, in order to give himself wholly to the Jesuit priesthood.

Those who believe that Hopkins might have become a greater poet if he had not turned priest should classify and weigh his undergraduate poetry. The most ambitious pieces are certainly secular, but they are heralds of failure, fragments which he never succeeded in worrying into completion: *Richard*, a blank verse narrative, *Floris in Italy*, a verse play. His future powers are more nearly anticipated in those poems of 1864–66 torn by uncertain faith or reaching after the spiritual ideal—'Heaven-Haven', 'The Half-way House' and 'Nondum'. The best is 'The Habit of Perfection':

> Shape nothing, lips; be lovely-dumb:
> It is the shut, the curfew sent
> From there where all surrenders come
> Which only makes you eloquent.
>
> Be shellèd, eyes, with double dark
> And find the uncreated light:
> This ruck and reel which you remark
> Coils, keeps, and teases simple sight.
>
> (Poems, p. 31)

The senses can seldom have been dismissed more sensitively or (in the best meaning of the word) sensuously. The originality of phrase and metaphor in which he afterwards excelled is here predicted by words like *the shut, curfew* (St James, chapter 3, vv. 5–6, warns us that the 'tongue is a fire', apt to escape control); *ruck* and *reel* have the direct appeal of the robust dialect words favoured by William Barnes, whose Dorset poetry Hopkins admired.

Hopkins left Oxford with a hard-earned First in 1867, and having finally decided on his vocation, he ceremonially burned his poems. The long training for the Jesuit priesthood followed. During the two years of his novitiate, spent in the quiet of Manresa House whose richly wooded grounds seemed an extension of the adjoining Richmond Park, he lived a life of meditation and devotional reading such as his 'Habit of Perfection' had aspired to, voluntarily isolated from the reading or composition of literature in a community severed from the 'ruck and reel' of national events. Then came three years of study in Lancashire—scholastic philosophy and ethics, mathematics and mechanics. Though he found sparse leisure for reading poetry or reviews, he drew inspiration from the great hills and noble fells (*Letters* I, p. 26; III, pp. 235, 238).

Since his entry into the Jesuit order Hopkins had in five years written no spontaneous poetry, only verse produced at the direct request of a superior—such as Greek iambics to welcome a new Bishop or pieces to adorn a statue, like 'Ad Mariam' and 'Rosa Mystica' in which Swinburne's melodious modes were used for sacred purposes. A landmark was reached in 1873 with his appointment for a year as Professor of Rhetoric at Manresa House, to teach some twenty advanced Jesuit students —a post which drove him to a fresh study of English literature and the reading of newly published volumes, e.g. by Matthew Arnold and Browning. A few pages of his notes have survived, on 'Rhythm and Other Structural Parts of Rhetoric' along with a fragment of a lecture on the distinction between 'Poetry and Verse' (*Journals*, pp. 267–290). These notes, though highly technical, reveal ideas about poetry which he was soon to put into effect. He emphasizes that poetry is a branch of speech, meant to be heard—a conviction which he applied most emphatically to his own productions (*Journals*, pp. 267, 289; *Letters* I, pp. 46, 79, 263, 272). And he speaks of alliteration as being used 'thickly in modern English verse : one may indeed doubt whether a good ear is satisfied with our verse without it' (*Journals*, p. 284).

The theological study which followed (1874–7), culminating in his ordination as priest, was in an environment which he found lyrically beautiful, overlooking the Welsh valley of the Elwy. It was in Wales that the final goad into poetry came in December 1875, when he was given official approval to write an ode on an event which had moved him deeply because it dramatized the new persecution of Catholics in central Europe, making England by contrast seem receptive to the Faith. Driven from Germany through the Falk Laws, five Franciscan sisters, tertiaries who cared for the poor and sick, had been sailing to a new life in Canada when their ship, the *Deutschland*, veered in a fierce snowstorm to death on a Kentish shoal.

> Into the snows she sweeps,
> Hurling the haven behind,
> The Deutschland, on Sunday; and so the sky keeps,
> For the infinite air is unkind,
> And the sea flint-flake, black-backed in the regular blow,
> Sitting Eastnortheast, in cursed quarter, the wind;
> Wiry and white-fiery and whirlwind-swivellèd snow
> Spins to the widow-making unchilding unfathering deeps.
>
> She drove in the dark to leeward,
> She struck—not a reef or a rock
> But the combs of a smother of sand : night drew her
> Dead to the Kentish Knock;
> And she beat the bank down with her bows and the ride
> of her keel;
> The breakers rolled on her beam with ruinous shock;
> And canvas and compass, the whorl and the wheel
> Idle for ever to waft her or wind her with, these she endured.
>
> (*Poems*, pp. 55–6)

While *The Times* and the German Reichstag demanded to know why rescue attempts were delayed thirty hours, and editorials in other papers questioned the captain's competence (e.g. *Illustrated London News*, Dec 11, *Saturday Review*, Dec 18 1875), Hopkins saw God extracting good from cruelty and suffering. All denominations had been shaken by the Presidential address to the British Association of Professor Tyndall (1874), identifying some religious views of Nature as surviving forms of primitive 'superstition'—Hopkins (*Letters*, III, p. 127) read a slightly abridged version—and by John Stuart Mill's

Three Essays on Religion (1874), which discerned no moral design or sense of justice in the Contriver of the cosmos. The Jesuit journal, *The Month*, was much concerned over agnostic assaults on religion and the persecutions in Europe. Hopkins the priest no longer harboured the doubts which had filled his undergraduate poem 'Nondum' with echoes of *In Memoriam*. Here he discerns, hidden behind the braggart Death and the roaring night, the unacknowledged Master of all, setting limits to the surge. God is hailed as

> The recurb and the recovery of the gulf's sides,
>> The girth of it and the wharf of it and the wall;
> Stanching, quenching ocean of a motionable mind;
> Ground of being, and granite of it : past all
>> Grasp God, throned behind
> Death with a sovereignty that heeds but hides, bodes but abides;
>> [*Poems*, p. 62, St. 32]

Those less familiar with Hopkins will most easily enjoy the narrative stanzas (11 to 17), but the full annotations in the fourth edition of the *Poems* should clear up most perplexities in the other portions. God is acknowledged as in the *inscape* of everything He has made; but we are usually blind to the divine instress except in the presence of great beauty—Hopkins mentions his favourite scenes, 'lovely-asunder Starlight' and 'the dappled-with-damson west' (st. 5)—or under the impact of the power strokes delivered by storm and lightning (st. 6). Yet in the confusing paradox of a world breached by the Fall and distorted by evil, the love of God can still operate through elements which the poet describes as 'endragonèd' (suggesting the Biblical arch-enemy of mankind) or issuing from 'cursed quarter'.[1] The lightning is also God's love: He is winter as much as spring, trying always to draw or drive men from their deluding self-sufficiency. In the final stanzas the poet's imagination passes beyond his vision of the King advancing over the wild Channel to receive His witness, the tall nun : he prays for His re-coronation in England, an exile restored.

It is, of course, possible to parallel a few of this poem's metaphors or phrases in the work of Hopkins's contemporaries. Swinburne's *Erechtheus* published while Hopkins was composing the 'Deutschland', carries similar imagery of sea and wreck—even lines with cognate rhythms (See Swinburne, *Collected Works*, 1924, Vol. II, pp. 353, 389, 399). Browning's Pope in *The Ring and the Book* may refer to the truth being flashed in a single lightning stroke, or to the purgatorial gloom.

> Where God unmakes but to remake the soul
> He else made first in vain.
>
> (X. 2119 ff.)

But in total effect the 'Wreck of the Deutschland' has no precedents in its rhythmic versatility, while its finest lines—including most of the long-drawn hexameters which end the stanzas—forge words into new and memorable units. The ambiguities of the ode retard but enrich even the modern student to whom sprung rhythm presents fewer vocal entanglements, but to Hopkins's fellow Jesuits the poem was unforgivably hobbled and knotty. (See N. H. MacKenzie: *Hopkins*, 1968, pp. 24–35.)

Having erected this memorial to strengthen faith, the poet naturally wished it to be seen, and unaware how far he had ventured ahead of general comprehension, he submitted the ode to the Jesuit journal, *The Month*. It was reluctantly refused. When that journal had been founded, its first editor had been warned by Newman that 'Catholics are not a reading set' (*The Month*, 29 June 1864) and required no predominantly literary review. Furthermore the Jesuits, following the lead of their founder, St Ignatius, had throughout their history avoided prominence and mistrusted brilliance, because earthly fame might lead a priest into the sin of pride. The Society, as Hopkins frankly explained to a friend urging the printing of his poems, valued literature only as a means to their main end, the advancement of the faith, and poetry 'has seldom been found to be to that end a very serviceable means' (*Letters*, II, p. 93). Hopkins completely accepted this evaluation as in the best interests of his Church, of his own highest nature and even of his poetry. His decision may seem regrettable to many who imagine that Victorian literature would have been leavened by his germinal innovations. We can only observe that among those contemporaries favoured with access to his work, most Catholics found it too unorthodox in literary terms, while to most Protestants it had the added deterrent of being too orthodox in Catholic terms. Victorian reviewers would certainly have pilloried Hopkins, a man who already shrank under the reputation of eccentricity. Robert Bridges's long delay in editing his poems brought one distinct gain, as Mellown has observed: it postponed their appearance until 1919, 'one of the most propitious years in which such "new" poetry could have been brought before the public, since only in the 1920's was a criticism developed which was appropriate for it. Hopkins was not so much born before his time, as before his critics' (*Modern Philology* LXIII (1965) p. 51).

There was nothing personal in the Jesuit rejection of his verse, since they published his *Silver Jubilee* along with a sermon by Father John Morris, S. J. that same year. But this was a somewhat inferior 'popular' piece in his own estimation, written to honour a bishop (*Letters*, I. p. 77). After a further elegy, on 'The Loss of the Eurydice' (April 1878), had been declined by *The Month*, and the rector of Stonyhurst had ruled that his 'May Magnificat' was below standard for display before the college's statue of the Virgin during her feast the following month, Hopkins ceased even to divulge to close colleagues that he ever wrote poetry on his own.

Fortunately the dampening effect of the Church-centred conservatism of his rectors was to some extent offset by a growing correspondence with two poets, Bridges and Dixon, with whom he interchanged detailed mutual criticism. Of immense value for the preservation of his poetic self was his friendship with Robert Bridges, whom he had known at Oxford. Different though they were in cast and calling, the two men were drawn into gradually mellowing harmony by their common pursuit of perfection in verse. Even before Hopkins had announced that he would no longer seek publication, nor permit it unless it came about through his superiors, Bridges as early as 1879 prepared an album in which to mount the autograph poems which Hopkins sent him, thus preserving them from the casualness of their author. And within a few years he also transcribed them into another album for private circulation among his friends, first scrupulously sending the book to Hopkins for checking and emendation.

That there were to begin with foolish misunderstandings on both sides we can see despite the destruction of Bridges's share of this fascinating correspondence (*The Letters of Gerard Manley Hopkins to Robert Bridges*). While Hopkins was studying theology (and incidentally privately learning Welsh) in the pastoral seclusion of Wales, the poet Bridges was facing the ugly duties of house-, and later casualty-physician in St Bartholomew's Hospital, London. His official report discloses that he had to see 30,940 patients in a single year! Hopkins, from graduation to the close of his life, seems to have lived under mental and physical tension which rendered even minor crises exhausting. It is ironic to find him writing from the peace of St Beuno's to St Bartholomew's: 'Dearest Bridges,—You have no call to complain of my delay in writing, I could not help it: I am not a consulting physician and have little time and now I am very very tired, ... and "scarce can go or creep" ' (*Letters*, I, p. 32). 'While others dance and play'—an adjoining phrase which he suppressed in this unidentified quotation from Haydn's popular song—hints at his delusions concerning Bridges's leisure. ('My mother bids me bind my hair', from *Twelve Canzonets*.) Bridges on his side at first showed cloven prejudices against his friend's Order. These Hopkins parried with humorous echoes, such as when he writes to Bridges (describing some fervent Anglicans), 'The Puseyites are up to some very dirty jesuitical tricks' (*Letters*, I, p. 58). Bridges was overharsh in castigating the 'oddities' to which Hopkins himself confessed, but Hopkins needed such reactions to keep eccentricity in check. Missing the chastening effect of a public upon a writer's experiments, he valued the comments of Bridges and Dixon: 'a poet', he said, 'is a public in himself' (*Letters*, I, p. 59). While he demanded absolute clarity in the verse of his friends, Hopkins himself needed to be told from time to time that some poem of his own resisted decipherment. If Bridges's taste was sometimes too classically circumspect to respond to audacities of phrase, such as 'leaves me a lonely began' ('To seem the stranger'), Hopkins was in artistic matters sufficiently self-assured in the rightness of his general practices to tell Bridges, for example, that his strictures upon the 'Wreck of the Deutschland' were mere bilgewater (*Letters*, I, pp. 50, 46–7). So too when towards the end of his life he developed new theories of musical composition, he firmly defended the music he had set to Collins's 'Ode to Evening': 'if you do not like it it is because there is something you have not seen and I see. That at least is my mind, and if the whole world agreed to condemn it or see nothing in it I should only tell them to take a generation and come to me again' (*Letters*, I, p. 214). In practice, however, where his poetry was involved he was apprehensive of its being so much as seen by literary reviewers like Andrew Lang, and in the early stages of a new venture he needed encouragement 'as much as crops rain' (*Letters*, I, pp. 218–9).

In their prosodic experiments Hopkins and Bridges were friendly rivals. Both had independently begun to develop Miltonic inversions before they exchanged poems (*Letters*, I, p. 38). Hopkins borrowed from music the term 'counterpoint' to describe the reversal of two successive feet, as in the opening

trochees of the iambic pentameter line: Generations have
trod, have trod, have trod ('God's Grandeur'). Here the iambic
plod at the end attains an onomatopoeic fitness because of the
disturbed metre in the first two feet. 'Sprung Rhythm', however, was a bold step well beyond simple counterpointing or
the substitution of trisyllabic for disyllabic feet. We may trace
the new rhythm 'haunting his ear' back to those lecture notes
already referred to, made for his Manresa students in 1873–4,
where he showed himself moving away from the simplici-
ties of reigning prosodists with their generalized patterns of
standard stressed and standard unstressed syllables. Hopkins's
subtle ear caught infinite nuances: 'no two weak accents in a
word are exactly equal'. He had recognized a metrical foot
as capable of having four or five syllables, 'grouped about one
strong beat' (*Journals*, p. 271), and further anticipated the note
on 'Sprung Rhythm' with which he afterwards prefaced the
experimental 'Wreck of the Deutschland' (See Gardner and
MacKenzie (edd.), *Poems of Gerard Manley Hopkins*, 1967, pp.
255–6) by pondering on the way in which a sensitive reader
might increase the emphasis upon the stressed syllable of a
long word to balance its family of unstressed syllables (*Journals*,
p. 271). He had quoted lines in which an accented monosyllabic
foot has replaced a trochee or iamb—another characteristic of
'Sprung Rhythm':

Toad that under *cold stone*

Days and nights has thirty one

(*Macbeth* IV. i. 6)

where editors have been tempted to amend *cold* into *coldest*
to 'preserve' the rhythm. In a line of 'Sprung Rhythm', as he
developed it from the 'Wreck of the Deutschland' onwards, a
metrical foot anywhere may consist of a single accented syllable, or have any reasonable number of unstressed syllables
(not merely one or two) following the stress. But although in
theory the five-stress lines of a sonnet could be constructed
with unlicensed abandon, Hopkins's fine ear tested the balance
of his phrases one against the other, marrying sense and sound
in a manner impossible with conventional prosody. In the
most characteristic 'sprung' lines, the voice 'springs' from one
stress to another, across a gap left by the omission of a slack
syllable redundant to the meaning. Thus in 'Inversnaid'

A windpuff-bonnet of fáwn-fróth
Turns and twindles over the broth

Of a pool so pitch-black, féll-frówning,
It rounds and rounds Despair to drowning.
(*Poems*, p. 89)

the two final stresses in lines 1 and 3 have no intervening
slacks. We can reduce them to conformity and commonplace
by substituting *táwny* for *fáwn*, and *fríghtful* for *fell*.

It is unfortunate that Hopkins's surviving journals break off
in the middle of a story just ten months before the wrecking
of the *Deutschland* exploded him back into poetry. But the
ones we have are invaluable as a background to his verse. They
preserve thousands of acutely worded notes (for he is a con-
noisseur of precise or uncommon words in his prose also) on
the appearance of waterfalls and ash trees, skies cloud-moulded
or pierced with stars, quaint dialect words or pronunciations,
comments on the architecture of churches or the merits of
individual pictures in an Academy Exhibition. Entering his in-
cessant discoveries in his journals reinforced his memory, so
that as he composed poems or sermons his language was saved
from the ruts by myriads of direct impressions. The prose
entries form an invaluable commentary on his verse. Thus
under April 21 and 22 1871 he records exceptional cloudscapes:
'the sky a beautiful grained blue, silky lingering clouds in flat-
bottomed loaves, others a little browner in ropes or in burly-
shouldered ridges swanny and lustrous, more in the Zenith
stray packs of a sort of violet paleness . . . Later/moulding
which brought rain: . . . April 22—But such a lovely damasking
in the sky as today I never felt before . . . slanted flashing
"travellers", all in flight, stepping one behind the other, their
edges tossed with bright ravelling' (*Journals*, p. 207). Six years
later a resplendent autumn sky reminded him of many of these
metaphors. As he returned in holiday mood from fishing in a
Welsh valley 'half an hour of extreme enthusiasm' resulted in
'Hurrahing in Harvest' (1877):—

Summer ends now; now, barbarous in beauty, the stooks rise
Around; up above, what wind-walks! what lovely behaviour

Of silk-sack clouds! has wilder, wilful-wavier
Meal-drift moulded ever and melted across skies?

(Poems, p. 70)

How the opening line, and even the title, have been tautened
from their first draft: 'Sonnet in Harvest—It is harvest; now
barbarous in beauty . . .'[2] All nature is buoyant as the clouds.
The stooks (Hopkins relishes the dialect word) rise as though
about to float; the poet's heart soars with elation; the azurous
hills are 'hung' (he discarded 'strong' and 'grand' in search of
a fresh exactitude). The mountains combine the lifting grace
of the stallion with the gentleness of the violet:

And the azurous hung hills are his world-wielding shoulder
Majestic—as a stallion stalwart, very-violet-sweet!—

a male/female image-cluster which Bridges considered an affectation. The last lines are reminiscent of Plato's *Phaedrus* in
which Socrates explains how the soul may grow wings, but
may lose them; how the philosopher, admiring the beauty of
the world and recollecting the divine beauty which is its
prototype, is raised with an enthusiasm like the spreading of
new wings in flight, only to find himself impotent to leave
the ground (246A–250C). So too Hopkins is honest enough to
end his sonnet in what some might think anticlimax, the sober
reservation in '*half hurls*':

These things, these things were here and but the beholder
Wanting; which two when they once meet,
The heart rears wings bold and bolder
And hurls for him, O half hurls earth for him off under his
feet.

Although to the end of his short life Hopkins could be
beckoned into corresponding excitement (see, e.g., his 'Ash-
boughs', p. 185, written on the same sheet of paper as his
'sonnets of desolation', about 1885), he had frequent periods of
deflation, such as preoccupies a sonnet contemporary with
'Hurrahing in Harvest', 'The Caged Skylark':

As a dare-gale skylark scanted in a dull cage
    Man's mounting spirit in his bone-house, mean house,
dwells—
    That bird beyond the remembering his free fells;
This in drudgery, day-labouring-out life's age.

(Poems, p. 70)

The alliteration and assonance point up the incongruities: the *skylark* is *scanted* ('constricted'—Hopkins rescues the sense of spatial limitation, still familiar in the adjective *scant* but neglected in the verb); the *dare-gale* bird is now *dull*; once able to soar or *drop* to its nest, it now *droops*. So too each human soul, 'flesh-bound' in 'bone-house' (a kenning dating from *Beowulf* (ll. 2508, 3147)) is seen as 'distressed', barred in, 'day-labouring' like the blind Milton, condemned to earth-bound drudgery like Samson in the prison-house of his enemies. (See *Samson Agonistes*, ll. 573, 1338, 1393; and *Sonnet*: 'On his blindness'.) Milton is a perpetual influence upon Hopkins in vocabulary and rhythm.

Written during that same fertile year, 1877, 'The Windhover' has become the most famous of his sonnets, its infinite suggestiveness attracting innumerable interpretations. It is ironic to find dogmatists trying to pontificate, from the embrasures of their fixed minds, what its *only* correct reading must be.

We may detect signs in it of many submerged contrasts: between the poet's timid heart hiding from conflict and the blast-defiant kestrel; between the pretty plumes of a bird dead-still and the stirring magnificence of one in which courage and action are seen to combine ('buckle') with its animal ('brute') beauty; between the hawk's aerobatic control in curving, flashing flight and the muscle-taxing endurance of the ploughman steering the share down its straight path, turning dull rust into sun-reflecting metal; between the blue-bleak coals, conserving their ebbing heat, and their fiery brilliance when they sacrifice all they have left in self-destroying splendour.

A more important antithesis became less evident during the sonnet's revision: the windhover is only the dauphin, not the King: a much-loved favourite ('minion'), not the centre of feudal loyalty. The dawnbird hints at, but is outshone by, the Dayspring Himself, the Sun of Righteousness, 'a billion/Times told lovelier, more dangerous'. The contemplation of created things leads the Jesuit priest to the Creator himself, just as (in 'God's Grandeur') the clouds at sunrise are construed as the shining wings of the Comforter, and the stars in 'The Starlight Night' as chinks letting the brightness of heaven escape, like knot-holes in a barn through which the lights of the harvest-home feast can be seen (ll. 13, 14).

After his ordination in 1877 Hopkins was given a succession of posts as the Society tried to find the most suitable niche for him. For a while he was stationed in London, his main duties being preaching at the West-End Jesuit Church in Farm Street. Then followed parish duties in Oxford, Lancashire and Glasgow. To this brief portion of his life, less than four years, belong a number of poems centring upon people rather than nature. 'Felix Randal' pictures the boisterous blacksmith at his 'random grim forge, powerful amidst peers'; 'At the Wedding March' touches, as Hopkins seldom did in his priestly poems, on the love between man and woman; a young Irish lad in the barracks at Cowley is the hero of 'The Bugler's First Communion'. But no real Margaret seems to have underlain his beautiful 'Spring and Fall: To a Young Child':

> Márgarét, áre you gríeving
> Over Goldengrove unleaving?
> Leáves, líke the things of man, you
> With your fresh thoughts care for, can you?
> Áh! ás the heart grows older
> It will come to such sights colder
> By and by, nor spare a sigh
> Though worlds of wanwood leafmeal lie;
>
> (*Poems*, p. 88)

His sermons also date from these central years. As with his verse, Hopkins tended to follow his own unique bents, sometimes to the amusement or disapproval of fellow Jesuits whose aesthetic side lay dormant. The sermons abound in energetic concepts and phrases, as when he suggests that Eve, thinking 'God her lord and landlord was envious and grudging, a rackrent', decided to 'seize crown-property', only to find herself turned out of Paradise with Adam in 'the first and most terrible of evictions' (*Sermons*, pp. 66–7).

The devotional writings printed with his sermons mostly belong to the next portion of his life, his year as a Tertian, during which he made notes towards a commentary upon the *Spiritual Exercises of St Ignatius*. Since his work is profoundly Ignatian, this section of the book (pp. 122–209) provides serious students of his poetry with considerable guidance.

After his tertianship, Hopkins was given advanced teaching posts—first at Stonyhurst College, and then, when the Jesuits were asked to rescue from failure the Catholic University College in Dublin, as Professor of Classics there from 1884 to his death in 1889. Ireland amidst her struggles towards independence was no haven of peace for any Englishman; the Catholic bishops who had mismanaged the College had insisted on stripping it of its library before handing over to the Jesuits, thus handicapping both students and staff. Moreover, Hopkins was passing through a spiritual experience of deep aridity: many have compared it to the Dark Night of the Soul which saints and mystics have attempted to describe. Among his papers after his death were found the intense personal 'sonnets of desolation' (as they are sometimes called). 'No worst, there is none', contains one of the most memorable sestets in English literature:

> O the mind, mind has mountains; cliffs of fall
> Frightful, sheer, no-man-fathomed. Hold them cheap
> May who ne'er hung there. Nor does long our small
> Durance deal with that steep or deep. Here! creep,
> Wretch, under a comfort serves in a whirlwind: all
> Life death does end and each day dies with sleep.
>
> *(Poems, p. 100)*

Another begins with self-charity, a mood very different from self-pity: 'My own heart let me more have pity on'. The desperation of a spirit which has exhausted all its own resources has nowhere been put more tersely than in the lines:

> I cast for comfort I can no more get
> By groping round my comfortless than blind
> Eyes in their dark can day or thirst can find
> Thirst's all-in-all in all a world of wet.
>
> (ibid, p. 102)

How is it that Hopkins seems to brand his name on every poem, scarcely a maverick line being found among his mature compositions? A student of Victorian literature seeking to contrast him with his contemporaries might go far towards an answer by placing one of his impressive later poems, 'Spelt from Sibyl's Leaves', alongside 'Childe Roland to the Dark Tower Came' by Browning, and Tennyson's 'Lucretius'. All three are mature works, and though not equally typical of their authors, they are made more comparable by a certain community of subject. Here we can merely begin the analysis.

Spelt from Sibyl's Leaves

Earnest, earthless, equal, attuneable, | vaulty, voluminous,
  . . . stupendous
Evening strains to be tíme's vást, | womb-of-all, home-of-all,
  hearse-of-all night.

Her fond yellow hornlight wound to the west, | her wild
   hollow hoarlight hung to the height
Waste; . . .

(Poems, p. 97)

The unusual verse movement arrests attention. Hopkins
created this sonnet out of eight-foot lines for the same reason
which made him afterwards extend three other sonnets by
means of codas—'Tom's Garland', 'Harry Ploughman' and
'That Nature is a Heraclitean Fire'. He was striving to match
in English the more dignified weight of the sonnet in Italian
—to him one of the most perfect structures in all literature
(Letters, II, pp. 85–98). Over two thirds of his major work went
into sonnet-craftsmanship: he seldom had leisure or impetus
for longer poems. Moreover, he felt that Tennyson and Browning became shapeless and less artistic when they spread themselves. 'Just think the blank verse these people have exuded',
he wrote (Letters, I, p. 101). Hopkins poured into his poems only
the essence, usually fractioned off at high temperature. And
since he defined poetry as 'speech framed to be heard for its
own sake and interest even over and above its interest of meaning', he filled it with 'repeating figures' (Journals, p. 289) to make
it musical and memorable. His poems almost invariably have
rhyme, preventing their stanzas from unravelling into amor-
phous lengths when heard instead of seen.

    As for diction, all three poets coin and compound in their
own fashion: each has his favourite words. Hopkins loved
consonant clusters, vigorous Anglo-Saxon monosyllables, with
lively dialect words such as pashed or degged for flavour; but
he knew the art of injecting a single polysyllable into a line
heavy with monosyllables.

Our tale, O óur oracle. | Lét life, wáned, ah lét life wind
Off hér once skéined stained véined varíety |upon, áll on
   twó spools; párt, pen, páck
Now her áll in twó flocks, twó folds—black, white; | right,
   wrong; reckon but, reck but, mind
But thése two; wáre of a wórld where bút these | twó tell,
   each off the óther;

(Poems, p. 98, ll. 10–13)

Browning's vast vocabulary, however, included most of Hopkins's regular words, even if he used them differently and often

hurried them down with less propriety or care for sound. It is a fallacy, too, to think that sprung rhythm led Hopkins into conversational cadences. Browning might simulate informal talk and Tennyson rhetorical speech, but with Hopkins the syntax and word-play are usually too elaborate to suggest the ordinary speaking voice. With great deliberation he fits every word—a fragment of mosaic—into a place which it alone can fill. The seven adjectives through which Hopkins seeks to come to terms with the devouring threat of evening (l. 1) each invite extensive commentary. We are given pause not by the rarity of some of these words, rather by the intense imagination with which they are applied: thus *equal* may remind us of the impartial, levelling quality of gathering darkness which made earlier scholars guess that *evening* might be cognate with the adjective *even* (see Johnson's Dictionary, ed. Todd, 1827.); *vaulty* reflects the way in which the shallow bowl of the sky may gain height as night comes on, its deep arch being here identified with that of a burial crypt (Cf. 'or night, still higher', 'The Wreck of the Deutschland', st. 26). The compounds describing night in line 2—*womb-of-all, home-of-all, hearse-of-all night* —have classical models among the innumerable Greek words in *pan-* and *pam-*, or in the *De Rerum Natura* (V. 259), where Lucretius writes of the earth as 'omniparens, eadem rerum commune sepulcrum'. Hopkins avoided the commonplace *womb . . . tomb* antithesis, (used, e.g., in Shakespeare's Sonnet 86, Swinburne's *Erechtheus*, Tennyson's *Lucretius*, l.243: 'the womb and tomb of all'). His *hearse-of-all* applied to enveloping night is more original and graphic: it refers to a type of 'hearse' still to be found in old cathedrals—a canopied framework, lit with hundreds of little tapers, mounted high above the bier of someone lying in state. Phrases in Hopkins bear closer inspection than those of most poets.

Towards the end of this sonnet there is an adaptation of a Welsh device with which Hopkins frequently harmonized his verse: *hér once skéined/stained véined/varíety'*. This imitates *cynghanedd sain*, in which a line is divided into three sections, the first two linked by rhyme and the second two by alliteration. (See Gardner, *Gerald Manley Hopkins*, II, pp. 143–158.) Closer approximations to Welsh alliteration (where a series of successive consonants may be repeated in identical order) are found in this poem: *west, waste; tool, tale; bleak, black; waned, wind.* These pairs also illustrate another device which he admired, 'vowelling off', or the 'changing of vowel down some scale' (*Journals*, p. 284). He had luxuriated in them in 'The

Wreck of the Deutschland', Stanza 8, where we encounter *lash, lush (plush); kept, capped; flesh (Gush), flush, flash* all in the narrow space of five lines.

Finally, the sprung rhythm of 'Spelt from Sibyl's Leaves' esablishes it as Hopkins's own make. The lines vary sensitively in pace and weightiness. Readers who do not trouble to give each half-line its four necessary stresses (the first line has a foot-long pause after 'voluminous') miss the intricacy of the effect. Note the drawn-out monosyllabic feet in line 2: 'tíme's | vást'—usually demoted to a trochee as though it were no more than 'Évening stráins to be tímeless'. Occasionally, as in the last line, the accents provided may seem eccentric: 'thóughts agáinst thoughts ín groans grínd'—where *in* is given pre-eminence above the two flanking words. But read as marked, the line seems distorted by the torture it describes. Once again Hopkins's *Letters* are full of illumination for us. 'Of this long sonnet above all remember what applies to all my verse, that it is, as living art should be, made for performance and that its performance is not reading with the eye but loud, leisurely, poetical (not rhetorical) recitation, with long rests, long dwells on the rhyme and other marked syllables, and so on. This sonnet should be almost sung: it is most carefully timed in *tempo rubato*' (*Letters*, I, p. 246).

Among the finest of his last poems is another extended sonnet, 'That Nature is a Heraclitean Fire . . .', (1888), which looks to the resurrection for the converting of this discordant mixture called 'man'—'This Jack, joke, poor potsherd, | patch, matchwood, immortal diamond' (*Poems*, p. 106)— into pure and entire diamond. In a frank poem, written a few weeks before his final illness, 'The shepherd's brow . . .', he enlarges upon the laughable pretensions of mankind. Here the heroic struggles of his 'terrible sonnets' such as 'Carrion Comfort' are viewed through a Swiftian reducing-glass:

> But man—we, scaffold of score brittle bones;
> Who breathe, from groundlong babyhood to hoary
> Age gasp; whose breath is our *memento mori*—
> What bass is *our* viol for tragic tones.
> He! Hand to mouth he lives, and voids with shame;
> (*Poems*, p. 107)

When Hopkins died in 1889, only 44 years old, the obituaries which praised his talent as an artist and critic showed no awareness that he was a poet. If he had lived to a riper age, we may assume that he would have continued to wrestle words, rhythm and verse-forms into new approximations to his thought, but there is little evidence that his rather restricted range of subjects would have expanded. He showed no wish to pass beyond the age-old circumvallating walls of the Catholic faith, though one of his fellow Jesuits, paying him tribute remarked: 'If I had known him outside, I should have said that his love of speculation and originality of thought would make it almost impossible for him to submit his intellect to authority' (*Letters and Notices* XX (March 1890), p. 173). If many Catholics now regard him as the one truly satisfying English poet, his fascination is also felt by those to whom his beliefs seem mistaken and his feelings sometimes misplaced. His intensity and technical virtuosity entitle him to the immense respect which he enjoys today: to claim that his poetry is beyond criticism, however,—as some enthusiasts continue to do—is to invite a precipitous and blind devaluation such as befell his fellow Victorians.

NOTES

1. See *Sermons*, p. 60—'it would have been no Paradise if it were liable to drought and storm'; also pp. 90–92 on the imperfect providence which permits disasters such as wrecks.

2. The misprinting from 1930 till the fourth edition of line 1 as 'the stooks arise' destroyed the leap of the sprung rhythm.

BIBLIOGRAPHY

The short titles used in references are given in brackets after the entry. All quotations from the published poems are taken from the 4th Edn.

Poems, 1st Edn., ed. R. Bridges, 1918; 4th Edn., ed. W. H. Gardner and N. H. MacKenzie, 1967 (*Poems*)

Letters . . . to Robert Bridges, ed. C. C. Abbott, 1935, revd., 1955. (*Letters*, I)

The Correspondence of Gerard Manley Hopkins and Richard Watson Dixon, ed. C. C. Abbott, 1935, revd. 1955. (*Letters*, II)

Further Letters of Gerard Manley Hopkins, including his correspondence with Coventry Patmore, ed. C. C. Abbott, 1938. 2nd Edn., revised and enlarged, 1956. (*Letters*, III)

Note-books and Papers, ed. H. House, 1937. Revised and enlarged as : *Journals and Papers*, ed. H. House, completed by Graham Storey, 1959. (*Journals*)

Sermons and Devotional Writings, ed. C. Devlin, 1959. (*Sermons*)

F. R. Leavis, *New Bearings in English Poetry*, 1932.

——, *The Common Pursuit*, 1952.

J. Pick, *Gerard Manley Hopkins—Priest and Poet*, 1942.

W. H. Gardner, *Gerard Manley Hopkins—A Study of Poetic Idiosyncrasy in Relation to Poetic Tradition*, Vol. I, 1944; II, 1949; revised 1966.

E. Ruggles, *Gerard Manley Hopkins—a Life*, 1944.

Kenyon Critics, *Gerard Manley Hopkins*, New York, 1945.

W. A. M. Peters, *Gerard Manley Hopkins—A Critical Essay towards the Understanding of his Poetry*, 1948.

N. Weyand and R. V. Schoder (ed.), *Immortal Diamond—Studies in Gerard Manley Hopkins*, 1949.

Y. Winters, *The Function of Criticism*, Denver, Col., 1957.

A. Heuser, *The Shaping Vision of Gerard Manley Hopkins*, 1958.

D. Downes, *Gerard Manley Hopkins—A Study of His Ignation Spirit*, 1959.

J. E. Keating, *The Wreck of the Deutschland—An Essay and Commentary*, Kent, Ohio, 1963.

N. H. MacKenzie, 'Hopkins among the Victorians—Form in Art and Nature.' In *English Studies Today—Third Series*, ed. G. I. Duthie, Edinburgh, 1964.

——, *Hopkins*, Edinburgh, 1968. ('Writers and Critics').

J. Hunter, *Gerard Manley Hopkins*, 1966.

G. H. Hartman (ed.), *Hopkins—A Collection of Critical Essays*, Englewood Cliffs, 1966.

P. Milward, *A Commentary on 'The Wreck of the Deutschland'*, Tokyo, 1968.

E. Schneider, *The Dragon in the Gate*, California, 1968.

D. McChesney, *A Hopkins Commentary*, 1968.

THE ROSSETTIS AND OTHER CONTEMPORARY POETS

JAMES SAMBROOK, *University of Southampton*

The Pre-Raphaelite Brotherhood was formed in 1848, that year of revolutions, by three painters, Dante Gabriel Rossetti (1828–82), Holman Hunt (1827–1910) and J. E. Millais (1829–96), a sculptor Thomas Woolner (1825–92), and three comparative nonentities whose main function appears to have been to bring the number up to a mystic seven. They had disbanded by 1853, and only Hunt stuck doggedly for the rest of his life to the original aims of the Brotherhood. These aims were— in revolt against academic rules of lighting and composition derived ultimately from Raphael—to paint always direct from the natural object, to use 'the bright colours of nature', and to choose subjects from contemporary life or to give all the realism of a contemporary scene to those historical and literary subjects which they took chiefly from Shakespeare, Keats and the Bible, or—in Rossetti's case—from Dante and Malory. They followed one of the innumerable paths 'back to nature'. In their case they sought nature by means of a minute particularization.

The Pre-Raphaelite Brotherhood founded a literary organ, *The Germ: Thoughts towards Nature in Poetry, Literature and Art,* which survived for four issues (January–May, 1850). This journal carried some admirable early poems by Dante Gabriel Rossetti, his sister Christina and Coventry Patmore, but in its pages appeared also two winsome cantos by Woolner of the work he later expanded into a *Maud*-like monodrama, *My Beautiful Lady* (1863).

> I love My Lady; she is very fair;
> Her brow is wan, and bound by simple hair:

Her spirit sits aloof, and high,
But glances from her tender eye
In sweetness droopingly.

(i, 1–5)

The last line adequately describes Woolner's style. The work
(which was popular in its day) is interesting now only as a
document from a sexually repressed society where sad love-
longing is sublimated into idealism. It is a verbal equivalent of
some of Arthur Hughes's paintings.

Despite *The Germ* and despite the fact that parallels may be
discovered between some P.R.B. paintings and some mid-Victorian poetry, we shall find that 'Pre-Raphaelite' is not a very
meaningful term in *literary* history. Rossetti had literary disciples and associates who picked up briefly from him a certain
style of Romantic archaism. This is not 'Pre-Raphaelitism' in
the original sense, and, in any case, the differences among these
disciples are more important than the similarities.

Dante Gabriel Rossetti's income came from painting: he
published verse in periodicals but did not make any collections
until fairly late in life, with *Poems* (1870, expanded 1881) and
Ballads and Sonnets (1881). Many of these poems had been
written as early as the 1840s, and of those the longest is the
unfinished narrative, 'The Bride's Prelude' (1881). This poem's
medievalism 'of lozenged arm-bearings', 'of chevesayle and
mantelet' is straight from Chatterton and Keats, but the narrative method of accumulating minutely observed descriptive
details corresponds in some way to Millais' and Hunt's crab-
like labour over their anecdotal canvases inch by painstaking
inch—at the cost of any central emphasis in the work. But
Rossetti's poem has a remarkable and finely realized cloistral,
airless atmosphere:

> The room lay still in dusty glare,
>   Having no sound through it
> Except the chirp of a caged bird
> That came and ceased: and if she stirred,
> Amelotte's raiment could be heard.

(151–5)

This is the effect of his elaborate, mysterious, tense, agora-
phobic water-colours such as 'The Wedding of St. George'
(painted 1857) or 'Sir Galahad at the Ruined Chapel' (1859).

Such paintings confirm Rossetti's declaration that 'imaginings . . . envelop me from the outer world'. He never finished

his oil 'Found' (begun 1853) which was his one attempt to paint a contemporary subject in the vein of Hunt's 'The Awakening Conscience'. The subject of a dramatic verse-monologue 'Jenny' (begun 1848) is comparable to that of 'Found', but the distinctive quality of the poem lies in the flickers of imaginative strangeness that brighten this study of a prostitute:

> When, wealth and health slipped past, you stare
> Along the streets alone, and there,
> Round the long park, across the bridge,
> The cold lamps at the pavement's edge
> Wind on together and apart,
> A fiery serpent for your heart
>
> (150–5)

and her client, the poet,

> Like a toad within a stone
> Seated while Time crumbles on . . .
> Even so within this world is Lust
> (282–97)

rather than in the pathos of its social commentary. 'The Burden of Nineveh' (1850) has a thoughtful, dry, ironic criticism of Mammonized English society; the Italian revolution of 1848 prompts 'On Refusal of Aid between Nations', and is referred to in a passionate Browningesque dramatic monologue, 'A Last Confession'; but all these are untypical of Rossetti's work as a whole.

Rossetti was half-Italian by birth. He wrote poems in Italian and his first large book was of English translations from pre-Petrarchan lyric poets, *The Early Italian Poets* (1861, rearranged as *Dante and his Circle*, 1874). These translations might be regarded as a scholarly counterpart to Pre-Raphaelitism; Petrarch was to European lyric poetry as Raphael was to figure painting; so that, by going to Dante's *Vita Nuova* and the courtly love poems of the Sicilian School, Rossetti was returning to the fresh dawn of art. In the prose tale 'Hand and Soul' (*The Germ*, 1850) a thirteenth-century painter has a vision of heaven where he worships a Beatrice-like figure who is a symbol not of Theology (as Beatrice was) but of Art. He 'became aware that much of that reverence which he had mistaken for faith had been no more than the worship of beauty'. Then he is commanded to paint a mystical lady who is the image of his own soul. God does not require the artist to moralize, but only to be true to his inner experience.

The Beatrice figure re-appears in Rossetti's best known poem 'The Blessed Damozel' (1850, later extensively revised), which he intended as a complement to Poe's 'The Raven' (1845). Rossetti sketches his setting in the manner of two men he excessively admired—John Martin (1789–1854), the wild, apocalyptic painter, and Philip James Bailey, author of the popular hyper-drama *Festus* (1839):

> It lies in Heaven, across the flood
> Of ether, as a bridge.
> Beneath, the tides of day and night
> With flame and darkness ridge
> The void, as low as where this earth
> Spins like a fretful midge.
>
> (Stanza 6)

This is grand, the names of Mary's heavenly seamstresses *are*, as the poet claims, 'five sweet symphonies', the aureate diction glitters, and one is reminded of the exquisite, but factitious, work of the Greek poets of Alexandria. Rossetti's conception of an after-life where the Blessed Damozel weeps in frustrated longing to be united with her lover—rather than with God— is not even remotely Christian. Heaven provides decorative, fancifully exotic and archaic 'furnishings' for the plaints of parted lovers. Rossetti consistently uses religion as an aesthetic mine. Significantly, he gave the title *Songs of the Art Catholic* to a manuscript collection of his verses which he sent to his friend William Bell Scott in 1847.

The Beatrice of Rossetti's life was Lizzie Siddal, to whom he was half-heartedly engaged for ten years before he dutifully married her in 1860. After less than two years of married life she poisoned herself with laudanum, and Rossetti in a fit of remorse buried his unique manuscript volume of poems in her coffin, whence it was exhumed seven years later for the poems to be included in the 1870 volume. He never laid her ghost, and in the 1860s and 70s painted four posthumous portraits of her as 'Beata Beatrix'. At the time of that marriage, though, he was infatuated with Jane, the wife of his friend William Morris. He had painted her in 1857 as Guenevere in the Oxford Union fresco which he described as follows:

Sir Lancelot prevented by his sin from entering the Chapel of the San Grael. He has fallen asleep before the shrine full of angels, and between him and it rises in his sleep the image of Queen Guenevere, the cause of all. (*Letters*, I, 337). Jane Morris continued to fascinate Rossetti to the end of his life. For sexual satisfaction he went to the vulgar and vital Fanny Cornforth who was following the oldest profession in the notorious Argyll Rooms when he met her in the 1850s. She sat for 'Found' and for many of the later 'epicurean' half-length portraits intended for the Renaissance palaces of Northern plutocrats when Rossetti, alive to his market, had become a somewhat flashily sensual type of Bradford Titian.

The guilt and the idealism of these personal relations appear in the sonnet sequence 'The House of Life', which represents a not altogether successful attempt to spiritualize love, using Dante's imagery and notions but lacking Dante's religion. So Rossetti rises no higher than religiosity in 'Heart's Hope' (sonnet v in the final version of the sequence, 1881), 'The Kiss' (vi), 'Secret Parting' (xlv), and 'Love's Redemption' in its 1870 version—it was revised as 'Love's Testament' (iii) in 1881:

> O Thou who at Love's hour ecstatically
>   Unto my lips dost evermore present
>   The body and blood of Love in sacrament;
> Whom I have neared and felt thy breath to be
> The inmost incense of his sanctuary.

This has a certain incantatory power, but the image remains vague and the idea vaguer.

This is not always the case. 'Silent Noon' (xix) has the Millais or Hunt qualities of fresh, crisp, static particularity. In its small way it approaches the one undoubted masterpiece of Pre-Raphaelite painting, 'The Blind Girl' by Millais:

> Your hands lie open in the long fresh grass,—
>   The finger-points look through like rosy blooms:
>   Your eyes smile peace. The pasture gleams and glooms
> 'Neath billowing skies that scatter and amass.
> All round our nest, far as the eye can pass,
>   Are golden kingcup-fields with silver edge
>   Where the cow-parsley skirts the hawthorn-hedge.
> 'Tis visible silence, still as the hour-glass.
>
> Deep in the sun-searched growths the dragon-fly
> Hangs like a blue thread loosened from the sky.

The painter's sharp perception and grasp of detail crystallize and communicate honestly an intense experience. So too in 'Sudden Light':

> I have been here before,
>   But when or how I cannot tell:
> I know the grass beyond the door,
>   The sweet keen smell,
> The sighing sound, the lights around the shore,

and in that fine rendering of exhausted sorrow, 'The Woodspurge'. Both these poems appeared among the Songs appended to the incomplete version of 'The House of Life' in *Poems*, 1870. Rossetti's most memorable poetry, like Wordsworth's, explores the landscape of memory; but all too often for Rossetti memory is a nightmare of remorse. He recognizes his failure to sustain his idealism in life, and is haunted by guilt over lost opportunities and failures in art due to lethargy, over visits to the Argyll Rooms, over Lizzie's death and over his love for Jane Morris. Remorse deepens into self-disgust and disintegration of personality:

> Look in my face; my name is Might-have-been;
> I am also called No-more, Too-late. Farewell;
>   ('A Superscription', xcvii 'The House of Life'),

> God knows I know the faces I shall see,
> Each one a murdered self, with low last breath.
> 'I am thyself,—what hast thou done to me?'
> 'And I—and I—thyself,' (lo! each one saith,)
> 'And thou thyself to all eternity!'
>   ('Lost Days', lxxxvi).

Four sonnets, written in 1868 and called collectively 'Willowwood' (xlix–lii), most poignantly speak for a man divided against himself. Here the past invades the present. Dumb, lonely figures—representing the lost days—stand beneath the trees, and the corpse of the wife rises to the surface of the hidden river. The images, at once personal and archetypal, convey a powerful sense of remorse brooding over the dead days. This 'thicket' image in 'Willowwood'—'the rustling covert of my soul'—is almost obsessive in Rossetti's work. It appears most strikingly in the pen and ink drawing 'How they met themselves', where two lovers in a wood (the models were Lizzie and himself on their honeymoon in Paris, 1860) meet their menacing *doppelgängers* who warn of impending

339

death. Around them the leaves and branches press down closely.

It is this sinister, demonic region where love meets death, rather than the angelic sphere of 'The Blessed Damozel', that Rossetti re-creates most convincingly. The image of the fatal woman runs through his painting from the Guenevere of 1857 to the last version of Proserpine in the year of his death; both were painted from Jane Morris. In the sonnet for his oil painting 'Pandora' (Jane Morris again) he sees 'In Venus' eyes the gaze of Proserpine'; love and death are united. In sonnet xlviii of 'The House of Life' a veiled woman reveals herself as 'Death-in-love'. The finest of Rossetti's several Coleridgean ballad imitations, 'Sister Helen' (1853, but much revised later) tells of a witch torturing and killing her false lover by melting a waxen image. Significantly, when Rossetti re-handles the matter of *Paradise Lost* and the *Iliad* in his ballads 'Eden Bower' and 'Troy Town' (1870), it is o compress it into the utterances of those mischief-working sirens, Lilith and Helen.

Rossetti once praised the Scottish painter W. D. Kennedy (1813–65) for re-creating 'the landscapes we have known in our dreams' (*Collected Works of D. G. Rossetti*, 1887, II, 496). These are Rossetti's landscapes in, for instance, 'Love's Nocturn' (1870):

> Vaporous, unaccountable,
> Dreamworld lies forlorn of light . . .
>
> There breathe perfumes; there in rings
> Whirl the foam-bewildered springs;
>   Siren there
> Winds her dizzy hair and sings . . .
>
> The black firwood sets its teeth.
> Part the boughs and look beneath,—
>   Lilies share
> Secret waters there, and breathe.
>   (8–9, 25–28, 102–5).

Perhaps the most intensely imagined work of Rossetti's is 'The Orchard-Pit', written about 1871 in prose and partly in verse, but unpublished in his lifetime. (In its present state it conveniently illustrates Rossetti's method of 'working up' a poem from a prose draft, just as some artists work up a painting from detailed sketches.)

Piled deep below the screening apple-branch
    They lie with bitter apples in their hands:
And some are only ancient bones that blanch,
And some had ships that last year's wind did launch,
    And some were yesterday the lords of lands.

In the soft dell, among the apple-trees,
    High up above the hidden pit she stands,
And there for ever sings, who gave to these,
That lie below, her magic hours of ease,
    And those her apples holden in their hands.

This in my dreams is shown me; and her hair
    Crosses my lips and draws my burning breath;
Her song spreads golden wings upon the air,
Life's eyes are gleaming from her forehead fair,
    And from her breasts the ravishing eyes of Death.[1]

Men say to me that sleep hath many dreams,
    Yet I knew never but this dream alone:
There, from a dried-up channel, once the stream's,
The glen slopes up; even such in sleep it seems
    As to my waking sight the place well known.

Rossetti turns his back on society, progress, the Condition
of England question, and all public themes in order to prowl
through the rustling coverts of his soul and flush out the
spectres of the pre-conscious mind. Albeit narrowly and neu-
rotically he continues, with a genuine imaginative power, to
work the introspective vein prospected by the great Romantic
poets at the beginning of the nineteenth century.

The religious enthusiasm of the Rossetti sisters, Christina
(1830-94) and Maria, more than compensated for the indifference of their brothers. William, the agnostic, was irritated
by Christina's 'perpetual church-going and communions,
her prayers and fasts, her submission to clerical direction, her oblations, her practice of confession.' (*Poetical
Works of C. G. Rossetti*, ed. W. M. Rossetti, 1904, p. lv.) From
the 1840s both sisters attended the famous, heady, High Church
services at Christ Church, Albany Street in London, and were
excited by the spectacle of attractive young women from
good families devoting themselves to austerity, discipline and
virginity in the Anglican sisterhood founded nearby by Dr.
Pusey. Maria joined a sisterhood as soon as she thought her

family duties permitted this, and Christina from the 1860s was an associate of the Highgate Penitentiary devoted to the re-formation of prostitutes. Neither sister ever married.

Christina strikes her characteristic note as a poet in 'An End' (*The Germ*, 1850), written when she was seventeen. It begins 'Love, strong as Death, is dead' and concludes:

> To few chords and sad and low
> Sing we so:
> Be our eyes fixed on the grass
> Shadow-veiled as the years pass,
> While we think of all that was
> In the long ago.

In her first published collection, *Goblin Market* (1862), which was widely recognized as revealing a new major woman poet to succeed Mrs. Browning who had died in the previous year, and in the later collections of her voluminous lyrical verse, *The Prince's Progress* (1866), *A Pageant* (1881), *Poems* (S.P.C.K., 1893) and *New Poems* (1895), Christina strikes these few chords again and again. However, they are not her only notes. There are nonsense verses, such as 'If a pig wore a wig', in her col-lection of nursery rhymes, *Sing-Song*, 1872 (though much of her writing for children—particularly in the prose stories—is grue-some and minatory). There is a slightly laboured playfulness in 'No, thank you, John' and a delicate wit in 'The Queen of Hearts'. A simple, clear note of sensuous rapture is heard in 'Maiden-Song', 'A Bride Song' and 'A Birthday' (*Macmillan's Magazine*, 1861):

> My heart is like a singing bird
> Whose nest is in a watered shoot;
> My heart is like an apple-tree
> Whose boughs are bent with thickset fruit;
> My heart is like a rainbow shell
> That paddles in a halcyon sea;
> My heart is gladder than all these
> Because my love is come to me.

More often, though, Christina images the joys of the senses as forbidden fruits—as in the opening lines of her richly imagined *Goblin Market*, a poetic fairy tale unobtrusively in-formed by the Christian doctrines of the Fall and Atonement, and sharpened by psychological insight into the nature of guilt and self-sacrifice.

Renunciation of the Flesh, the World and the Devil is the

subject of a tensely dramatic dialogue, 'The Three Enemies' (1862), but nearly all her verse, early and late, is in a sense a dialogue between the resolved soul and created pleasure. There are echoes from Albany Street when she writes of the nun's vocation in dramatic monologues such as the splendidly passionate 'The Convent Threshold' (1862) or 'Soeur Louise de la Miséricorde' (1881). In the fourteen sonnets entitled 'Monna Innominata', with epigraphs from Dante and Petrarch, and the twenty-eight entitled 'Later Life' (both 1881) she tells how earthly love dies to be reborn as love of Heaven. The nightmare images of her sonnet 'The World' (1862) reveal a very horror of the flesh. The effort that her renunciation of earthly loves cost her is sometimes apparent. 'Noble Sisters' and 'Sister Maude' (1862, but omitted by Christina from subsequent editions) are allegories of a conflict within the divided personality : one sister drives away the other sister's lover. In 'Up-Hill' (*Macmillan's Magazine*, 1861, and the first poem to bring considerable public attention to Christina) the familiar Pilgrim's Progress figure becomes an emblem of world-weariness in a particularly sinister way :

Does the road wind up-hill all the way?
Yes, to the very end.
Will the day's journey take the whole long day?
From morn to night, my friend.

But is there for the night a resting-place?
A roof for when the slow dark hours begin.
May not the darkness hide it from my face?
You cannot miss that inn.

In her second lyric under the title 'The heart knoweth its own bitterness' (written 1857, but not published in full until 1895) Christina, by contrast, is not the weary pilgrim but a splendidly passionate creature, distraught in a world that can provide no satisfaction for her love :

To give, to give, not to receive!
    I long to pour myself, my soul,
Not to keep back or count or leave,
    But king with king to give the whole.
I long for one to stir my deep—
    I have had enough of help and gift—
    I long for one to search and sift
Myself, to take myself and keep.

343

You scratch my surface with your pin,
　　You stroke me smooth with hushing breath :-
Nay pierce, nay probe, nay dig within,
　　Probe my quick core and sound my depth.
You call me with a puny call,
　　You talk, you smile, you nothing do :
　　How should I spend my heart on you,
My heart that so outweighs you all? . . .

Not in this world of hope deferred,
　　This world of perishable stuff :–
Eye hath not seen nor ear hath heard
　　Nor heart conceived that full 'enough' :
Here moans the separating sea,
　　Here harvests fail, here breaks the heart :
　　There God shall join and no man part,
I full of Christ and Christ of me.

Hymns and prayers account for an ever increasing proportion of her verse in later years. They consist, as we should
expect, of highly rigorous self-examinations as she treads the
hard, up-hill road to Christ. With age and sickness her cry
'Lord, I am waiting' grows ever more insistent; but she had
been waiting ever since, at the age of fourteen, she had placed
all her hopes in Heaven :

　　　　filling there and satisfying
　　Man's soul unchanging and undying,
Earth's fleeting joys and beauties far above,
　　　　In heaven is Love.
　　　　　　　　　　　　　('Earth and Heaven')

Her introspection, unlike her brother's, is disciplined sternly to
orthodox and intelligible religious ends.

The Pre-Raphaelite Brothers liked the ballad rhythms and
medieval décor in *Poems* (1844) by Coventry Patmore (1823–
96), and invited him to contribute to *The Germ* (1850). He wrote
a brief succession of bright verbal vignettes, 'The Seasons' :

　　The crocus, in the shrewd March morn,
　　　　Thrusts up his saffron spear;
　　And April dots the sombre thorn
　　　　With gems, and loveliest cheer.

　　Then sleep the seasons, full of might;
　　　　While slowly swells the pod,
　　And round the peach, and in the night
　　　　The mushroom bursts the sod.

> The winter comes : the frozen rut
> Is bound with silver bars;
> The white drift heaps against the hut;
> And night is pierced with stars.

This word-painting is good, but untypical. Patmore is remembered as the thrice-married celebrant and singer of the connubial sacrament; above all as the author of *The Angel in the House* (1854–6) which sold a quarter of a million copies before its author's death. This verse-novel, prompted by Patmore's love for his first wife, tells in smooth but never tedious octosyllabics how Felix Vaughan, a respectable young gentleman with six hundred pounds a year, courts and marries Honoria, eldest daughter of the Dean of Sarum, without meeting any serious obstacle. Patmore mirrors the domesticity of the Victorian middle-class with a Betjemanic fidelity :

> Geranium, lychnis, rose array'd
> The windows, all wide open thrown;
> And some one in the Study play'd
> The Wedding-March of Mendelssohn.

>> (Book I, Canto i, 'The Cathedral Close', 2).

He dignifies the commonest tastes and sentiments of his readers—hence the poem's popularity—but more than this, he accompanies the unruffled narrative of commonplace incidents with a subtle psychological commentary :

> And ever her chaste and noble air
> Gave to love's feast its choicest gust,
> A vague, faint augury of despair.
>> (I, vi, 'The Dean', 4).

> Why, having won her, do I woo?
> Because her spirit's vestal grace
> Provokes me always to pursue,
> But, spirit-like, eludes embrace.
>> (II, xii, 'Preludes', 1).

Patmore, like Dante Gabriel Rossetti, pursues a love that can never be completely satisfied by its carnal object, but, unlike Rossetti, he can relate this pursuit of the ideal love easily (one is sometimes tempted to say, complacently) to life and to a total religious scheme of things. Accepting the sacramental doctrine that, in the words of Newman's *Apologia*, 'material phenomena are both the types and the instruments of real things unseen,' he sees sexual union in Christian marriage as the shadow of God's love for the human soul. This doctrine is expounded in 'The Wedding Sermon' which concludes *The Victories of Love* (1860–3, a sequel to *The Angel in the House*) and is further developed in the odes written at various times after the death of his first wife in 1862, and published as *The Unknown Eros* (1877–8).

Some of these odes, 'Eros and Psyche', 'Psyche's Discontent', 'Wind and Wave', display a frank sexuality that shocked many of Patmore's first readers. 'Pain' and 'De Natura Deorum' which describes the joys of the wife—

> Ah, Child, the sweet
> Content, when we're both kiss'd and beat!

appear to have traces of sado-masochism, but Patmore would claim, with St Bernard of Clairvaux, that these image the soul's desire to submit fully to God. The sexual relation symbolizes the spiritual. In 'Sponsa Dei' Patmore expresses with a craggy directness this idea that, as man is to woman, so God is to the soul, an ardent, tyrannical lover:

> Who is this only happy She,
> Whom, by a frantic flight of courtesy,
> Born of despair
> Of better lodging for his Spirit fair,
> He adores as Margaret, Maude, or Cecily? ...
>
> What if this Lady be thy Soul, and He
> Who claims to enjoy her sacred beauty be,
> Not thou, but God; and thy sick fire ...
> A reflex heat
> Flash'd on thy cheek from His immense desire,
> Which waits to crown, beyond thy brain's conceit,
> Thy nameless, secret, hopeless longing sweet,
> Not by-and-by, but now,
> Unless deny Him thou!

This is the culmination of the philosophy of *The Angel in the House*. The Mariolatry that appears in some other odes (e.g. 'Deliciae Sapientiae de Amore' and 'The Child's Purchase') can be attributed to Patmore's conversion to Roman Catholicism in 1865, on his second marriage. Some earlier, tender odes— 'The Toys', 'Tired Memory', 'Departure' and, most notably the delicate and tremblingly beautiful 'The Azalea'—convey in direct, simple terms the widower's lonely sadness. There is a repellently different tone in the bitter, reactionary political odes such as '1867', referring to Disraeli's Reform Act:

In the year of the great crime,
When the false English Nobles and their Jew,
By God demented, slew
The Trust they stood twice pledged to keep from wrong.

In the face of creeping democracy Patmore hurls his impotent invective and stands aside:

> Here, in this little Bay,
> Full of tumultuous life and great repose,
> Where, twice a day,
> The purposeless, glad ocean comes and goes,
> Under high cliffs, and far from the huge town,
> I sit me down.
> For want of me the world's course will not fail:
> When all its work is done, the lie shall rot;
> The truth is great, and shall prevail,
> When none cares whether it prevail or not.

He turns away to meditate, in characteristically disciplined, energetic and grave Pindarics, upon the religion that had provided him with the intellectual convictions and the imaginative symbols by which he had idealized Victorian domestic life and love.

The best work of Robert Stephen Hawker (1803–75) belongs to the 1860s. So he finds a place in this chapter even though his first book, *Tendrils*, appeared in 1821, and his best known poem, the rousing Trelawny ballad 'The Song of the Western Men', in 1826. Apart from this ballad, his verse, which was usually published in small pamphlets, went largely unnoticed. The only sizeable collection made in his lifetime was *Cornish Ballads and Other Poems* (1869). His *Footsteps of Former Men in Far Cornwall* (1870) is a gathering of prose biographical sketches of Cornish 'characters' whose eccentricities were, in many cases, matched by those that Hawker himself developed in his forty years as a patriarchal, almost missionary, vicar of the isolated, uncivilized parish of Morwenstow in North Cornwall. He had known the Tractarians in his undergraduate days at Oxford. At Morwenstow he sought to revive what he took to be the usages of the ancient Celtic Church, but his most significant innovation was the Harvest Festival, connecting church ceremonial with the land.

Hawker is a local poet in a locality where every rock and ruin is instinct with legend. Folk-lore prompts, for instance, the simple, lively ballad, 'Featherstone's Doom', about the Cornish wrecker whose troubled spirit is doomed to live beneath Blackrock, near Bude, and twist a rope of sand. But more often he writes of the Christian legends and local saints—in, for instance, 'The Sisters of Glen Nectan' (which he accused Wilkie Collins of plagiarizing), 'The Doom Well of St Madron' (Arthurian), 'The Saintly Names' and 'St Nectan's Kieve'. In 'Morwenna Statio' and 'The Vine' he makes ecclesiological tours of his own parish church reading sermons in its stones, but he loved the shrine more than the pulpit. To Sabine Baring-Gould's antiquarian query about the burial-place of St Morwenna he replied:

> What! Morwenna not lie in the holy place at Morwenstow! Of that you will never persuade me—no, never. I know that she lies there. I have seen her, and she has told me as much, and at her feet ere long I hope to lay my old bones.

'A Rapture on the Cornish Hills' records a mystical experience, but far more distinctive is 'Aishah-Schechinah' (1860) which is a meditation upon the mystery of the Incarnation:

> The zone, where two glad worlds for ever meet,
> > Beneath that bosom ran:
> Deep in that womb the conquering Paraclete
> > Smote Godhead on to man.

Hawker translated the Hebrew words of his title as 'The Woman Numinous', and refers often in his works to the 'Numyne', which he defines as 'the Spiritual or Etherial Element . . . Within its texture the other and grosser elements of Light and Air, ebb and flow, cling and glide. Therein dwell the forces, and thereof Angels and all Spiritual Things receive their Substance and Form'.[2]

This definition occurs in one of the many learned footnotes to his longest poem, *The Quest of the Sangraal* (1864), a blank verse narrative with a Cornish setting. Of all the many Victorian retailers of the Grail story Hawker is most fully alive to the Christian truth of the legend. Whereas Tennyson represents the quest as a morbid, enthusiastic mysticism that will destroy the system of rational virtue in the Round Table, Hawker sees it as the fullness of spiritual vitality. Tennyson's Arthur is full of gloomy foreboding; Hawker's Arthur is the first to raise the cry 'Ho! for the Sangraal, vanished vase of

God!' For Hawker the Grail is a specific object, 'The vessel of the Pasch, Shere Thursday night', as well as an emblem of life and fertility and an awesome sign of God's indwelling with men. So he writes of Joseph of Arimathea:

> He dwelt in orient Syria: God's own land . . .
> His home was like a garner, full of corn
> And wine and oil: a granary of God . . .
> All things were strange and rare: the Sangraal
> As though it clung to some etherial chain,
> Brought down high heaven to earth at Arimathèe.
>   (Lines 88, 91–2, 95–7)

(There is a comparable directness and lack of affectation in the devotional drinking-song, 'King Arthur's Waes-hael', added among the appendices to *The Quest of the Sangraal*.) Like Tennyson, Hawker speaks to his contemporaries and offers, in the last lines of his poem, an allegory of the spiritual history of modern Britain, but his work is far more 'medieval' in its heartfelt faith and its unforced symbolism than anything produced by Tennyson or by any contemporary except Christina Rossetti, who uses little medieval décor, and Patmore, who uses hardly any.

William Morris (1834–96) was born into the Victorian plutocracy, but nostalgia for an imagined, changeless medieval world was the chief urge of his busy life from the boyhood when he rode through Epping Forest in a toy suit of armour to the maturity when he recounted *A Dream of John Ball* in the pages of the Socialist journal he had founded. As an Oxford undergraduate he joined Edward Burne Jones, Richard Watson Dixon and others who had felt the backwash from the Tractarians and had resolved to form a celibate Brotherhood, the 'Order of Sir Galahad', to conduct a 'Crusade and Holy Warfare' against the materialism and rationalism of the age. They read *The Germ*, founded, in imitation, *The Oxford and Cambridge Magazine* (1856), and were inspired by Dante Gabriel Rossetti with artistic and literary ambitions.

Morris's first collection of verse, *The Defence of Guenevere* (1858), was dedicated to Rossetti and includes at least four poems directly inspired by Rossetti's 'medieval' water-colours of 1854–7. Morris uses painterly techniques to convey feeling through the pose of a figure or the placing of significant detail:

> I look'd down on the floor,
> Between my feet . . .   less and less
>
> I saw the melted snow that hung in beads
>   Upon my steel-shoes; less and less I saw
> Between the tiles the bunches of small weeds.
>
> ('Sir Galahad, a Christmas Mystery')

Other pieces deploy the devices of traditional ballads, with just a little too obtrusive an antiquarianism:

> He had a coat of fine red gold,
>   And a bascinet of steel;
> Take note his goodly Collayne sword
>   Smote the spur upon his heel.
>
> ('Welland River')

In this picturesque, 'medieval' world re-created from Malory and Froissart Morris found an escape fom the ugliness and commercialism of contemporary society, and discovered, too, a violence that, perhaps in his case, compensated for his middle-class environment. Such violence may be found in the more intensely imagined pieces—'The Defence of Guenevere' itself, 'Sir Peter Harpdon's End', 'Concerning Geffray Teste Noire' and 'The Haystack in the Floods':

> Right backward the knight Robert fell,
> And moaned as dogs do, being half dead,
> Unwitting, as I deem: so then
> Godmar turn'd grinning to his men,
> Who ran, some five or six, and beat
> His head to pieces at their feet.

Sometimes the piety of the Age of Faith appears as an ironic appendage:

> 'Swerve to the left, son Roger,' he said,
>   'When you catch his eyes through the helmet-slit,
> Swerve to the left, then out at his head,
>   And the Lord God give you joy of it.'
>
> ('The Judgment of God')

The cool, 'flat' tone in which Morris narrates an episode even as brutal as the conclusion of 'The Haystack in the Floods' reveals the sensibility of the designer rather than, say, the moralist. His main occupations from 1861, when he founded his decorative art firm, were in the applied arts of design, where his work supplemented that of Owen Jones and Pugin to bring about a revolution in public taste. But, significantly, Morris himself very rarely designed three-dimensional objects; his talent was as a designer of flat, and usually repetitive, patterns for fabrics and wallpapers (see P. Floud 'William Morris as an artist: A new View' and 'The Inconsistencies of William Morris', *The Listener* 7 and 14 October 1954).

The literary equivalent to this talent appears as a kind of verbal tapestry in the verse romances of his middle years, *The Life and Death of Jason* (1867) and a re-telling of two dozen medieval and classical stories in *The Earthly Paradise* (1868–70). In these any central significance is dispelled by the meticulous attention to visual detail. 'The Hill of Venus' (*Earthly Paradise*), for instance, is a kind of pageant-poem which closely corresponds in content, organization and style to any typical Burne-Jones frieze with its procession of pale, androgynous figures. In the introductory verses to *The Earthly Paradise* Morris asks his readers to 'Forget six counties overhung with smoke' and proclaims himself the 'idle singer of an empty day' who strives

> to build a shadowy isle of bliss
> Midmost the beating of the steely sea.

This gesture of 'aesthetic withdrawal' re-appears in the languid, sweetly melancholy morality play *Love is Enough* (1872) where the five receding planes of action constitute a kind of Chinese box of dreams 'dreamed within another dream'.

Morris claimed that his discovery of the Icelandic sagas, which taught men to endure stoically the worst of this world rather than dream of a better, served to wake him from his dreams to a sense of reality. In two renderings of the Sigurd story and one of the *Laxdaela Saga*—as, too, in *The Pilgrims of Hope* (1885–6), a socialist narrative poem with a contemporary setting—the theme of a husband despised by a wife who has taken a more splendid lover may conceivably echo the relationship between Jane Morris and Rossetti. The cantering measure of *The Story of Sigurd* (1877) is at least brisker than the variously languid metres of *The Earthly Paradise*, but there is hardly any more emotional urgency. In his later years he turned increasingly to prose, and between 1888 and his death wrote eight somniferous, pseudo-medieval romances in archaic English.

Two of these were among the books printed splendidly at Morris's Kelmscott Press in the 1890s. The Kelmscott books, like the tiles, fabrics and wallpapers of Morris and Co., were supplied to a narrow luxury-market when, paradoxically, Morris's political activities were directed towards the creation of an equal, classless society. His socialism grew out of his views upon the relationship between art and society which originated in his reading Ruskin at Oxford, but he went far beyond Ruskin in claiming that the regeneration of art could come about only after the overthrow of the capitalist, competitive economic structure which underlay contemporary ugliness and squalor. In the expository prose of two collections of essays, *Hopes and Fears for Art* (1882) and *Signs of Change* (1888), and other scattered lectures and essays in his socialist journal *The Commonweal* (founded 1885) Morris analyses social ills with pungency and economy, but his complementary imaginative work, *News from Nowhere* (1890), which beautifully and wistfully paints a Rousseau/Godwinesque-anarchist-pastoral-arts-and-crafts ideal society, is only a compensatory dream, not far removed in tone and function from his medieval romances.

Morris was a man of action. His work in decorative arts and crafts and in politics has played some part in cultural developments of the twentieth century, and, indeed, in helping to define 'culture' for us, but his poetry represents only one, and not the most important, aspect of his personality and achievement.

Richard Watson Dixon (1833–1900) was a member of the Oxford Brotherhood of Rossetti's disciples and the originator of *The Oxford and Cambridge Magazine*, but, unlike Morris and Burne-Jones, he persisted in the first intention of all three to enter the Anglican ministry. Much of the verse in his first collection, *Christ's Company* (1861), reflects the ritualizing, 'aesthetic' afterglow of the Tractarian Movement. In hagiographical pieces such as 'The Holy Mother at the Cross' and the lengthy 'St. John' (as too, in *S. John in Patmos*, 1863) he dresses and somewhat muffles a strictly orthodox body of Christian doctrine in Keatsian vestments. More esoteric are the inner landscapes of 'The Soul's World' and 'Despair', or those mysterious, half-apprehended visions of sin in 'The Wizard's Funeral' and 'Dream':

> With scarlet corded horn,
> With frail wrecked knees and stumbling pace,
> The scapegoat came:
> His eyes took flesh and spirit dread in flame
> At once, and he died looking towards my face.

352

In the lyrics appended to *Historical Odes* (1864) the mood is of regret and resignation, perhaps connected with the ending of his intense intellectual and emotional life within the Brotherhood—the state that he had once called 'meteorosophia'. His feelings are expressed directly in 'To Summer' and 'Ode on Departing Youth', but more obliquely in 'Inscience':

> The wind, like mist of purple grain
> Arises o'er the Arab plain;
> Strange constellations flashing soar
> Above the dreadful Boreal shore.
>
> But never purple cloud I see
> Swelling above immensity;
> And never galaxy doth peer
> Through the thick mists that wrap me here.

From 1875 to his death he worked obscurely in North-Country vicarages upon his large-scale, learned and often witty, anti-Froude *History* of the Church of England. His long *terza-rima* narrative poem, set in the tenth century, *Mano* (1883), has an imaginative coherence and depth which, like that of Hawker's *The Quest of the Sangraal*, comes from the combination of scholarship and religious insight. In his privately printed *Odes and Eclogues* (1884) and *Lyrical Poems* (1887) there are plaintive, introspective odes on 'Conflicting Claims' and 'Advancing Age', and other poems, notably 'The Spirit Wooed', 'The Fall of the Leaf' and a handful of songs which look at external nature in a distinctively innocent, fresh and unselfconscious way. See, for instance, the end of 'Winter Will Follow':

> And yet again the bird that sings so high
> Shall ask the snow for alms with piteous cry,
> Take fright in his bewildering bower, and die.

From 1878 he had been corresponding with Hopkins, and the comfort and encouragement he gave to Hopkins was a significant indirect contribution to English poetry. Dixon, indeed, was the only contemporary who came close to a full understanding of Hopkins's verse, because he had known the kind of spiritual struggles which underlay it. Hopkins found in Dixon's verse, 'an extreme purity, a directness of human nature, and absence of affectation which is most rare', and added, 'I feel in reading him what a gentleman he is and it brings on the feeling that I am a blackguard.' (*Letters of G. M. Hopkins to R. Bridges*, ed. C. C. Abbott, 1935, p. 139). Dixon received even less public attention than Hawker (whose mind and career his resembled—except in their more colourful aspects). The high praise he earned from Hopkins and Bridges is a tribute to the saintliness of the man and the truth of his vision, rather than to the skill of the artist, for Dixon never fully mastered the techniques of versification—a failure that is all the more glaring when he is set beside his friends, Rossetti, Swinburne, Hopkins and Bridges.

Algernon Charles Swinburne (1837–1909), while an Oxford undergraduate, wrote poems, such as 'Queen Yseult', 'Joyous Garde' and 'Lancelot', that read like addenda to *The Defence of Guenevere*, but he quickly passed, comet-like (with his tiny body and glory of flame-coloured hair) out of the orbits of Rossetti and Morris. His verse tragedies, *The Queen Mother* and *Rosamund* (1860), are ill-conceived imitations of George Chapman. By contrast, *Atalanta in Calydon* (1865), is the most spirited and least academic of the Victorian attempts to imitate Greek tragedy. The rush and lilt of the famous first chorus 'When the hounds of spring are on winter's traces' splendidly achieve the intensity of Dionysian rapture. However, the implacable and inscrutable God whose purposes are questioned in Biblical cadences in the fourth chorus, 'Who hath given man speech?', is Hebraic rather than Hellenic, while the appeal from the tyranny of that 'supreme evil God' to 'the holy spirit of man' is the libertarian humanism of the nineteenth century. The rich and intoxicating rhythms of this play may be compared with the flatness of Morris's rime royal in 'Atalanta's Race' in *The Earthly Paradise*: Swinburne's rhythms express, or rather embody, youth, vigour, defiance, the great and general idea of liberty.

The third chorus of *Atalanta in Calydon*, 'We have seen thee, O Love', hails the 'perilous goddess' Aphrodite as mother of love and death. In the tragedy *Chastelard* (1865, but begun at Oxford in 1860) Mary Stuart appears as 'Fair fearful Venus' who

> reddens at the mouth with blood of men,
> Sucking between small teeth the sap o' the veins,
> Dabbling with death her little tender lips.
>
> (V, ii)

Vampire figures are not uncommon in Romantic literature, but they are rarely as egregious as Swinburne's or as obviously linked to overt sexual abnormalities. For at his poetic prime Swinburne, apart from being a chronic drunkard, was a masochist who liked to be whipped by two ladies in a brothel in St. John's Wood. Between 1861 and 1881 he worked with loving care upon his epic of flagellation, *The Flogging Block* (unpublished).

That a man's weaknesses may be the condition of his poetic vigour seems to be the case in *Poems and Ballads* (1866) where Swinburne works out his sado-masochistic impulses in heady lyrical verse, and, in passing, tilts at the grey, repressive eunuch-morality of Christians—followers of the 'pale Galilean'. The libertarian feeling that underlay *Atalanta in Calydon* explodes here into a tuneful riot of variegated but cerebral lechery. A recurrent imagined situation is of submission to a cruel, lustful, destructive woman—Dolores ('daughter of Death and Priapus/Our Lady of Pain'), the Empress Faustine, Lucrezia Borgia in 'A Ballad of Life' or the Venus of Tannhaüser in 'Laus Veneris'. There is Lesbian cannibalism in 'Anactoria', where Sappho exclaims,

> That I could drink thy veins as wine, and eat
> Thy breasts like honey!

The cult of the androgyne appears in four 'Hermaphroditus' sonnets, influenced by the 'charming monster' in Théophile Gautier's *Mademoiselle de Maupin*. Medieval necrophilia is the subject of 'The Leper'. In the Proserpine poems Swinburne's sense of sexual isolation develops into a defiant, and of course melodious, fatalism:

> Pale beyond porch and portal
>   Crowned with calm leaves, she stands
> Who gathers all things mortal
>   With cold immortal hands
>   ('The Garden of Proserpine')

> For there is no God found stronger than death; and
>   death is a sleep.
>   ('Hymn to Proserpine')

Swinburne had preached the doctrine of aestheticism in his review of Baudelaire's *Fleurs du Mal* in *The Spectator* (1862), had related it to his own *Poems and Ballads* in his de-

355

fence of that work, *Notes on Poems and Reviews* (1866), and had given prominence to the slogan 'Art for art's sake' in his critical study, *William Blake* (1868). In the 'Prelude' to *Songs before Sunrise* (1871) he announces a new 'public', political purpose in his work. He had been an admirer of Mazzini and a dedicated republican from his Oxford days, and in this volume he commemorates the Italian liberation movement. Nevertheless, his prostrated hero-worship and loving attention to the sufferings of the persecuted are, psychologically, not completely out of keeping with *Poems and Ballads*. However, the effort at sublimation makes atheism, not sexual deviation, the foremost motif. The 'Hymn of Man', a companion of the earlier 'Hymn to Proserpine', hurls the language of the Bible back into the teeth of God:

> Thou are smitten, thou God, thou art smitten; thy death
>   is upon thee, O Lord.
> And the love-song of earth as thou diest resounds through
>   the wind of her wings—
> Glory to Man in the highest! for Man is the master of
>   things.

In 'Hertha', 'Genesis' and 'Christmas Antiphones' Swinburne again preaches this Positivist religion of humanity.

The best of Swinburne is in the volumes of 1865 to 1871. Undistinguished sequels to the successes of those years appeared in *Erectheus* (1876), more exactly imitating Greek tragedy than *Atalanta in Calydon* did, and the vast *Bothwell* (1874) and *Mary Stuart* (1881), fluently versifying Froude to complete the trilogy begun by *Chastelard*. The best things in *Poems and Ballads, Second Series* (1878) are a set of distinguished translations from Villon and the premature elegy on his idol Baudelaire, 'Ave atque Vale' (written 1867). In this last Swinburne distantly and faintly echoes the heady excitements of his own 'Fleurs du Mal', the *Poems and Ballads* (1866), while recognizing Baudelaire's far profounder conception of the nature of evil:—

> Thou sawest, in thine old singing season, brother,
>   Secrets and sorrows unbeheld of us:
>   Fierce loves, and lovely leaf-buds poisonous,
> Bare to thy subtler eye, but for none other
>   Blowing by night in some unbreathed-in clime;
>   The hidden harvest of luxurious time,
> Sin without shape, and pleasure without speech;

> And where strange dreams in a tumultuous sleep
> Make the shut eyes of stricken spirits weep;
> And with each face thou sawest the shadow on each,
> Seeing as men sow men reap.

Swinburne was drinking himself to death, but in 1879 he was taken home by Theodore Watts-Dunton and restored to sobriety and social respectability—to live out his remaining thirty years as the hermit of Putney and to write another twenty books of verse and critical prose.

Swinburne wrote too much. His great agglomerations of words leave too little for the mind to grasp. Even his best work is marred by what he called 'a tendency to the dulcet and luscious form of verbosity'. Our general impression in reading his published verse—that sound predominates over sense—is confirmed by his manuscripts. His drafts of 'Ilicet' in *Poems and Ballads* (1866) show that in his hunt for the correct five-syllable adjective in the verse 'Of the old unalterable gods' he rejected in turn 'unprofitable', 'unperishable', unfathomable', inexorable', 'unconquerable' and (indeed) 'inevitable'. Such care is evidence, though, of a very fine ear for the tonal values of words. Swinburne, for all the great bulk of his writings, has little to say, but he never forgets his own declaration that the poet's 'first and last duty is to sing', and, in a sense, the melody of his lyrical poems *is* their meaning. Thus the persona of the nightingale is well-chosen in 'Itylus':

> Sister, my sister, O fleet sweet swallow,
> Thy way is long to the sun and the south;
> But I, fulfilled of my heart's desire,
> Shedding my song upon height, upon hollow,
> From tawny body and sweet small mouth
> Feed the heart of the night with fire.

James Thomson (1834–82) died in poverty, having sustained a precarious and dipsomaniac existence as schoolmaster, clerk and hack-journalist (1860–75) for Charles Bradlaugh's 'Atheistic-Republican-Malthusian' *National Reformer*. In the pages of that journal he thumbed his nose at God with such pieces as 'The Story of a Famous Old Firm' (1865) and 'Christmas Eve in the Upper Circles' (1866), and occasionally contrived the more penetrative satire that is found in 'Proposals for the Speedy Extinction of Evil and Misery' (1871). This last essay is founded upon Swift's *Modest Proposal*; Thomson suggests that current ills should be cured by universal suicide. Such grim

357

ridicule of the Victorian idea of progress perplexed the perfectibilian secularists who were his friends.

Thomson's verse, printed in various journals, went unnoticed until, near the end of his life, he published two collections in 1880 and 1881. The initials 'B.V.' (Bysshe Vanolis) over which he published much of his verse proclaimed his admiration for Shelley and for the melancholy German who wrote under the pen-name Novalis; but, except in such trifles as 'The Lord of the Castle of Indolence' (1860) where he imitates his poet-namesake and Keats in *their* imitations of Spenser, Thomson is not an obtrusively 'literary' poet, as, for instance, Morris and Swinburne are.

The 'banjo music' (in Edmund Blunden's phrase) of the Cockney conversation-pieces, 'Sunday at Hampstead' (1866) and 'Sunday up the River' (1869), and the ghost-story shivers of 'In the Room' (1872), where dingy lodging-house furniture chatters around a suicide's corpse, are inconsiderable, but 'The Doom of a City : a Fantasia' (written 1857, before he had turned atheist, published posthumously) is worth attention, if only because it is Thomson's longest poem. Its action opens in a real city where the narrator paces at night

through desert streets, beneath the gleam
Of lamps that lit my trembling life alone,
(Part I, line 26)

This episode may owe a hint to the admirably atmospheric nightscape of 'Glasgow' in *City Poems* (1857) by Alexander Smith (1830–67). (Wordsworth, of course, had already provided the Victorians with the frightening image of man 'single in the wide waste of the city'.) But the action of Thomson's poem soon moves to a dream-city where the narrator hears God's judgements against a London that is in danger of going the way of Tyre, Carthage and Venice, because its enormous wealth rests upon bitter social and economic inequalities, gambling, greed, fraud, and so forth. The poem is a commonplace allegory, preaching the gospel according to Carlyle—

Finite souls and all things live by progress solely,
All *are* but what they *do*.
(III, 619)—

but there is something of an original imaginative vision in the dream-cityscape, which conveys powerfully a nightmare sense of sterility and futility.

In his one great poem 'The City of Dreadful Night' (published serially in *The National Reformer* 1874) he combines the real city and the dream into an image that evokes the condition of solitary man in urban surroundings, while at the same time it performs its chief function in objectifying the poet's own religious despair and sense of psychological disintegration. Arnold had known that the inescapable city was a breeding ground for 'this strange disease of modern life'. Thomson displays the ravages of this disease, not as 'sick hurry and divided aims', but, more sensationally, as the divided selves and the 'Infections of incurable despair' (xv, 21) of the various inhabitants of his City. One of these city-dwellers is the traveller through the desert (iv) who has seen his better self, corpse-like, carried off by his dead mistress, leaving the other 'viler' self to stride on in fear and anger into the City. Another is a deformed, bestial, crawling figure (xviii), who seeks to retrace the thread of his life and become 'An infant cradled on its mother's knee', an infant who would scream 'if it saw this loathsome present me'. Others are the frail form (ii) who endlessly revisits, like a purposeless machine, the places where Faith, Hope and Love died, and the necrophiliac in his luxurious surroundings (x) uttering a melodious dirge. The city is a condition of mind such as that displayed in the later, overtly personal poem 'Insomnia' (1882); it is the hell of Thomson's own consciousness :-

> The City is of Night, but not of Sleep;
> There sweet sleep is not for the weary brain;
> The pitiless hours like years and ages creep,
> A night seems termless hell. This dreadful strain
> Of thought and consciousness which never ceases,
> Or which some moments' stupor but increases,
> This, worse than woe, makes wretches there insane.
>
> (i, 71–7)

Some passages seem to offer what is in some sense a 'criticism of life'. In a grimly ironic parody of the Positivists' view of intellectual history (xx), the angel (theism), the warrior (science) and the unarmed man (nihilism) fall in turn before the sphinx Necessity. A Messiah-like figure preaches in the great cathedral (xiv-xvi),

> Good tidings of great joy for you, for all :
> There is no God; no Fiend with names divine
> Made us and tortures us . . .

> I find no hint throughout the Universe
> Of good or ill, of blessing or of curse;
> I find alone Necessity Supreme.
>
> (xiv, 40–1, 73–5),

and in the last section of the poem the Titanic 'Patroness' of the City, a figure modelled on Dürer's 'Melencolia', offers her 'confirmation of the old despair'. But in drawing this strange and awesome female Thomson, in fact, is obeying the command given to the artist in Rossetti's 'Hand and Soul', that is, to paint the image of his own soul. Thomson's passion and vision, like Rossetti's, serve an intense subjectivism. Both use poetry to grapple with inner experience rather than to address audiences. Believing that art is dream rather than a public address system, they manage to illuminate significantly some of the general neuroses of their age.

NOTES

1. It was Rossetti's uncle, J. W. Polidori, who told the famous story of Shelley at Geneva in 1816 suddenly shrieking and rushing from the room. Polidori had, with cold water and ether, to restore him to normality. It transpired that as Shelley had been staring at Mary Shelley he had been shocked into uncontrollable horror by seeing a vision of a woman he had once heard of who had eyes for nipples. See *Diary of Dr. John William Polidori*, ed. W. M. Rossetti, 1911, p. 128.

2. Hawker, like R. W. Dixon and, no doubt, many other Christians perturbed by the assertions of scientific materialism, obtained religious comfort from the scientific theory of a luminiferous ether, propounded by Sir David Brewster (1781–1868), inventor of the kaleidoscope.

BIBLIOGRAPHY

A *General*

M. Beerbohm, *Rossetti and his Circle*, 1922. A series of twenty-four satirical water-colour drawings by a critic of exquisite analytic vision.

M. Praz, *The Romantic Agony*, 1933. Deals in some detail with Swinburne—especially his sado-masochism, but its analysis of certain kinds of beauty is relevant to the work of D. G. Rossetti, Morris and Thomson.

C. M. Bowra, *The Romantic Imagination*, Cambridge, Mass., 1949, Chapters IX–XI.

R. Ironside, *Pre-Raphaelite Painters*, 1948. Contains over a hundred well chosen reproductions of paintings and drawings by artists of the P.R. Brotherhood and their close associates.

Graham Hough, *The Last Romantics*, 1947. Chapters II and III contain the best modern criticism of D. G. Rossetti, the P.R. Brotherhood and William Morris.

W. D. Fredeman, *Pre-Raphaelitism, A Bibliocritical Study*, Cambridge, Mass., 1965. A good bibliography for D. G. Rossetti, but very patchy in its coverage of other painters and writers.

J. D. Hunt, *The Pre-Raphaelite Imagination 1848–1900*, 1968.

B *D. G. Rossetti*

Works, ed. W. M. Rossetti, 1911. The best and most complete edition. The Table of Contents conveniently provides a chronological outline of Rossetti's writings.

Dante Gabriel Rossetti: Poems, ed. O. Doughty, 1957.

Letters, ed. O. Doughty and J. R. Wahl, 5 volumes, 1965—

H. C. Marillier, *Dante Gabriel Rossetti, an Illustrated Memorial of his Art and Life*, 1899. The standard full-length study of Rossetti's graphic art.

O. Doughty, *A Victorian Romantic, Dante Gabriel Rossetti*, 2nd ed. 1960. The most detailed and best balanced of the many *Lives* of Rossetti.

R. G. Grylls, *Portrait of Rossetti*, 1964. Lively; written in order to disprove Doughty's 'hostile interpretation of Rossetti's motives'.

C C. G. Rossetti

Poetical Works, ed. W. M. Rossetti, 1904.

D. M. Stuart, *Christina Rossetti*, 1930.

L. M. Packer, *Christina Rossetti*, Berkeley, California, 1963. The most fully documented biography, but marred by a great deal of unsupported conjecture.

D Patmore

Poems, ed. F. Page, 1949. Incomplete, but the standard modern edition.

F. Page, *Patmore, a Study in Poetry*, 1933. Amply fulfils its intention 'to expound a temper' rather than 'to collect a system'.

J. C. Reid, *The Mind and Art of Coventry Patmore*, 1957. A learned and exhaustive study of Patmore's thought.

E Hawker

R. S. Hawker, *Cornish Ballads and Other Poems*, ed. C. E. Byles, 1904.

M. F. Burrows, *Robert Stephen Hawker, a Study of his Thought and Poetry*, 1926. Pedestrian, but thorough.

F Morris

Collected Works, ed. May Morris, 24 vols., 1910–15. Standard edition, with valuable Introductions by the editor.

Letters, ed. P. Henderson, 1950. A selection.

William Morris: Stories in Prose, Stories in Verse, Shorter Poems, Lectures and Essays, ed. G. D. H. Cole, 1934. The best one-volume selection.

William Morris: Selected Writings and Designs, ed. Asa Briggs, with a Supplement by Graeme Shankland, 1963.

P. Henderson, *William Morris, His Life, Work and Friends*, 1967. A well-proportioned account of Morris's activities.

E. P. Thompson, *William Morris, Romantic to Revolutionary*, 2nd ed. 1961. Mostly on Morris's political activities.

P. Thompson, *The Work of William Morris*, 1967. On Morris as designer.

G Dixon

Poems by Richard Watson Dixon, a Selection, ed. R. Bridges, 1909.

J. Sambrook, *A Poet Hidden: the Life of R. W. Dixon*, 1962.

H *Swinburne*

Poems, 6 vols., 1904.

Tragedies, 5 vols., 1905.
> These two collections are incomplete, but textually are far more accurate than the 'Bonchurch' edition.

Algernon Charles Swinburne: the Complete Works, ('Bonchurch Edition'), ed. E. Gosse and T. J. Wise, 20 vols., 1925–7. Textually corrupt—inevitably so in view of Wise's association with it. It includes Gosse's tactful *Life* of Swinburne.

The Swinburne Letters, ed. C. Y. Lang, New Haven, 6 vols., 1959–62.

New Writings by Swinburne, ed. C. Y. Lang, New York, 1964.

Swinburne: a Selection, ed. Edith Sitwell, 1960. Contains the best of the verse, including *Atalanta in Calydon* entire. The Introduction is full of creative understanding.

G. Lafourcade, *La Jeunesse de Swinburne, 1837–1867*, Paris, 2 vols., 1928. Monumental in its day, and never superseded.

G. Lafourcade, *Swinburne, a Literary Biography*, 1932. The best study of Swinburne in English.

Max Beerbohm, 'No. 2, The Pines', *And Even Now*, 1926.

I *James Thomson ('B.V.')*

Poetical Works, ed. B. Dobell, 2 vols., 1895. Prefaced by a *Memoir*.

Poems and Some Letters, ed. Anne Ridler, 1963. The most substantial selection of poems.

The Speedy Extinction of Evil and Misery; Selected Prose of James Thomson (B.V.) ed. W. D. Schaefer, Berkeley, California, 1967.

Imogene B. Walker, *James Thomson 'B.V.': a Critical Study*, Ithaca, 1950. The most thorough and studious critical account of Thomson.

W. D. Schaefer, *James Thomson 'B.V.': Beyond 'The City'*, Berkeley, California, 1965. Contains an extremely useful bibliography. Makes enthusiastic claims for Thomson as a religious, political, social and economic thinker and literary critic.

ASPECTS OF THE FIN DE SIÈCLE

BERNARD BERGONZI, *University of Warwick*

Towards the end of the nineteenth century, many writers felt that literature and art had moved into a new phase, and that even though Queen Victoria continued to be very much alive the Victorian era was already passing away. Although there was, and is, agreement that the change took place, critics remain divided about the best way of describing this phase of cultural history, and about the point in time when it began to emerge. To talk simply of the 'nineties' is tempting: the period was indeed remarkably compact, with a very characteristic literary flavour, and its mythology has survived for over seventy years. The 'nineties', whether qualified as 'naughty' or 'mauve' or 'yellow', can still exert a striking appeal, as is evident in the recent vogue for Beardsley prints and *art nouveau* decoration. And yet to refer to a single decade in this way can be misleading, since many of the essential attitudes of the nineties had their roots in the eighties or even the seventies; specifically, the Aesthetic Movement, which is sometimes referred to as though it were synonymous with the innovations of the nineties, was essentially a manifestation of the previous decade; as early as 1881 Oscar Wilde was caricatured in the Gilbert and Sullivan opera, *Patience*. The word 'Decadence' has a broader application, but suffers from its ambiguity; some of the time it suggests a combination of physical lassitude and psychological and moral perversity—as exemplified for instance in J-K. Huysmans's novel, *À Rebours*, which was much admired in the nineties—although more properly it should refer only to language. Arthur Symons wrote in the Introduction to *The Symbolist Movement in Literature* (1899), 'the term is in its place only when applied to style; to that ingenious deformation of the language, in Mallarmé, for instance, which can be compared with what we are accustomed to call the Greek and Latin of the Decadence.' A few years before Symons had been happy to use 'decadence' in the broader and looser sense, as in his poem, 'Intermezzo', which describes the dancer 'Nini Patte-en-l'Air' as the 'Maenad of the Decadence'.

I have decided in this essay to use the phrase *fin de siècle*, which clearly points to the preoccupations of the last years of the nineteenth century, without being limited to a single decade, and which can cover such particular manifestations as 'aestheticism' and 'decadence'. From the early nineties onward, *fin de siècle* was something of a catch-phrase; there is a characteristic instance in Wilde's *The Picture of Dorian Gray*, published in 1891:

'*Fin de siècle*,' murmured Lord Henry.
'*Fin du globe*,' answered his hostess.
'I wish it were *fin du globe*,' said Dorian with a sigh. 'Life is a great disappointment.'

(Chapter XV)

In the poem just referred to, Symons attributes to Nini Patte-en-l'Air,

> The art of knowing how to be
> Part lewd, aesthetical in part
> And *fin-de-siècle* essentially.

Holbrook Jackson quotes various other entertaining instances of the phrase in his book, *The Eighteen Nineties* (first published in 1913 and still an indispensable guide to the period). It occurs more portentously in Max Nordau's *Degeneration*, of which the English translation appeared in 1895; writing with ponderous, pseudo-scientific assurance, Nordau uses the phrase *fin de siècle* to define and dismiss practically everything that was significant in late-nineteenth century art and literature: Wagner, Ibsen, Zola, the French symbolists, were all seen as symptomatic of a prevalent mental and physical degeneration. The English translation of *Degeneration* was something of a *succès de scandale*; it ran through several impressions in 1895, no doubt because it coincided with the trials of Oscar Wilde, but was quickly forgotten. Bernard Shaw attacked the book at length in *The Sanity of Art*.

The phrase *fin de siècle* was applied to a wide range of trivial behaviour, provided it was sufficiently perverse or paradoxical or shocking Yet insofar as *fin de siècle* refers to a serious and consistent cultural attitude, it had two essential characteristics: the conviction that all established forms of intellectual and moral and social certainty were vanishing, and that the new situation required new attitudes in life and art; and the related belief that art and morality were separate realms, and that the former must be regarded as wholly autonomous; hence the aesthetic doctrine or 'art for art's sake'. As I have remarked, it is difficult to define the point at which these attitudes begin clearly to emerge. If the *fin de siècle* represented a break with established Victorian attitudes, then the break was not particularly clean: in a literary sense there are lines of development that link the *fin de siècle* poets with the major Romantics—with Blake, with Coleridge and with Keats. Arthur Hallam's review of Tennyson's early poems—whose influence was acknowledged by Yeats—was an important intermediary: Hallam praised a poetry of pure images, without any admixture of rhetoric, in a thoroughly proto-symbolist fashion. One writer has attempted to pin down the emergence of the doctrine of aestheticism:

> The actual doctrine appears first in Swinburne's review of Baudelaire's *Fleurs du Mal* in the *Spectator* for September 6th, 1862 (reprinted in Swinburne's *Works*, Volume XIII, p. 419) and in Pater's essay on Winckelmann, which was published in the *Westminster Gazette* in 1867. Swinburne's *William Blake* (1868) gave prominence to the phrase 'art for art's sake' and five years later the phrase was embodied in the provocatively enigmatic conclusion to Pater's *Renaissance*.
> (Ian Fletcher in *Romantic Mythologies*, ed. I. Fletcher, 1967, p. 181)

The mention of Walter Pater takes us clearly within the ambience of the *fin de siècle*. For over thirty years Pater was one of the most influential of English writers, both for his manner of writing and for what was supposed to be his essential message. Oscar Wilde in *De Profundis* refers to reading Pater's *The Renaissance* (originally titled, in the first edition of 1873, *Studies in the History of the Renaissance*) in his first term at Oxford, calling it 'that book which has had such a strange influence over my life'. Arthur Symons, in a memorial essay written after Pater's death, said that *The Renaissance* 'even with the rest of Pater to choose from, seems to me sometimes the most beautiful book of prose in our literature'. James Joyce, in many passages in his early books, *Dubliners* and *A*

Portrait of the Artist as a Young Man, reveals a consciousness
that has been saturated in Pater's prose. W. B. Yeats, looking
back in the nineteen-twenties to his companions of the nineties,
wrote :

> If Rossetti was a subconscious influence, and perhaps the
> most powerful of all, we looked consciously to Pater for
> our philosophy. Three or four years ago I re-read *Marius the
> Epicurean,* expecting to find I cared for it no longer, but it
> still seemed to me, as I think it seemed to us all, the only
> great prose in modern English ...
>
> (*Autobiographies,* 1955, p. 302)

Such valuations are hard for the present-day reader to accept,
since he is accustomed to a prose that is expressive rather than
musical, and he is likely to echo Max Beerbohm's complaint
about Pater :

> I was angry that he should treat English as a dead language,
> bored by that sedulous ritual wherewith he laid out every
> sentence as in a shroud—hanging like a widower, long over
> its marmoreal beauty or ever he could lay it at length in his
> book, its sepulchre.
>
> (*Works and More,* 1946, p. 115)

Beerbohm's point is well taken, and yet it is in a sense unfair
to Pater; his prose makes its effects cumulatively, and its appeal
can grow with familiarity; one also becomes aware of a curious
counterpointing between Pater's elaborately cadenced, ritualistic prose, and his sceptical, relativistic, even iconoclastic
intelligence. G. S. Fraser has recently published an instructive
article on the method of Pater's prose (in *The Art of Victorian
Prose,* ed. G. Levine and W. Madden, New York, 1968, pp. 201–
223).

From an art-historical point of view, *The Renaissance* is an
important work, since Pater was one of the first English writers
to deal in an analytical and historically conscious fashion with
some of the major artists of the Italian Renaissance, thus antici-
pating the later, more systematic researches of Berenson and
other scholars. At the same time Pater ranges widely, in a way
that illustrates the cultural time-travelling and eclecticism that
typified the aesthetic movement of the seventies and eighties. At
one end of the scale he writes about two thirteenth-century
French stories, and at the other he discusses the eighteenth-
century German antiquarian, Johann Winckelmann. The most
famous lines in *The Renaissance*—indeed, in all of Pater's work

—form the celebrated purple passage about the Mona Lisa, which Yeats rather perversely arranged in *vers libre* to print as the first exhibit in the *Oxford Book of Modern Verse*. It is unfortunate that this passage has come to be regarded merely as a virtuoso stylistic exercise; it occurs as the climax of Pater's essay on Leonardo, and is carefully led up to and prepared for by the developing strategy of the essay. Furthermore, what Pater says about the Mona Lisa is at least as important as the way he says it. For him she is a symbol of the modern consciousness that is burdened by a multiplicity of knowledge and experience; she is an embodiment of the timeless frequenting of many cultures that modern historical knowledge has made possible; she anticipates *The Waste Land* and the *Musée Imaginaire*:

> She is older than the rocks among which she sits; like the vampire, she has been dead many times, and learned the secrets of the grave; and has been a diver in deep seas, and keeps their fallen day about her; and trafficked for strange webs with Eastern merchants: and, as Leda, was the mother of Helen of Troy, and, as Saint Anne, the mother of Mary; and all this has been to her but as the sound of lyres and flutes, and lives only in the delicacy with which it has moulded the changing lineaments, and tinged the eyelids and the hands. The fancy of a perpetual life, sweeping together ten thousand experiences is an old one; and modern philosophy has conceived the idea of humanity as wrought upon by, and summing up in itself, all modes of thought and life. Certainly Lady Lisa might stand as the embodiment of the old fancy, the symbol of the modern idea.

In the almost equally celebrated 'Conclusion' to *The Renaissance*, Pater continues to stress the 'modern idea': 'to regard all things and principles of things as inconstant modes or fashions has more and more become the tendency of modern thought'. Here we see the authentically *fin de siècle* note. As an historical relativist, Pater was sceptical about the possibility of ultimate values and truths; human life was fleeting and uncertain, and instead of pursuing abstractions, man should constantly strive to refine and purify his sensations and impressions:

> Every moment some form grows perfect in hand or face; some tone on the hills or sea is choicer than the rest; some mood of passion or insight or intellectual excitement is

irresistibly real and attractive to us,—for that moment only. Not the fruit of experience, but experience itself, is the end. A counted number of pulses only is given to us of a variegated, dramatic life. How may we see in them all that is to be seen in them by the finest senses? How shall we pass most swiftly from point to point, and be present always at the focus where the greatest number of vital forces unite in their purest energy?

To burn always with this hard, gemlike flame, to maintain this ecstasy is success in life. In a sense it might even be said that our failure is to form habits: for, after all, habit is relative to a stereotyped world, and meantime it is only the roughness of the eye that makes any two persons, things, situations seem alike. While all melts under our feet, we may well grasp at any exquisite passion, or any contribution to knowledge that seems by a lifted horizon to set the spirit free for a moment, or any stirring of the senses, strange dyes, strange colours, and curious odours, or work of the artist's hands, or the face of one's friend. Not to discriminate every moment some passionate attitude in those about us, and in the very brilliancy of their gifts some tragic dividing of forces on their ways is, on this short day of frost and sun, to sleep before evening.

The traditional *carpe diem* theme is reinforced by a profound, modern scepticism which rejects any 'theory or idea or system which requires of us the sacrifice of any part of this experience'. The moral antinomianism that Pater's 'Conclusion' seemed to be advancing was found deeply subversive; and Pater, who in his personal life was an orderly, withdrawn, somewhat timid scholar, removed it from the second edition of *The Renaissance*: 'As I conceived it might possibly mislead some of those young men into whose hands it might fall.' He finally restored the 'Conclusion', slightly modified, to the third edition of his book, with the added comment, 'I have dealt more fully in *Marius the Epicurean* with the thoughts suggested by it.'

Marius the Epicurean, published in 1885, is nominally a novel, but Pater's talents for fiction were limited, and there is little sense of character or dramatic interplay in *Marius*. The central figure is a Roman gentleman living in the second century A.D., a conscientious, rather solemn young man, who attempts to live according to the best principles of paganism, as outlined in the Epicurean philosophy. *Marius the Epicurean* is subtitled, 'His Sensations and Ideas', and although Marius's attitude to life is continuous with that presented in the 'Conclusion' to *The Renaissance*, his Epicureanism is a very high-minded affair, far removed from mere sensuous hedonism; Marius cultivates the pleasures of the mind and spirit rather than of the senses. But the insufficiency of Epicureanism weighs increasingly on Marius, and he is drawn to an enchanting community of early Christians. He is captivated by the beauty of their ritual, and the sweetness and light of their beliefs, and he dies in their care, without having been formally converted. Provided one does not expect the normal satisfactions of fiction from *Marius* and gives oneself time to adapt to its infinitely leisurely cadences, *Marius* can be read as a work of a genuine if muted charm, where action is at a minimum, but where the reader is slowly borne along by the billowing movement of Pater's prose and caught up by degrees into Marius's unfolding consciousness. Although Pater endeavours to make the historical detail correct, it is evident that an earnest nineteenth-century enquirer lies beneath Marius's Roman exterior, and that the Roman Empire of the Antonines thinly conceals the late-Victorian British Empire. The book develops at length the historical superimpositions hinted at in the description of the Mona Lisa.

Pater's major writings reveal another crucial element in the *fin de siècle* state of mind: the mistrust of theory and system, and the corresponding stress on sensation and impression, led in the nineties to a taste for the brief concentrated lyric, and, in prose, for the short story. In the twentieth century, the tendency became more systematic, in the 'images' and 'epiphanies' and other moments of fragmentary illumination in the literature of the Modern Movement. *Marius* had a more immediate effect in projecting the attractiveness of ritual as a way of life, independently of religious affiliation. Yeats remarked of it:

> I began to wonder if it, or the attitude of mind of which it was the noblest expression, had not caused the disaster of my friends. It taught us to walk upon a rope tightly stretched through serene air, and we were left to keep our feet upon a swaying rope in a storm.
>
> *(Autobiographies, p. 302)*

There was one writer who absorbed Pater's lesson not wisely but too well, who achieved a tragic celebrity with relatively slender talents, and whose name is still a veritable symbol for the whole *fin de siècle* period and state of mind. This, of course, is Oscar Wilde: he is difficult to place in literary history, since, as he admitted, he devoted his genius to his life rather than his art. Wilde survives as a figure of pure and fascinating mythology, where the works inevitably seem secondary to the legend of the man. The essential judgments were made, sharply but justly, soon after Wilde's death by Arthur Symons, who was the finest critic of his day:

> His intellect was dramatic, and the whole man was not so much a personality as an attitude. Without being a sage, he maintained the attitude of a sage; without being a poet, he maintained the attitude of a poet; without being an artist, he maintained the attitude of an artist. And it was precisely in his attitudes that he was most sincere.
>
> (*Studies in Prose and Verse*, 1904, p. 125)

Admittedly, Wilde wrote copiously in verse and prose, but the more one reads through his collected works the more one is conscious of its largely derivative quality. Most of the verse draws heavily on a variety of Victorian poets, while his most famous piece of fiction, *The Picture of Dorian Gray*, though a lively story, is a pale imitation of Huysmans's *A Rebours*. The dialogues first published in Wilde's book, *Intentions*, 'The Critic as Artist' and 'The Decay of Lying', offer a witty and accessible source of ideas about art that were fundamental to symbolist aesthetics and which have been developed in the literature and criticism of the twentieth century. Yet they are all taken over from other critics: 'Reading *Intentions* one finds here a bit of Arnold, here a patch of Pater or William Morris, and, in this unlikely company, even Carlyle' (Ruth Z. Temple in *Edwardians and Late Victorians*, ed. R. Ellmann, New York, 1960, p. 42).

If one wishes to find what is most enduring in Wilde's work one is likely to turn to his comedies, *Lady Windermere's Fan*, *A Woman of No Importance*, *An Ideal Husband* and *The Importance of Being Earnest*, which were produced between 1892 and 1895. All are excellent pieces of theatre and splendidly witty. Yet the first three tend to be melodramatic and contain a rather uneasy mixture of farce and morality: *The Importance of Being Earnest* is Wilde's comic masterpiece, and indeed one of the great comedies of the English theatre. Its qualities have been well described by Ian Gregor in an important article on Wilde's comedies ('Comedy and Oscar Wilde', *Sewanee Review* LXXIV (1966), pp. 501–21); he says of this play, 'what he gives us is a completely realized idyll, offering itself as

371

something irrevocably *other* than life, not a wish-fulfilment of life as it might be lived'. For the rest, some of Wilde's shorter tales preserve their self-conscious charm; and among the poems, 'The Ballad of Reading Gaol' stands out as an impressive achievement, although it is over-long and suffers from Wilde's tendency to turn the elements of tragedy into a repetitive decoration. To quote Symons again:

> In this poem, where a style formed on other lines seems startled at finding itself used for such new purposes, we see a great spectacular intellect, to which, at last, pity and terror have come in their own person, and no longer as puppets in a play.
>
> (op. cit., p. 124)

Symons himself was one of the most interesting figures of the *fin de siècle* period. He was born in 1865 and emerged in the eighties as a self-taught but learned young literary man, who was widely read in several languages. In addition to his distinction as a critic, he was a prolific minor poet, a translator, an essayist on all forms of art and an *entrepreneur* of foreign literary influences. In this last respect Symons was of crucial importance, notably as the author of *The Symbolist Movement in Literature* (1899), a book which discussed the work of such French poets as Rimbaud, Verlaine, Laforgue and Mallarmé. This book had a decisive influence on the development of twentieth-century poetry in English. It was dedicated to Yeats who became a close friend of Symons in the nineties; Symons, who was very much at home in Paris literary circles, introduced Yeats to Mallarmé and other French symbolists and to their work, thereby expanding and reinforcing Yeats's existing interest in poetic symbolism, which he had developed from his reading of Blake and his dabblings in magic and the occult. Yeats himself influenced Symons away from mere 'decadence' as a literary concept, towards a quasi-occult understanding of symbolism, reinforced with a Paterian sense of ritual; in the introduction to *The Symbolist Movement* Symons wrote that literature 'becomes itself a kind of religion, with all the duties and responsibilities of the sacred ritual'. A few years later, T. S. Eliot as an undergraduate at Harvard was to find Symons's book extremely fruitful:

> I myself owe Mr Symons a great debt. But for having read his book I should not, in the year 1908, have heard of Laforgue and Rimbaud; I should probably not have begun to read

Verlaine, and but for reading Verlaine, I should not have heard of Corbière. So the Symons book is one of those which have affected the course of my life.

(Quoted in F. O. Matthiessen, *The Achievement of T. S. Eliot*, New York, 1959, pp. 27–28)

Yeats and Symons were associated in a group of poets calling themselves the Rhymers' Club that met during the nineties; in Yeats's words, the Club 'for some years was to meet every night in an upper room with a sanded floor in an ancient eating-house in Fleet Street called the Cheshire Cheese'. The Rhymers, as their name denoted, aimed at the unpretentious pursuit of pure song, purged of Victorian rhetoric or moralizing, and their habit of meeting regularly in such surroundings was an attempt to combine French literary café life with Johnsonian conviviality. These poets were later to be mythologized by Yeats as the 'tragic generation': two of the Rhymers, Ernest Dowson and Lionel Johnson, were to die in their thirties, and another, John Davidson, committed suicide in 1909 at the age of forty-three. Symons, although he lived to be nearly eighty, was afflicted by madness in his later years. The Rhymers did not have the temper of literary revolutionaries, but they aimed to break with the recent past in a way that has been memorably described by Yeats:

The revolt against Victorianism meant to the young poet a revolt against irrelevant descriptions of nature, the scientific and moral discursiveness of *In Memoriam*—'When he should have been broken-hearted', said Verlaine, 'he had many reminiscences'—the political eloquence of Swinburne, the psychological curiosity of Browning, and the poetical diction of everybody. Poets said to one another over their black coffee —a recently imported fashion—'We must purify poetry of all that is not poetry', and by poetry they meant poetry as it had been written by Catullus, a great name at that time, by the Jacobean writers, by Verlaine, by Baudelaire. Poetry was a tradition like religion and liable to corruption, and it seemed that they could best restore it by writing lyrics technically perfect, their emotion pitched high, and as Pater offered instead of moral earnestness life lived as 'a pure gem-like flame' all accepted him for master.

(*The Oxford Book of Modern Verse*, p. ix)

As I have remarked, the brief concentrated lyric could serve as the literary crystallization of a Paterian sensation; the most obvious stylistic influences at work in such poetry were the Elizabethan lyric and the short poems of Verlaine. Even now, so long after they wrote, it is not easy to get the poets of the nineties in critical focus. It is tempting to mythologize them as men, as Yeats did, and to regard their verses as infinitely poignant human records; alternatively, one can dismiss them as poseurs of patently limited talent, whose literary achievement is minuscule, when it is not wholly unnoticeable. Looked at as objectively as possible, the poets of the nineties do have certain definable qualities in their favour. They were at their best extremely skilful craftsmen, who could bring off subtle and striking rhythmic effects, and who were surprisingly successful in importing a Verlainian music into their poems. And by following the example of Baudelaire they were able to enlarge the subject-matter of poetry, even though Baudelaire was systematically misunderstood in the nineties as a romantically decadent celebrant of 'sin' rather than as the tormented Catholic moralist that he was later to appear to T. S. Eliot. At all events, the sensibility of the nineties was inclined to write about prostitutes, or other sources of casual amour: 'the chance romances of the streets, the Juliet of a night', in Symons's words. However much the poets may have romanticized these matters, by touching on them at all they were acknowledging an element in the social reality of Victorian London that had not, so far, received much literary recognition. Despite the narrowness of their poetic means, poets such as Dowson and Symons broadened the spectrum of poetic material in a way that anticipates Eliot, and which shows the influence not merely of French poetry, but of French fiction. Where they were weakest was in the resources of their diction. Dowson's well-worn (and hard-wearing) anthology favourite, 'Non sum qualis eram bonae sub regno Cynarae', illustrates these considerations:

> Last night, ah, yesternight, betwixt her lips and mine
> There fell thy shadow, Cynara! thy breath was shed
> Upon my soul between the kisses and the wine;
> And I was desolate and sick of an old passion,
>   Yea, I was desolate and bowed my head:
> I have been faithful to thee, Cynara! in my fashion.
>
> All night upon mine heart I felt her warm heart beat,
> Night-long within mine arms in love and sleep she lay;
> Surely the kisses of her bought red mouth were sweet;

374

But I was desolate and sick of an old passion,
    When I awoke and found the dawn was gray:
    I have been faithful to thee, Cynara! in my fashion ...

It is evident that Dowson's Swinburnian or Pre-Raphaelite diction is strained to breaking point in his attempt to convey a
novelistic complexity of the erotic life. But I would argue that
the poem's achievement is that it can take the strain: Dowson's intentions are reinforced by a remarkable verbal energy
that underlies the seemingly debilitated surface of the poem
and by his virtuoso manipulation of rhythm.

Symons treats of a similar theme, more succinctly and
equally musically, in 'Leves Amores II', a poem which conveys
an intensely 'realistic' experience with all the immediacy demanded by twentieth-century poetics.

> The little bedroom papered red,
> The gas's faint malodorous light,
> And one beside me in the bed,
> Who chatter, chatters, half the night.
>
> I drowse and listen, drowse again,
> And still, although I would not hear,
> Her stream of chatter, like the rain,
> Is falling, falling on my ear.
>
> The bed-clothes stifle me, I ache
> With weariness, my eyelids prick;
> I hate, until I long to break,
> That clock for its tyrannic tick.

Symons was an intensely visual poet, who often anticipates the
effects demanded by the Imagists of c. 1912; as for instance, in
'At Dieppe: After Sunset', written in 1890:

> The sea lies quieted beneath
> The after-sunset flush
> That leaves upon the heaped grey clouds
> The grape's faint purple blush.
>
> Pale, from a little space in heaven
> Of delicate ivory,
> The sickle-moon and one gold star
> Look down upon the sea.

Symons was a passionate frequenter of the music-halls of London and Paris, and he constantly celebrates them in his verse.
His interest in ballet-girls was not merely amorous; he was a

great exponent of the *fin de siècle* interest in the dance as a momentary fusion of art and ritual, a pure expressive image lifted out of discourse and the flux of everyday life. This topic has been discussed by Frank Kermode in *Romantic Image* and pursued in detail in 'Poet and Dancer Before Diaghilev', an essay which combines theatrical and literary history (included in Kermode's *Puzzles and Epiphanies*, 1962).

Another of the Rhymers, Lionel Johnson, has left an unflattering comment both on Symons's proto-imagist methods and his propensity for sordid subjects:

> [Symons] is a slave to impressionism, whether the impression be precious or not. A London fog, the blurred, tawny lamplights, the red omnibus, the dreary rain, the depressing mud, the glaring gin-shop, the slatternly shivering women: three dexterous stanzas telling you that and nothing more. And in nearly every poem, one line or phrase of absolutely pure and fine imagination. If he would wash and be clean, he might be of the elect.
>
> (Quoted in *Literary Essays of Ezra Pound*, ed. T. S. Eliot, 1960, p. 365)

Johnson was a poet of more austere temperament than Dowson or Symons; his indulgence was alcohol rather than harlots. Like his contemporaries, Johnson was a disciple of Pater, but he followed the implications of *Marius the Epicurean* to their logical conclusion and joined the Roman Catholic Church. Catholicism was very much in the air in the nineties: Dowson also became a Catholic, of an intensely aesthetic, wistful kind, though he does not seem to have shared Johnson's attachment to reading the Fathers of the Church and otherwise speculating on doctrinal niceties (graphically described by Yeats in the *Autobiographies*). Aubrey Beardsley was converted to Catholicism towards the end of his short life, and Oscar Wilde became a Catholic on his death-bed. Another convert was the poet John Gray, not one of the Rhymers, who was a close friend of Wilde and who was falsely alleged to be the original of Dorian Gray: he interestingly broke the *fin de siècle* pattern of the 'tragic generation' by becoming a priest and not dying young. Gray ended his days in 1934 at the age of sixty-eight as a well-loved parish priest in Edinburgh. The temper of this aesthetic Catholicism is well illustrated in two poems on the same theme by Dowson and Johnson, which also serve to contrast the temperaments of the two poets.

'Benedictio Domini'

Without, the sullen noises of the street!
   The voice of London, inarticulate,
Hoarse and blaspheming, surges in to meet
   The silent blessing of the Immaculate.

Dark is the church, and dim the worshippers,
   Hushed with bowed heads as though by some
      old spell,
While through the incense-laden air there stirs
   The admonition of a silver bell.

Dark is the church, save where the altar stands,
   Dressed like a bride, illustrious with light,
Where one old priest exalts with tremulous hands
   The one true solace of man's fallen plight.

Strange silence here: without, the sounding street
   Heralds the world's swift passage to the fire:
O Benediction, perfect and complete!
   When shall men cease to suffer and desire?

                           Dowson.

'The Church of a Dream'

Sadly the dead leaves rustle in the whistling wind,
Around the weather-worn, gray church, low down the vale:
The Saints in golden vesture shake before the gale;
The glorious windows shake, where still they dwell enshrined;

Old Saints by long dead, shrivelled hands, long since designed:
There still, although the word autumnal be, and pale,
Still in their golden vesture the old saints prevail;
Alone with Christ, desolate else, left by mankind.

Only one ancient Priest offers the Sacrifice,
Murmuring holy Latin immemorial:
Swaying with tremulous hands the old censer full of spice,
In gray, sweet incense clouds; blue, sweet clouds mystical:
To him, in place of men, for he is old, suffice
Melancholy remembrances and vesperal.

                           Johnson.

Both poems convey a Paterian feeling for liturgy, but where
Dowson is fervid and aspiring, Johnson is cold and melancholy.
Johnson was, if anything, a more accomplished verbal artist
than Dowson or Symons, but compared with theirs, his poetry,
which dwells on religious topics or fragments of Celtic legend

(although born a Welshman, Johnson transformed himself into an honorary but patriotic Irishman), is somewhat stiff and lacking in human interest. He is seen at his best in such accomplished anthology pieces as 'By the Statue of King Charles at Charing Cross' and 'The Dark Angel'.

In attacking Symons for his taste for low urban subjects, Johnson was drawing attention to another poetic preoccupation of the *fin de siècle*: if a tormented eroticism was one way of extending the range of poetry, a fascination with the multifarious life of the modern city was another. London was not, of course, a completely untouched poetic subject; Tennyson momentarily caught the anomic quality of urban life in a superb image in *In Memoriam*:

> He is not here; but far away
>   The noise of life begins again,
>   And ghastly thro' the drizzling rain
> On the bald street breaks the blank day.

Wordsworth treated London positively in 'Sonnet Written on Westminster Bridge' and negatively in the middle books of the *Prelude*; and there are dark visions of London life in Blake and the Augustan satirists. Yet the great exemplar for the *fin de siècle* poets was Baudelaire, whose poems about Paris had shown the intense but sombre poetic possibilities of the huge modern metropolis. A more romantic source of urban imagery was Whistler and other painters; Wilde wrote in 'The Decay of Lying':

> Where, if not from the Impressionists, do we get those wonderful brown fogs that come creeping down our streets, blurring the gas-lamps and changing the houses into monstrous shadows? To whom, if not to them and their master, do we owe the lovely silver mists that brood over our river, and turn to faint forms of fading grace curved bridge and swaying barge?

He had already shown a similar response in his poem, 'Impression du Matin', published in 1881:

> The Thames nocturne of blue and gold
>   Changed to a Harmony in grey:
>   A barge with ochre-coloured hay
> Dropt from the wharf: and chill and cold
>
> The yellow fog came creeping down
>   The bridges, till the houses' walls

378

Seemed changed to shadows and St Paul's
Loomed like a bubble o'er the town.

Among the Rhymers there were similarly romantic treatments
of the urban scene; Richard Le Gallienne's 'A Ballad of London' indulges in the characteristic *fin de siècle* preference for
the artificial over the natural:

Ah, London! London! our delight,
Great flower that opens but at night,
Great City of the midnight sun,
Whose day begins when day is done.

Lamp after lamp against the sky
Opens a sudden beaming eye,
Leaping alight on either hand
The iron lilies of the Strand . . .

Symons wrote copiously about London—his third book of
poems, published in 1894, is appropriately called *London Nights*
—and his treatment ranges between the romantic and the intensely realistic; he is usually most effective when he is
most purely descriptive:

The grey and misty night,
Slim trees that hold the night among
Their branches, and, along
The vague Embankment, light on light.

One of the most striking of the poets associated with the
Rhymers was John Davidson, a melancholy Scotsman of philosophical inclinations—he was one of the first people in England
to be interested in Nietzsche—whose treatment of urban themes
was realistic to the point of grimness. Perhaps Davidson's best
known poem is 'Thirty Bob a Week', the monologue of an impoverished clerk hopelessly struggling to keep up appearances
and make ends met:

For like a mole I journey in the dark,
A-travelling along the underground
From my Pillar'd Halls and broad Suburbean Park,
To come the daily dull official round;
And home again at night with my pipe all alight,
A-scheming how to count ten bob a pound.

T. S. Eliot wrote interestingly about his admiration for this
poem:

I am sure that I found inspiration in the content of the poem, and in the complete fitness of content and idiom: for I also had a good many dingy urban images to reveal. Davidson had a great theme, and also found an idiom which elicited the greatness of the theme, which endowed this thirty-bob-a-week clerk with a dignity that would not have appeared if a more conventional poetic diction had been employed. The personage that Davidson created in this poem has haunted me all my life, and the poem is to me a great poem for ever.

(*John Davidson: A Selection of His Poems*, ed. M.
Lindsay, 1961, pp. xi–xii)

Davidson coldly appraised the newer aspects of the spreading metropolis in 'A Northern Suburb':

> In gaudy yellow brick and red,
>   With rooting pipes, like creepers rank,
> The shoddy terraces o'erspread
>   Meadow, and garth, and daisied bank.
>
> With shelves for rooms the houses crowd,
>   Like draughty cupboards in a row—
> Ice-chests when wintry winds are loud,
>   Ovens when summer breezes blow.

In such poems as these Davidson suggests a poetic equivalent to the fiction of George Gissing. In a late poem, written not long before he died, Davidson turned to the fairly well-worn subject of the Thames and treated it in a way that is both realistic and richly textured:

> As gray and dank as dust and ashes slaked
> With wash of urban tides the morning lowered;
> But over Chelsea Bridge the sagging sky
> Had colour in it—blots of faintest bronze,
> The stains of daybreak. Westward slabs of light
> From vapour disentangled, sparsely glazed
>
> The panelled firmament; but vapour held
> The morning captive in the smoky east.
> At lowest ebb the tide on either bank
> Laid bare the fat mud of the Thames, all pinched
> And scalloped thick with dwarfish surges. Cranes,
> Derricks and chimney-stalks of the Surrey-side,
> Inverted shadows, in the motionless,
> Dull, leaden mirror of the channel hung.

The poets associated with the Rhymers were not the only ones who expressed a *fin de siècle* sensibility. I have already referred to John Gray, the author of *Silverpoints* (1893), a slender volume designed with infinite preciousness by the artist Charles Ricketts; Gray's poetry was of a matching preciousness —Lionel Johnson dismissed him as a 'sometimes beautiful oddity'—although some of it has a curious distinction; like Symons, Gray was very familiar with the French symbolists, and translated some of their verse, usually in a more restrained and laconic fashion than Symons. (For a further account of Gray, see my introduction to his *Park: A Fantastic Story*, Aylesford, 1966, reprinted in *The Aylesford Review*, VII (1965–6), pp. 206–15. For a comparison of Gray and Symons as translators from the French, see Ruth Z. Temple, *The Critic's Alchemy*, New Haven, 1953, pp. 322–30.) Another Catholic, Francis Thompson, continues to be well-known, at least on the strength of his 'Hound of Heaven' : Yeats remarked of him in relation to the Rhymers, 'Francis Thompson came once but never joined'. Thompson's life of indignity and suffering makes him a signal embodiment of the late-nineteenth myth of the *poète maudit*, and his Catholicism was more existential and less Paterian or aesthetic than that of his contemporaries. In literary respects, too, his perspective was somewhat different from theirs; his models were the Metaphysicals, particularly Crashaw, and Shelley, whom he saw, curiously, as fulfilling their promise. The influence of these poets is evident in 'The Hound of Heaven', which remains a vigorous if over-forceful record of spiritual adventure. In 'In No Strange Land' Thompson writes more calmly of mystical experience :

> O world invisible, we view thee,
> O world intangible, we touch thee,
> O world unknowable, we know thee,
> Inapprehensible, we clutch thee!
>
> Does the fish soar to find the ocean,
> The eagle plunge to find the air—
> That we ask of the stars in motion
> If they have rumour of thee there?

Another poet chiefly remembered as the author of a famous anthology piece is W. E. Henley; the poem is, of course, 'Invictus' :

Out of the night that covers me,
Black as the Pit from pole to pole,
I thank whatever gods may be
For my unconquerable soul.

The rhetoric now seems a little stagey and unconvincing, though the poem's defiant spirit reflects Henley's own life-long struggle against physical disability. His most interesting work is the early sequence of poems called 'In Hospital', which dates from the eighteen-seventies; its exact descriptive realism gives it a surprisingly modern flavour. Henley also experimented with *vers libre*, and in his 'London Voluntaries' he treated a familiar topic, although in a more rhapsodic spirit than most of the Rhymers would have thought appropriate. Although his verse reflected something of the *fin de siècle*, in his role as publicist, critic and editor, Henley was decidedly out of sympathy with anything that smacked of aestheticism or decadence. He favoured a robust, extravert attitude in literary matters, and in politics he was a vehement imperialist. Henley was a friend of R. L. Stevenson, with whom he collaborated in several works, and as editor of the *Scots Observer*, the *National Observer*, and the *New Review*, he sponsored such new arrivals on the literary scene as Kipling and Wells. The nineties was a great period for literary magazines: *The Yellow Book*, which ran from 1894 to 1897, is generally regarded as the quintessential expression of the *fin de siècle* spirit, although this was only true, if at all, of the first four numbers, of which Aubrey Beardsley was art editor; after the *debâcle* of Wilde in 1895, Beardsley was removed from his post, and *The Yellow Book*, although unchanged in appearance, became a sober middle-of-the-road publication. The spirit of the nineties was better captured in *The Savoy*, which was edited by Arthur Symons, and although it ran for only a few months during 1896, it was described by Holbrook Jackson as 'the most ambitious and, if not the most comprehensive, the most satisfying achievement of *fin de siècle* journalism in this country' (*The Eighteen Nineties*, Harmondsworth, 1950, p. 47). Beardsley's drawings were prominent in *The Savoy*, which also published one of his occasional ventures into literature, the consciously decadent romance, *Under the Hill*. A prominent contributer to the early *Yellow Book* was Max Beerbohm; his love of witty paradox and his preference for the artificial as against the natural—his essay, 'The Pervasion of Rouge' is characteristic—made him thoroughly *fin de siècle*, but he always wrote in a spirit of ironical, mocking detachment, and his essays have lasted better than the work of his more fervid contemporaries. The wealth of literary periodicals in the nineties meant that the short story as a literary form was encouraged, and excellent work was done in this medium by Kipling and Wells and James. Closer to the *fin de siècle* spirit were English disciples of Maupassant like Hubert Crackanthorpe and Ella D'Arcy.

Considered as a literary period the eighteen-nineties was rich and various, and much of its best work was written outside the ambience of the *fin de siècle* mood. A comprehensive survey of the period would certainly acknowledge, for instance, in poetry, Kipling's *Barrack-Room Ballads*, Housman's *A Shropshire Lad* and Alice Meynell's *Poems*, as well as the poets I have discussed. In fiction, the major achievements of the nineties include Gissing's *New Grub Street*, Stevenson's *Weir of Hermiston*, George Moore's *Esther Waters*, James's *Spoils of Poynton* and *The Awkward Age*, and Hardy's *Tess of the Urbervilles* and *Jude the Obscure*. The last-named of these does, in fact, embody a good deal of the *fin de siècle* state of mind, notably in the presentation of the neurasthenic 'new woman', Sue Bridehead, and in the grotesque child, 'Father Time'. H. G. Wells's *The Time Machine* is a highly distinguished piece of fiction which, as I have argued elsewhere (*The Early H. G. Wells*, Manchester, 1961) is pervaded by *fin de siècle* feelings, little as one would normally associate them with Wells. And the picture would need to be completed by some consideration of Shaw's achievement in *Plays: Pleasant and Unpleasant*.

Yet to concentrate on what I have tried to isolate, however imperfectly, as the *fin de siècle* mentality is to stress what from Pater onward was known as the 'modern' and to emphasize those elements in late-nineteenth century literary theory and practice that were to be picked up by the Modern Movement in the early twentieth. In one sense the activity exemplified by the Rhymers did not last beyond the end of the century. As Yeats put it:

> Then in 1900 everybody got down off his stilts; henceforth nobody drank absinthe with his black coffee; nobody went mad; nobody committed suicide; nobody joined the Catholic church; or if they did I have forgotten.
>
> (*The Oxford Book of Modern Verse*, p. xi)

(Yeats, in his habitual mythologizing, *had* forgotten: Symons went mad and Davidson committed suicide.) And yet in a deeper sense, the continuities between Pater and Joyce, and between Symons or Davidson and Eliot, are apparent. Yeats himself, who has appeared in this essay as a commentator rather than a creative participant, is the supreme example of a great writer of our century who was nurtured in the nineties, and who transcended the *fin de siècle* spirit without abandoning it. But that is a matter for another chapter and another volume.

BIBLIOGRAPHY

A *General Studies*

Arthur Symons, *The Symbolist Movement in Literature*, 1899, New York, 1958, with an introduction by Richard Ellmann.
—— *Studies in Prose and Verse*, 1904.
Holbrook Jackson, *The Eighteen Nineties*, 1913. This is still the most comprehensive and detailed survey of the nineties.
W. B. Yeats (ed.), *The Oxford Book of Modern Verse*, Oxford, 1936.
—— *Autobiographies*, 1955.
R. Z. Temple, *The Critic's Alchemy: A Study of the Introduction of French Symbolism into England*, New Haven, 1953.
F. Kermode, *Romantic Image*, 1957. A short but immensely suggestive study of *fin de siècle* iconography and its relation to twentieth-century poetics.
—— *Puzzles and Epiphanies*, 1962.
R. Ellmann (ed.), *Edwardian and Late Victorians* (English Institute Essays 1959), New York, 1960.
G. Hough, *The Last Romantics*, 1961. An outstandingly good study of the period.
B. Charlesworth, *Dark Passages: the Decadent Consciousness in Victorian Literature*, Madison, Wisconsin, 1965.
I. Fletcher (ed.), *Romantic Mythologies*, 1967.
D. Stanford (ed.), *Poets of the Nineties*, 1965. A quite representative modern anthology, but the editorial matter is not reliable.

B *Particular Authors*

Max Beerbohm, *Works and More*, 1946.
D. Cecil, *Max*, 1965.
John Davidson, *A Selection of His Poems*, ed. Maurice Lindsay, 1961.
The Poetical Works of Ernest Dowson, ed. Desmond Flower, 1967.
The Letters of Ernest Dowson, ed. D. Flower and H. Maas, 1967.
John Gray, *Silverpoints*, 1893.
—— *Spiritual Poems*, 1896.
Two Friends: John Gray and André Raffalovich, ed. Brocard Sewell, Aylesford, 1963.

W. E. Henley, *Works*, 5 Vols., 1921.
J. H. Buckley, *W. E. Henley*, Princeton, 1945.
The Complete Poems of Lionel Johnson, ed. I. Fletcher, 1953.
Walter Pater, *Works*, 10 vols., 1910.
I. Fletcher, *Walter Pater*, 1959.
Arthur Symons, *Collected Works*, 7 vols, 1924.
R. Lhombreaud, *Arthur Symons*, 1963.
Francis Thompson, *Works*, ed. W. Meynell, 3 vols., 1913.
J. C. Reid, *Francis Thompson: Man and Poet*, 1959.
The Works of Oscar Wilde, ed. G. F. Maine, 1948.
H. Pearson, *The Life of Oscar Wilde*, 1954.

THE VICTORIAN THEATRE

CECIL J. L. PRICE, *University College of Swansea*

The Victorian theatre made a comparatively small contribution to nineteenth-century literature. The output of plays was enormous, for there were far more theatres in existence than had ever been known before, and, with the growth of population and improvement in public transport, large audiences to fill them. All kinds of entertainment were presented from 'legitimate' theatre (straight plays, unaccompanied by music) to equestrian dramas, melodrama, punning farce, and music-hall sketch. The demand was great, and many of the suppliers were either resident dramatists at the playhouses or non-resident hacks. Their financial rewards were generally meagre, and were supplemented by acting. They were forced to bring out plays quickly, and found it easier and more profitable to dramatize a novel or translate a French melodrama than to attempt anything original. Even creating a new play was largely a matter of devising situations for the stock scenes and machinery of the theatre concerned, as well as for particular members of its company acting well-defined characters like the heavy father, Irish boy, soubrette, walking gentleman, or dastardly villain.

An amusing but significant picture of the dramatist's lot at the beginning of the period was drawn by Dickens in *Nicholas Nickleby* (1838–9), a year after Victoria's accession to the throne. Crummles and his band of players were highly-coloured but not very untrue to life, and the manager's method of obtaining a new attraction was only too typical. Nicholas was asked to translate and adapt a French play for him, to introduce a dance for the 'Infant Phenomenon', and to bring the scenes to a close 'with a picture'. By the standards of the day and of the next thirty years, this was a comparatively simple demand for a piece of dramatic fretwork. Conditions like these did not favour the dramatist and it was only in the seventies that they really began to improve.

In the intervening period they were strongly affected by the low social position of the theatre. Attendance at the old patent houses, Drury Lane and Covent Garden, was still socially possible, and Victoria herself encouraged the work of Charles Kean, manager of the Princess Theatre; but the minor theatres, homes of melodrama and burlesque, were left to the 'fast' and the raffish. Arthur Machen put the position clearly:— 'In the days of Thackeray, the theatre lived not for itself, but as a symbol of gaiety' (*Far off Things*, 1923, p. 60), and we have to remember that the word 'gay' had a strongly pejorative sense and was obviously at the other extreme from the prevailing admiration for earnestness. Refinement, respectability and religious zeal, all kept people away, and the theatre suffered, as Matthew Arnold suggested (*Letters of an Old Playgoer*, 1919, pp. 23–4), because it did not attract an audience really representative of the society of its day. Opera alone retained social favour, partly because of the idea that music could only have an elevating effect and partly because of Victorian delight in the ostentatious (See A. Hauser, *Social History of Art*, 1951, Vol. II, p. 809).

The theatres had their hardest struggle for existence in the fifties and early sixties, but gradually began to win favour again and by the end of the century had done much to consolidate their position as centres of artistic excellence. The general quality of plays was higher, and the financial reward greater. If a play were a London success, it was sent on tour throughout the country and brought in even more money. Syndicates were formed to promote and control productions, and introduced new problems for the dramatist, but, at least, a successful playwright could now give time and thought to his work. In its turn the public was willing to give more time and thought to the productions, and the standards of reviewing in the newspapers rose considerably. Ibsen became known here, and the stage began to rival the pulpit.

Yet if the common man of our own day were to be asked what he knew of the Victorian theatre, he would mention first *Maria Marten* and *Sweeney Todd*. In the popular imagination, they epitomize the nineteenth-century desire for the sensational as well as some of the lurid means of satisfying it: the murder and the dream in the one; 'I'll polish them off', in the other. Pressed again our informant might recall *The Bells* as a play always associated with Henry Irving, though it was really an adaptation of Erckmann-Chatrian's *Le Juif Polonais*. Only after further thought would Wilde, Shaw and Pinero come to mind, and the last two might well be seen to have contributed more to the twentieth- than to the nineteenth-century theatre.

The common man would be right, for though the eighties and nineties saw the production of a few splendid comedies that are among the glories of our dramatic literature, the period as a whole was dominated by melodrama. If, then, we are to look for a dramatist who is truly representative of the period, we must select Dion Boucicault (1820–90), whose literary contribution is almost nil but who influenced the theatre of his time very considerably.

He is credited with 145 plays, many of them adaptations or written in collaboration with novelists and actors. The best of his early attempts was in comedy, *London Assurance* (1841), and its style—imitating, at some distance, *The School for Scandal*—is indicated in the name of one of its characters, Lady Gay Spanker. The dialogue moves briskly through a complicated plot; character is sufficiently noted to allow the players to give an illusion of a kind of life; and the whole play has a characteristic jauntiness. Boucicault went on to make a reputation as an adapter of French melodrama. The best-remembered is *The Corsican Brothers*, which gave Charles Kean splendid acting opportunities of a spectacular kind. Kean's passion for detail and his delight in tableaux and 'strong' scenes affected Boucicault considerably, but with this difference: he reconstructed in detail contemporary rather than historical themes, believing as he did that the public was most interested in 'the actual, the contemporaneous, the photographic' (See F. Rahill, *The World of Melodrama*, 1967, p. 184). He thought about the negro problem in the United States and wrote *The Octoroon* (1859), in which the heroine generously committed suicide rather than allow her white lover to suffer from his association with her. This is presented against an 'authentic' background of slave auctions and lynching, as well as the exciting spectacle of a steam-boat exploding in flames.

From the literary point of view, Boucicault's greatest successes were his highly romantic pictures of Irish country life in *The Colleen Bawn* (1860) and *The Shaughraun* (1875). There were 'sensation scenes' in them, but much of the interest lay in language, character and sentiment—W. S. Gilbert, for example, mentions in *Patience* 'The pathos of Paddy as rendered by Boucicault'. Middle-class people were still stilted and stunted, but the country folk had undoubted vitality. Some of the phrases remind us of Synge. Danny the boatman says of Eily:

> The looking glass was never made that could do her justice; and if St. Patrick wanted a wife, where could he find an angel that 'ud compare with the Colleen Bawn. As I row her on the lake, the little fishes come up to look at her; and the wind from heaven lifts up her hair to see what the devil brings her down here at all—at all.
>
> (I.i.)

If this reminds us of Christy Mahon's phrases about Pegeen, some lines in *The Shaughraun* recall Pegeen's interview with the Widow Quin:

> *Mrs. O'Kelly* Run in quick, before he sees you, and I'll take the churn.
> *Claire* Not I!—I'll stop where I am. If he was the Lord-Lieutenant himself I'd not stir or take a tuck out of my gown.
>
> (I.i.)

Boucicault acted the parts of Myles na Coppaleen and Conn the Shaughraun himself and gave them an unusual gusto. In so doing he transformed the stock character of the Irish boy (long amusing for his Irish 'bulls') into a fiery and quick-witted schemer. Boucicault cannot be ignored, if only because Synge, Shaw and O'Casey were strongly influenced by, or reacted against, his example.

Another playwright who was to influence his successors considerably—though in a more literary way—was T. W. Robertson (1829–71). It is easy to exaggerate his achievement, for it marks only the beginning of a movement away from the broad effects of melodrama and farce towards a more subtle realization of everyday life upon the stage. Allardyce Nicoll quotes approvingly one of Boucicault's remarks: 'Robertson differs from me, not fundamentally, but scenically; his action takes place in lodgings and drawing rooms—mine has a more romantic scope' (*A History of Late Nineteenth Century Drama, 1850–1900*, 1946, Vol. I, p. 120). This seems to me only partly true. The more romantic scope of the setting and action meant that a rhetorical and declamatory manner was still appropriate: exaggeration and high-flown speeches were condoned.

Robertson worked towards a greater naturalism, with very brief speeches carefully linked. The contrast between the two styles may be seen in Pinero's *Trelawney of the 'Wells'* (1898), where Tom Wrench represents Robertson, and the old-style actors complain of Tom's play that 'there's not a speech in it, my dear—not a real speech; nothing to dig your teeth into' (Act IV).

Of course, Robertson's earliest work is in the old vein, and even in *David Garrick* (1863) where he begins to show some faint signs of individuality, there is much that is conventional. The dialogue is largely made up of questions and exclamations, and the central scene is one in which Garrick pretends to be drunk. As a portrayal of a great actor, the play has no psychological interest; but it is unusual for its time in detailed stage directions and the naturalistic set with its clutter of ornaments, books and furniture.

In *Society* (1865) Robertson realizes his aims far more surely. Chodd junior declares that his cheque book can buy him anything, and has to be brought to realize that a wife is not always gained by such simple means. Maud is in love with the well-born but unfortunate Sidney Daryl, and her mother strongly opposes the match (and supports Chodd) until she learns that Sidney has not only been secretly bringing up her dead son's daughter, but has been elected to parliament and has succeeded to a title. This sounds stagey enough, but *Society* is original in the way it indicates the love between Maud and Sidney: in place of the usual declamatory raptures, muted tones suggest passionate feeling.

In *Caste* (1867) Robertson took another social theme, but handled it with greater subtlety. The serious point of view is as moderate in tone as one would expect from a dramatist who is trying to move away from the melodramatic; and it is put forward by the hero, George:

Caste is a good thing if it's not carried too far. It shuts the door on the pretentious and the vulgar; but it should open the door very wide for exceptional merit. Let brains break through its barriers, and what brains can break through love may leap over.

(Act III)

A more comic outlook is expressed in the encounter between George and Eccles:

Eccles (sighing) Ah, sir, the poor and lowly is often 'ardly used. What chance has the working man?

George None when he don't work.

Eccles We are all equal in mind and feelings.

George (aside) I hope not . . allow me to offer you this trifling loan.

Eccles Sir, you're a gentleman. One can tell a real gentleman with half a sov.—I mean with half an eye—a real gentleman understands the natural emotions of the working man.

(I.i.)

For Eccles, a gentleman is one who has money to give away. Shaw's Doolittle, Burgess, and Snobby Price share in the character and the point of view.

Eccles is a petty thief and gambler, but he is no melodramatic villain. Robertson's concentration is upon contrast, but of the meditative, comic and sentimental type. Polly defends her father with the words, 'He has his faults, but his good points, when you find 'em, are wonderful.' So Eccles does not change his ways, but cheerfully accepts the invitation to go to 'Jersey, where spirits are cheap', so that he can drink himself to death in a year. The audience must accept him as he is, even in the final tableau: 'Eccles falls off the chair in the last stage of drunkenness, bottle in hand. Hawtree, leaning one foot on the chair from which Eccles has fallen, looks at him through eyeglass.' There is no moralizing here, merely a quizzical glance at the toper.

Robertson's plays are altogether less strident than those of Boucicault and other dramatists of his day. Of course, he often depends on the emotional shorthand of the theatre, particularly the accepted clichés of conventional themes. Look at the exchange between the Marquise de St Maur and Esther:

Marquise (rising) You are insolent—you forget that I am a lady.

Esther You forget that I am a mother. Do you dare to offer to buy my child—*his* breathing image, *his* living memory —with money? There is the door—go.

(Act III)

Usually the tone was more restrained, as suited 'cup and saucer' comedy. He was able to suggest a natural situation, too, by keeping several dialogues in motion at the same time, and by interrupting a straight narrative by one character with the preoccupations of another.

In *Caste* and his later plays (*Play*, 1868; *School*, 1869; *War*, 1871) he is most successful in the comic scenes. The titles suggest an absorption in social ideas that is not entirely justified. He is acute enough to make some good points in passing, but he is usually more interested in effective theatre than in forceful thinking. With this qualification in mind, we may agree with the critic who said that his plays 'are entitled to a place with the novels of Trollope as sober records of mid-Victorian England' (E. Reynolds, *Early Victorian Drama, 1830–1870*, 1936, p. 92).

Another writer who made a very personal contribution to the Victorian theatre was W. S. Gilbert (1836–1911). Robertson encouraged him in his writing, but Gilbert's work owed far more to the extravaganzas of J. R. Planché (1796–1880) and the farces of H. J. Byron (1834–84). Gilbert's serious plays, such as *The Palace of Truth* (1870), *Sweethearts* (1874), *Broken Hearts* (1875) and *Dan'l Druce the Blacksmith* (1876) are almost forgotten, and the only one in print is *Pygmalion and Galatea* (1871), a great success in its own day. It possesses that mingling of light irony and more melancholy feeling which was to be characteristic of his masterpieces, the libretti for the *Savoy* operas. The dramatist's art is rather confined in the operatic medium, but Gilbert skilfully provided variety of interest in spectacular entrances and contrasting choruses. Thirteen comic operas were produced between 1875 and 1896, and a number of them are still extraordinarily popular. They have given more phrases and characters to the common stock of English quotation than all the other Victorian plays combined.

Two of the comic operas were outstanding in their satirical wit: *H.M.S. Pinafore* (1878) and *Patience* (1881). The first took off vigorously the nautical drama of the early part of the nineteenth century. The 'Ruler of the Queen's Navee' is not a good-hearted jolly Jack Tar but a man whose soul has been 'fettered to an office stool'. The sentimental Little Buttercup has (like most middle-aged ladies in the Victorian theatre) a shameful secret to disclose: in her youth she practised baby-farming. The Captain, too, teaches the 'principle that a British sailor is any man's equal, excepting mine.' Yet all this is deftly handled with the lightest of touches. In *Patience* much the same methods are used to laugh at pretentious aestheticism, but Gilbert is careful to balance the arguments. The chorus of twenty love-sick maidens is set off against the chorus of blustering dragoons.

The accusation against the aesthetes that 'the meaning doesn't matter if it's only idle chatter of a transcendental kind' is compared with the reproach to the philistines, 'Of course you will pooh-pooh whatever's fresh and new, and declare it's crude and mean.' Yet the final effect is an amusing burlesque of the ideas of Oscar Wilde in his early phase: if we wish to understand them, we must 'cling passionately to one another, and think of faint lilies.'

In *The Mikado* Gilbert reached his highest achievement. Mock gravity and complicated humour mark Ko-ko's

> self-decapitation is an extremely difficult, not to say dangerous thing to attempt; . . . it's suicide and suicide is a capital offence.
>
> (Act I)

Witty ingenuity is to be found in his handling of feminine rhyme in 'Taken from a county jail.' The patter-songs (like 'I've got a little list') are brilliantly executed, and Gilbert's remarkable ability in mixing pathos with absurdity is evident in 'Willow, tit-willow'. Against the ferocity of the Mikado himself and his judicial 'object all sublime' are placed the artless prattle of the 'Three little maids from school', and the sentiment of 'A wandering minstrel I'. Real depth of feeling is not to be expected here or in his other comic operas: they are brilliantly limited to what will delightfuly entertain.

It is strange to reflect that Gilbert is the only writer to use verse with complete success in the Victorian theatre. It is true that his range was confined to the comic, ironic and sentimental, and would have been scorned by poets whose ambitions lay in historical tragedy. Yet he knew his theatre; they did not show that they knew theirs. R. H. Horne (1803–84) and J. W. Marston (1819–90) had tried to imitate the most sublime moments of the Elizabethans and failed. Tennyson's *Becket* (1893) gave Irving an acting part but is of little interest otherwise. W. B. Yeats (1865–1939) brought out *The Countess Cathleen* (1892) and *The Land of Heart's Desire* (1894), but their blank verse and commonplace metaphor made them slow and wordy, poeticized closet-drama rather than true verse-plays.

The dramatists who still remain to be considered all achieved their theatrical success in prose comedy. The nearest in spirit to Gilbert's flippant and satirical jesting is Oscar Wilde (1854–1900), especially in his one undisputed masterpiece, *The Importance of Being Earnest*. His earlier plays, however, are more akin to those of Pinero and H. A. Jones.

The fact that they turn upon the disclosure of a shameful secret might be of much psychological interest in the study of Wilde himself, were this device not so common in the Victorian theatre. He also brings into these pictures of fashionable society that other well-worn figure, a woman with a past—Mrs. Erlynne (*Lady Windermere's Fan*, 1892), Mrs. Arbuthnot (*A Woman of No Importance*, 1893) and Mrs. Cheveley (*An Ideal Husband*, 1895). In fact, he is content to make use of the usual human furniture of the comedies of his day and of some of its more melodramatic conventions, but he is different from many of his contemporaries in being more interested in dialogue than character and in wit rather than situation. This sometimes leads to an uneasy sequence of ideas that weakens the theme.

An obvious example of this is to be found in *A Woman of No Importance*. Mrs. Arbuthnot's secret was that she had been seduced by Lord Illingworth and that Gerald, her son by him, knows nothing of his parentage. Mrs. Arbuthnot only divulges the information at the end of Act III, when Gerald threatens to shoot Illingworth. At this point the audience is entirely on Gerald's side, and is pleased when it learns, in the following act, that he is to marry the wealthy Hester. In the plot of the play Gerald and Hester stand for right thinking and Mrs. Arbuthnot represents right feeling: in theatrical terms, they must be adequately rewarded. For Wilde this was the mechanical part of the play, but in inserting his celebrated epigrams he sometimes forgot that what the witty characters said was at odds with their role. An illustration may be found in Illingworth's statement, 'Nothing is serious except passion' (Act I), though his character, as it is developed, seems to suggest that he thinks nothing at all is serious.

Even though the persiflage of the aristocrats remains much longer in the memory than the correctness of hero and heroine, we are sometimes conscious that the wit itself owes something to old devices. Definition is one of them, and there are long rallies on the subject of the ideal husband at one point and on the secret of life at another. At times mechanical contrivance is too obvious:

Illingworth What do you call a bad man?
Mrs. Allonby The sort of man who admires innocence.
Illingworth And a bad woman.
Mrs. Allonby Oh! the sort of woman a man never gets tired of.

(Act I)

The humour here lies in the adjectives, since they are merely the opposite of what is expected. Exchange them and the replies are commonplace. The trick was a useful one but Wilde used it too often.

A Woman of No Importance has much less unity of tone and effect than *The Importance of Being Earnest* (1895) and has never been so successful on the stage. The latter shows the same command of form, but this time the handling of the theme is masterly. Illingworth had said that the problem of poverty in the East End was 'the problem of slavery. And we are trying to solve it by amusing the slaves' (Act I). No such acknowledgement of the real world and its troubles is to be found in *The Importance of Being Earnest*, and its reasoning is unclouded by sincerity. Pleasure alone matters; ideals are merely fancies. Gwendolen displays these feelings perfectly in Act I:

> We live, as I hope you know, Mr. Worthing, in an age of ideals. The fact is constantly mentioned in the more expensive monthly magazines, and has reached the provincial pulpits, I am told; and my ideal has always been to love some one of the name of Ernest.

The challenge is put out gaily and draws attention to Wilde's delight in absurdity and twisted logic:

> *Algernon* Please don't touch the cucumber sandwiches. They are ordered specially for Aunt Agatha. [*Takes one and eats it.*]
> *Jack* Well, you have been eating them all the time.
> *Algernon* That is quite a different matter. She is my aunt.

But the most famous example of brilliant flippancy is the scene between Lady Bracknell and Jack concerning his appearance in a handbag.

Wilde's summary verdict on the play was a just one: 'I like the play's irresponsibility and its *obiter dicta*, but it is essentially an acting play' (*Letters*, ed. R. Hart-Davis, 1962, p. 786). Its vitality in the theatre is remarkable, and its appeal is to the comic side of the intellect. Shaw thought it heartless and a proof of Wilde's perversion, but while we inhabit the world it portrays we are aware only of the joy we obtain from the run of the dialogue and the soaring wit. Within those limits style alone matters; persiflage is all.

A. W. Pinero (1855–1934) made an early reputation as a writer of farce. The best was *Dandy Dick* (1887), which, in spite of the facetiousness at the expense of the aitchless lower classes, had a neat plot and a number of warmly funny characters and situations. He could laugh quite safely at some of the old stage clichés:

Sheba Shall we grant them a dignified interview?
Salome Yes. Curl your lip, Sheba.
Sheba You curl your lip better than I—I'll dilate my nostrils.
(Act II)

When he turned to social satire, he was less successful, and plays like *The Times* (1891) compared unfavourably in tone and effect with, say, *New Men and Old Acres* (1869) by Tom Taylor and A. W. Dubourg. He is much better in the handling of sentiment. In the first act of *Trelawney of the 'Wells'* (1898) the consequential actors and actresses of the old school are seen bidding farewell to their young colleague, Rose. Mr and Mrs Telfer, the leaders, are particularly ludicrous in their pomposity, but at the end of the play face a very uncertain future with a courage that lifts them from caricature into life. Naturally, they deplore the efforts of Tom Wrench (who represents T. W. Robertson) to catch the accents of ordinary speech and are bewildered when he says he wants to 'fashion heroes out of actual, dull, every-day men' (Act I). Pinero then proceeds to show us that these ordinary stage-folk really have a quiet heroism about them in their acceptance of their fate and their warmth of heart. These qualities give them an imaginative life denied to the wealthier people they meet. Courage, too, marks Sophy in *The Gay Lord Quex* (1899), more especially in the brilliant third act. She is an independent self-made young manicurist and thinks she can protect her foster-sister Muriel against Quex. She finds herself out-manoeuvred and Quex forces her to write a letter that he can hold against her. We recognize this as an old theatrical trick, but then see that Pinero's later development of the situation springs from character. Sophy realizes that she is betraying Muriel, so she makes the quixotic gesture of tugging the bell-rope, knowing that it may bring the servants and compromise her reputation. Quex admires her spirit and answers her gesture by giving up the letter. All this is most effectively worked out, with changes of mood that are always acceptable. Sophy is ordinary, very ordinary, but she has some extraordinary qualities too. Pinero really interests us in her and can even show her spying at a key-hole without forfeiting our sympathy. He is a dramatist with considerable technical resource, and it is a pity that his dialogue now seems flat and, in the worst sense, too ordinary.

The theatrical progress of Henry Arthur Jones (1851–1929) is a little like that of Pinero, though his early reputation was gained in melodrama rather than farce. *The Silver King* (1882) had a long run and is still remembered for its celebrated line, 'Oh God! put back Thy universe and give me yesterday!' (II. iv), Wilfred Denver made a fortune in the American mines and returned home to exact vengeance from men who had made it appear that he was a murderer. The theme lent itself to strong situations and Jones exploited them, but when he came to apply himself to more serious subjects, he found that he was unable to avoid a certain conventionality of outlook as well as a tendency to over-emphasis. These defects even mar what are probably the best of his twenty-four plays: *The Case of Rebellious Susan* (1894), *The Liars* (1897) and *Mrs. Dane's Defence* (1900). The three bear out the statement by Sir Richard (in *The Case of Rebellious Susan*) that women cannot 'break the seventh commandment, without leaving any ill effects upon society' (Act I). Susan has to forgive her unfaithful husband and forget the attentive young diplomat; Lady Jessica must give up the idea of an elopement; Mrs. Dane must not expect to marry again. Jones puts his point of view in the mouth of Sir Daniel Carteret:– 'The rules of the game are severe. If you don't like them, leave the sport alone' (*Mrs. Dane's Defence*, Act IV). But the pronouncement comes a little too pat and we have the uncomfortable feeling that Sir Daniel is not talking about sport but about blood-sport. Besides, after some brilliantly contrived situations, moments of real crisis, clever bursts of dialogue and one famous cross examination, the endings are tame, even timid. Jones was a first-rate story-teller with a talent for edged dialogue, but he did not really understand character or ideas. For him Nora Helmer and Hedda Gabler had lived in vain.

This is not really surprising for Ibsen's plays on social questions (*Pillars of Society*, 1875–7; *A Doll's House*, 1878–9; *Ghosts*, 1881; *An Enemy of The People*, 1882), were slow to impress themselves on the English theatre. Their champion was William Archer (1856–1824), who was able to influence taste both through his translations and his work as dramatic critic for several periodicals. His articles in the *London Figaro* (1878–81) interested George Bernard Shaw (1856–1950), and Shaw's daily reading in the British Museum (*Das Kapital* in French, and an orchestral score of *Tristan and Isolde*) piqued Archer's curiosity. They became close friends and were to raise the standards of theatrical criticism to a height seldom reached before or since. They also collaborated in two acts of a play: Archer thought up the plot and Shaw supplied the dialogue. Seven years later Shaw completed it alone for production. It was called *Widowers' Houses* (1892).

The occasion was of importance in theatrical history, for the play was put on by J. T. Grein (1862–1935), who was director of the Independent Theatre, an organization formed to give special performances of work of literary and artistic merit rather than merely commercial possibilities. Grein had attracted considerable attention in March 1891, when he had put on Ibsen's *Ghosts*: most critics had been abusive, hearing only the references to venereal disease and missing the profoundly moral point of the play. *Widowers' Houses* discussed a rather different kind of problem: who was to blame for the slums—landlords, the poor or society as a whole? Sartorius, the landlord, is a self-made man who has known poverty himself and is able to justify his methods without difficulty. The opposite point of view is put by his employee, Lickcheese:

> Hardly a penny of that but there was a hungry child
> crying for bread it would have bought.

(Act II)

For two acts the debate has strong moral force, but it falls off in the third act where the question is resolved in rather stagey terms. Nevertheless, this 'blue book drama', as it was called, was ahead of its time in its searching discussion of the ethics of the ownership of slum property. The shrewdest comment upon it was written by Oscar Wilde:—'I like your superb confidence in the dramatic value of the mere facts of life' (*Letters*, ed. R. Hart-Davis, 1962, p. 339). Encouraged by this, Shaw went on writing plays, though they were not produced. *The Philanderer* is dull (as Archer said it was), but it is not 'vulgar and worthless' (*Collected Letters of G. B. Shaw*, ed. Dan H. Laurence, 1965, p. 711). *Mrs. Warren's Profession* is much more successful. Vivie is the 'new woman':

> *Praed* Are you to have no romance, no beauty in your life?
> *Vivie* I don't care for either I assure you.
> *Praed* You can't mean that.
> *Vivie* Oh yes I do. I like working and getting paid for it.
> When I'm tired of working I like a comfortable chair, a
> cigar, a little whisky, and a novel with a good detective
> story in it. ...

(Act I)

Yet she is appalled to hear of her mother's (Mrs. Warren's) secret: that she was a prostitute and now draws a comfortable living from a chain of brothels abroad. Mrs. Warren defends herself much as Sartorius had done. She had been born in poverty and had resolved to better herself, but the path she had taken was not that recommended by Samuel Smiles: she preferred a brothel to the horrors of a white-lead factory. Vivie can forgive her this, but not her secretiveness and pretence of respectability, living one life and believing in another. The reactions are interesting, though the leading characters are highly unsympathetic. Shaw challenged the romantic view that the fallen woman was a victim (as in *La Dame aux Camélias*) of her own passionately generous nature and suggested that sober truth indicated she was mercenary. Pinero's Paula (in *The Second Mrs Tanqueray*) might be a scapegoat (see M. Meisel, *Shaw and the Nineteenth Century Theatre*, 1963, pp. 143–58), but Mrs. Warren could only be a calculating shop-keeper, ready to justify her prices. So Shaw called the play 'a cold-bloodedly appalling one' (*Collected Letters*, p. 566). It would be very much worse, however, if we believed in the characters. As it is, we accept them as puppets in an intellectually exciting debate.

Shaw regarded these early plays as 'dramatic pictures of middle class society from the point of view of a Socialist who regards the basis of that society as thoroughly rotten economically and morally' (*Collected Letters*, p. 632). On the same occasion he made a strong distinction between them and the four subsequent plays, which were not 'realistic' but dealt 'with life at large'. In other words, he moved now from a discussion of social evils to a delighted mockery of accepted Victorian conventions.

Arms and the Man (1894) was the first of his plays to be given in the West End, but ran for only eleven nights. It was quite well received by the critics, and the American rights were bought by the actor, Richard Mansfield. Shaw, however, had no means of knowing that even this very modest degree of success was to be denied him in the commercial theatre for another decade. It is easy to understand why *Arms and the Man* was not more successful. Jingoism was still common, and an attack on the romantic view of Ruritanian (actually Bulgarian) military men could well be taken as mockery of real heroes like 'the soldiers of the Queen'. Shaw seems to intend it to be just such a satire on inflamed patriotic feeling: the only good soldier is a sensible man who does not hazard his life without cause, who indulges in no heroics, and who finds chocolate as useful as cartridges. Bluntschli, who epitomizes this point of view, is a middle-class Swiss, eminently practical, and even apologetic about his efficiency. His attitude is contrasted with the heroic antics of Sergius, who has to learn to pronounce the true lesson of the play:

Oh, war! war! the dream of patriots and heroes!
A fraud, Bluntschli. A hollow sham, like love.

(Act III)

The attitudinizing common in popular military plays of the day is dismissed. Aristocratic dowries are laughed at when Bluntschli bids for Raina's hand with the contents of his hotels. Stage conventions of all kinds are held up to ridicule. Even the device of demonstrating a character's ill-breeding by showing him or her listening at a keyhole is examined, and Bluntschli says, 'It's all a question of the degree of provocation' (Act III).

From this most good-humoured of comedies Shaw went on to create the second of his 'Four Pleasant Plays', *Candida* (1895). Here, too, he attacked romantic fustian and conventional situations. When her husband is away from home and Marchbanks, the young poet, is with her, Candida has no adulterous *affaire* with him but listens placidly while he woos her by the only method he knows—reading his poems. Similarly, in the bargaining scene, she points out that her eloquent husband is not the strong man he would wish to appear to be: his ready-made phrases prevent him from knowing the truth. She is not wholly dependent upon him; he is upon her.

By comparison with these two beautifully constructed plays, *You Never Can Tell* (1897) is something of a disappointment. The opening seems to suggest an attempt at the manner of *The Importance of Being Earnest*, and in the amusing prattle of the twins Shaw comes nearer to it than anywhere else in his work. He still shows his remarkable ability to write prose that leaps from the actor's tongue and to create characters like the waiter whose common sense delights us, but the satire upon Victorian family life goes on too long, and Mrs Clandon, her husband, McComas and Bohun are uninteresting. Gloria, too, though triumphing over Valentine in their sex-combat, is unattractive.

In the same year Shaw wrote what is undoubtedly one of his best stage plays, *The Devil's Disciple*. The direction his thoughts were taking is to be seen in a letter to Ellen Terry:

'A good melodrama is a more difficult thing to write than all this clever-clever comedy.'

(*Collected Letters*, p. 617)

When he set about writing, he cheerfully admitted that the new play was based on Adelphi Theatre tricks—'the reading of the will, the heroic sacrifice, the court martial, the execution, the reprieve at the last moment.' (A. Henderson, *George Bernard Shaw, Man of the Century*, New York, 1956, p. 473). Specific resemblances have also been found to Boucicault's *Arrah-na-Pogue* (1864) (A. Nicoll, op. cit., pp. 90–91). Yet what is at once clear is that Shaw has given these stock situations a new force. Dick Dudgeon, the reprobate, does not know why he takes the parson's place and brings the threat of execution upon himself. It seems a wry jest, but he grows in moral stature as he faces the consequences. The contrast between his apparent bravado, Burgoyne's suavity and Judith's bewilderment is brilliantly conceived.

The last two plays that Shaw wrote in the Victorian period were *Caesar and Cleopatra* (1898) and *Captain Brassbound's Conversion* (1899). If they were by other nineteenth-century dramatists, they would be acclaimed as thoughtful and imaginative, but they are by Shaw at less than his best. He is much too discursive in them and appears to be aiming at something greater than he achieves. What is noticeable is that he was to return to some of the character-types and their relationships for two of his greater plays. The Caesar-Cleopatra association is to be revealed with greater insight in Undershaft and Barbara; Brassbound was to be transformed into Shotover.

Shaw had to wait until the famous seasons (1904–7) at the Court Theatre before the public had any real chance of seeing his plays in London. By that time he was ready to conquer the literary and theatrical worlds, and to bring his magnificent intelligence and superb prose to the creation of some of the finest comedies of the twentieth century. Yet his roots were in the earlier period and, theatrically speaking, he was certainly the most eminent of the Victorians.

BIBLIOGRAPHY

D. Boucicault, *The Dolmen Boucicault*, ed. D. Krause, Dublin, 1964.
W. S. Gilbert, *The Savoy Operas*, 1926.
A. W. Pinero, *Plays*, 1891–1930.
G. B. Shaw, *Plays, Pleasant and Unpleasant*, 2 vols., 1898.
—— *Three Plays for Puritans*, 1901.
—— *Our Theatre in the Nineties*, 3 vols., 1932.
—— *Collected Letters, 1874–97*, ed. Dan H. Laurence, 1965.
O. Wilde, *Works*, ed. R. B. Ross, 12 vols., 1909.
—— *Letters*, ed. R. Hart Davis, 1962.

W. Archer, *English Dramatists of To-Day*, 1882.
D. Cook, *Nights at the Play*, 2 vols., 1883.
C. Scott, *The Drama of Yesterday and To-Day* 2 vols., 1899.
B. Stoker, *Henry Irving*, 2 vols., 1932.
W. Winter, *The Life and Art of Richard Mansfield*, 2 vols., 1910.
M. Arnold, *Letters of an Old Playgoer*, 1919.
J. D. Jones, *The Life and Letters of H. A. Jones*, 1930.
A. Nicoll, *A History of Early Nineteenth Century Drama, 1800–50*, Cambridge, 2 vols., 1930.
—— *A History of Late Nineteenth Century Drama, 1850–1900*, Cambridge, 2 vols., 1946. The standard works with very full bibliographies.
C. Archer, *William Archer: His Life, Work and Friendships*, 1931.
R. A. Cordell, *Henry Arthur Jones and the Modern Drama*, 1932.
E. Reynolds, *Early Victorian Drama (1830–1870)*, Cambridge, 1936. A thoughtful examination.
W. Dunkel, *Sir Arthur Pinero*, 1941.
St. J. Ervine, *Bernard Shaw. His Life, Work and Friends*, 1956.
G. Rowell, *The Victorian Theatre: A Survey*, 1956. Includes a helpful bibliography.
V. Holland, *Oscar Wilde, A Pictorial Bibliography*, 1960.
N. Schoonderwoerd, *J. T. Grein, Ambassador of the Theatre*, Assen, 1963.
H. Schmid, *The Dramatic Criticism of William Archer*, Bern, 1964.
F. Rahill, *The World of Melodrama*, 1967. Particularly good in its comparison of French sources.

TABLE OF DATES

The following tables provide a conspectus of the period, relating literature to other events of the time. They do not contain the dates of all the works of all the authors dealt with in the preceding pages.

Dramatic works usually appear under the year of performance.

Important foreign works of literature are shown at the foot of the Literature column in the appropriate year.

	PUBLIC AFFAIRS
1832	Grey P. M.
	Parliamentary Reform
1833	Factory Act ("Children's Charter")
	Oxford Movement
1834	Melbourne and Peel P.Ms
	Tolpuddle Martyrs transported
	Abolition of slavery in British Empire
	Poor Law
1835	
1836	
1837	Accession of Queen Victoria

LITERATURE AND DRAMA	SCIENCE, ARTS, &c.
Crabbe, Goethe, Bentham Sir Walter Scott died Tennyson, *Poems* (Lady of Shalott, Lotos Eaters, &c.) Disraeli, *Contarini Fleming*	Morse—telegraph
Browning, *Pauline* Carlyle, *Sartor Resartus* Newman *et al, Tracts for the Times* (to 1841)	
Coleridge, Charles Lamb died Crabbe, *Poetical Works*	Faraday—electrical self-induction Braille—alphabet for blind
Cobbett died	Donizetti, *Lucia di Lammermoor* (opera)
Dickens, *Sketches by Boz*, 1st Ser. Browning, *Paracelsus* Wordsworth, *Yarrow Revisited* Strauss, *Der Leben Jesu* Gogol, *Dead Souls*	
Dickens, *Sketches by Boz*, 2nd Ser. *Pickwick Papers*	First train in London
Carlyle, *French Revolution* Dickens, *Oliver Twist* Thackeray, *Yellowplush Papers*	Froebel's kindergarten Pitman's shorthand

1838   Anti-Corn Law League (Manchester)
Beginnings of Chartism

1839   Chartist Riots
Anglo-Chinese Opium War

1840   Union of Canada Act
Penny Post
Queen's marriage to Prince Albert

1841   Peel P.M.
New Zealand declared British
Sovereignty over Hong Kong
Livingstone in Africa
Delane—editor of *Times*

1842   Chartist Riots
Income Tax
Mines Act (no women or children under 10 underground)
Copyright Act (42 years or 7 years after author's death)

1843   Natal British

1844   Factory Act (restricts hours for women and children)
Co-operative Movement (Rochdale Pioneers)
Royal Commission on Health of Towns

1845   Newman becomes Roman Catholic
Irish Potato Famine

1846   Repeal of Corn Laws
Railway boom
Daily News (ed. Dickens)
Irish potato crop fails again
Russell P.M.

Dickens, *Nicholas Nickleby* Surtees, *Jorrocks' Jaunts and Jollities*	National Gallery Liebig and beginnings of biochemistry

Carlyle, *Chartism*
Sydney Smith, *Works*
Thackeray, *Catherine*
	Daguerre—photography
	Turner, *Fighting Temeraire*
	    (painting)
	Grand National at Aintree and
	    Cesarewitch at Newmarket

Browning, *Sordello* Mérimée, *Colomba* Poe, *Tales of the Grotesque*	Kew Gardens Houses of Parliament
Browning, *Pippa Passes* Carlyle, *Heroes and Hero Worship* Dickens, *Old Curiosity Shop* Emerson, *Essays*	Ross discovers Southern Continent *Punch* Bradshaw's *Railway Guide* Cook's tours

Tennyson, *Poems* (Morte d'Arthur,
    &c.)
Wordsworth, *Poems*
Longfellow, *Ballads*
	Mudie's Circulating Library
	Mendelssohn, 'Scottish'
	    Symphony (op. 36)

Southey died (Wordsworth succeeded as Poet Laureate) Carlyle, *Past and Present* Dickens, *Christmas Carol* J. S. Mill, *Logic* Macaulay, *Critical and Historical Essays* Ruskin, *Modern Painters* (to 1860)	Brunel's Thames Tunnel Thurber's 'typewriter' Wagner, *Flying Dutchman* (opera) Donizetti, *Don Pasquale* (opera)
Dickens, *Martin Chuzzlewit* Disraeli, *Coningsby* E. B. Barratt (Browning), *Poems* Thackeray, *Barry Lyndon* Dumas, *Three Musketeers* *Count of Monte Cristo*	Chambers, *Vestiges of Creation*
Disraeli, *Sybil* Mérimée, *Carmen*	Armstrong—hydraulic crane British Museum Liszt, *Préludes* Wagner, *Tannhäuser* (opera)
Brontës, *Poems* G. Eliot, *Strauss's Life of Jesus* Balzac, *Cousine Bette* Melville, *Typee*	E. Howe—sewing machine (U.S.A.) Mendelssohn, *Elijah* (oratorio) Berlioz, *Damnation of Faust* Liszt, 1st Hungarian Rhapsody Schumann, 2nd Symphony

1847   Ten Hours Factory Act

1848   Communist Manifesto
         Chartist petition
         Revolution throughout Europe
         Public Health Act

1849   Christian Socialism (F. D. Maurice and Kingsley)

1850   Public Libraries Act
         Roman Catholic hierarchy in Great Britain
         Gorham Judgment in C. of E. (on baptismal regeneration)

1851   Napoleon III's *coup d'etat* in France
         Australian gold-rush
         Great Exhibition, Hyde Park
         Owens College, Manchester

1852   Revival of Convocation (C. of E.)
         Derby and Aberdeen P.Ms

1853

C. Brontë, *Jane Eyre*	Simpson—chloroform
A. Brontë, *Agnes Grey*	
E. Brontë, *Wuthering Heights*	
Tennyson, *The Princess*	
Emily Brontë died	Pre-Raphaelite Brotherhood
A. Brontë, *Tenant of Wildfell Hall*	Millais, *Ophelia* (painting)
Dickens, *Dombey and Son*	
Gaskell, *Mary Barton*	
J. S. Mill, *Principles of Political Economy*	
Thackeray, *Vanity Fair*	
Anne Brontë, died	Menai Bridge
Arnold, *Strayed Reveller*	Monier—reinforced concrete
C. Brontë, *Shirley*	
Clough, *Ambarvalia*	
Froude, *Nemesis of Faith*	
Macaulay, *History of England* (to 1861)	
Ruskin, *Seven Lamps of Architecture*	
Household Words (ed. Dickens)	
Wordsworth died	Natural Sciences School at Oxford
(Tennyson succeeded as Poet	Clausius—2nd Law of
Laureate)	Thermodynamics
Dickens, *David Copperfield*	Millais, *Christ in the House of His
E. B. Browning, *Poems* (Sonnets from	Parents* (painting)
the Portuguese, &c.)	Paxton's Crystal Palace
Browning, *Christmas Eve and Easter	Schumann, 3rd Symphony
Day*	
Carlyle, *Latter-Day Pamphlets*	
Kingsley, *Alton Locke*	
Rossetti *et al*, *The Germ* (1–4)	
Tennyson, *In Memoriam*	
Thackeray, *Pendennis*	
Wordsworth, *The Prelude*	
Hawthorne, *The Scarlet Letter*	
Kingsley, *Yeast*	King's Cross station
Meredith, *Poems* (Love in a Valley)	Verdi, *Rigoletto* (opera)
Ruskin, *Stones of Venice* (to 1853)	Corot, *Danse des Nymphes*
Melville, *Moby Dick*	(painting)
Arnold, *Empedocles on Etna*	Niagara Falls Bridge
Thackeray, *Henry Esmond*	Paddington Station
H. B. Stowe, *Uncle Tom's Cabin*	
Arnold, *Poems* (Scholar Gypsy,	Verdi, *Il Trovatore*
Sohrab and Rustum)	*La Traviata* (operas)
C. Brontë, *Villette*	
Gaskell, *Ruth*	
Cranford	
Thackeray, *English Humourists*	
Hawthorne, *Tanglewood Tales*	
Le Nerval, *Les Chimères*	

1854	Crimean War (Balaclava, Inkerman)
	Dogma of the Immaculate Conception
	Northcote-Trevelyan Report on Civil Service
1855	Palmerston P.M.
	Sebastopol captured
	Florence Nightingale in Crimea
	Newspaper tax abolished
	Livingstone discovers Victoria Falls
1856	Treaty of Paris (ending Crimean War)
	Limited Liability Act
1857	Indian Mutiny
	Matrimonial Causes Act (divorce courts)
	Ritual cases in Church courts
1858	Derby P.M.
	Removal of Jewish disabilities
1859	Palmerston P.M.
	Franco-Austrian War over Italy
1860	Italian unification
	Lincoln U.S. President
	Food and Drugs Act

Dickens, *Hard Times*
Patmore, *Angel in the House*, Pt. 1.

Maurice's Working Men's College, London.

Charlotte Brontë died
Arnold, *Poems*, 2nd Ser.
Browning, *Men and Women*
Gaskell, *North and South*
Kingsley, *Westward Ho*
Tennyson, *Maud*
Thackeray, *The Newcomes*
Trollope, *The Warden*

Froude, *History of England* (and to 1870)
Patmore, *Angel in the House*, Pt. 2.
Reade, *It is Never Too Late to Mend*
Flaubert, *Madame Bovary*
Hugo, *Contemplations*

Bessemer's steel process

C. Brontë, *The Professor*
E. B. Browning, *Aurora Leigh*
Buckle, *History of Civilisation in England*
Dickens, *Little Dorrit*
Gaskell, *Life of C. Brontë*
Trollope, *Barchester Towers*
Baudelaire, *Les Fleurs de Mal*

Transatlantic cable
National Portrait Gallery

Carlyle, *Frederick the Great*
Clough, *Amours de Voyage*
G. Eliot, *Scenes of Clerical Life*
Morris, *Defence of Guenevere*
Trollope, *Dr Thorne*
          The Three Clerks

Covent Garden Opera
Frith, *Derby Day* (painting)
Manet, *Le Concert aux Tuileries* (painting)

De Quincey, Leigh Hunt, Macaulay died
Dickens, *Tale of Two Cities*
FitzGerald, *Omar Khayyám*
G. Eliot, *Adam Bede*
Meredith, *Richard Feverel*
Mill, *On Liberty*
Smiles, *Self-Help*
Tennyson, *Idylls of the King* (to 1872)
Thackeray, *The Virginians*
All the Year Round (ed. Dickens)
Goncharov, *Oblomov*
Hugo, *Légende des siècles*

Darwin, *Origin of Species*
Gounod, *Faust* (opera)
Wagner, *Tristan und Isolde* (opera)

Collins, *Woman in White*
G. Eliot, *Mill on the Floss*
Patmore, *Angel in the House*, Pt. 3.
Peacock, *Gryll Grange*
Essays and Reviews
Cornhill Magazine, ed. Thackeray
Burckhardt, *Renaissance in Italy*
Boucicault, *Colleen Bawn*

1860   Italian unification

1861   American Civil War
        Death of Prince Consort

1862   Colenso denies authenticity of Mosaic books

1863

1864

1865   Russell P.M.
        Assassination of Lincoln
        End of American Civil War

Boucicault, *Colleen Bawn*

Mrs. Browning, Clough died
Arnold, *On Translating Homer*
Dickens, *Great Expectations*
G. Eliot, *Silas Marner*
Meredith, *Evan Harrington*
Mill, *Representative Government*
Palgrave, *Golden Treasury*
Reade, *The Cloister and the Hearth*
H. Spencer, *Education*
Trollope, *Framley Parsonage*

Pasteur's germ theory of disease
Morris's wallpapers and tapestries
Royal Academy of Music
Brahms' Piano Concerto No. 1.

Collins, *No Name*
G. Eliot, *Romola*
Meredith, *Modern Love*
C. Rossetti, *Goblin Market*
Ruskin, *Unto This Last*
Thackeray, *Philip*
Trollope, *Orley Farm*
Hugo, *Les Misérables*
Turgenev, *Fathers and Sons*

Verdi, *La Forza del Destino* (opera)
Sarah Bernhardt's debut in Paris
Cricket tour to Australia

Thackeray died
Gaskell, *Sylvia's Lovers*
Huxley, *Man's Place in Nature*
Lyell, *Antiquity of Man*
Mill, *Utilitarianism*
Reade, *Hard Cash*
Renan, *La Vie de Jesus*

Manet, *Luncheon on the Grass*
   (painting)
Football Association

Landor, Clare, Surtees died
Browning, *Dramatis Personae*
Gaskell, *Cousin Phillis*
Meredith, *Emilia in England* (later
   Sandra Belloni)
Newman, *Apologia pro Vita Sua*
Tennyson, *Enoch Arden*
Trollope, *The Small House at Allington
   Can You Forgive Her?*

'Pasteurisation'
Geneva Convention (Red Cross)
Bruckner, Mass No. 1 in D minor
Tchaikovsky, *Romeo and Juliet
   Overture*

Mrs Gaskell died
Arnold, *Essays in Criticism*, 1st Ser.
'Lewis Carroll', *Alice in Wonderland*
Meredith, *Rhoda Fleming*
Swinburne, *Atalanta in Calydon*
Pall Mall Gazette and *Fortnightly
   Review*

Lister—antiseptic surgery
Rimsky-Korsakov, 1st Symphony
Whymper climbs Matterhorn

1866   Derby P.M.
        Austria at war with Prussia and Italy
        Dr. Barnardo's Homes
        Riots in Ireland

1867   Disraeli P.M.
        Dominion of Canada
        Second Reform Bill

1868   Gladstone P.M.

1869   Suez Canal
        Irish Church disestablished

1870   Franco-Prussian War
        Elementary Education Act
        Dogma of Papal Infallibility

1871   Abolition of religious tests at Oxford and Cambridge
        Trade Unions legalised
        Newnham College, Cambridge
        Stanley meets Livingstone
        Bank Holidays established

414

Peacock died
Collins, *Armadale*
Gaskell, *Wives and Daughters*
G. Eliot, *Felix Holt*
Reade, *Griffith Gaunt*
Swinburne, *Poems and Ballads*
Trollope, *The Belton Estate*
Daudet, *Lettres de Mon Moulin*
Dostoievsky, *Crime and Punishment*
Ibsen, *Brand*
Hugo, *Les Travailleurs de la Mer*
Verlaine, *Poemes saturniens*

Nobel—dynamite
Mendel's laws of heredity
Smetana, *Bartered Bride* (opera)
Henry Irving on London stage

Arnold, *New Poems*
Bagehot, *English Constitution*
Carlyle, *Shooting Niagara*
Meredith, *Vittoria*
Trollope, *Last Chronicle of Barset*
Marx, *Das Kapital*, I
Ibsen, *Peer Gynt*
Zola, *Thérèse Raquin*

Strauss, 'Blue Danube' Waltz

Browning, *The Ring and the Book*
Collins, *Moonstone*
Morris, *Earthly Paradise* (& 1869, 1870)

Wagner, *Mastersingers* (opera)
Grieg, Piano Concerto in A minor
Brahms, *German Requiem*
Renoir, *Lise* (painting)

Arnold, *Culture and Anarchy*
Mill, *On the Subjection of Women*
Tennyson, *Holy Grail*
Trollope, *Phineas Finn*
Flaubert, *L'Education sentimentale*
Verlaine, *Fêtes galantes*

Brahms, *Hungarian Dances*
Wagner, *Rhinegold* (opera)
Galton and eugenics
Mendeleeff's periodic tables of chemical elements

Dickens died
Arnold, *St Paul and Protestantism*
Dickens, *Edwin Drood*
Disraeli, *Lothair*
Newman, *Grammar of Assent*
Reade, *Put Yourself in His Place*
D. G. Rossetti, *Poems*

Cramme's dynamo
J. D. Rockefeller, Standard Oil Co.
Wagner, *Die Walküre* (opera)

T. W. Robertson died
Arnold, *Friendship's Garland*
Darwin, *Descent of Man*
G. Eliot, *Middlemarch*
L. Carroll, *Through the Looking Glass*
Meredith, *Harry Richmond*
Ruskin, *Fors Clavigera*
Swinburne, *Songs before Sunrise*

Whistler, *Artist's Mother* (painting)
Verdi, *Aïda* (opera)

1872   Secret Ballot

1873   Financial crisis in Europe and America
        Sankey and Moody Revival meetings

1874   Disraeli P.M.

1875   Britain buys Suez Canal shares

1876   Bulgarian Atrocities

1877   Russo-Turkish War
        Annexation of Transvaal

1878   Congress of Berlin
        Irish Land League (Parnell)
        Salvation Army

1879   Gladstone's Midlothian Campaign

1880   Gladstone P.M.
        Transvaal declares itself a republic

F. D. Maurice died
Butler, *Erewhon*
Hardy, *Under the Greenwood Treee*
Ruskin, *Munera Pulveris*

Edison's telegraph

J. S. Mill, Lytton died
Arnold, *Literature and Dogma*
Mill, *Autobiography*
Pater, *Studies in the Renaissance*
Trollope, *Eustace Diamonds*
Tolstoi, *Anna Karenina*

Cezanne, *Straw Hat* (painting)
Remington typewriters

Hardy, *Far from the Madding Crowd*
Thomson, *City of Dreadful Night*
Trollope, *Phineas Redux*

Monet, *Impression: Sunrise*
 (painting)
Wagner, *Götterdammerung*
Verdi, *Requiem*

Charles Kingsley died
Tennyson, *Queen Mary*
Trollope, *The Way We Live Now*

Bizet, *Carmen* (opera)
Gilbert & Sullivan partnership
Tchaikovsky, 1st Piano Concerto

G. Eliot, *Daniel Deronda*
Meredith, *Beauchamp's Career*
Morris, *Sigurd the Volsung*
Tennyson, *Harold*
Trollope, *The Prime Minister*
James, *Roderick Hudson*

Edison's phonograph
Gauguin's landscapes at Salon,
 Paris
Brahms' 1st Symphony
Wagner's *Siegfried* (opera)

Bagehot died
Meredith, *Idea of Comedy*
Zola, *L'Assommoir*
Ibsen, *Pillars of Society*

Rodin, *Bronze Age* (sculpture)

Browning, *La Saisiaz*
Hardy, *Return of the Native*
Swinburne, *Poems and Ballads* II

London electric street lighting
Eddystone Lighthouse
Tchaikovsky, *Swan-Lake* (ballet)

Browning, *Dramatic Idyls* I
Meredith, *Egoist*
Spencer, *Principles of Ethics*
Stevenson, *Travels with A Donkey*
Ibsen, *Doll's House*

London telephone exchange
Australian frozen meat
Rodin, *John the Baptist* (sculpture)

'George Eliot' died
Browning, *Dramatic Idyls* II
Disraeli, *Endymion*
Gissing, *Workers in the Dawn*
Hardy, *Trumpet Major*
Tennyson, *Ballads and Other Poems*
Trollope, *The Duke's Children*
Dostoievsky, *Brothers Karamazov*
Maupassant, *Boule de Suif*
Zola, *Nanna*

Dvorak, 1st Symphony
Tchaikovsky, 1812 *Overture*

1881   Married Women's Property Act
Irish Land Act
Revised Version of New Testament

1882   Phoenix Park murders in Dublin.
British intervention in Egypt

1883

1884   Third Reform Bill
Oxford English Dictionary (to 1928)

1885   Salisbury P.M.
Fall of Khartoum

1886   Gladstone and Salisbury P.Ms

1887   Queen's Jubilee
Stanley discovers Lake Nyanza

1888   County Councils established

Disraeli, Carlyle died 'Mark Rutherford', *Autobiography* D. G. Rossetti, *Ballads and Sonnets* Trollope, *Dr Wortle's School* Ibsen, *Ghosts* James, *Portrait of a Lady* Verlaine, *Sagesse*	Monet, *Sunshine and Snow* (painting) Offenbach, *Tales of Hoffman* (opera)
Darwin, D. G. Rossetti, James Thomson (B.V.) Trollope died Shaw, *Cashel Byron's Profession* Swinburne, *Tristram of Lyonesse* Maupassant, *Une View*	Daimler's petrol engine Manet, *Le Bar aux Folies-Bergeres* (painting) Brahms, Piano Concerto No 2 Wagner, *Parsifal* (opera)
FitzGerald died Trollope, *Autobiography* Lang &c., *Iliad* Nietzsche, *Thus spake Zarathustra*	Brahms, Symphony No. 3 Dvorak, *Stabat Mater* (oratorio) Royal College of Music
Charles Reade died Gissing, *The Unclassed* Tennyson, *Becket* Huysman, *A Rebours* Ibsen, *Wild Duck* Mark Twain, *Huckleberry Finn*	Seurat, *Bathers at Asnières* (painting) Burne-Jones, *King Cophetua and the Beggar Maid* (painting)
Meredith, *Diana of the Crossways* Pater, *Marius the Epicurean* Ruskin, *Praeterita* Tennyson, *Tiresias* Zola, *Germinal*	Gold in Transvaal Degas, *Woman Bathing* (painting) Sullivan, *Mikado* (opera) Brahms, Symphony No. 4
Gissing, *Demos* Hardy, *Mayor of Casterbridge* Kipling, *Departmental Ditties* Tennyson, *Locksley Hall Sixty Years After* Ibsen, *Rosmersholm* James, *Bostonians* *Princess Casamassima* Nietzsche, *Beyond Good and Evil*	Severn Tunnel Canadian Pacific Rly. completed
Gissing, *Thyrza* Hardy, *Woodlanders* Pater, *Imaginary Portraits* Strindberg, *The Father*	Verdi, *Otello* (opera)
Matthew Arnold died Arnold, *Essays in Criticism* II Gissing, *A Life's Morning* Kipling, *Soldiers Three* *Plain Tales from the Hills* Yeats, *Fairy and Folk Tales of the Irish Peasantry* Strindberg, *Miss Julie* Verlaine, *Amour* Zola, *La Terre*	Eastman's Kodak box camera Dunlop's pneumatic tyre Van Gogh's *Yellow Chair* and *Sunflowers* (paintings) Rimsky-Korsakov, *Scheherazade* (music) Football League

1889   London Dock Strike

1890   Beginnings of municipal housing

1891   Free elementary education

1892   Gladstone P.M.

1893   Independent Labour Party

1894   Rosebery P.M.
        Death Duties

Browning, G. M. Hopkins, Wilkie Collins died Browning, *Asolando* Gissing, *The Nether World* Pater, *Appreciations* Swinburne, *Poems and Ballads* III Tennyson, *Demeter* Yeats, *Wanderings of Oisin*	Dvorak, Symphony No. 4 Franck, Symphony in D minor
Newman died Frazer, *Golden Bough* (to 1915) W. James, *Principles of Psychology* Morris, *News from Nowhere* Ibsen, *Hedda Gabler*	Borodin, *Prince Igor* (opera) First 'tube' railway
Gissing, *New Grub Street* Hardy, *Tess of the D'Urbervilles* Henley, *Lyra Heroica* Kipling, *The Light That Failed* Shaw, *Quintessence of Ibsenism* Wilde, *Picture of Dorian Grey*	Tchaikovsky, *Nutcracker* (ballet)
Tennyson died Gissing, *Born in Exile* Henley, *Song of the Sword* Kipling, *Barrack-Room Ballads* Shaw, *Widowers' Houses* Tennyson, *Death of Oenone* Yeats, *Countess Kathleen* Ibsen, *Master Builder*	Toulouse-Lautrec, *At the Moulin Rouge* (painting)
Davidson, *Fleet Street Eclogues* Gissing, *The Odd Women* Pinero, *The Second Mrs. Tanqueray* F. Thompson, *Poems* (Hound of Heaven &c.) Wilde, *A Woman of No Importance*	Benz's four-wheel car Manchester Ship Canal *The Studio* (with Beardsley drawings) Dvorak, New World Symphony Tchaikovsky, *Symphony Pathetique* Verdi, *Falstaff* (opera)
Froude, Stevenson, Christina Rossetti, Pater died Davidson, *Ballads and Songs* Gissing, *In the Year of Jubilee* Meredith, *Lord Ormont* Moore, *Esther Waters* Shaw, *Arms and the Man* Swinburne, *Astrophel* Yeats, *Land of Heart's Desire*	*Yellow Book* (Beardsley art editor) Debussy, *L'Après-midi d'un Faune* (music) Edison's Kinetoscope Parlour, New York

1895 Salisbury P.M.
      Jameson Raid (into Transvaal)

1896

1897 Queen's Diamond Jubilee
      2nd Colonial Conference
      Workmen's Compensation Act

1898 Kitchener defeats dervishes at Omdurman
      Anglo-French clash at Fashoda

1899 South African War
      Board of Education

1900 Relief of Ladysmith and Mafeking

Conrad, *Almayer's Folly*
Gissing, *Eve's Ransom*
Hardy, *Jude the Obscure*
L. Johnson, *Poems*
Meredith, *Amazing Marriage*
Wells, *Time Machine*
Wilde, *Importance of Being Earnest*
Yeats, *Poems*

National Trust
Röntgen's X-rays
Freud's first work on
   psychoanalysis
Marconi's 'wireless' telegraphy
Mahler, Symphony No. 2
R. Strauss, *Til eulenspiegel*

Morris, Patmore died
Housman, *A Shropshire Lad*
Pinero, *Benefit of the Doubt*
Chekhov, *Seagull*

Nobel Prizes
Langley's flying machine
Morris & Burne Jones' Kelmscott
   Chaucer

Conrad, *Nigger of the Narcissus*
Davidson, *New Ballads*
Kipling, *Captains Courageous*
F. Thompson, *New Poems*
Shaw, *Candida*
Wells, *Invisible Man*
James, *Spoils of Poynton*
   What Maisie Knew

Ross discovers malaria bacillus
Klondike Gold Rush
Tate Gallery

'Lewis Carroll' died
Gissing, *Human Odds and Ends*
Hardy, *Wessex Poems*
Shaw, *Plays Pleasant and Unpleasant*
   Caesar and Cleopatra
Wells, *War of the Worlds*

The Curies discover radium
Rodin, *Kiss* (sculpture)

Gissing, *Crown of Life*
Pinero, *Trelawny of the Wells*
Tolstoi, *Resurrection*

Elgar, *Enigma Variations* (music)
Sibelius, Symphony No. 1

Ruskin, Wilde, Dowson died
Conrad, *Lord Jim*
Henley, *For England's Sake*
Pinero, *Gay Lord Quex*
Shaw, *Three Plays for Puritans*
Wells, *Love and Mr. Lewisham*

Max Planck's quantum theory
Elgar, *Dream of Gerontius* (oratorio)
Mahler, 4th Symphony
Sibelius, *Finlandia Overture*

INDEX

(Compiled by Miss Ruth Green)

Figures in heavy type indicate main reference,
those in italics bibliography.